MW01274298

The New
Face of War

Books by Robert W. Chandler

War of Ideas: The U.S. Propaganda Campaign in Vietnam

Tomorrow's War, Today's Decisions: Iraqi Weapons of Mass
   Destruction and the Implications of WMD-Armed
   Adversaries for Future U.S. Military Strategy

Counterforce: Locating and Destroying Weapons of Mass
   Destruction

The New Face of War

Weapons of Mass Destruction
and the Revitalization of America's
Transoceanic Military Strategy

Robert W. Chandler

with John R. Backschies

AMCODA PRESS
McLean, Virginia

AMCODA Press
1390 Chain Bridge Road, #204
McLean, Virginia 22101

Manufactured in the United States of America

printing number
10 9 8 7 6 5 4 3 2 1

Cover/interior design and production:
    Cindy Dyer, Dyer Design

Chandler, Robert W.
    The new face of war / Robert W. Chandler with John R. Backschies

    Bibliography
    Includes index
    ISBN 0-9650770-2-0 (acid-free paper)

                                        97-68443
                                           CIP

This is the third of AMCODA's "Trilogy on Weapons of Mass Destruction and 21st Century Warfare." Discounts are available when ordering all three of the information-packed books. Write AMCODA Press Publications Service, 1390 Chain Bridge Road, Suite 204, McLean, VA 22101 • Call toll free 1-888-262-6322 • Fax 703-883-0499.

In Memoriam:

Major General Robert E. Linhard, U.S. Air Force
Realist, Strategist, Patriot, Friend

"Now nothing can be more important than that the work of a soldier should be well done."

— Plato, *Republic* Book II

CONTENTS

PART IV
Global Reconnaissance-Strike Complex

PART V
The Eleventh Plague

FIGURES

TABLES

PREFACE

The global technological transformation of warfare, underway since the end of the Cold War, was accelerated by the Persian Gulf War. Curiously, the strategic implications of the U.S.-led eviction of Iraq from Kuwait did not begin to unfold until long after the last shots were fired and the grand victory parade in Washington, D.C., became a fading memory. First, applying the lessons of Saddam Hussein's proliferation handbook, rogue regimes and other countries potentially hostile toward the United States worked to obtain weapons of mass destruction (WMD)—nuclear, biological, and chemical weapons—and advanced conventional weapons and technologies. Secondly, like falling dominoes, more than 100,000 veterans of Operation Desert Storm succumbed to still undefined illnesses, Gulf War Syndrome. And, thirdly, terrorists ignited a huge conventional explosion against American forces based in Saudi Arabia in June 1996, killing nineteen and injuring nearly 500 U.S. airmen.

These three events come together to raise serious questions about the validity of the U.S. transoceanic power projection strategy in the new era. Will the current U.S. military strategy—dependent on fourteen days' warning and assured access to overseas seaports and airfields—work? Has the Department of Defense adjusted defense policies, strategy, and military objectives to account for the WMD-armed enemy's possible surprise attacks and anti-access operations designed to delay and block U.S. deployments? Are the uniformed services prepared to fight in chemically and biologically contaminated environments? What are the implications of using WMD terrorism as a military weapon against American forces in peace and war?

John R. Backschies, one of the best and brightest of the post-Cold War generation defense specialists, joined me more than two years ago in thinking through the military risks associated with WMD proliferation, combat operations in contaminated environments, and terrorism as a military weapon. We agreed quickly that the cumulative impact of these three events was *fundamental,* meaning that the new risks had a significant impact on both U.S. military strategy and forces. This book benefitted from our collaboration. John's assistance in laying out the logic of key chapters and his review and comments were extraordinarily helpful. Hence, his name on the title page is in recognition of his contributions and my debt of gratitude.

My thanks to Gary A. Van Valin for taking time from his primary election campaign for Congress to critique several chapters of the manuscript. A friend and colleague for many years, Gary's experience in national security issues and his superior intellect were very helpful in striking just the right balance in making several of the key arguments for reshaping the current U.S. military strategy.

Cindy Dyer unleashed her considerable artistic and creative talents in designing the book, its graphics and tables, and cover. I am deeply grateful for her efforts—the final product stands in silent testimony to her skill, dedication, and creativity.

Finally, most thanks are extended to my very dear wife, Esperanza, for putting up with disrupted family activities for more than a year. She listened to key arguments in the book, asked difficult questions, and offered commentary that could only come from one who has experienced the terror of war and the stresses and strains of an American military spouse. Her heart and mind are most clearly expressed in the discussion of Gulf War Syndrome.

Nearly a thousand research sources were analyzed in preparation of this book; 500 documents are cited. Any errors or omissions are my sole responsibility.

Robert W. Chandler

U.S. Strategy at a Crossroads

INTRODUCTION: PART I

The United States, like Gulliver, is a giant vulnerable to smaller nations. But unlike Gulliver, who was tied down while blissfully unaware of his surroundings, our government knows the new dangers presented by the world's rogue regimes. Now is the time to take decisive action to protect ourselves from the proliferation of weapons of mass destruction and their delivery systems.

Source: U.S., Congress, Senate, Committee on Governmental Affairs, *The Proliferation Primer,* A Majority Report of the Subcommittee on International Security, Proliferation, and Federal Services (Washington, D.C.: January 1998), p. 1.

CHAPTER 1

"The Roaring Twenty-First Century"

R. James Woolsey, former Director of Central Intelligence, has aptly characterized the upcoming era of global politics as "the roaring twenty-first century."[1] The "roaring" sound emanates from the frantic activities of aspiring proliferators as they satisfy their dark urges to build robust arsenals of nuclear, biological, and chemical weapons and the means to deliver them. These "equalizers" are needed to break America's transoceanic power projection strategy and neutralize Washington's overwhelming conventional military superiority. The proliferating states, amassing stores of weapons of mass destruction (WMD) to coerce their neighbors and dissuade intervention by outside countries, are in the process of compelling the United States to deal with a new risk calculus. This revised risk calculation is based on a new set of strategic conditions driven by the realities that weapons of mass destruction offer non-Western countries far greater firepower than they had previously. The newly WMD-armed states are developing innovative operational concepts to take advantage of the up-gunning that these weapons offer. Since fewer nuclear, biological, and chemical weapons are needed to inflict *mass* destruction and numerous military and civilian casualties, WMD proliferators will have an easier task exploiting the U.S. dependence on time by giving little or no strategic warning. Similarly, WMD proliferation opens the door to denying the United States easy access to regional seaports, airfields, and military bases. Since American military forces will be vulnerable to attack when they come within striking range of WMD, regional adversaries also will possess the ability to multiply the casualty risks confronting the United States.

These military risks are growing in the face of an ongoing "splintering process" that is similar to, but not yet as significant as, the great schism between conventional and nuclear strategy after 1945. Nuclear strategy rep-

---

[1] R. James Woolsey, remarks at the National Defense University Foundation and American Defense Preparedness Association breakfast seminar (Washington, D.C.: Capitol Hill Club, April 24, 1997).

---

resented an entirely new field. The threat of nuclear war was so much more severe than conventional conflict that deterrence and prevention of nuclear warfighting dominated the strategy. Conventional conflict could be waged only to the extent that military operations could be conducted independent of nuclear war and the potential for escalation could be controlled.[2]

The magnitude of the contemporary WMD proliferation is no less important than the incipient proliferation of nuclear weapons in the 1940s. The regional impact of WMD proliferation is profound in terms of changing the political and military relationships among regional powers. Weapons of mass destruction offer proliferators the potential for exerting political coercion short of war as well as direct attack options against their neighbors. The strategic consequences of WMD proliferation for regional states today are as fundamental as those for the United States resulting from the Soviet atomic test in August 1949. India's and Pakistan's 1998 nuclear tests underscore this observation and extend its application to regional proliferation of biological and chemical weapons worldwide.

The existence of WMD and the means to deliver them accurately across great distances—ranging from strike aircraft and modern missiles to commando operations and state-sponsored terrorism—changes the very context of regional warfare. The weapons themselves are not novel—they have existed actually or latently for some time. What is new is the spread of these weapons of *mass* destruction to dictatorial regimes of questionable stability and whose leaders may hold few inhibitions about using these weapons against domestic challengers, neighboring countries, or American military forces. Biological weapons, for instance, could inflict casualties on the order of nuclear weapons when delivered against unprotected civilian populations. Another difference is that WMD have been elevated to the political or strategic level for use in manipulating American perceptions of the risks of military action in overseas theaters. WMD also make possible entirely new operational concepts for aggression against neighboring countries, both as coercive tools to influence foreign policy decisions and as highly lethal supplements to conventional military operations.

The political or strategic effectiveness of WMD is obtained from the proliferator's psychological manipulation of their latent threat. Over time, one should anticipate that WMD-armed adversaries will become quite adept in the political "use of non-use"—or strategic use—of their nuclear,

---

[2] Martin van Creveld, *Nuclear Proliferation and the Future of Conflict* (New York: Free Press, 1993), pp. 53-62.

biological, and chemical weapons in manipulating American perceptions of the risks incurred when deploying military forces overseas. To paraphrase Hebrew University's Martin van Creveld, a conventional-only strategy in the coming decades will only be possible to the extent that weapons of mass destruction are ignored. The United States would dismiss these growing military capabilities at its own peril.[3]

The emergence of WMD in the post-Cold War era has split military strategy between traditional conventional and integrated conventional-WMD operations. A conventional war is possible only insofar as military operations can be separated from WMD. There is no guarantee that a conventional war against a WMD-adversary will not escalate to biological and chemical attacks against U.S. forces. Nuclear attacks also are possible—they would change the entire scope of a conflict and the chain of events that would follow.

The current U.S. military strategy is based on a longstanding conventional model, although biological and chemical weapons are generally recognized as posing novel threats and risks to U.S. deployments and operations. Two key doctrinal elements shape this strategic approach: (1) the *counter-offensive* to recover lost territory and restore the status quo ante, and (2) *two wars* occurring roughly at the same time in widely separated regions. Both of these Cold War-derived planning factors require large numbers of tactical fighters and heavy armored and mechanized divisions following a lengthy massing of forces in the overseas theater.

Despite these new threats emerging onto the world scene, U.S. conventional warfighting strategy has undergone little change. American military forces at the threshold of "the roaring twenty-first century" are linear extensions of Cold War conventional forces. Since militaries can be expected to fight the way they are armed, U.S. regional military strategy in the early twenty-first century can be expected to prosecute a well-established conventional warfare approach. New technologies incorporated into the U.S. armed forces since the end of the Persian Gulf War in 1991—including advanced intelligence collection sensors and computing for precise target location, stealth aircraft, and precision munitions—have not spawned new operational concepts to deal with the mushrooming threat of WMD. Rather, they have been used to achieve greater efficiency in the conduct of yesterday's operational doctrines centered on the conventional counter-offensive and two nearly overlapping major theater conflicts.

---

[3]*Ibid.,* pp. 53-62. Professor van Creveld assessed the impact of nuclear weapons.

Two major reviews of U.S. defenses were conducted in 1997—neither took a full accounting of the increasing WMD threat to America's long-standing transoceanic power projection strategy. The Pentagon's May 1997 Quadrennial Defense Review (QDR) validated the counter-offensive and the overlapping two-wars as cornerstones of the post-Cold War conventional strategy. In order to fight and win two wars occurring at roughly the same time, in which a counter-offensive is needed in each conflict, the QDR justified ten Army divisions (six of them heavy armored or mechanized units), twelve Air Force fighter wings, twelve aircraft carriers, and three Marine Amphibious Forces.[4] Eliot Cohen, a former senior defense analyst who also was the director for the *Gulf War Air Power Survey,* lamented the "Pentagon's brain-dead two-war strategy" and a QDR that "stretches Pentagon resources too thin." Professor Cohen was all too correct when he described the defense review process as a demonstration of "how the habits and logic of bureaucracy can turn the work of even the most intelligent, hard-working, and patriotic civil servants into pabulum."[5]

The congressionally mandated National Defense Panel conducted an independent review of the U.S. military force structure. The Panel's December 1997 report offered a trenchant risk assessment and expressed several very useful ideas on how the existing conventional strategy might be adjusted over time to mitigate the new realities presented by WMD-armed adversaries. A dearth of specific force recommendations that could have put the United States on a pathway toward developing a sensible conventional-WMD strategy and force structure weakened the Panel's influence.[6]

Although the conventional warfare model has reached a dead end, it still dominates force structure decisions in the Pentagon. Largely ignoring the growing WMD threat, the current military strategy does not account for the burgeoning military risks facing the United States. Are we vulnerable to militarily inferior but highly innovative WMD-armed adversaries capable of attacking the current U.S. military strategy? Can even a scantily-armed WMD adversary bring future transoceanic force deployments to a screeching halt with nary a shot being fired?

---

[4] William S. Cohen, Secretary of Defense, *Report of the Quadrennial Defense Review* (Washington, D.C.: Department of Defense, May 1997), p. 30.

[5] Eliot Cohen, "Calling Mr. X," *New Republic* (January 19, 1998), pp. 17-18.

[6] U.S., National Defense Panel, *Transforming Defense: National Security in the 21st Century* (Arlington, Va.: December 1997), p. 7.

America's Next First Battle

The first quarter of the twenty-first century is shaping up as a possible rock'em sock'em, bare knuckles brawl between the United States and a host of non-Western countries in various parts of the world. The equalizer capabilities available to regional militaries—WMD, advanced conventional weapons, and long distance ballistic and cruise missiles—offer new opportunities to offset and neutralize American military power. Five WMD proliferators of special concern to the United States are North Korea, Iran, Iraq, Syria, and Libya. Despite the best efforts by the United States and other Western countries to prevent the transfer of WMD materials, technologies, and weapons themselves through export controls and international arms control agreements, interdiction cannot halt the proliferation of WMD. The proliferating countries have proven very adept at finding alternative suppliers and technologies, using denial and deception practices, and a growing capability to produce their own critical components and weapons. Terrorist groups and cults also are seeking to acquire or develop their own biological and chemical weapons.[7]

China and Russia are the world's two key WMD suppliers. Nevertheless, proliferating countries, as they gain expertise in producing WMD, often become the suppliers to other non-Western states. North Korea, for instance, is a major exporter of ballistic missiles. It also offers technical assistance to countries building their own missile production plants. In addition, ever since the demonstration effect of American conventional warfare prowess in the Gulf War, potential adversaries have been buying advanced conventional strike aircraft, missiles, munitions, and reconnaissance assets from a bustling world arms market. Several have turned to indigenous production as a means of protecting their access to advanced technologies.

The future promises an acceleration of these WMD and advanced conventional weapons proliferation trends. Over time, the technological benefits of the West's "revolution in military affairs" should be expected to spread to non-Western countries. Potential adversaries will possess weapons with far greater range, accuracy, and lethality. For example, ballistic missiles with an accuracy of about fifteen feet, according to The Air University's David Blair, are likely to proliferate around the world early in the next century. This development will have a significant impact on

---

[7]U.S., Central Intelligence Agency, "The Acquisition of Technology Relating to Weapons of Mass Destruction and Advanced Conventional Weapons" in *Inside Missile Defense,* 3-14 (July 16, 1997), pp. 5-6.

---

deploying American tactical fighters overseas. In 1998, for instance, it would take from fifteen to forty-eight of the currently used 1980s-vintage missiles armed with runway-cratering munitions—and accuracy of about 150 feet—to close a typical air base. In the future, only three to five missiles with a fifteen-foot accuracy would be required to close the same airfield. Even fewer missiles could destroy the airfield's fuel, maintenance and other essential support.[8]

A similar situation exists for aircraft carriers, even when they are deployed with the electronic protection of Aegis cruisers. Ballistic missiles, anti-ship missiles, submarines, advanced anti-ship mines, and other threats will be increasingly used to prevent American battle groups from entering littoral waters near the enemy's coastline. If Iraq had had as few as six diesel submarines, Admiral James Owens, former deputy chairman of the Joint Chiefs of Staff, explains, it "could have made a significant difference in the Persian Gulf."[9] North Korea, China, and Iran have been making heavy investments in submarines and anti-ship cruise missiles and mines to keep American aircraft carriers out of their coastal waters. Other countries are sure to follow suit.

In addition to providing technical assistance to some WMD programs, China is a source of military assessments of the U.S. power projection strategy and forces. The greater understanding of the American conventional strategy by non-Western leaders contributes to the development of asymmetric military strategies by WMD-armed countries. China's Academy of Military Sciences, for instance, has studied the 1990-91 Persian Gulf War for lessons on how Saddam Hussein used his forces effectively as well as military strengths he possessed but of which he did not take advantage. Chief among Baghdad's lost opportunities, according to Beijing, was the failure to use ballistic missiles to strike U.S. logistical facilities in Saudi Arabia and elsewhere in the region prior to the counter-offensive aimed at ejecting Iraq's military forces from Kuwait. According to the Chinese, in order to mount effective challenges to the projection of U.S. forces to an overseas theater, the regional "defender" needs to find ways to strike U.S. command, control, communication, and intelligence capabilities—including

---

[8] David Blair, "How to Defeat the United States: The Operational Effects of the Proliferation of Weapons of Precise Destruction" in *Fighting Proliferation: New Concerns for the Nineties,* ed. by Henry Sokolski (Washington, D.C.: Government Printing Office (Air University Press), September 1996), p. 87.

[9] As quoted in Blair, "How to Defeat the United States," p. 87.

The New Face of War

space-based assets—and locate and destroy U.S. stealth aircraft and cruise missiles.[10]

General Ronald R. Fogleman, former U.S. Air Force Chief of Staff, was straightforward about the burgeoning military risks:

> Saturation ballistic missile attacks against littoral forces, ports, air-fields, storage facilities, and staging areas could make it extremely costly to project U.S. forces into a disputed [region], much less carry out operations to defeat a well-armed aggressor. Simply the threat of such enemy missile attacks might deter the U.S. and coalition part-ners from responding to aggression in the first instance.[11]

In past conflicts, America's first battles reflected unique qualities re-sulting from the lack of recent and relevant combat experience of the forces involved. Typically, military personnel brought little more than a set of expectations and predictions. The problem is that the violent shock of battle is unlike anything imagined, making the first casualty of war the precon-ceived operational plans to deal with just such a contingency. This shock effect should be expected to be multiplied manifold when U.S. forces con-front sustained biological and chemical attacks. Drawing upon studies of America's first battles in past wars, one should expect to find weakness in command and control resulting from confusion, demoralization, and ex-haustion; mind-numbing delays in conducting appropriate counteractions when doctrine or the preconceptions for the first battle do not fit the actual circumstances; "frantic improvisation" when American forces find them-selves engulfed in biologically and chemically contaminated environments; and offensive action to dominate defensive operations, giving chance a greater play—the greater the role given to chance the greater will be the military risks.[12]

These effects of past first battles can be expected to be multiplied many times over when fighting in a WMD environment. The enemy's use of

---

[10] "Gulf War Provides Ample Information for Chinese Military Thinkers," *Inside Missile Defense* (March 12, 1997), p. 13.

[11] As quoted in Dr. Andrew F. Krepinevich, Jr., *Testimony Before the Airland Subcommittee, Senate Armed Services Committee on the Future of Tactical Aviation* (Washington, D.C.: Center for Strategic and Budgetary Assessments, March 5, 1997), p. 4.

[12] John Shy, "First Battles in Retrospect" in *America's First Battles: 1776-1965,* ed. by Charles E. Heller and William A. Stofft (Lawrence, Kan.: University of Kansas Press, 1986), pp. 328-45.

---

biological and chemical warfare agents, for example, against American forces while they are deploying through seaports and airfields would induce an extraordinary jolt by inflicting what could be massive casualties from odorless, colorless substances emanating from unknown sources. Since military units may not yet be fully deployed and assembled with only a part of their equipment, "frantic improvisation" might be a good guess of how the forces would respond. Biological and chemical attacks during U.S. deployment operations would certainly multiply the military risks. The specter of Gulf War Syndrome casts a dark shadow over the projection of U.S. military forces overseas. Questions logically arise as to how well Americans might fight in biologically and chemically contaminated environments when so far from home and with no relief in sight.

New Power Projection Calculus

Early tactical fighter and troop deployments may not be the best way to counter future threats. An innovative WMD-armed adversary seeking to exploit his strengths might strike U.S. forces with little or no warning and deny them access to forward bases. Fixed facilities and massed formations might be targeted, and the enemy can be expected to employ imaginative tactics and techniques to derail the American power projection strategy.[13]

The truth of the matter is that WMD proliferation is today's problem and that an imaginative WMD-armed adversary would be capable of shutting down U.S. power projection operations early in the coming decade, perhaps as early as 2005 or even before. Nevertheless, the United States plans to fight the next war in exactly the same manner as it fought yesterday's Persian Gulf War. The deployment of thousands of ground troops and hundreds of short-range land- and sea-based fighters to the theater are called for by the conventional strategy. This massive transoceanic power projection operation is predicated on accepting the early loss of territory until the U.S. can deploy sufficient forces to the theater. Hence, a counter-offensive to retake lost ground following a lengthy buildup of land and air forces is still the dominant strategy. Success hinges on unrestricted access to and use of ports, airfields and military bases.

Wholly in line with the conventional strategy that tends to consider WMD as an operational threat amenable to tactical or technological solutions, the Pentagon's modernization plan has a near-absolute emphasis on

---

[13] U.S., National Defense Panel, *Transforming Defense,* p. 11.

---

short-range tactical aviation, heavy land forces, and aircraft carriers. The strategic usefulness of WMD in manipulating risk perceptions through the political use of non-use of force are largely ignored. Since WMD attacks against forward U.S. installations could kill thousands, the specter of such casualties could cause the president to balk at taking decisive action. Such threats could also prompt would-be overseas hosts to U.S. forces to deny access to their territory for basing, overflight, and refueling.

In sum, the regional proliferation of WMD has altered the U.S. risk calculus of projecting power overseas by raising the prospective price of rushing American forces into the death grip of WMD-armed adversaries. American policy makers and military planners need to recognize these risks and adjust the nation's strategy and forces accordingly. The U.S. military strategy, like it or not, must be transformed in light of the proliferation of weapons of mass destruction. Strategic emphasis now needs to be placed on fighting from long-range with systems that are not sensitive to surprise attack or access denial. Moreover, the enormous destructive capacity and killing power of WMD compels an adoption of a strategy focused intensely on the earliest hours and days of a crisis. An integrated conventional-WMD strategy must be designed and supported with the forces necessary to halt an armored invasion far short of the attacker's objectives and to locate and destroy as much of the enemy's WMD as possible before they are delivered against friendly forces and populations.

Adapting U.S. military strategy to project military power overseas in the face of WMD-armed adversaries is no longer tomorrow's problem. Nevertheless, the Department of Defense has not yet fully recognized that the WMD threat compels an abandonment of its outmoded conventional warfare paradigm and adaptation to more versatile conventional-WMD power projection operations in the earliest hours of an attack. "In short," the National Defense Panel correctly asserted, "we must radically alter the way in which we project power."[14]

A "Splintering" of Warfare

WMD-armed adversaries can be expected to use their new-found equalizer weapons innovatively through asymmetric applications of military power against weaknesses in America's conventional military strategy. The current conventional warfare model is dependent on time, and lots of it, and

---

[14] *Ibid.,* p. 33.

---

unhindered access to theater seaports, airfields, and operating bases. This is the wrong paradigm for dealing with WMD-armed adversaries. First, currently planned transoceanic power projection operations will not work when the adversary has the capability to threaten or actually attack regional seaports, airfields, and other reception facilities. Secondly, delays in inserting U.S. forces can lead to a greater loss of territory, higher friendly casualties, and more time for the aggressor to achieve his objectives and present the U.S. with a fait accompli. To retain its coherence and relevance to events in overseas theaters, the U.S. transoceanic power projection strategy must be immunized against such effects of WMD as quickly as possible. One way of vaccinating American military strategy is to develop timely and effective asymmetric initiatives for exploiting the enemy's weaknesses.

An appropriately framed integrated conventional-WMD strategy would abandon the counter-offensive as the doctrinal centerpiece of U.S. military strategy and shift both thinking and resources toward an early defense operational concept. Halting an invasion quickly would minimize the loss of territory and friendly casualties. A parallel effort to locate and destroy enemy WMD could relieve the threat on seaports and airfields sufficiently to facilitate the introduction of land warfare forces, tactical fighters, and ships. In a word, the United States needs to recognize the "splintering" of strategy between conventional and conventional-WMD warfare.

Standing in the path of innovation to deal with WMD are powerful bureaucratic forces inside the Pentagon that favor a business-as-usual, conventional strategy. Rejecting the idea that the advent of WMD dictates new strategic and operational doctrines, the Defense Department, like Gulliver depicted in the Introduction to Part I, is "blissfully unaware," or chooses to ignore, the dynamic new circumstances challenging the longstanding U.S. conventional military strategy. For starters, the Defense Department's budget-based approach to strategy-making is bankrupt. Budget-driven strategy confuses weapons with war and applies outdated concepts to contemporary problems—its balance sheet algorithms factor out the psychological dynamics of America's next first battle. Army General J. H. Binford Peay III, formerly the commander-in-chief of U.S. forces ensuring security of the Persian Gulf, offered a trenchant observation and warning at his retirement in September 1997: "I am convinced that we are living in the 'interwar years'—a period akin in so many ways to that of the 1920s and '30s, when Americans failed to recognize the war clouds gathering in Europe and Asia, embraced isolationism and refused to maintain a properly equipped, trained and ready military."[15]

At the strategic level of warfare the proliferating countries are preparing to play a careful strategy game of chess designed to evoke desired U.S. responses. The United States, on the other hand, so far has been playing checkers in a losing tactical game of pursuing yesterday's conventional strategy in the face of the new WMD threats mushrooming on the horizon. The name of the strategic game between the proliferators and the United States is the political use of non-use of military forces to manipulate the threat perceptions of the other. Will America's strategic will to protect the nation's regional security interests break under the strain of the adversary's innovative uses of WMD to threaten, delay, and even block U.S. overseas deployments? Or, will the United States recognize the new face of warfare and boldly transform its power projection strategy and force structure to counter and neutralize the enemy's initiatives at the outset of future conflicts? Five corollary questions should be answered by U.S. policy makers and military planners:

- How can the United States best deter the use of conventional weapons and weapons of mass destruction against U.S. forces and those of its allies?

- Will the specter of numerous casualties early in the conflict prompt American political and military leaders to pause and think twice about dispatching expeditionary forces overseas?

- What can the United States do to counter the enemy's anti-access operations designed to block American use of regional seaports, airfields, and littoral waters?

- What can the United States do early to halt an aggressor's military forces invading neighboring countries?

- How can the United States best locate and destroy the enemy's WMD sufficiently to enable sustained combat operations by theater-based tactical fighters on land and at sea?

---

[15] Ernest Blazer, "Inside the Ring: Unready Signs," *Washington Times* (October 2, 1997), p. A5.

The New Face of War defines a new warfare paradigm based on a recognition of the need for a break with past doctrinal concepts and developing a workable conventional-WMD strategy. The book explains how events likely to emerge in 1998-2005 will offer the United States an extraordinary opportunity to adapt its military strategy and forces to the realities of the growing WMD threat. The challenges to the U.S. transoceanic power projection strategy will occur sooner than most experts will admit. Forget about the Administration's illusions of America basking in a "strategic lull" or that defenses can be relaxed somewhat since a "peer competitor" is unlikely to emerge until at least 2015.[16] The WMD threat exists today and all indications promise a continuing trend at an accelerating pace.

Indeed, one answer is already clear enough: A "peer competitor" is not necessary to knock the United States off of its superpower pedestal. When North Korea, China, Iran, and other countries are capable of successfully challenging U.S. primacy in the areas covered by the range of their deliverable nuclear, biological, and chemical weapons, the longstanding American conventional strategy of projecting military forces across the oceans to distant overseas theaters will be placed into jeopardy.[17]

Part II—*Proliferation of Weapons of Mass Destruction and Other Advanced Technologies*—provides the details on the proliferation of WMD and advanced conventional weapons around the world. Several countries either possess or soon will have in their arsenals sufficient biological and chemical warfare weapons, and perhaps even a few nuclear weapons, to challenge U.S. projection of its forces overseas. WMD in the hands of terrorists, aided and abetted by state sponsors, can be transformed into a unique military delivery system against U.S. forces early in a conflict. Meanwhile, the open questions surrounding the origins and course of Gulf War Syndrome loom over any U.S. decision to send American forces abroad to engage WMD-armed adversaries.

---

[16] "It would be fair to say that, at least for now, the U.S. is in a *strategic lull,* but faced with a more complex and diverse set of smaller threats. By the phrase 'strategic lull,' we mean that the U.S. currently has *no global peer.* Also, the most likely conflicts are the least threatening (the U.S. could stay out of them); the most challenging are unlikely to occur soon." [emphasis added] See U.S., National Defense University, *1997 Strategic Assessment* (Washington, D.C.: Government Printing Office, 1997), pp. 241-42.

[17] James Chace, "The Pentagon's Superpower Fantasy?," *New York Times* (March 16, 1992), p. A17.

Part III—*A New Power Projection Calculus*—assesses the implications of WMD proliferation for the U.S. conventional strategy. Two lessons of the 1990-91 Persian Gulf War that should have been learned are still absent from the planning assumptions used by the Defense Department. One lesson is the overwhelming dependence of the U.S. armed forces on time to deploy, set up, and employ tactical fighter and heavy land warfare forces in an overseas theater. A second lesson that should have been learned is the dependence of the U.S. conventional strategy on unfettered and easy access to overseas bases, airfields, and other military facilities. These American dependencies offer a regional adversary, using WMD in conjunction with conventional operations, the opportunity to increase the tempo of aggressive operations beyond the pace that deploying U.S. forces can match.

The reader will find a logical, step-by-step unveiling of how proliferation of WMD and advanced conventional weapons, plus state-sponsored WMD terrorism as a weapon of war, are challenging the current U.S. conventional strategy. Apparently oblivious to the military risks looming on the horizon, the Clinton Administration continues to tinker at the margins of the current strategy rather than devise a new one suitable for meeting tomorrow's challenges. A yawning gap exists between the Defense Department's rhetoric and action. The Pentagon has not yet recognized the "splintering" of its past strategy nor taken the steps to form a new framework for developing a conventional-WMD strategy and military forces.

Part IV—*Global Reconnaissance-Strike Complex*—assesses the implications of WMD proliferation analyzed and described in Part III and offers a new strategy and force structure to deal with the emerging WMD threat. The strategy is based on a system-of-systems architecture of existing forces or those entering production. The creation of a Global Reconnaissance-Strike Complex will underwrite an integrated conventional-WMD strategy in which long-range precision strike assets—B-52s, B-1s, B-2s, and cruise missiles— make an early-response "halt and enable" operational concept possible. This warfare model demonstrates how innovative use of long-range precision strike forces and cruise missiles can halt an enemy armored invasion and reduce WMD to levels that may make it possible for deployment of tactical fighters, ground units, and ships to overseas theaters.

In order to enact and facilitate the entire Global Reconnaissance-Strike Complex, four lines of inquiry are prosecuted: (1) bridging the gap in long-range precision strike, 1998 to 2015; (2) developing a long-range plan for a follow-on bomber, 2016 to 2030; (3) defining the functional and organizational changes necessary to enact a new central operational concept; and (4) making force structure trade-offs to free the resources necessary to revitalize America's transoceanic military strategy.

Part V—*The Eleventh Plague*—offers conclusions and recommendations. The analysis suggests how the United States might go about immunizing its strategy against weapons of mass destruction by organizing and equipping the force to conduct long distance warfare.

Proliferation of Weapons of Mass Destruction and Other Advanced Technologies

INTRODUCTION: PART II

As we move into the twenty-first century, the military threats to American interests and allies abroad are increasing in both number and complexity. Indeed, with advanced military technologies proliferating at a dizzying pace, the basic nature of warfare is undergoing a radical transformation. Most troubling for the United States is the regional proliferation of nuclear, chemical and biological weapons—the so-called weapons of mass destruction (WMD)—and their means of delivery. Defense Secretary William S. Cohen's 1997 report to Congress on the *Quadrennial Defense Review* recognizes the reality of this grave new challenge, stating that "...the threat or use of chemical and biological weapons...is a likely condition of future warfare, including in the early stages of war to disrupt U.S. operations and logistics."

What will a twenty-first century proliferator look like? The answer is clear: "Something like Iraq in 1990-91." After all, Saddam Hussein wrote a virtual "how-to" book for any country interested in acquiring nuclear, biological, and chemical weapons and missile delivery systems. Iraq's proliferation activities before the Persian Gulf War blazed a new trail for aspiring proliferators. The Iraqi leader sent students abroad to study science and engineering and who would later provide a cadre of expertise essential to the progress of the WMD programs. He built a web of front companies and re-transferred technology from country to country in elaborate schemes to deceive Western export controls. Iraqi experts reengineered weapons for domestic production and modified others. In some cases, small turn-key pilot-plants on critical technologies were purchased from foreign sources and later were up-scaled for domestic production.

The seven chapters in Part Two examine global proliferation activities and alternative pathways open to aspiring proliferators of nuclear, biological, chemical, and advanced conventional weapons as well as those pursuing ballistic and cruise missile programs. A special chapter examines Gulf War Syndrome and its implications for U.S. operations in contaminated environments. Super-terrorism, or the use of WMD by terrorists as a weapon of warfare, is assessed in a second special chapter.

Part Two provides an essential building block for understanding how proliferation activities by rogue regimes and other countries around the world are multiplying the risks to successful execution of America's longstanding transoceanic power projection strategy. The strategic assessments in Part Two lay the groundwork for an examination of the implications of the growing threat to the U.S. military strategy and forces.

CHAPTER 2

Nuclear and Radiological Weapons

"**I**f Saddam Hussein had delayed his invasion of Kuwait for two or three years until Iraq had nuclear weapons, he very likely would be in possession of Kuwait and quite possibly the Saudi oil fields also," says Samuel P. Huntington, a Harvard University professor and former member of the National Security Council.[1] This judgment by a serious, no-nonsense observer of the world scene foretells serious consequences for the United States and its allies. It says to Americans that the leaders of several non-Western countries[2] may perceive great geopolitical prizes at the end of a nuclear weapons rainbow. Thus, significant incentives underwrite their attempts to bridge the nuclear fault line between the United States and themselves.

For the proliferators, nuclear weapons provide a means of establishing dominance over neighboring regional states while at the same time deterring intervention by the United States and other outside powers. Indeed, non-Western countries drew special lessons from the Gulf War.

> For the North Korean military these were: "Don't let the Americans build up their forces; don't let them put in air power; don't let them take the initiative; don't let them fight a war with low U.S. casualties." For a top Indian military official the lesson was even more explicit: "Don't fight the United States unless you have nuclear weapons." That lesson has been taken to heart by political leaders and

---

[1] Samuel P. Huntington, *Clash of Civilizations and the Remaking of World Order* (New York: Simon & Schuster, 1996), p. 186.

[2] Semantic Alert: The political-military jargon of the Cold War of "East -West," "North- South," "Third World," and the like seem out of place in the new era. A more relevant frame of reference is offered by Professor Huntington in terms of contemporary civilizations and world order. Western civilization includes Europe and North America, plus New Zealand and Australia. Hence, the "non-Western countries" include those in the other major civilizations: Sinic (China, related cultures in Korea and Vietnam, and Chinese communities in Southeast Asia), Japanese, Hindu, Islamic, Latin American, and African. *Ibid.,* pp. 40-48.

---

military chiefs throughout the non-Western world, as a plausible corollary: "If you have nuclear weapons, the United States won't fight you."[3]

"Going nuclear" for a non-Western state poses a number of strategic and operational questions for the United States. What can the proliferating country do with a few nuclear weapons, say five to ten deliverable bombs and warheads? What do these military capabilities mean for them and for us? How will their possession of few nuclear weapons change their operational concepts? How far has their armed forces gone in integrating conventional and nuclear military operations? With due consideration to the technologies, systems, forces and doctrine at the core of their conventional-nuclear operations, how effective will they be?

One thing is clear about nuclear proliferation: for the proliferator, these weapons hold the potential of serving as an "equalizer" to the conventional military superiority of the United States. The non-Western nuclear states do not have to attack American forces or their regional allies directly to elicit significant strategic advantages. North Korea, for instance, might threaten the destruction of a Japanese city to deter U.S. intervention in South Korea.[4] A new nuclear state in the Persian Gulf or Middle East might threaten to strike a European city, if the U.S. and its allies persist in deploying military forces near its borders. Assessing the potential impact of such political uses of force on the U.S. strategy remains elusive for American planners. Since the international community may be opposed to unilateral nuclear solutions, it is not at all clear that the United States would be able to bring its own sizable advantage to bear against a country holding just a few atomic weapons.

During the Cold War, the United States and its European allies faced-down Moscow's overwhelming conventional military superiority and Soviet divisions poised along NATO's borders by threatening the first use of nuclear weapons to shore up its deterrence and defense posture. Hence, it was not surprising when the Russians announced in May 1997 that they had adopted a nuclear first use policy. "We're not speaking of making a first

---

[3] *Ibid.*, pp. 186-87

[4] William Kincade, *Nuclear Proliferation: Diminishing Threat?*, INSS Occasional Paper 6 (U.S. Air Force Academy, Colo.: Institute for National Security Studies, December 1995), p. 40.

The New Face of War

strike in order to secure advantage," explained Boris Berezovsky, the deputy head of Russia's security council, "but if we are driven into a corner and are left with no other option, we will resort to nuclear weapons."[5]

South Asia Arms Race

India and Pakistan jolted the world in May 1998 when New Delhi tested five nuclear devices and Islamabad answered with six underground tests of its own. India said that its action was in response to Pakistan's April test firing of 900-mile range nuclear capable missiles, which can cover all of India's main population centers, and the belief that China—New Delhi's principal military threat—had positioned tactical nuclear weapons near the Indian border in Tibet.

India's first three explosions tested three kinds of weapons: those to be fired by artillery or dropped from tactical fighters, a mid-size blast for bombs that might be dropped by bombers, and full hydrogen bomb from a fission device, showing that India's thermonuclear technology worked. A second round of Indian explosions tested low yield devices. Prime Minister Atal Bihari Vajpayee declared that "we have the capacity for a big bomb now," and added that "ours will never be weapons of aggression."[6]

Pakistan answered India's challenge on May 28 with five nuclear tests between two and twelve kilotons; a sixth underground explosion took place on May 30. Foreign Secretary Shamshad Ahmad said that the six devices tested by Pakistan "correspond to weapons configuration compatible with delivery systems" developed by the country.[7] "Our security...was gravely threatened," Pakistan's Prime Minister Nawaz Sharif explained. "Our hand was forced by the present Indian leadership's reckless actions. We could not ignore the magnitude of the threat."[8] While Pakistan denied that actual

---

[5] David Hoffman, "Yeltsin Approves Doctrine of Nuclear First Use If Attacked," *Washington Post* (May 10, 1997), p. A21.

[6] Kenneth J. Cooper, "Premier Says India Capable of 'Big Bomb,'" *Washington Post* (May 16, 1998), pp. A1, A23. See also Toni Marshall, "India Announces Nuclear Tests: Move Could Spark Response By Its Bitter Rival, Pakistan," *Washington Times* (May 12, 1998), pp. A1, A11; Lorraine Woellert, "After Atomic Tests, Economic Fallout?," *Washington Times* (May 13, 1998), p. A14; Kenneth J. Cooper, "India Conducts 2nd Round of Nuclear Tests," *Washington Post* (May 14, 1998), pp. A1, A28; and Kenneth J. Cooper, "Leader Says India Has A 'Credible' Deterrent," *Washington Post* (June 17, 1998), p. A21.

[7] John Ward Anderson and Kamran Khan, "Pakistan Again Explodes Bomb," *Washington Post* (May 31, 1998), pp. A1, A23.

[8] John Ward Anderson and Kamran Khan, "Pakistan Sets Off Nuclear Blasts," *Washington Post* (May 29, 1998), pp. A1, A32.

---

weaponization of its delivery systems with nuclear weapons had taken place, it was quite clear that Islamabad's military was poised just "a screwdriver turn away" from nuclear bombs.

The arms race dynamics in South Asia are based on three main driving forces. First is the longstanding conflict between India and Pakistan, including three major wars, two major near-war crises, and an ongoing struggle over Kashmir whose sovereignty has been open to question since 1947. The second driving force of the arms race is the fact that India's most potent possible enemy is the nuclear-armed China, and Pakistan's most powerful enemy is a militarily superior India. This three-cornered dynamic is also motivated by China's military assistance to Pakistan, including nuclear technology and ballistic missiles, and India's concern that it could face a two-front war with Pakistan in the west and China to the north.[9] A third factor of the arms race is the deep Indian resentment against the West, and particularly the United States, for declaring that the five nuclear powers, including China, could have nuclear weapons and India and other countries could not. General Krishnaswami Sundarji, former Chief of the Indian Army, put the issue quite plainly at a U.S. arms control conference in 1993: "The trouble with you Americans is you think that just because I have a brown face I should not have nuclear weapons."[10]

In 1995, General Sundarji presented the conditions for a non-nuclear India with great clarity. The United States and Russia would have to cut back their arsenals to ten percent of their force levels at that time; Britain, France, and China would cap their arsenals at the levels existing in mid-1995, and "all the five so-called legitimate nuclear powers give up privileged treatment in production of fissile material, or avoiding intrusive international inspection of all facilities." He argued that the five nuclear powers accept a "non-discriminatory" comprehensive test ban treaty, make no first use pledges, and place their nuclear weapons under control of the United

---

[9] John H. Sandrock, *Arms Control and Nonproliferation: South Asia* (McLean, Va.: Science Applications International Corporation, November 19, 1993), pp. 3-8.

[10] General Krishnaswami Sundarji, Army of India (retired), remarks at the U.S. Defense Nuclear Agency's *International Conference on Controlling Arms* (Richmond, Va.: Defense Nuclear Agency, June 7-10, 1993). Later, when the writer jokingly reminded General Sundarji of his comments, he said: "I remember that and I stand by every word." See also M. R. Narayan Swamy, "India Lashes West for 'Hypocrisy' of Anti-Nuclear Stance," *Washington Times* (May 21, 1998), p. A19, and Selig S. Harrison, "India's Muscle Flexing Is Over: Let the Bargaining Begin," *Washington Post* (May 17, 1998), pp. C1, C7.

Nations. This scenario, General Sundarji contends, "...will eliminate the danger to civilization as we know it from mass use of nuclear weapons."[11] On the other hand, if the world's nuclear regime continues to be "thoroughly discriminatory and cynical" and the United States feels compelled to retain a large nuclear arsenal, "the message to regional powers with more live and immediate threats, some of them nuclear, would be loud and clear. There is no alternative to nuclear weapons and ballistic missiles if you are to live in security and with honor."[12] He added that "nuclear weapons can only be deterred by nuclear weapons...it is enough if India goes for minimum deterrence." All that is required is an assured capability of a second strike. "Hence, nuclear arms racing is truly counter productive."[13]

The Stockholm International Peace Research Institute (SIPRI) estimates that at the end of 1995 India possessed 330 kilograms of plutonium (plus or minus twenty percent) or enough for twenty to twenty-five nuclear weapons. Having exploded five nuclear devices in 1998, India is positioned to develop a strong military nuclear program. Sixty to eighty weapons would be required to defend against China and fewer for conflict with Pakistan.[14]

Pakistan is motivated to acquire and use nuclear weapons to counter India's nuclear capability and superior conventional military capabilities. The Pakistani people view nuclear weapons as an equalizing factor vis-a-vis India, and, since they are the holders of the "Islamic Bomb," the weapons serve as a status symbol. SIPRI estimated that at the end of 1995 the Pakistanis possessed 210 kilograms of highly enriched uranium (plus or minus twenty five percent) or enough for five to ten nuclear weapons. Some fifteen to twenty-five nuclear weapons might be required to hold several

---

[11] General Krishnaswami Sundarji, Army of India (retired), "Strategic Stability in the Early 2000s: An Indian View of a South Asian Model" in *NATO Advanced Research Workshop: Strategic Stability in the Post-Cold War World and the Future of Nuclear Disarmament,* ed. by Melvin L. Best, Jr., John Hughes-Wilson, and Andrei A. Piontkowsky (Brussels, Belgium: NATO Scientific and Environmental Affairs Division, April 6-10, 1995), p. 152.

[12] *Ibid.,* p. 153.

[13] *Ibid.,* p. 162.

[14] John H. Sandrock, "South Asian Proliferation Drivers" in *Adjusting to Change: Understanding Proliferation Risks,* a Defense Nuclear Agency-Sponsored Strategic Options Assessments Conference (McLean, Va.: Strategic Planning International, Inc.,1994), pp. A82 thru A92; U.S., Foreign Broadcast Information Service, *Proliferation Issues,* p. 26; David Albright, "A Proliferation Primer," *Bulletin of Atomic Scientists* (June 1993), p. 22; and David Albright, Frans Berkhout and William Walker, "Fact Sheet: Plutonium and Highly Enriched Uranium 1996: World Inventories, Capabilities and Policies" (March 13, 1997) (photocopy).

---

major Indian targets at risk, including Delhi and Bombay. Despite pledges to the United States to cease its assistance to Pakistan's nuclear and missile programs, China continued to sell nuclear weapons-related equipment to Pakistan in 1996 and 1997, including the sale of ring magnets essential to uranium enrichment and a special industrial furnace and advanced diagnostic equipment with military applications in nuclear facilities.[15]

India's and Pakistan's nuclear tests in May 1998 were clearly linked with weapons delivery systems in their respective arsenals. Both are now nuclear weapons states. Yet, the five nuclear powers (the "Big Five") acknowledged by the Nuclear Non-Proliferation Treaty—Britain, France, Russia, China, and the United States—refused to grant India and Pakistan the status of being recognized nuclear weapons states. The Nuclear Non-Proliferation Treaty, which is ratified by 186 countries, restricts the "nuclear club" to these five powers. Neither India nor Pakistan are members of the Treaty. The Big Five took the position that admitting India and Pakistan to the "Club" would reward them for testing nuclear weapons and encourage other countries to follow suit. A joint statement of the Big Five acknowledged nuclear powers called on both South Asia countries to sign the Nuclear Non-Proliferation Treaty and the Comprehensive Test Ban Treaty.

Pakistan said the "approach has been manifestly lopsided, unjust and unrealistic" since it did not offer concrete measures by the international community to seek a resolution of the Kashmir issue.[16] India rejected any outside involvement in its dispute with Pakistan over Kashmir. Vasundhara Raje, India's Minister of State for External Affairs, detailed China's assistance to Pakistan's nuclear weapons program to parliament: "China has provided assistance, inter alia, in setting up an unsafeguarded research reactor and plutonium reprocessing facility, providing ring magnets, heavy water, diagnostic equipment, etc." India chastised the Big Five nuclear powers for failing to recognize and take action to address this clear violation of the Nuclear Non-Proliferation Treaty.[17]

---

[15] Sandrock, "South Asian Proliferation Drivers" in *Adjusting to Change: Understanding Proliferation Risks,* pp. A94 thru A95; Albright, Berkhout and Walker, "Fact Sheet: Plutonium and Highly Enriched Uranium 1996;" and Bill Gertz, "Arms Agency Finds Beijing Broke Pledge," *Washington Times* (August 16, 1997), pp. A1, A4.

[16] "Both India and Pakistan Reject U.N. Call to Sign Nuclear Treaty," *Armed Forces Presswire (June 7, 1998).*

[17] Hari Ramachandran, "India Criticizes Big Five on China," *Washington Times* (June 6, 1998), pp. A1, A7.

In the wake of the nuclear tests in South Asia, Henry Kissinger urged U.S. policy to move forward on the basis of geopolitical analysis rather than "Wilsonian universalism." "India and Pakistan are testing because living as they do in a tough neighborhood, they will not risk their survival on the exhortations coming from countries basing their own security on nuclear weapons," Kissinger observed. "Therefore, American policy should move from treating India and Pakistan as the problem to incorporating them into the solution as partners in a nonproliferation regime and in easing political tension in South Asia." American objectives, the former secretary of state counselled, should be focused on containing further nuclear proliferation and addressing political and arms control issues affecting the region, "including protecting a second-strike capability and the prevention of accidents."[18]

Nuclear Proliferators

A rationale similar to those motivating India and Pakistan to become nuclear weapons states might be expressed by leaders of other non-Western states in succumbing to the powerful incentives for obtaining nuclear weapons. There are some good reasons to believe nuclear proliferation will plague the world community for some years to come. Russian analysts correctly identify four basic driving forces behind the attempts of non-Western countries to obtain nuclear weapons. One, the "fear factor," is a particularly strong proliferation driving force when states are confronted by a potential regional adversary possessing weapons of mass destruction or conventional military superiority. Another is the "containment factor" of making it very clear to a future enemy that even with its military superiority it is not immune from a devastating counterstrike. The "victory factor" is offensively oriented to achieve an overwhelming and quick advantage in a conflict through the actual or threatened use of nuclear weapons. And, finally, the "extreme measure factor" is associated with the opportunity to threaten or use nuclear weapons when facing the prospect of complete military defeat.[19]

---

[18] Henry Kissinger, "India and Pakistan: After the Explosions," *Washington Post* (June 9, 1998), p. A15, and Richard D. Fisher and John T. Dori, *The Strategic Implications of China's Nuclear Aid to Pakistan,* Executive Memorandum No. 532 (Washington, D.C.: Heritage Foundation, June 16, 1998).

[19] U.S., Foreign Broadcast Information Service, *Proliferations Issues – Russian Federation: Foreign Intelligence Service Report – A New Challenge After the Cold War: Proliferation of Weapons of Mass Destruction,* JPRS-TND-93-007 (March 5, 1993), p. 5.

In addition to the five acknowledged nuclear weapons states, India, and Pakistan, three groups of countries are of interest in nuclear proliferation matters. First are the *opaque countries* or those already possessing nuclear capabilities but who do not officially acknowledge the fact. A second group is the *threshold countries* or those whose leadership has already made the policy decision to obtain nuclear weapons, and the necessary technical and scientific facilities are being assembled over time toward fielding a militarily significant arsenal (five to ten weapons) in the near future.[20] And, third, *near-threshold countries* are those that have initiated actions to develop or otherwise obtain nuclear weapons but do not yet have the requisite technical and scientific expertise nor the industrial infrastructure needed to produce weapons in the near-term. See Figure 2.1.

Opaque Countries. Two states make up this group—they possess nuclear weapons or the standby capabilities to produce them quickly.

- *Israel* began plutonium separation at its reactor at Dimona in the mid-1950s and expanded its capabilities in the 1960s with French assistance. SIPRI[21] estimates that Israel possessed 460 kilograms of plutonium (with a twenty-five percent plus or minus uncertainty band) at the end of 1995 or an amount sufficient for sixty to 110 nuclear weapons. Five to ten nuclear weapons can be manufactured per year. By the mid-1990s, Israel is believed to have possessed between 100 and 200 weapons, with one estimate as high as 240 weapons.[22] The problem for Israel is the vulnerability of its Zachariah missile base and nuclear storage area to just a few nuclear-tipped non-Western ballistic missiles. "By being vulnerable to a ballistic missile with a

---

[20] Five to ten nuclear weapons are "militarily significant" since even so few weapons should be enough to coerce neighbors to do the possessor's bidding—like denying the U.S. access to its military facilities—and to strike the few major ports and airfields that might be used by U.S. forces being introduced into the theater. Even after nuclear strikes aimed at denying the U.S. access, enough weapons should be left over to hold their neighbors' urban areas at risk to deter American retaliation and compel the United States to limit its war aims.

[21] The Stockholm International Peace Research Institute (SIPRI) maintains databases on arms producing countries and conventional arms transfers. Information from these databases is published annually in the *SIPRI Yearbook* and is made available to researchers visiting the Institute.

[22] David Albright, Frans Berkhout, and William Walker, *Plutonium and Highly Enriched Uranium 1996: World Inventories, Capabilities and Policies* (Stockholm International Peace Research Institute and Oxford University Press, 1997) and "Fact Sheet: Plutonium and Highly Enriched Uranium 1996, and U.S., Foreign Broadcast Information Service, *Proliferation Issues*, p. 29.

The New Face of War

Figure 2.1

Global Nuclear Possession and Potential Proliferation

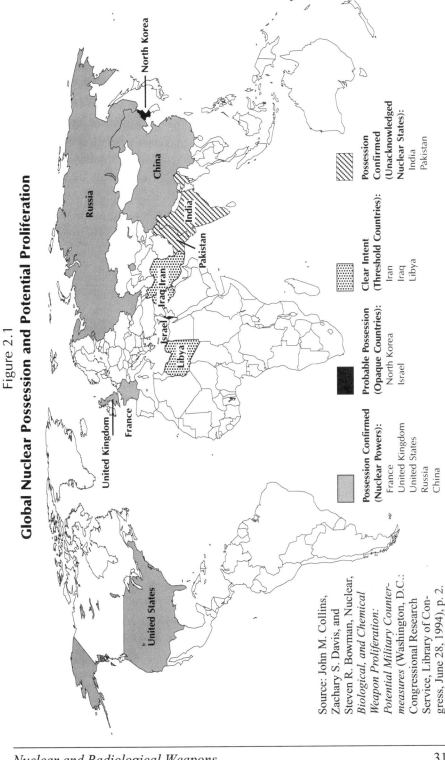

Source: John M. Collins,
Zachary S. Davis, and
Steven R. Bowman, *Nuclear,
Biological, and Chemical
Weapon Proliferation:
Potential Military Counter-
measures* (Washington, D.C.:
Congressional Research
Service, Library of Con-
gress, June 28, 1994), p. 2.

**Possession Confirmed
(Nuclear Powers):**
France
United Kingdom
United States
Russia
China

**Probable Possession
(Opaque Countries):**
North Korea
Israel

**Clear Intent
(Threshold Countries):**
Iran
Iraq
Libya

**Possession
Confirmed
(Unacknowledged
Nuclear States):**
India
Pakistan

crude nuclear device," writes defense analyst Harold Hough, "Israel may be forced to launch a pre-emptive nuclear strike rather than risk losing the ability to respond with nuclear weapons."[23]

- Many believe North Korea possesses some thirty kilograms of plutonium (plus or minus twenty percent) and from two to five nuclear weapons. On-again, off-again U.S. intelligence estimates ranged as high as three possible weapons and then dropped back to zero weapons, apparently based on domestic political pressures inside the United States. Even if the weapons do not exist, the North Koreans can be expected to wring out of the United States, Japan, and South Korea economic and security guarantees through skillful manipulation of perceptions. If the weapons do exist, the North Koreans could sell them to third parties for hard currency, deter attacks, fight and win wars, and assure the regime's survival.[24]

Threshold countries. Iraq, Iran, Taiwan, Japan and South Korea. Owing to the wartime and post-war destruction of *Iraq's* nuclear facilities, Baghdad's program is in abeyance awaiting the end of the U.N. on-site inspections. The Iraqis still possess the know-how and have the scientists and engineers necessary to restart its quest to obtain or produce nuclear weapons (see details below). *Iran* continues its efforts to build the industrial base necessary to produce nuclear weapons around 2005 to 2007. Iran's dependence on foreign assistance in the science and technology needed to build a viable program is inhibiting its progress. Nonetheless, many analysts believe Tehran is moving closer to possessing nuclear weapons and will produce them just after the turn of the century.

Taiwan, Japan and South Korea are included as threshold countries because of inconsistencies in their peaceful nuclear programs. Each country possesses nuclear power reactors, scientific equipment, laboratories, and skilled scientists and engineers that would allow development of nuclear weapons, if the policy decision was made to do so. A secret program in

[23] Harold Hough, "Could Israel's Nuclear Assets Survive a First Strike?," *Jane's Intelligence Review* (September 1997), pp. 407-10.

[24] Richard E. Darilek, "What Drives North Korea's Nuclear Program" in *Adjusting to Change: Understanding Proliferation Risks,* a Defense Nuclear Agency-Sponsored Strategic Options Assessments Conference (McLean, Va.: Strategic Planning International, Inc., 1994), pp. A72 thru A81, and Albright, Berkhout and Walker, "Fact Sheet: Plutonium and Highly Enriched Uranium 1996."

The New Face of War

Taiwan to produce nuclear weapons was halted in December 1987. Colonel Chang Hsien-yi, deputy director of Taiwan's nuclear research institute, stole vital documentation and turned it over to the U.S. Central Intelligence Agency. A long-time C.I.A. agent, Colonel Chang defected to the U.S. and helped to smuggle reams of documentation out of Taiwan. Confronted by irrefutable evidence, Taiwanese officials acceded to American demands and halted the nuclear program.[25] Public policy groups in the United States ten years later speculate that Taiwan might be within twelve to twenty-four months of building a nuclear bomb.[26]

In 1994, Japan "misplaced" 154 pounds of plutonium, enough to make nine nuclear bombs, or rather it was found stuck inside the fuel processing machinery of the country's plutonium program. South Korea shut down its military nuclear program in the mid-1970s under pressure from the United States. By the 1990s, however, South Korea had developed an advanced program for the production of nuclear energy, which employs nearly 5,000 scientists and practical workers. Many of the prerequisites for a military nuclear program are already in the country.[27] Each of these countries have reason to hedge their dependence on the United States in the face of the growing regional power of China.

Japan also faces the potential of a nuclear-armed unified Korea in the near-term. Greenpeace International puts the issue plainly: "A nation with a store of separated plutonium is a nation with a nuclear option."[28] This general statement applies equally to Japan and South Korea as well as others worldwide.

Near-threshold countries. The nuclear "wanna-be's" include some despotic states that are distinctly unfriendly toward the United States. Others are countries with established non-nuclear positions but whose intentions could change when threat conditions mount or changes in the ruling regime move the country in new directions. Among the most likely proliferators under such circumstances are Egypt and Algeria. Turkey could reevaluate its non-nuclear position, if a nuclear-armed Iraq or Iran emerges

---

[25] Tim Weiner, "US Spy Halted Taiwan N-Bomb," *New York Times* (December 22, 1997).

[26] "Nuclear Taiwan," *CQ Washington Alert* (December 22, 1997).

[27] U.S., Foreign Broadcast Information Service, *Proliferation Issues,* p. 37; Charles J. Hanley, "Iran's Nuclear Effort Behind Schedule," *Washington Times* (May 5, 1997), p. A13; and "General Warns On Iran Nukes," *Washington Times* (June 27, 1997), p. A10.

[28] *The Plutonium Trade: A Troubling New Era of Proliferation* (Greenpeace International, March 1, 1993), p. 1.

---

on its borders. Saudi Arabia was strongly rumored during the Persian Gulf War to be seeking to purchase nuclear weapons, although there are no reports of a completed transaction. Nonetheless, the lax controls inside Russia over fissile material and, increasingly, nuclear weapons, combined with the economic straits of many of those Russians entrusted to guard the weapons and material, give reason for pause. The transfer of nuclear weapons or bomb-grade nuclear materials could put weapons into the hands of rogue regimes very quickly. Iran, for instance, is said to be experiencing difficulty with its nuclear program and "is in the market for nuclear materials."[29]

Courtesy of Saddam Hussein, potential proliferators everywhere now have a textbook for developing nuclear and radiological weapons. The Iraqi leader blazed a new trail for proliferators to follow. Moreover, the scientists and engineers that put together Iraq's nuclear weapons program are still available to assist in the "how-to" aspects of building a bomb. If a country can obtain a sufficient amount of weapons grade fissile material from external sources, it will have substantially eased the bomb-making process.

Nuclear Smuggling

The single greatest challenge to producing nuclear weapons is acquiring a sufficient amount of fissile material. This barrier has crumbled since 1994 with the leakage of nuclear materials from the former Soviet Union. "There is now a clear and present danger that the essential ingredients of nuclear bombs could fall into the hands of radical states or terrorist groups," John P. Holdren, an adviser to President Clinton, explains.[30]

Highly enriched uranium (HEU) or plutonium are the materials that can sustain a nuclear chain reaction resulting in a tremendous release of energy in a short period of time—a nuclear explosion. As little as eight kilograms (17.6 pounds) or twenty-five kilograms (55 pounds) of HEU could be used by terrorists or proliferating countries to produce a nuclear explosion.[31]

---

[29] "Iran's Weapons Development, Limping Poor Economy Saps Alleged Nuclear Program," *MSNBC* (December 10, 1997).

[30] As quoted in James L. Ford, "Nuclear Smuggling: How Serious a Threat?," *Strategic Forum*, No. 59 (Washington, D.C.: National Defense University, January 1996), p. 1.

[31] U.S., General Accounting Office, *Nuclear Nonproliferation: Status of U.S. Efforts to Improve Nuclear Material Controls in Newly Independent States,* GAO/NSIAD/RCED-96-89 (Washington, D.C.: March 1996), p. 2.

The uranium route is centered on separating the uranium-235 (HEU) isotope from the more common uranium-238. Several alternative processes can be used to enrich uranium; they all involve complex and expensive facilities.[32] A country could also obtain weapons-usable materials by buying, stealing or otherwise obtaining it from supplier countries or international crime syndicates.

Weapons-grade plutonium is created when the naturally occurring uranium-238 isotope, which cannot be used for weapons purposes directly, is irradiated in a nuclear reactor. The irradiation will convert a part of the uranium-238 into plutonium-239. To make the plutonium-239 useful for nuclear bomb-making, it must be separated from the unconverted uranium and irradiated byproducts through chemical reprocessing. Plutonium separated from the spent fuel of a commercial nuclear power reactor (i.e., reactor grade) is also weapons-usable, although further enrichment processing might be preferred. By 2003, the world's plutonium supply from dismantled warheads will be sufficient to make 40,000 nuclear bombs; another 65,000 bombs could be made from the highly enriched uranium taken from dismantled warheads. In addition, the growing stockpiles of reactor-grade plutonium in Japan and Western Europe will be sufficient to produce 47,000 bombs.

Once a sufficient amount of weapons-grade fissile material is obtained, the process of devising a nuclear device is rather simple. Separated U-235 would give a proliferating state or terrorist organization a capability to produce workable nuclear bombs in short order. Even a primitive, low-yield device from reactor-grade plutonium would be sufficient to set off an explosion that could destroy a city and produce extensive radioactive fallout.[33]

When government officials in Kazakhstan realized in 1994 that they had inherited about 1,000 pounds of highly enriched uranium—sufficient for about twenty weapons—from the breakup of the Soviet Union, they

---

[32] Uranium enrichment technologies include thermal diffusion, gaseous diffusion, gas centrifuge, aerodynamic processes, chemical exchange processes, laser processes, and electromagnetic processes. For details see Appendix 4-B in U.S., Congress, Office of Technology Assistance, *Technologies Underlying Weapons of Mass Destruction,* OTA-BP-ISC-115 (Washington, D.C.: Government Printing Office, December 1993), pp. 176-80.

[33] Guy B. Roberts, *Five Minutes Past Midnight: The Clear and Present Danger of Nuclear Weapons Grade Fissile Materials,* INSS Occasional Paper 8 (U.S. Air Force Academy, Colo.: Institute for National Security Studies, February 1996), pp. 2-3, and Joanne Charnetski and Tariq Rauf, "Let Canada Cremate Nuclear Swords," *Defense News* (October 3-9, 1994), pp. 23-24.

---

found that the Iranians already were trying to get their hands on it. Instead, the Kazakhs sold the material to the United States for $20 million, and it was subsequently flown to America on military transports for disposal.[34]

In 1994, weapons-grade samples of fissile material were recovered by Western authorities in five separate cases: (1) 5.6 grams of plutonium-239 (99.7% pure) in Tengen, Germany; (2) 0.8 grams of uranium-235 (88% pure) in Landshut, Germany; (3) 350 grams of plutonium-239 (87% pure) in Munich, Germany; (4) 1.0 gram or more of plutonium suitable for military use (unconfirmed) in Verona, Italy; and (5) 2.7 kilograms (six pounds) of uranium-235 (88% enriched) in Prague, Czech Republic.[35]

The safeguarding of nuclear warheads and weapons-usable fissile materials in Russia is among the highest U.S. national security concerns. The estimated inventory in the former Soviet Union includes 30,000 nuclear warheads, 1,200 metric tons of weapons-usable highly enriched uranium and 200 metric tons of separated plutonium in weapons or available for weapons. Most of this bomb-making material lacks adequate security and supply control and accounting. Many research centers and weapons production centers have been required to provide their own security since military guards have been removed from many facilities. This material is located at eighty to 100 civilian research, naval nuclear propulsion, and civilian-controlled nuclear weapons-related facilities.[36]

The prospect for illicit theft and diversion of fissile materials is great. Since they are not very radioactive, they are relatively safe to handle, and they are stored in containers that can be easily carried by one or two persons or in components from dismantled weapons. The theft potential of weapons themselves is also high. Tactical nuclear weapons and nuclear torpedoes are most at risk because of their size and lack of adequate physical security. The torpedoes, for instance, have easily removable locks.[37]

---

[34] Graham Allison, "Testimony to the Senate Committee on Government Affairs, Permanent Subcommittee on Investigations" (Cambridge, Mass.: Harvard University, March 13, 1996) (photocopy).

[35] Ford, "Nuclear Smuggling," p. 2.

[36] U.S., General Accounting Office, *Nuclear Nonproliferation,* pp. 3-5; Thomas B. Cochran, "Nuclear Weapons and Fissile Material Security in Russia," testimony before the Committee on Foreign Affairs, Subcommittee on International Security, International Organizations and Human Rights (National Resource Defense Council, Inc., June 27, 1994) (photocopy); and Christoph Bluth, "Russia's Nuclear Forces: A Clear and Present Danger," *Jane's Intelligence Review* (December 1997), p. 551.

[37] U.S., General Accounting Office, *Nuclear Nonproliferation,* p. 5, and Bill Gertz, "Russian Renegades Pose Nuke Danger," *Washington Times* (October 22, 1996), p. A18.

The deteriorating standard of living among most Russians, including the military and others entrusted to safeguard nuclear weapons and materials, could lead to the theft and smuggling of fissile material out of the country. The commander of the Siberian Military Region sent President Boris Yeltsin a telegram on February 14, 1997, informing him that the "officers and men have reached the limits of survival. No one has been paid in six months. Many families do not even have enough money to buy bread." Shortly afterward, defense minister Igor Rodionov sent an even more ominous warning to President Yeltsin: "Russia will soon reach a limit beyond which we will not be able to control missiles and nuclear systems." For the right perspective, imagine William S. Cohen, the U.S. Secretary of Defense, giving this assessment to President Clinton.

Previously, more than 400 nuclear power plant employees went on strike in December 1996 over unpaid wages; a dozen workers occupied the control room and threatened to shut down St. Petersburg's energy supply if the wages were not paid. This is another event indicating that the possibility remains high of illicit transfers of fissile material.

Organized crime and corruption have emerged as Russia's top problems. President Boris Yeltsin estimates that as many as forty percent of private businessmen and sixty percent of all Russian companies have ties with organized crime. There are about 8,000 criminal gangs in Russia and the other former Soviet republics. Some 200 of these are global conglomerates that have worked out a division of labor with American, Sicilian, and Columbian crime syndicates. Criminal activities by the Russian gangs have been detected in seventeen American cities. The most powerful members pursue criminal activity in arms and drug trafficking, gambling, banking, petroleum exports, automobile theft and smuggling, precious metals trading, and similar ventures.[38]

Alexander Lebed, former Russian general and security council secretary, claimed during a CBS *60 Minutes* interview in September 1997 that, when he tried to account for more than 100 suitcase-sized nuclear weapons held by the armed forces, he could locate only forty-eight. General Lebed suggested that the one-kiloton weapons could be in Georgia, Ukraine, or the

---

[38] William H. Webster and others, *Russian Organized Crime* (Washington, D.C.: Center for Strategic and International Studies, 1997), pp. 2-3, and Graham H. Turbiville, Jr., *Weapons Proliferation and Organized Crime: The Russian Military and Security Force Dimension,* INSS Occasional Paper 10 (U.S. Air Force Academy, Colo.: Institute for National Security Studies, June 1996), p. 5.

Baltic states. Russian authorities disputed the claim, including the existence of such weapons. Congressman Curt Weldon has the right perspective: "Increases in crime, corruption and incompetence and institutional decay are so advanced in Russia that the theft of nuclear weapons, unthinkable in the Soviet war machine of the Cold War, seems entirely plausible in the Russia of today."[39] Reportedly, the U.S. intelligence community acknowledging that it could not disprove Lebed's claim, also could find "no credible evidence" that warheads have been diverted, stolen or sold.[40] "As a representative of the Defense Ministry," announced Russian spokesman Vladimir Uvarenko, "I declare there are no nuclear bombs in Russia out of control of the Russian armed forces."[41] Senator Richard Lugar, on the other hand, questions Russia's nuclear accounting procedures: "The Russian inventory system is so antiquated and inefficient that the Russians do not have an accurate count of nuclear weapons or materials."[42]

Alexi Yablokov, a former member of the Russian Security Council, explained in his October 1997 testimony at the U.S. House of Representatives that he was "absolutely sure they have been made." He explained that the weapons were developed by the KGB secret police in the 1970s and that they were not really "suitcase bombs." They are not flat and it takes two people to carry them—the munitions are more like steamer trunk nuclear bombs.[43] "These are ideal weapons to conduct nuclear terrorism," General Lebed explains. "We must seriously look for them [the missing weapons] or else humankind cannot rest in peace."[44]

The general lawlessness and growth of organized crime syndicates in Russia have resulted in substantial trafficking in illegal goods. No material seized or reported stolen has come from nuclear warhead stocks. Yet, smugglers are becoming increasingly sophisticated in the amount of fissile

---

[39] Bill Gertz, "'Suitcase' Weapons Exist, Built for 'Terrorist Purposes,'" *Washington Times* (October 3, 1997), p. A11.

[40] R. Jeffrey Smith and David Hoffman, "No Support Found for Report of Lost Russian Suitcase-Sized Nuclear Weapons," *Washington Post* (September 5, 1997), p. A19, and General Alexander Lebed, Remarks on *60 Minutes,* CBS Television (September 7, 1997).

[41] "Russia's Defence Minister Denies Nuclear Bombs Are Missing," *Reuters* (September 5, 1997).

[42] Senator Richard Lugar, remarks on *ABC News* (television) (October 2, 1997).

[43] Gertz, "'Suitcase' Weapons Exist," p. A11.

[44] "Lebed Again Says Russia Has Lost Some of Its Nuclear Weapons, " *Reuters Information Service* (September 19, 1997).

The New Face of War

materials traded (from gram to kilogram or greater quantities). The nuclear-theft clock is ticking. George Tenet, Director of the C.I.A., put Russian nuclear security into a proper perspective in June 1997 when responding to questions from the U.S. Senate Intelligence Committee: "The intelligence community remains very concerned about their security because of continuing social and economic difficulties, corruption in the military and potential activities of organized crime groups."[45] There is no evidence that incontrovertibly links organized crime to the diversion, smuggling, or sale of fissile materials, but given the level of criminal activity in Russia it is only a matter of time, if not already, until the gangs are in control.[46]

Pathways to Nuclear Weapons Proliferation

A country aspiring to obtain nuclear weapons might be able to purchase or steal nuclear weapons under certain conditions. On the other hand, it could take the steps necessary to produce its own nuclear weapons. And as general knowledge, fissile materials and technologies associated with nuclear weapons become more available, the proliferation process appears more doable every day. The high costs and resources required will keep many of the "wanna-bes" out of the running. It is very difficult and expensive to obtain the necessary plutonium and HEU, and the aspiring nuclear proliferator would always face the possibility of discovery. Moreover, the costs for a clandestine indigenous nuclear weapons program could be substantially higher than one conducted in the open. Open proliferation may be unattractive since it would likely attract international scrutiny.[47]

Regardless of which proliferation pathway is chosen, several technical hurdles stand in the way of a successful nuclear program: enough fissile material to form a super-critical mass for each nuclear weapon that will permit a chain reaction; creating a weapon design that will bring that mass together in a fraction of a second; and building a device small enough to be carried on chosen delivery vehicles (e.g., ballistic or cruise missile, strike aircraft).

---

[45] "CIA 'Very Concerned' By Russian Nuclear Safeguards," *Russia Today* (December 4, 1997).

[46] Cochran, "Nuclear Weapons and Fissile Material Security in Russia;" Roberts, *Five Minutes Past Midnight,* pp. 13-14; and Tom Hunter, "Russia's Mafiyas: The New Revolution," *Jane's Intelligence Review* (June 1997), p. 250.

[47] U.S., Congress, Office of Technology Assessment, *Technologies Underlying Weapons of Mass Destruction,* pp. 119-80.

Integrating nuclear weapons with delivery systems and preparing for their use is the third stage in developing a nuclear capability. Many of these countries believed to be armed with nuclear weapons or the manufacturing base to produce them quickly also possess strike aircraft, and many either have or are pursuing longer-range ballistic missiles. Other civilian or military vehicles also could be used for delivery.

As shown in Table 2.1 and Figure 2.2, the steps necessary to produce and deploy nuclear weapons are complex but not insurmountable. The process breaks down into three basic phases: acquisition of nuclear weapons materials, weapons fabrication, and weapons testing and deployment.

Table 2.1
Steps Needed to Produce and Deploy Nuclear Weapons

- **Acquisition of Nuclear Weapons Materials**
  - Mining of uranium-bearing ore
  - Milling to extract uranium concentrate in the form of yellowcake or other uranates
  - Chemical processing to convert yellowcake into usable compounds

- *Uranium-234 based weapons:*
  - Enrichment of uranium to high levels of uranium-235
  - Conversion of enriched uranium product to uranium metal

- *Plutonium-based weapons:*
  - Uranium fuel fabrication in the form of metal or oxide
  - Reactor construction and operation
  - Reprocessing of spent fuel to extract plutonium metal
  - Conversion of plutonium product to plutonium metal

- **Weapon Fabrication (plutonium and uranium weapons)**
  - Design and fabrication of fissile core
  - Design and fabrication of nonnuclear components (chemical explosives, detonator, fuze, neutron initiator, reflector, etc.)
  - Weapon assembly

- **Weapon Testing and Deployment**
  - Physics tests
  - Development of delivery system and integration with warhead
  - Weapons transport and storage
  - Possible development of doctrine and training for use

Source: U.S., Congress, Office of Technology Assessment, *Technologies Underlying Weapons of Mass Destruction,* OTA-BP-ISC-115 (Washington, D.C.: Government Printing Office, 1993), p. 130.

The New Face of War

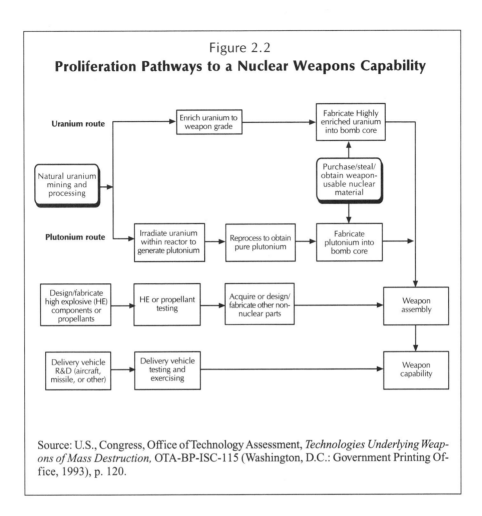

Figure 2.2

Proliferation Pathways to a Nuclear Weapons Capability

Source: U.S., Congress, Office of Technology Assessment, *Technologies Underlying Weapons of Mass Destruction,* OTA-BP-ISC-115 (Washington, D.C.: Government Printing Office, 1993), p. 120.

In addition to the potential for "loose nukes" and the stealing of fissile material in Russia, low-enriched uranium that is used to fuel hundreds of nuclear power reactors worldwide can also be used as feedstock in a proliferator's uranium enrichment process, accelerating the production of highly enriched uranium for weapons. In addition, civilian nuclear reactors routinely convert part of their uranium fuel into plutonium as they operate. The plutonium obtained by separating unconsumed uranium fuel and radioactive byproducts through reprocessing can be reused in nuclear reactors, as well as used to make nuclear weapons. This is the fundamental reason the International Atomic Energy Agency (IAEA) imposes a strict system of nuclear safeguards—to prevent diversion of plutonium derived from reprocessing to weapons programs.[48]

Once a sufficient amount of weapons-grade materials are acquired for plutonium or uranium weapons, the second step, weapons fabrication, involves the design and production of the fissile core, nonnuclear components (chemical explosives, detonator, fuze, neutron initiator, reflector, etc.), and weapons assembly. The core of fissile material is formed into a super-critical mass[49] by chemical high explosives (HE) or propellants. Detonators are timed electronically by a fuzing system to explode the HE; initiators inject a burst of neutrons into the fissile core at the appropriate moment to start the nuclear chain-reaction.

Non-Western states attempting to obtain nuclear weapons are not starting from scratch. The basic concepts of nuclear bombs are widely known, the requisite technology is based on the applications available in the 1940s, and the relevant physics for a workable bomb design is available in published sources, including unclassified and declassified documents. The successful design of nuclear explosive devices or weapons requires individuals with expertise in metallurgy, chemistry, physics, electronics, and explosives. Non-Western proliferators can use computer simulation and design codes for assistance in designing first-generation nuclear weapons.[50]

Proliferation Template:
Iraq's Nuclear Weapons Program

Twenty-eight International Atomic Energy Agency (IAEA) inspection teams visited Iraq from the conclusion of the 1991 Persian Gulf War through the end of 1995 to inspect facilities, interview key personnel, inventory nuclear materials, identify prohibited items, and carry out destruction and removal operations.[51] The inspectors found a large and complex clandestine nuclear

---

[48] *Ibid.*, pp. 128-31

[49] The *critical mass* is the minimum mass of fissile material needed to sustain a nuclear chain reaction which depends on the density, shape and type of fissile material as well as the effectiveness of a *reflector* or *tamper* at reflecting neutrons back into the fissioning mass.

[50] U.S., Congress, Office of Technology Assessment, *Technologies Underlying Weapons of Mass Destruction,* pp. 149-52.

[51] The United Nations Security Council Resolution 687 was adopted on April 3, 1991, setting the terms for a formal ceasefire in the Gulf War. Under the terms of the Resolution, Iraq was to declare all locations, amounts, and types of nuclear weapons materials, subsystems, components, or research, development, support, or nuclear production facilities. To ensure compliance, Iraq was compelled to place all nuclear weapons materials under the exclusive control of IAEA and accept on-site inspection and destruction, removal, or rendering harmless all such items.

---

weapons program carried out at ten dedicated sites (Table 2.2). Each site had several major buildings, representing a very large investment—millions of dollars worth of specialized equipment.[52]

In addition to the ten core sites shown in Figure 2.3, the IAEA included nine whose activities encompassed three main areas: uranium mining, production, and processing; uranium enrichment; and weaponization. The massive industrial enterprise supporting the nuclear program involved many more locations. The number of facilities was higher than what might be expected because of the extraordinary complexity and compartmentation of the clandestine program.

When the Iraqis decided to embark on a clandestine nuclear weapons program, while Iraq was still a member of the Non-Proliferation Treaty, they created a front organization with the code name Petrochemical Project 3 or "PC 3." The broad-based effort to design assistance, and an investment of some $10-$12 billion. The highly compartmentalized program was operated through an interlocking relationship between the Iraqi Atomic Energy Commission (IAEC) and the Ministry of Military Industry and Industrialization.

Iraq's clandestine nuclear program was designed from the start to secrete its bomb-making efforts from the IAEA and U.S. spy satellites. Although it may be shocking to Western nuclear weapons experts, the Iraqis turned to "old" technology. Iraqi scientists essentially replicated the technologies at the Oak Ridge Plant in Tennessee, which helped to produce the first U.S. atomic bombs. The Iraqis built huge antiquated machines called "calutrons" for enriching uranium to weapons-grade levels. An elaborate complex of nuclear research and development facilities was established in various parts of the country. This effort was supported by 2,000 foreign-trained scientists, 18,000 engineers, and numerous Jordanian front companies to obtain needed materials from abroad. Evidence of these activities in Western intelligence was fragmentary. After the war, the Defense Intelligence Agency concluded that "prior to Desert Storm, little was known about Iraq's highly compartmented nuclear weapons program."[53]

---

[52] International Atomic Energy Agency, *IAEA Inspections and Iraq's Nuclear Capabilities* (Vienna, Austria: April 1992), pp. 5–13.

[53] As quoted in Michael R. Gordon and General Bernard E. Trainor, *The Generals' War: The Inside Story of the Conflict in the Gulf* (Boston: Little, Brown, 1995), pp. 181-82, 457.

Table 2.2
Iraq's Ten Core Nuclear Facilities

Nuclear Site	Description
Al Tuwaitha Nuclear Research Center	Main site for Iraqi nuclear program. Activities included: several research reactors, plutonium separation and waste processing, uranium metallurgy, neutron initiator development, and work on a number of methods of uranium enrichment.
Tarmiya	Main site for the enrichment of uranium. Site included both 1200 mm and 600 mm separators. Much of the equipment was disassembled by the Iraqis and the components hidden from IAEA inspection teams.
Al Atheer Center	This site was designed and constructed as the major facility for nuclear weapons development and testing. Activities at the site included: uranium casting and metallurgy, core assembly, explosive lens assembly, and detonics testing. A high explosives test bunker near the site was used for hydrodynamic experiments.
Al Furat	This site was intended for the design, assembly, and testing of gas centrifuges for uranium enrichment. A 100 centrifuge cascade was planned.
Al Jesira factory	Uranium feed stock production facility. Products included uranium dioxide, uranium tetrachloride, and uranium hexaflouride.
Akashat Mine	Uranium ore production site; associated with Al Qaim site.
Al Qaim	Production of yellowcake (refined uranium ore); ore supplied by foreign and domestic sources.
Rashdiya	Centrifuge development center; engaged in centrifuge design and testing.
Ash Sharqat	Site intended as a duplicate of the Al Tarmiya enrichment facility.
Petrochemical -3 Center	Complex of five office buildings in central Baghdad housing Iraqi nuclear weapons design effort.

Source: United Nations, Security Council, Special Commission on Iraq, information paper (October 16, 1995).

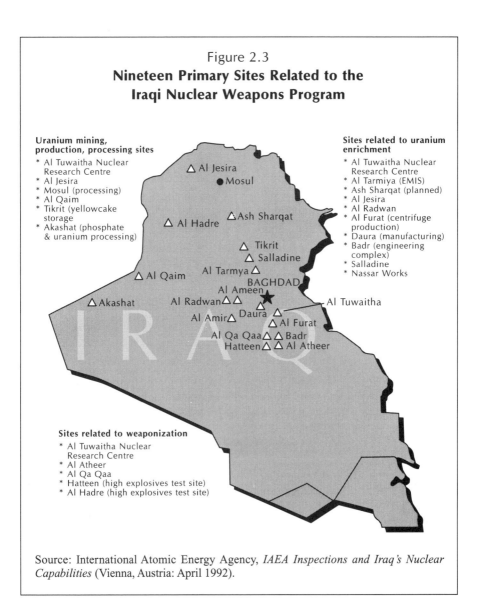

Figure 2.3
**Nineteen Primary Sites Related to the
Iraqi Nuclear Weapons Program**

Uranium mining, production, processing sites
* Al Tuwaitha Nuclear Research Centre
* Al Jesira
* Mosul (processing)
* Al Qaim
* Tikrit (yellowcake storage
* Akashat (phosphate & uranium processing)

Sites related to uranium enrichment
* Al Tuwaitha Nuclear Research Centre
* Al Tarmiya (EMIS)
* Ash Sharqat (planned)
* Al Jesira
* Al Radwan
* Al Furat (centrifuge production)
* Daura (manufacturing)
* Badr (engineering complex)
* Salladine
* Nassar Works

Sites related to weaponization
* Al Tuwaitha Nuclear Research Centre
* Al Atheer
* Al Qa Qaa
* Hatteen (high explosives test site)
* Al Hadre (high explosives test site)

Source: International Atomic Energy Agency, *IAEA Inspections and Iraq's Nuclear Capabilities* (Vienna, Austria: April 1992).

Many Western scientists and nuclear experts now believe Iraq was twelve to eighteen months away from producing a nuclear bomb. "When it comes to nuclear weapons," one American recalls about pre-Gulf War U.S. intelligence reports, "it's easy to dismiss a country like Iraq." An Israeli expert called the inability of Western governments to detect the Iraqi nuclear program a "colossal intelligence failure," including their lack of knowledge about the existence of PC 3, development of implosion-type weapons involving three ongoing uranium enrichment programs, and a massive foreign procurement program shrouded behind an array of sophisticated deception practices. Hans Blix, director of IAEA, which conducted inspections of Iraq's declared nuclear facilities before the Gulf War, observes that "there was suspicion certainly [but] to see the enormity of it is a shock."[54]

PC 3 was a complex, comprehensive nuclear weapons development program characterized by parallel approaches to fissile material production and by theoretical and experimental design work. The Iraqis were pursuing three industrial-scale methods of uranium enrichment: electromagnetic isotope separation (EMIS), chemical processes, and gas centrifuge. A fourth approach, the gaseous diffusion method, was discarded in the 1980s after the Iraqis concluded it was too risky. At the R&D level, at least as far as the IAEA inspectors know, the Iraqis also tried Atomic Vapor Laser-Isotope Separation (AVLIS) and Molecular Laser Isotope Separation (M-LIS).[55]

The nuclear program was supported by broad-based international procurement efforts. For instance, IAEA inspectors, found numerous catalogues from foreign suppliers. The Iraqis devised a multitude of plausible cover explanations for purchases from overseas. While the Ministry of Industry and Military Industrialization maintained general control over the weapons program, PC 3 was assigned specific command of nuclear weapons.[56]

The Al Tuwaitha Nuclear Research Center was the nerve center of the Iraqi clandestine weapons complex. It was made up of more than 100 buildings and included research reactors, hot cells, radiochemistry and radioisotope production laboratories, workshops, a radioactive waste treatment facility, a material testing laboratory (ceramics and metals), nuclear physics laboratories, a complex of chemistry and chemical engineering research and development, and other nuclear weapons-related activities. Many of the buildings were destroyed during the Gulf War and two functioning research reactors were destroyed or heavily damaged.[57]

---

[54] As quoted in R. Jeffrey Smith and Glenn Frankel, "Saddam's Nuclear-Weapons Dream: A Lingering Nightmare," *Washington Post* (October 13, 1991), pp. A1, A44, A45.

[55] U.S., Congress, Office of Technology Assessment, *Technologies Underlying Weapons of Mass Destruction*, pp. 120–21, 140–43.

[56] United Nations, Security Council, *First Report on the Sixth IAEA On-Site Inspection in Iraq Under Security Council Resolution 687 (1991)*, U.N. Doc. S/23122 (October 8, 1991), pp. 3–7.

[57] United Nations, Security Council, *Consolidated Report On the First Two IAEA Inspections Under Security Council Resolution 687 (1991) of Iraqi Nuclear Capabilities*, U.N. Doc. S/22788 (July 15, 1991).

The Geological Survey Institute in Baghdad developed the process and pilot plant operations to recover uranium from carbonate ore from the Abu Sukhayr Mine. Uranium ore commonly is mined along with other mineral-bearing ores; only one part in 500 is uranium. Milling facilities extract the uranium concentrate known as "yellowcake." The next step in the process is to convert the yellowcake to a form of uranium suitable for enrichment.[58]

The Iraqis were developing simultaneously three methods of uranium enrichment, including gas centrifuge, chemical processes from France, and electromagnetic isotope separation. The research and development activities for the Iraqi centrifuge enrichment program were conducted at Al Tuwaitha along with some manufacturing tests at Al Furat. Machinery of required parts took place at the Saddam Works, the Nassar Works, and the Rashdiah Engineering Center for centrifuge research and development. These were to be used at Al Furat, which was planned as the center for centrifuge assembly and testing.[59]

Iraqi scientists also were experimenting with French-developed techniques that would yield weapons-grade uranium. These techniques involved the liquid-liquid solvent extraction (Chemex) process. Previously, the Iraqis experimented with the Japanese Asahi ion-exchange process but abandoned it after judging it too risky.[60]

The Tarmiya EMIS plant, located approximately twenty-five miles north of Baghdad, was designed by the Iraqis to support industrial-scale uranium enrichment operations. The installation housed two EMIS operations and was largely destroyed during the Gulf War. A twin of the Tarmiya plant was still under construction at Ash Sharqat, 125 miles northwest of Baghdad. This installation also was bombed during the Gulf War, and sustained heavy-to-moderate bomb damage.[61]

---

[58] U.S., Congress, Office of Technology Assessment, *Technologies Underlying Weapons of Mass Destruction*, pp. 137–38.

[59] United Nations, Security Council, *Report of the Seventh IAEA On-Site Inspection in Iraq Under Security Council Resolution 687 (1991)*, U.N. Doc. S/23215 (May 22, 1992), p. 23.

[60] U.S. Congress, Office of Technology Assessment, *Technologies Underlying Weapons of Mass Destruction*, pp. 151, 178.

[61] Barbara Ebert, "Iraq: Its Nuclear Past As a Way of Assessing Its Nuclear Future," unpublished report (Vienna, Va.: Science Applications International Corporation, April 1994), pp. 6–7 (photocopy); International Atomic Energy Agency, "Fact Sheet" (January 1994), p. 3; U.S., Department of the Air Force, *Gulf War Air Power Survey: Operations and Effects and Effectiveness*, Vol. II, Part 1 (Washington, D.C.: Government Printing Office, 1993), p. 228; and United Nations, Security Council, Report on the Twelfth IAEA On-Site Inspection in Iraq Under Security Council Resolution 687 (1991), U.N. Doc. S/24223 (July 2, 1992), p. 30.

A principal facility for Iraq's gas centrifuge program, as far as we knew at the end of 1997, was under construction at Al Furat, approximately twenty miles southwest of Baghdad. While the centrifuge program was second in priority to the EMIS program and was started much later, Iraqi authorities realized its potential and aggressively pursued obtaining the equipment necessary for this program, which relied heavily on imports of foreign technology and equipment from the West. Iraq was scheduled to start operations of its first pilot cascade of 100 centrifuges in mid-1993.[62]

The greatest surprise for Western nuclear experts was the Iraqi success in using EMIS. Using computer controls and fiberoptic links, the Iraqis developed highly automated isotope separators. EMIS is considered the worst of all methods to enrich uranium because the process requires enormous quantities of electricity to power the large magnets or calutrons. But Iraq has plenty of electrical power from petroleum and hydroelectric sources. This technology was discarded by the West long ago. Indeed, "calutrons are the Model-Ts of the Nuclear Age."[63]

Experiments on the EMIS system and in uranium recovery and UCl_4 production were conducted at Al Tuwaitha. Manufacturing facilities were centered at Al Ameer—prototype EMIS components; Al Radwan and Al Amir—magnet cores, return irons, ion sources, and collector parts; SEHEE (Daura)—vacuum chamber parts; Salladine and the Dijjla laboratory—assembling of electrical control panels; and Al Tuwaitha—manufacturing of coils. An EMIS facility was operating at Tarmiya and another one was planned at Ash Sharqat; Al Jesira produced the UCl_4 required.[64]

The Iraqis had an ongoing weaponization program at five main facilities. Efforts to develop high explosive triggers for the bombs took place at Al Qa Qaa, Hatteen, Al Atheer, and Al Hadre. Development of an implosion device was underway at Al Tuwaitha.[65]

While initial efforts at weaponization were begun at Al Tuwaitha, this work was later shifted to Al Atheer, which became the primary center

---

[62] Ebert, "Iraq: Its Nuclear Past As a Way of Assessing Its Nuclear Future," p. 7, and International Atomic Energy Agency, "Fact Sheet," p. 4.

[63] Smith and Frankel, "Saddam's Nuclear-Weapons Dream," p. A33. See also Peter D. Zimmerman, "Proliferation: Bronze Medal Technology Is Enough," *Orbis* (Winter 1994), pp. 76–77.

[64] United Nations, Security Council, *Report on the Seventh IAEA On-Site Inspection in Iraq,* p. 22.

[65] *Ibid.,* p. 8.

for Iraq's weapons design, development and testing efforts. Because this installation was unknown to U.S. planners, it was virtually untouched during the war.

The Iraqis were examining the implosion technique for their nuclear weapons. A shell of chemical high-explosive surrounding the nuclear material is designed to be detonated nearly simultaneously at multiple points to compress the nuclear material rapidly to form a super-critical mass. The implosion technique requires substantially less nuclear material than the gun-assembly method.[66]

Seventeen other facilities provided support for Iraq's nuclear weapons program. A couple of these were storage locations for key components, others had the precision machine tools necessary in the manufacture of key elements, some provided electronic and computer support, and a range of other technical support activities are included. The data on these facilities gleaned from the IAEA on-site inspection reports tell only a part of the story.

Documentary evidence revealed that two Iraqi facilities had had a program for developing an implosion-type nuclear weapon; other documents linked nuclear weapons to a surface-to-surface missile project. The extensive weaponization program had been centered on Al Tuwaitha and Al Atheer, including work with neutron irradiators and plans for external irradiating high-explosive components, exploding bridge wire detonators and firing sets for multiple detonator systems.[67]

Producing a nuclear weapon is a formidable task, even for a country such as Iraq, which has large and well-developed electronic, chemical, and metallurgical manufacturing capabilities. Development of a nuclear weapon, even crude ones such as those used against Hiroshima and Nagasaki, for example, involves thousands of parts. The Los Alamos National Laboratory detailed the components needed to make a nuclear weapon and where to obtain them: the document is 500 pages long.[68] For this reason, a number of other facilities were involved in Iraq's nuclear program that would not at

---

[66] U.S., Congress, Office of Technology Assessment, *Technologies Underlying Weapons of Mass Destruction,* pp. 173–75.

[67] United Nations, Security Council, *Report by the Executive Chairman of the Special Commission Established by the Secretary-General Pursuant to Paragraph 9 (b) (i) Security Council Resolution 687 (1991),* U.N. Doc. S/23165 (October 25, 1991), p. 23.

[68] David Albright and Mark Hibbs, "Iraq and the Bomb: Were They Even Close?," *Bulletin of the Atomic Scientists* (March 1991), pp. 18–19.

---

first glance appear to be critical facilities. In many cases, however, they contained precision machine tools or computer equipment the Iraqis would find necessary to complete the project, and thus would be legitimate military targets.

As IAEA inspectors delved deeper into Iraq's nuclear program, they often found references to other locations that could have played a role in the program. Subsequent inspection of these facilities, including a bicycle plant that had received high voltage electronic tubes, an electronics factory, and a prison, revealed that their functions were consistent with their stated uses, and they were not involved in the nuclear program. All told, as shown in Figure 2.4, fifty-six nuclear facilities were identified in the IAEA on-site in-

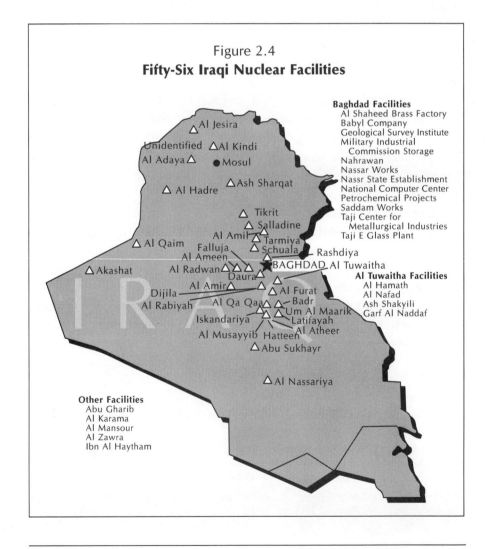

Figure 2.4
Fifty-Six Iraqi Nuclear Facilities

Baghdad Facilities
Al Shaheed Brass Factory
Babyl Company
Geological Survey Institute
Military Industrial
  Commission Storage
Nahrawan
Nassar Works
Nassr State Establishment
National Computer Center
Petrochemical Projects
Saddam Works
Taji Center for
  Metallurgical Industries
Taji E Glass Plant

Al Tuwaitha Facilities
Al Hamath
Al Nafad
Ash Shakyili
Garf Al Naddaf

Other Facilities
Abu Gharib
Al Karama
Al Mansour
Al Zawra
Ibn Al Haytham

The New Face of War

spection reports; the actual number of potential nuclear targets would probably be much higher when dual-use and other support facilities are included. The actual number of nuclear targets was at least seven times greater than those included on the target lists during the Gulf War.

Radiological Weapons. It was not until 1995 that the U.N. discovered Iraq had worked on producing radiological devices. Previously, radiological weapons and their use in armed conflict were thought to be primarily a theoretical possibility. The Soviet Union's "crisis group" for the Persian Gulf War appraised the real possibility of Iraq using radiological weapons against Israel. Since it was known that Iraq had shut down its nuclear reactor during the Coalition's bombing campaign, it meant that the nuclear fuel had been removed. For this reason the Soviet experts could not rule out the possibility of Iraq's radiological weapons use.[69]

Iraq conducted an experiment in late 1987 to determine the military effectiveness of using irradiated materials. The idea was that the radiation effect would kill or incapacitate through inhalation exposure from the irradiated materials in the air. A few pounds of zirconium oxide, which had been irradiated, were stored in lead-shielded metal containers and exploded at a chemical weapons test site. The project was purportedly shelved due to poor test results and the problems in handling and transporting the irradiated materials (the lead-lined containers each weighed about a ton).

At about the same time, the Nuclear Research Center at Al Tuwaitha began exploring radiological weapons as a means of area denial for use in the last stages of the 1980-88 Iran-Iraq War. Three modified "Nassar 28" aerial bombs filled with irradiated zirconium oxide were tested: one was exploded at ground level as a static test, two were armed with impact fuzes and dropped from an aircraft. The results were disappointing since the radioactive material remained concentrated in and around the craters.

According to Iraq, 100 casings of a small caliber aerial bomb were produced for the purpose of radiological weapons. Twenty-five of the bombs were destroyed by Iraq in the summer of 1991. Iraq claims that no order

---

[69] Russia, Foreign Intelligence Service Report, *A New Challenge After the Gulf War* in U.S., Foreign Broadcast Information Service, *Proliferation Issues,* JPRS-TND-93-007, p. 12, and "U.N. Official: Iraq Worked On Radiological Arms," *Washington Post* (November 8, 1995), p. A25.

---

was given to move forward on radiological weapons and the project was dropped.[70]

The potential for development of radiological weapons is present wherever radiological materials are stored. Intended to kill through radiation or contamination rather than blast and shock, radiological weapons could consist of small amounts of highly irradiated fissile material (e.g., uranium-235, plutonium-239) or non-fissile radioactive material (e.g., uranium-238, cesium-137, cobalt-60).[71] While such weapons are not believed to exist, the Chechen military leader Shamil Basayev warned in October 1995 that five containers of radioactive materials were being sent to Russia and two of them were wired with explosives. The Japanese Aum Shinrikyo sect that was responsible for the sarin gas released on the Tokyo subway may also have had radiological weapons in mind when members of the radical sect sought Russian nuclear technology.[72]

Radiological weapons have the potential to cause widespread contamination that would inflict numerous fatalities and serious casualties. Robin Ranger and David Wiencek of Britain's Lancaster University report that radiological weapons could come in the form of bombs or artillery shells that were also packed with ordinary explosives or they could be dispersed in liquid or solid aerosol form by aerial spraying.[73]

Terrorists could attempt to spread radioactive isotopes to contaminate property and the environment. Since it has been proven that a nuclear blast can be achieved by using reactor-grade plutonium rather than weapons-grade, a truck could be used to deliver a low-yield "dirty device."[74]

---

[70] United Nations, Security Council, *Tenth Report of the Executive Chairman of the Special Commission Established By the Secretary-General Pursuant to Paragraph 9 (b) (i) of Security Council Resolution 687 (1991), and Paragraph 3 of Resolution 699 (1991) On the Activities of the Special Commission,* U.N. Doc. S/1995/1038 (December 17, 1995), pp. 16-18, and United Nations, Security Council, *Report of the Secretary-General On the Activities of the Special Commission Established By the Secretary-General Pursuant to Paragraph 9 (b) (i) of Resolution 687 (1991),* U.N. Doc. S/1996/258 (April 11, 1996), pp. 21-22.

[71] Robin Ranger and DavidWiencek, *The Devil's Brew II: Weapons of Mass Destruction and International Security* (Lancaster, United Kingdom: Centre for Defence and International Security Studies, Lancaster University, 1997), p. 62.

[72] Turbiville, *Weapons Proliferation and Organized Crime,* p. 30.

[73] Ranger and Wiencek, *Devil's Brew II,* p. 63.

[74] Roberts, *Five Minutes Past Midnight,* p. 3, and Oleg Bukharin, "Problems of Nuclear Terrorism" in *The Monitor,* 3-2, Center for International Trade and Security at the University of Georgia (Spring 1997), p. 9.

The New Face of War

. . . . .

How could U.S. and foreign intelligence services have been so far off the mark concerning Iraq's large nuclear weapons program? Part of the reason is that the U.S. consistently underestimated Iraq's nuclear capabilities before the Gulf War. According to one newspaper account, the U.S. Department of Energy and Department of State were firm in their views in 1989 and 1990 that the Iraqis lacked the technical competence for rapid nuclear weapons development and that several years of effort would be required to achieve a meaningful breakthrough. Although the C.I.A. disagreed with this judgment, it did not offer a dissenting view in the government estimates. Such faulty estimates laid the mental groundwork for American military commanders and their planners to misperceive Iraq's true nuclear weapons potential.[75]

Seven years after the Gulf War and years of painstaking on-site inspections, the IAEA said in April 1998 that it had not found evidence of nuclear weapons or the means to produce them in Iraq for more than a year. The U.S. view is that the IAEA still cannot unequivocally state that Iraq's nuclear program has been eliminated.[76] Many analysts believe Iraq still has a nuclear weapons program. The basic scientific and industrial facilities needed to build a bomb remain in place. The staff responsible for Iraq's earlier program are still present, and hundreds of them are supported by the state as full-time employees. While much of the equipment and materials for building a nuclear bomb have been destroyed, a great deal remains hidden. By late 1997, Israeli intelligence reported indications of "technical co-operation" between Iraq and Syria, former enemies, on joint WMD development. It was too early to speculate whether nuclear weapons might be a potential cooperative project.[77]

Transfer of Nuclear Technology

China's assistance to Pakistan's nuclear program has deep roots, going back at least to the 1980s. Western intelligence experts believe the Chinese gave the Pakistanis a design for a twenty-five kiloton implosion device. China is

---

[75] R. Jeffrey Smith, "Iraq's Nuclear Prowess Underestimated by U.S.," *Washington Post* (October 13, 1991), p. A45.

[76] John M. Goshko, "U.N. Teams Find No Sign of Iraqi Nuclear Arms," *Washington Post* (April 14, 1998), p. A11.

[77] Al J. Venter, "How Saddam Almost Built His Bomb," *Jane's Intelligence Review* (December 1997), p. 562.

---

believed to have given Pakistan enough weapons-grade uranium to fuel two nuclear weapons. In 1996, it was reported that China had sold 5,000 unsafeguarded ring magnets to Pakistan for suspected use in enriching uranium in gas centrifuges. In May 1996, just two months after China had test-fired missiles in waters near Taiwan and Washington responded by dispatching two aircraft carriers as a sign of its concern, the U.S. State Department announced neither China nor Pakistan would be sanctioned for the ring magnets. A new agreement was reached with China as the U.S. presidential elections got underway.

China has provided nuclear technology to Iran since the 1980s, including the transfer of designs and technology for reactor construction and training for at least fifteen Iranian nuclear engineers from Iran's nuclear research center at Esfahan; a secret Iranian-Chinese cooperation agreement was signed sometime after 1988. China has sold Iran a facility to convert uranium ore into uranium hexaflouride gas, which could be enriched to weapons-grade material. Reportedly, Chinese technicians have built the Iranians a calutron system—electromagnetic isotope separation (EMIS)—for enriching uranium at the Karaj nuclear research facility. This system is similar to the one used by Iraq until discovery by U.N. inspectors after the Persian Gulf War.[78]

North Korea is reported to have made a deal to sell Iran several nuclear weapons as well as provide designs for a weapons-grade plutonium reprocessing plant. North Korea and Iran are thought to have had exchanges of civilian and military personnel engaged in the nuclear field; North Korean nuclear scientists are believed to be working in Iran. It also has been reported that North Korea sold Iran equipment necessary for uranium mining.[79]

Russia is building a 1,000-megawatt turn-key light-water reactor at Bushehr on the Persian Gulf coast, which will finish a project started by Germany in 1979 but later suspended. This is the first of two planned atomic reactors. The United States and Israel objected to the nuclear power

---

[78] Shirley A. Kan, *Chinese Proliferation of Weapons of Mass Destruction: Background and Analysis* (Washington, D.C.: Congressional Research Service, Library of Congress, September 13, 1996), pp. 27-35.

[79] Kenneth Katzman and Rinn-Sup Shinn, *North Korea: Military Relations With the Middle East* (Washington, D.C.: Congressional Research Service, Library of Congress, September 27, 1994), pp. 6-7.

The New Face of War

stations since they could be used to support a nuclear weapons program. Russia rejects suggestions that Iran is trying to build nuclear weapons.[80]

Saddam Hussein, according to some experts, retains nuclear weapons-building capabilities. Some estimate that the Iraqi's could build a nuclear weapon within a year of the U.N. lifting the inspection regime and economic sanctions. The Iraqis have the expertise available, and many believe they have hidden key documentation and components essential for a rapid reconstitution of their nuclear program.[81]

---

[80] David Hoffman, "Russia Expanding Role in Iranian Power Plant," *Washington Post* (February 22, 1998), p. A30.

[81] Al J. Venter, "Experts Differ On Iraq's A-bomb Threat," *Jane's Intelligence Review and Jane's Sentinel Pointer* (June 1998).

CHAPTER 3

Biological Weapons

Biological warfare is often called "public health in reverse" and for a good reason. Using bacteria, viruses and biological toxins, this form of warfare is all about killing humans in large numbers through disease, viral infection or poisoning. Iraqi leaders finally admitted in 1995, after years of pressure by the U.N. following the Gulf War, that they had secretly produced enough deadly microbes to kill everyone on earth several times over.

The 139 signatories to the 1972 Biological Weapons Convention agreed not to develop, produce, stockpile, acquire or retain biological agents or toxins and weapons. Yet, some countries of proliferation concern to the United States have not signed the Convention and are believed to be pursuing or already possess biological weapons; others are signatories and may nonetheless have secret programs. The implications seem clear: no matter where U.S. military forces may deploy in the world, they will face the threat of biological warfare.

Biological warfare has been a part of human conflict since antiquity. In 600 B.C., for instance, Solon, the legislator of Athens, contaminated the river Pleisthenes with hellebore (a purgative herb), which gave the defenders of Kirrha violent diarrhea and led to their defeat. When plague broke out among the Tartar army during its siege of Kaffa in 1346, disease-infected corpses were hurled over the city walls. The resulting plague caused the defenders to surrender. Russian troops may have used the same biological warfare technique in 1710 during a war against Sweden. During the 1754-67 French and Indian War in North America, the English provided the Indians loyal to the French with smallpox-ladened blankets; the epidemic casualties that followed led to the loss of Fort Carillon.

Japan's infamous Unit 731 set up a biological warfare program in Manchuria in 1937. In an isolated area, Pingfan, forty miles south of the city of Harbin, the Japanese constructed more than 150 buildings and 3,000 personnel worked at the site. Among the biological agents studied were botulism, cholera, dysentery, gas gangrene, influenza, tularemia, and epidemic haemorrhagia fever. More than 3,000 prisoners, mostly Chinese (seventy percent) and Russians, were sacrificed as human guinea pigs to support the

---

Japanese program. In 1943, 1,485 prisoners of war (more than a thousand Americans, British, Australians, and New Zealanders were included) were sent to Markdown, 350 miles from Pingfan, also to serve as guinea pigs. They were inoculated with thyroid, smallpox, and dysentery cholera. During the first winter, 430 prisoners died, mostly Americans. In 1944, the Japanese planned to deny the U.S. use of Saipan's airstrip by scattering plague-infected fleas along the runway—fortunately, a U.S. submarine sunk the transport ship before the attack was executed. By 1945, the Japanese had stockpiled nearly 900-pounds of anthrax and set up a factory producing 100 million plague-infected fleas every few days with the goal of breeding a billion fleas. When Russian troops swept across Manchuria during the fall of 1945, Unit 731 did its best to eliminate the facility. Remaining prisoners were executed, main buildings were destroyed, and thousands of infected rats were set loose, causing an epidemic lasting into 1946.[1]

The threat of biological warfare has increased dramatically over the last two decades of the twentieth century. Some of the proliferators may be attracted by the prospect of being able to produce large numbers of casualties from a distance. A 1970 World Health Organization study, for instance, reported that "if a biological agent such as anthrax were used, an attack on a city by even a single bomber disseminating 50 kg [110 pounds] of the dried agent in a suitable aerosol form would affect an area far in excess of 20 square km, with tens to hundreds of thousands of deaths."[2] Biological weapons may also be regarded by proliferators as a deterrent to those countries possessing nuclear or biological weapons. On the other hand, they may also be viewed as tools of intimidation and blackmail to persuade neighboring states to acquiesce to the possessor's strategic demands. Or, more ominously for the United States, Jonathan B. Tucker at the Monterey Institute of International Studies says that "a biological arsenal might serve as the basis of an 'asymmetric strategy' in which, instead of confronting a superior conventional military power head-on, the weaker state employs biological weapons to inflict high casualties, spread terror, and undermine the enemy's will to fight."[3]

---

[1] U.S., Department of the Army, *Handbook: Medical Management of Biological Casualties,* 2d ed. (Fort Detrick, Md.: Medical Research Institute of Infectious Diseases, 1996), pp. 4-5, and Deedee White, *Characterization and Historical Review of Chemical/Biological Weapons: Mid-Term Review* (San Diego, Calif.: Science Applications International Corporation, 1992).

[2] "Health Aspects of Chemical and Biological Weapons" (Geneva: World Health Organization, 1970) as quoted in L. Dunn and others, *Global Proliferation: Dynamics, Acquisition Strategies, and Responses,* Volume IV: Biological Weapons Proliferation (Newington, Va.: Center for Verification Research, 1992), p. IV-3.

[3] Jonathan B. Tucker, "The Biological Weapons Threat," *Current History* (April 1997), p. 170.

Which countries possess biological weapons? Estimates vary between ten and fourteen countries as either having shown interest in or having offensive biological programs or the ready biotechnology base available to produce germ weapons. Russia is known to have biological weapons. Eight countries probably possess germ weapons: China, India, Pakistan, North Korea, Taiwan, Iran, and Iraq. Egypt and Libya are suspected of having biological programs.[4] According to Russian government sources, Israel and South Korea each possess a strong biotechnology base which, if necessary, could be easily redirected to production of biological weapons.[5] See Figure 3.1. Since these programs are often conducted in secret and they are easily hidden from the prying eyes of outsiders, it is difficult to make a firm estimate.

The acceleration of the global diffusion of biotechnology expertise and industries makes many biological weapons technologies widely available and relevant to legitimate civil uses as well as a ready conversion base for germ weapons. The peaceful uses of biotechnology—fertilizers and pesticides, new vaccines and therapies—are often needed in the non-Western world, making control of dual-use technologies impractical. The ongoing advances in the biological sciences, including genetic engineering, which includes the transfer of discrete, well-characterized genes to a microorganism, can lead to improved production of existing products or even new ones in the pharmaceutical industry. An essential aspect of the highly competitive international trade in pharmaceuticals is secrecy for the protection of proprietary information often obtained following years of expensive research. Yet, genetic engineering has long-term implications for biological warfare programs. Biotechnology enables the development of new microorganisms and products with unorthodox characteristics. It is within reach to produce new-design biological warfare substances in militarily significant quantities.[6]

---

[4] John M. Collins, Zachary S. Davis, and Steven R. Bowman, *Nuclear, Biological, and Chemical Weapons Proliferation: Potential Military Countermeasures* (Washington, D.C.: Congressional Research Service, Library of Congress, 1994), p. 2, and Barbara Starr, "Egypt and Syria Are BW Capable, Says Agency," *Jane's Defence Weekly* (August 21, 1996).

[5] Russia, Foreign Intelligence Service Report, *A New Challenge After the Gulf War* in U.S., Foreign Broadcast Information Service, *Proliferation Issues,* JPRS-TND-93-007, pp. 21-38.

[6] L. Dunn and others, *Global Proliferation: Dynamics, Acquisition Strategies, and Responses,* Vol. IV - Biological Weapons Proliferation (Newington, Va.: Center for Verification Research, December 1992), pp. IV-10 through IV-17.

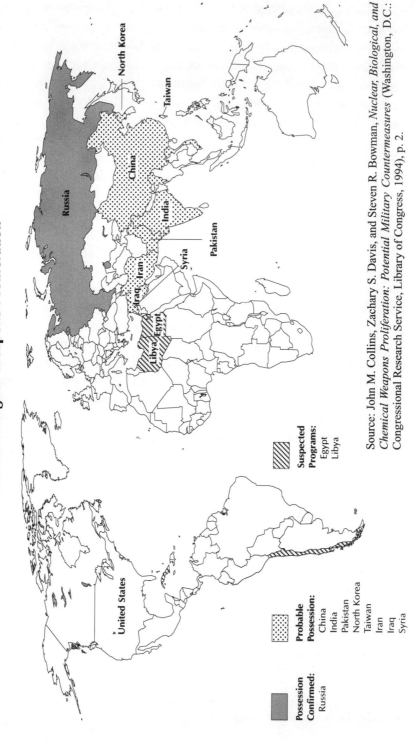

Figure 3.1
Global Biological Weapons Proliferation

Possession Confirmed: Russia

Probable Possession: China India Pakistan North Korea Taiwan Iran Iraq Syria

Suspected Programs: Egypt Libya

Source: John M. Collins, Zachary S. Davis, and Steven R. Bowman, *Nuclear, Biological, and Chemical Weapons Proliferation: Potential Military Countermeasures* (Washington, D.C.: Congressional Research Service, Library of Congress, 1994), p. 2.

The New Face of War

The 1972 Biological Weapons Convention has not been effective in stopping the development of biological weapons. Not only are some fifty countries not members—including Syria, Israel and Egypt—its compliance measures have proven ineffective. Jonathan Tucker identified two primary weaknesses. The first is the dual-use dilemma that allows countries to produce and stockpile microbial pathogens and toxins for biomedical research and vaccines that can be turned into offensive biological warfare programs. "Thus," says Tucker, "the line between treaty-permitted and -prohibited activities is largely a question of intent." A second weakness in the Biological Weapons Convention is its lack of formal verification measures. Despite efforts since 1986 to define some voluntary transparency measures and a legally binding protocol, countries are divided over the intrusiveness of verification and potential usefulness of confidence-building measures.

Supply-side controls, such as those by the Australia Group which tries to impede biological weapons proliferation through the harmonization of national export controls on microorganisms and toxins and dual-use equipment, are increasingly ineffective. See Table 3.1. The dual-use nature of biological warfare materials and equipment presents a giant loophole to be exquisitely

---

Table 3.1
Australia Group — Biological Weapons

Control List of Dual-Use Biological Equipment (Selected)
- Complete containment facilities (Biosafety Levels 3 and 4)
- Fermenters
- Centrifugal separators
- Cross-flow filtration equipment
- Freeze-drying equipment
- Aerosol inhalation chambers

List of Biological Agents for Export Control (Selected)
- Dengue fever virus
- Monkey pox virus
- Venezuelan Equine Encephalitis virus
- Clostridium botulinum bacteria
- Bacillus anthracis bacteria
- Botulinum toxins
- Clostridium perfringens toxins
- Ricin

---

exploited by proliferators through spiderweb networks of front companies designed to circumvent even the best of national export controls.[7]

Any country having a modest pharmaceutical industry can produce biological warfare agents relatively easily and inexpensively. The world biotechnology industry is more information-intensive than capital-intensive. Widely available published literature contains much of the data needed to produce biological warfare agents. Equipment for the biotechnology industry is widely available and much of it can be put to work in support of a biological weapons program. Hence, the proliferation of scientific and engineering knowledge and equipment availability lie at the base of biological warfare. Indiscriminate dispersal of biological agents would not be difficult and could cause large numbers of casualties. On the other hand, it is more difficult to develop munitions that will spread biological agents in ways that will produce predictable or controllable military effects. Only about thirty of several hundred pathogenic microbes that can afflict humans are considered as likely warfare agents. Biological agents for military use would preferably include the characteristics summarized in the Table 3.2 below.

Table 3.2
Desirable Attributes: Biological Warfare Agents

1. *Infect reliably* in small doses
2. *High virulence* (no undue loss of potency during production, storage or transport)
3. *Short incubation* between infection and onset of symptoms
4. *Minimal contagiousness* (avoid triggering an uncontrolled epidemic that could boomerang)
5. *No widespread immunity* by the target population
6. *Insusceptible to common medical treatments*
7. *Suitable for economic production* in military significant quantities
8. *Ease of transport and stability* under wartime field conditions
9. *Ease of dissemination*
10. *Survive environment stresses* during dissemination long enough to infect
11. *Available protection for attacking troops* (vaccine, antibiotics, protective clothing)

Source: U.S., Congress, Office of Technology Assessment

---

[7] Tucker, "Biological Weapons Threat," pp. 171-72. See also, U.S., General Accounting Office, *Arms Control: U.S. and International Efforts to Ban Biological Weapons,* GAO/NSIAD-93-113 (Washington, D.C.: Government Printing Office, 1992).

Three basic types of biological agents are bacteria, viruses, and biological toxins. *Bacteria* are single-celled microscopic organisms that include anthrax, plague, tularemia, Q-fever and others. *Viruses* are extremely small submicroscopic agents containing genetic material, either RNA or DNA, with a protective coat that facilitates transmission from one cell to another. To replicate, agent interaction with host cell genetic material is generally required. Some examples include Venezuelan equine encephalitis and viral hemorrhagic fevers. *Biological toxins,* as contrasted to man-made toxins in chemical agents, are products of living organisms that produce adverse clinical effects in human beings and animals.

Bacterial Agents. Some bacterial agents can be transformed into spores, nature's resting place of the bacterium that can germinate when conditions are favorable. The spore of the bacterial cell is more resistant to cold, heat, drying radiation, and chemicals than the bacterium itself.

Anthrax. This is a zoonotic disease with cattle, horses, and sheep being the chief hosts, though other animals can also be infected. The disease may be contracted by handling of contaminated hair, wool, hides, flesh and other direct contact. The spores are very stable and may be viable for years in the soil and water. When this agent is stabilized for weaponization, it can be delivered as an aerosol cloud from a line source, such as an aircraft or unmanned aerial vehicle flying upwind of its intended targets, or it can be spread from a point source through a spray device. The hardy anthrax spore can survive explosive dissemination from a bomb or shell and a large area could be covered by dispersal of multiple spray bomblets from a missile warhead at a predetermined height above the ground.

Following an incubation period of one to six days, presumably dependent upon the dose of inhaled anthrax spores, a fever, malaise, and fatigue may be present, followed by a period of improvement ranging from hours to days. Next is the abrupt development of severe respiratory distress; shock and death usually follow within twenty-four to thirty-six hours. Almost all cases where medical treatment was begun after patients became symptomatic from the inhalation of anthrax have been fatal, regardless of treatment. A vaccine is available but researchers possess insufficient data to judge its efficacy against anthrax inhalation; studies in rhesus monkeys, however, suggest that good protection can be afforded.[8]

---

[8] U.S., Department of the Army, *Handbook: Medical Management of Biological Casualties,* pp. 16-22.

Two major accidents involving anthrax provide additional insight to the threat that this biological agent poses to the U.S. armed forces. The accidental release of twenty-two pounds of dry anthrax spores occurred on April 3, 1979, on the outskirts of Sverdlovsk[9], a city of 1.2 million people in the Soviet Union. Several days after the explosion, seven or eight persons were admitted to the hospital with high fever (107°), blue ears and lips, choking, and breathing difficulties. All died within hours. Several workers in a ceramics factory downwind were exposed when ventilators sucked in bacilli—within days, many died. Initial disinfection and decontamination efforts were largely ineffective, though mass immunization with anthrax vaccine was partially effective. Many within the contaminated area contracted pulmonary anthrax through inhalation; additional cases were possible through skin contact and consumption of food contaminated with fallout spores. All told, at least sixty-six people died from the unintentional dispersal of anthrax spores.[10]

A second accidental case occurred during the summer of 1942 when British experiments to measure the effects of anthrax went awry on the Gruinard Island off the northwest coast of Scotland. The dissemination container held a slurry of anthrax spores and was ignited by an explosive charge. Sheep tethered in concentric circles around the bomb began to die the next day. Additional tests were conducted over the next two years. After each test, the sheep were dragged to the edge of cliffs and flung over the side, and explosives were used to bring the hilltop down on the carcasses. In at least one instance, the carcasses of dead sheep floated across to the mainland in a heavy storm, triggering an outbreak of anthrax on the Scottish mainland. Decontamination efforts by burning heather were only partially successful. Anthrax spores are estimated to still be alive under a foot of soil. Meanwhile, rabbits on the island turned black and are now immune.[11]

Tularemia. Tularemia—also known as rabbit fever and deer fly fever— is a zoonotic disease that humans can acquire through inoculation of skin or mucous membranes with blood or tissue fluids of infected animals, or bites of infected deer flies, mosquitoes, or ticks. Typhoidal tularemia occurs after inhalation of infectious aerosols. Pneumonia is most common with the typhoidal form of tularemia. The fatality rate for tularemia is five percent.

---

[9] Sverdlovsk has been renamed to Ekaterinberg, Russia.

[10] Al J. Venter, "Sverdlovsk Outbreak: A Portent for Disaster," *Jane's Intelligence Review,* 10-5 (May 1998), pp. 36-41, and White, *Characterization and Historical Review of Chemical/Biological Weapons.*

[11] White, *Characterization and Historical Review of Chemical/Biological Weapons.*

After an incubation period of two to ten days, onset is acute. Ulceroglandular disease usually manifests as regional lymphadenopathy, fever, chills, headache, and malaise. A live, attenuated tularemia vaccine is available as an investigatory new drug. The vaccine has been administered to 5,000 persons without significant adverse reactions. Vaccine-induced protection could be overwhelmed by extremely high doses.

Some countries are suspected of having weaponized this agent in either a wet or dried form. The agent could be delivered against U.S. forces in a manner similar to anthrax or other bacteria.

Viral Agents. Viruses lack a system for their own metabolism and are therefore dependent on their host cells: viruses are intercellular parasites. This means that a virus requires living cells in order to multiply.

Venezuelan Equine Encephalitis or VEE. The disease is characterized by inflammation of the meninges of the brain and of the brain itself; a small percentage of infections develop encephalitis. This acute disease is of short duration and the fatality rate is less than one percent. Onset of VEE is usually sudden following an incubation period of one to five days. A spiking fever, general malaise, and severe headache are among the initial symptoms, followed by nausea, vomiting, cough, sore throat and diarrhea. This acute phase lasts from twenty-four to seventy-two hours.

The U.S. weaponized VEE in the 1950s and 1960s and other countries have or are suspected to have weaponized this agent. It could be produced in wet or dry form and stabilized for weaponization. Many consider VEE as the most likely viral agent that would be used against U.S. forces in a biological attack. Smallpox and viruses that cause hemorrhagic manifestations could also be employed as biological warfare agents.

Biological Toxins. These toxins include any toxic substance of natural origin produced by animal, plant or microbe. They differ from chemical agents in that they are not man-made. Biological toxins tend to be more toxic per weight than many chemical agents.

Botulinum Toxins. This is a group of seven related neurotoxins, A through G, produced by the bacillus Clostridium botulinum. These toxins could be dispersed by aerosol over troop concentrations. When inhaled, these toxins produce a clinical picture similar to foodborne intoxication. The clinical syndrome produced by one or more of these toxins is known as "botulism." Botulinum toxin is one of the most toxic compounds known to man, requiring only 0.001 microgram per kilogram of body weight to kill fifty percent of the animals studied. Botulinum toxin is 15,000 times more toxic than VX and 100,000 times greater than sarin, two well-known chemical agents that will be discussed in Chapter Four.

Ricin. This is a potent toxin derived from beans of the castor plant. Castor beans are found worldwide and it is quite easy to produce ricin from them. Each year about one million tons of castor beans are processed to produce castor oil. The waste mash resulting from this process is about five percent ricin by weight. Ricin is stable and extremely toxic. In 1978, for example, Georgi Markov, a Bulgarian exile, was assassinated in London when a ricin pellet was implanted in his body from a special weapon designed to look like an umbrella.

When inhaled as a small particle aerosol, pathologic changes may occur within eight hours and acute hypoxic respiratory failure in thirty-six to seventy-two hours. When ingested, ricin causes severe gastrointestinal symptoms and vascular collapse and death.

Pathways to Biological Weapons Proliferation

Non-Western countries might stick close to easily produced biological agents, such as anthrax, plague, cholera, tularemia, and botulinum. The scientific expertise necessary to mass-produce natural biological and toxin agents should be readily available. As illustrated in Figure 3.2, eight basic steps are prerequisite to acquiring a militarily significant biological weapons program: (1) provide for the conduct of *work in secret,* including one or more facilities, personnel, and security measures; (2) *research* on microbial pathogens and toxins; (3) *pilot production* of agent in laboratory containers or small fermenter systems; (4) a *military assessment* of the agent should include such factors as stability, infectivity, course of infection, dosage, and feasibility of aerosol dissemination; (5) *research, design, development, and testing* of munitions and other dissemination equipment; (6) *production* of agent scaled-up, perhaps in stages, and *freeze-drying;* (7) *stabilize* agent through microencapsulation or other means and *fill into* munitions, spray tanks, and other delivery systems; and (8) *stockpile* filled or unfilled munitions and delivery vehicles.[12]

Almost all the equipment needed for large-scale production of pathogens and toxins is dual-use—civil and military applications—and widely available on the world market. Much of it is already used in breweries, pesticide plants, pharmaceutical companies, and others. Spore cultures of

---

[12] U.S., Congress, Office of Technology Assessment, *Technologies Underlying Weapons of Mass Destruction,* pp. 83-84.

---

66   *The New Face of War*

Figure 3.2
Proliferation Pathways Toward Biological Weapons

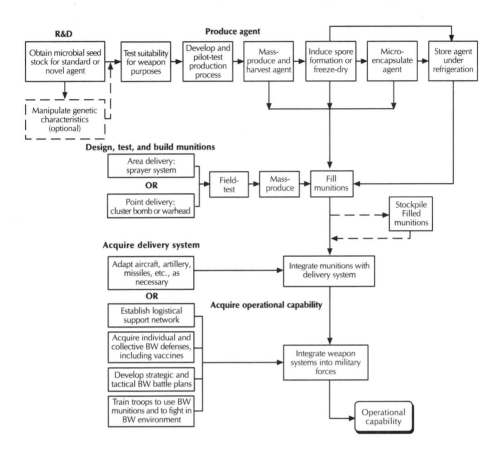

Source: U.S., Congress, Office of Technology Assessment, *Technologies Underlying Weapons of Mass Destruction,* OTA-BP-ISC-115 (Washington, D.C.: Government Printing Office, 1993), p. 83.

pathogenic (disease-producing) organisms can be purchased from international suppliers that provide culture samples to universities, hospitals and laboratories.[13] Nonetheless, there some sizable technical difficulties that must be hurdled satisfactorily to produce biological warfare agents.

Biological warfare agents are plentiful and widely accessible. Pathogenic microorganisms are indigenous to many countries and can be cultured from

- Infected wild animals – plague in rodents
- Living domestic animals or infected remains – Q-fever in sheep, anthrax in cattle
- Soil in endemic areas – trace amounts of anthrax bacteria and other pathogens
- Spoiled food

This points out a fundamental problem in trying to block biological weapons programs. So much of the scientific and technical expertise and the associated commodities and technology have legitimate applications to the commercial fermentation and biotechnology industries. The world biotechnology industry is growing as more developing countries turn to industrial microbiology for such things as the production of fermented beverages, vaccines, antibiotics, ethanol (from corn and sugar cane), enzymes, yeast, vitamins, food colors and flavorings, amino acids, and single-cell protein as a supplement for animal feeds. In a word, it is impossible for Western nations to prevent the diffusion of knowledge and technology to potential proliferating countries. More than 100 countries have the capability to develop biological warfare agents.

Key components of a biological warfare production plant include fermenters and the capability to sterilize and dispose of biological wastes on a large-scale. Fermentation can be conducted on a batch basis or in a continuous culture from which organisms are constantly removed and an equal volume of culture medium is added. The yield of a continuous culture is about ten times greater than the batch process. The batch approach is technically less complex and it makes maintenance of the agent potency easier.

---

[13] Dunn, *Global Proliferation,* Volume IV: Biological Weapons Proliferation, pp. IV-19 through IV-26.

Containment measures are among the greatest needs of a biological warfare program to ensure lethal agents do not escape from the production facility. In the Western countries, Biosafety Levels 3 and 4 facilities are required to work on highly infectious microbial agents. The high-containment standards for Level 3 require all personnel be immunized against the infectious agent with which they are working, and they must wear protective clothing, goggles, and face masks. At a Biosafety Level 4, the highest level of containment, the human operator is separated from the infectious agents. These facilities include sealed boxes with rubber-glove ports that provide absolute containment while the infectious disease is being manipulated.

Biological warfare agents need to be processed into a form that enhances their stability in storage and after dissemination to ensure they remain viable long enough to infect their human targets. Rapid freezing and dehydration under a high vacuum is one popular method since it avoids the need to maintain the microorganism in dangerous liquid suspensions during storage and movement. This freeze-drying or *lyophilization* process reduces the solution of bacteria and a sugar stabilizer to a small cake of dried material that can be milled into any state of fineness. A lyophilizer is required for this process and it is widely available in the pharmaceutical industry.

Another stabilizing approach is microencapsulation. This process emulates natural spore formation by coating droplets of pathogens or particles of toxins with a thin dry coat of gelatin, cellulose or another protective material.

Biological warfare agents would be disseminated either as a liquid slurry or a dry powder of freeze-dried organisms or toxin. To have military utility they must produce consistent and reliable results. Delivery systems can range from an agricultural sprayer mounted on a truck to a specialized cluster munition on a ballistic missile warhead. Many biological agents can invade the body through the lungs and then travel through the bloodstream to other parts of the body. Biological aerosols, a simple piece of machinery akin to the home vaporizer, can be used to produce large-scale respiratory infections. The aerosol creates a stable cloud of suspended microscopic droplets, each containing from one to thousands of bacterial or virus particles.

Detection of clandestine biological warfare programs is a difficult task. Intelligence analysts will need to integrate data from many sources, both technical and human. Production and weaponization signatures are difficult to detect and storage of components for biological munitions can be masked easily by integrating them with the activities of conventional munitions. Human intelligence use of agents, defectors and emigres, and whistleblowers offer some potential.[14]

Some countries or terrorist groups are unlikely to reach the high safeguards of a U.S. government laboratory. Nonetheless, large volumes of biological agents can be handled in a fairly unsophisticated environment. Since much of the equipment needed to produce biological agents is commercially available, licenses are not required, and most of the toxic strains that might be used can be found naturally or ordered commercially, a very deadly capability is possible. The biological threat is multiplied several times over when one couples the availability of expertise, equipment and biological agents. The biological production process can also include experiments that can make the toxins insensitive to known antitoxins and vaccines.

Proliferation Template: Iraq's Biological Weapons Program

Iraq initiated its biological warfare program in 1985-86, developing anthrax and botulinum toxin. Weapons field trials were held in 1988 involving tests of biological agents on sheep, monkeys, donkeys, and dogs. Production of 1,500 liters of anthrax agent began the following year and was increased rapidly to 8,425 liters, plus 6,000 liters of concentrated botulinum toxin at Al Hakam in 1990.[15]

Six major sites associated with Iraq's biological warfare program were directed from the Baghdad Biological Research Center. See Figure 3.3.

- **Salman Pak:** This facility was the hub of laboratory-scale research on anthrax, botulinum toxin, Clostridium perfringens (gas gangrene), mycotoxin, aflatoxin, and ricin. Researchers conducted toxicity evaluations of these agents and assessed their growth characteristics and survivability. Initial scale-up production research also was conducted. Salman Pak was destroyed by the Iraqis in 1991, two weeks before the U.N. inspectors arrived.

---

[14] U.S., Congress, Office of Technology Assessment, *Technologies Underlying Weapons of Mass Destruction,* pp. 71-117.

[15] Bill Gertz, "Horror Weapons," *Air Force Magazine,* (January 1996), p. 46.

The New Face of War

- **Al Hakam:** This site was specifically designed and constructed to serve as Iraq's main biological agent production facility. Thousands of liters of anthrax and concentrated botulinum toxin were produced at this facility before the Gulf War as well as hundreds of liters of Clostridium perfringens. This facility was destroyed by the U.N. Special Commission in the spring of 1996.

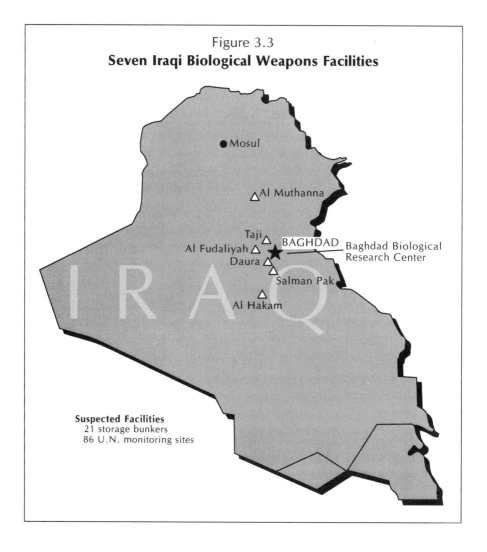

Figure 3.3
Seven Iraqi Biological Weapons Facilities

- **Daura Foot and Mouth Disease Vaccine Facility:** This facility was incorporated into the biological warfare program in the fall 1990. Initial research was conducted on viral warfare agents, including hemorrhagic conjunctivitis, human rotavirus, and camel pox. At least 5,400 liters of concentrated botulinum toxin were also produced over a two-month span from November 1990 to mid-January 1991.
- **Agricultural and Water Resources Research Center at Fudaliyah:** Converted from a scientific agricultural research station, this facility was dedicated to the production of aflatoxin, a cancer-causing agent. Some 1,850 liters were produced at this site.
- **Taji Single Cell Protein Plant:** This facility was converted in the late 1980s for the production of concentrated botulinum toxin. Some 400 liters had been produced in time for the Gulf War.
- **Muthanna State Establishment:** The initial location for Iraq's biological warfare program in 1985-86, researchers conducted initial toxicity evaluations of several biological agents and examined their growth characteristics and survivability. Four agents were investigated: anthrax, botulinum toxin, aflatoxin, and ricin. Small amounts of botulinum toxin were also produced at Muthanna. Biological warfare equipment was moved to Salman Pak in 1987. Subsequently, the facility provided weaponization expertise to the biological warfare program as well as chemical munitions technology and testing.[16]

Iraq experimented with new biological agents useful for warfare while producing several well-known ones:
- **Anthrax:** The Iraqis, according to their declarations, produced 8,500 liters of concentrated anthrax with some 6,000 liters filled into fifty bombs and ten Scud warheads.[17]

---

[16] United Nations, Special Commission on Iraq, "Major Sites Associated with Iraq's Past WMD Programs" (New York: UNSCOM, October 3, 1995) (photocopy), and Anthony H. Cordesman, *Weapons of Mass Destruction in Iraq: A Summary of Biological, Chemical, Nuclear* and *Delivery Efforts and Capabilities* (Washington, D.C.: Center for Strategic and International Studies, November 12, 1996), p. 4.

[17] United Nations, Security Council, *Report of the Secretary-General on the Status of the Implementation of the Special Commissions Plan for the Ongoing Monitoring and Verification of Iraq's Compliance with Relevant Parts of Section C of Security Council Resolution 687 (1991)*, U.N. Doc. S/1995/864 (October 11, 1995), pp. 1–29.

- **Botulinum Toxin:** The Iraqis produced some 19,000 liters of concentrated botulinum toxin; almost 10,000 liters of this stockpile was filled into 100 bombs and thirteen extended-range Scud warheads.[18]
- **Clostridium perfringens:** This is a new agent that causes gas gangrene or the rotting of flesh in war casualties requiring amputation of affected limbs. When placed within artillery and mortar rounds, this biological agent would be spread by shrapnel which would cause wounds to develop gas gangrene.[19] Iraq produced 340 liters by the time the Gulf War broke out.[20]
- **Aflatoxin:** This poisonous substance is common to fungus-contaminated food grains and is known to cause liver cancer many months to years after the victims have been exposed and possibly could cause death. Iraq began studying aflatoxin in May 1988 at Al Salman where the toxin was produced by growth of the fungus aspergillus in 5.3 quart flasks. A year later aflatoxin production was moved to Fudaliyah where some 1,850 liters were processed between the spring and the end of 1990. Having conducted three trials using aflatoxin warheads in 122-millimeter rockets and R400 aerial bombs between November 1989 and August 1990, large-scale weaponization was begun in December 1990, including sixteen R400 aflatoxin bombs and two Scud warheads (extended range version).[21]
- **Tricothecene Mycotoxins:** Iraq conducted research into tricothecene mycotoxins and may have field tested them.[22] These agents allegedly were used in aerosol form to produce lethal and non-lethal casualties in Laos (1975-81)—6,300 deaths; Kampuchea (Cambodia) (1979-81)—1,000 deaths; and Afghanistan (1979-81)—3,000 deaths. The victims, civilians and guerrillas, were not protected with masks and chemical protective clothing. While controversy surrounds the use of this "Yellow Rain," enough evidence has been collected to judge their use as highly probable. Early symptoms begin within minutes of exposure

---

[18] *Ibid.*

[19] Gertz, "Horror Weapons," p. 46.

[20] United Nations, Security Council, *Report of the Secretary-General,* U.N. Doc. S/1995/864, pp. 1–29.

[21] *Ibid.* See also Alan George, "Saddam Stockpiled 'Cancer Time Bombs,'" *Washington Times* (October 1996), p. A17, and John Hanchette and Norm Brewer, "U.N., Intelligence Reports Show Iraq Could Have Spread Deadly Aflatoxin," *Gannet News Service* (December 7, 1996).

[22] Gertz, "Horror Weapons," p. 46.

---

and include burning skin pain, redness, tenderness, blistering, and progression to skin necrosis with leathery blackening and sloughing of large areas of skin in lethal cases. Death may occur in minutes, hours or days.[23]

- **Hemorrhagic conjunctivitis virus:** The Iraqis examined this new disease agent that causes extreme pain and temporary blindness, resulting from bleeding eyeballs.[24] Viral hemorrhagic fevers make up a diverse group that have roots in several different viral families. The viruses can be spread in many ways, and for some, the respiratory portal of entry to the human body is a possibility. This indicates the potential for aerosol dissemination, although no evidence exists of weaponization in Iraq or elsewhere.[25]
- **Rotavirus:** Iraq conducted research into this potential agent that causes severe diarrhea and can lead to dehydration and death.
- **Camel Pox:** This disease is endemic to Iraq and does not appear to affect Iraqis. For foreigners, however, it causes fever and skin rash, including pus-filled skin eruptions.[26]

Iraq field-tested biological aerial bombs as early as 1988 at Al Muthanna. Sprayers and 155-millimeter artillery shells were also tested. Live firings of 122-millimeter rockets with botulinum toxin and aflatoxin were conducted in May 1990. The Iraqis began a crash military biological program just prior to their seizure of Kuwait aimed at killing Israel's entire population using germ weapons. Two MIG fighters outfitted with remote control each would carry 250 gallons of germ warfare agent. One of the pilotless aircraft was flight-tested with simulated biological agents, but the attack was never attempted.

Following Iraq's August 2, 1990, invasion of Kuwait, its biological weapons warfare program shifted into high gear. A program was initiated in December 1990 to develop a biological spray tank to spew up to 2,000 liters of anthrax over a target from an aircraft or a remotely piloted vehicle. Field tests were considered a failure but three additional spray tanks were prepared and stored. A dozen special nozzles made to spray germs from air-

---

[23] U.S., Department of the Army, *Medical Management of Biological Casualties*, pp. 98-102.

[24] Gertz, "Horror Weapons," p. 46.

[25] U.S., Department of the Army, *Medical Management of Biological Casualties*, pp. 61-74.

[26] Gertz, "Horror Weapons," p. 46.

craft and helicopters remain unaccounted for. Approximately 157 bombs and twenty-five Scud warheads were filled with botulinum toxin, anthrax, and aflatoxin. These weapons were stored at four locations throughout the war. Only twenty-five of the bombs could be accounted for; the whereabouts of the Scud warheads are unknown.[27]

It is open to question just how effective Iraq's bombs and Scud warheads would have been in delivering anthrax and other biological agents. Anthrax is most effective as a weapon of war when it is delivered in aerosolized form. Since aerosols do not settle appreciably, the germ agents have to be released more or less at the altitude of a persons nose. This means that bombs and warheads must descend slowly enough to allow release of the anthrax spores at just the right time before impact.[28]

In August 1991, two weeks before the U.N. visited Salman Pak, which served as the hub of the Iraqi biological warfare program, the Iraqis leveled much of the site. Two buildings were bulldozed. Equipment was removed. Ashes and melted binders suggested that documentation had been destroyed. One telling piece of equipment was found twenty miles away—the test chamber, large enough to hold primates, was found in a garbage dump; it had been crushed with a bulldozer.

In November 1994, the U.N. inspectors discovered a secretive Iraqi group known as the "Technical and Scientific Materials Import Division" which was a part of the Organization of Military Industrialization. Israel provided the U.N. inspectors key trade documents for ten tons of microbial food that confirmed Iraq's germ warfare program. Bacteriologists use special blends of sugars, proteins, and minerals to feed and breed germs. This "growth media" is commonly used in hospital and clinic laboratories to identify illnesses. As explained by reporters William Broad and Judith Miller, a swab of material from the back of a patient's throat would be placed in a small dish of growth media. The presence of germs would be indicated by the growth of the bacterial colonies.

Only a small amount of growth media is needed for such diagnostic purposes. Yet, the Iraqis had been importing growth media by the ton. The amount imported was judged to be sufficient for hundreds, even thousands

---

[27] William J. Broad and Judith Miller, "Iraq's Deadliest Arms: Puzzles Breed Fears," *New York Times* (February 26, 1998), pp. A1, A10, A11.

[28] Matthew Meselson, "How Serious Is the Biological Weapons Threat?," *Defense & Arms Control Studies Seminar* (Cambridge, Mass.: Center for International Studies, Massachusetts Institute of Technology, November 29, 1995).

---

of biological weapons. All told, the Iraqis had imported forty tons of growth media, at least thirty times greater than needed for medical purposes. The U.N. inspectors were able to trace a little more than half of the growth media; more than seventeen tons is missing.[29]

The U.N. Commission, despite Iraq's disclosures in August 1995, still does not believe that a full and correct accounting of the biological weapons program has been given. U.N. on-site inspectors were convinced in late 1997, after tracking twenty-five supposedly destroyed germ-loaded Scud warheads for more than two years in the context of elaborate cat-and-mouse games with Iraqi officials, that it was "extremely doubtful that any of the warheads were destroyed." Some forty gallons of anthrax and botulinum toxin Iraq claims were filled in twenty-one of the warheads could theoretically kill between 100,000 and one million people.[30] In its tireless quest for a complete disclosure of Iraq's proscribed biological weapons program, the Commission continues to conduct intrusive on-site inspections while monitoring eighty-six dual-use (civil and military uses) sites throughout the country.[31] See Table 3.3.

In the event of war, these eighty-six facilities logically would be listed as "suspected" biological weapons targets by intelligence and operational planners. The number of locations points to the difficulty of destroying a priority target set when extensive dual-use materials and equipment are involved. During the Gulf War, the Coalition air forces struck Al Kinde, which was dedicated to civilian production, but never hit Al Hakam, a producer of botulinum toxin, one of the deadliest biological agents known to humankind.

Iraq's main production plant for botulinum, Al Hakam, was never identified by Western intelligence. Air attacks were carried out instead against the Al Kinde veterinary company in Abu Ghurayb and Latifiyah, neither of which was a part of the biological warfare program. Even the twenty-one storage bunkers identified as possible storehouses for biological weapons

---

[29] Broad and Miller, "Iraq's Deadliest Arms," p. A10.

[30] R. Jeffrey Smith, "Iraq's Drive for a Biological Arsenal," *Washington Post* (November 21, 1997), pp. A1, A48.

[31] United Nations, Security Council, *Report of the Secretary-General,* U.N. Doc. S/1995/864, pp. 1–29, and *Report of the Secretary-General On the Activities of the Special Commission Established By the Secretary-General Pursuant to Paragraph 9 (b) (i) of Resolution 687 (1991),* U.N. Doc. S/1997/301 (April 11, 1997), p. 17; "Saddam Hopes BW Confession Is Enough To Convince USA," *Jane's Defence Weekly* (September 2, 1995), p. 27; and "Iraq Finally Admits Building Biological Weapon Arsenal," *Jane's Defence Weekly* (July 15, 1995), p. 3.

Table 3.3
Biological Monitoring Sites

Sites Monitored	Number
Sites known to have played significant role in the past biological weapons program	11
Vaccine or pharmaceutical facilities	5
Research and university sites that have significant technology or equipment	35
Breweries, distilleries and dairies with dual-purpose capabilities	13
Diagnostic laboratories	8
Acquisition and distribution sites of biological supplies and equipment	5
Facilities associated with biological equipment development	4
Product development organizations	4
Total	**86**

Source: United Nations, Security Council, *Report of the Secretary-General On the Status of the Implementation of Iraq's Compliance With Relevant Parts of Section C of Security Council Resolution 687 (1991),* U.N. Doc. S/1995/864 (October 11, 1995), pp. 19–20; *Report of the Secretary-General,* U.N. Doc. S/1996/258 (April 11, 1996), p. 20; and *Report of the Secretary-General On the Activities of the Special Commission Established By the Secretary-General Pursuant to Paragraph 9 (b) (i) of Resolution 687 (1991),* U.N. Doc. S/1997/301 (April 11, 1997), p. 17.

appear to have been nominated as targets on little more than guesses rather than hard evidence. This should not be surprising, since there were more than 3,000 storage structures in Iraq. By limiting the target set to bunkers, planners would have approximately 800 targets. Since the presence of air conditioning units at some bunkers could be a telltale sign of biological weapons, these bunkers could be nominated for high priority destruction. After the war, it was discovered that the suspect bunkers held only conventional weapons.[32]

---

[32] U.S., Department of the Air Force, *Gulf War Air Power Survey: Operations and Effects and Effectiveness,* Vol. II, Part 1, pp. 230–31; Gordon and Trainor, *The Generals' War,* p. 182; and Broad and Miller, "Iraq's Deadliest Arms," p. A10.

The point is that neither Western intelligence nor U.N. inspectors after the war had a clue of the scope and magnitude of the Iraqi biological warfare program. Through use of clever deception measures, hiding equipment, lies, and ordering equipment that could be plausibly used for non-military purposes, the Iraqis were able to spin an image of a country without an offensive biological warfare program and certainly one that did not weaponize munitions and warheads with bacteria and toxins.

The ambiguity and elusiveness of the biological warfare program in Iraq spells trouble for the future. The 19,000 liters of botulinum alone are theoretically enough to kill *fifteen billion* people. Actual use, of course, would confront dissemination inefficiencies but millions still could be killed.[33] The enormity of this kind of killing power in the hands of a person like Saddam Hussein makes one wonder of the consequences if Coalition forces had pursued the Iraqi leader and his elite units into the streets of Baghdad. Even worse is the thought that Western actions could have triggered biological weapons use without even knowing of their existence.

The elusiveness and ambiguity of the biological warfare target set also are reflected by the large number of sites in Iraq being monitored by the U.N. Special Commission. This monitoring is a result of the dual-purpose items and activities at these sites and the ease with which civilian facilities can be converted to biological weapons purposes. For the military planner, these dual-purpose sites should be included in the biological warfare target set, perhaps labelling them "suspected" sites and awaiting intelligence confirmation before striking them. The most important components, however, are the 300-plus scientists and technicians that underwrite Iraq's biological capabilities. Most of the workers and many dual-use facilities are located in urban areas.

In November 1997 Iraq suddenly and inexplicably expelled U.S. members of U.N. inspection teams, prompting a walk-out by the international body. Inspectors said Iraq had imported 750 tons of chemicals needed to produce the chemical nerve agent VX—less than a quarter-ounce of the gas could paralyze or kill millions of people.[34] The Iraqis are also reported to

---

[33] R. Jeffrey Smith, "Iraq Had Program For Germ Warfare," *Washington Post* (July 6, 1995), pp. A1, A17.

[34] "Team Was Close to Uncovering Iraqi Nerve Gas, Report Says," *USA Today* (November 3, 1997).

The New Face of War

have developed a doomsday option, if the U.S. air attacks are launched against them. A remote-controlled Polish M18 crop-duster aircraft capable of traveling hundreds of miles was reported to have been developed for delivery of up to a ton of anthrax bacteria or enough to kill tens of thousands of people if dropped on a city.[35]

According to Ahmad Alawi, an activist opposed to Saddam Hussein, Iraq in late 1997 was producing biological agents capable of causing outbreaks of bubonic plague in humans and animals. The Iraqis were also accused of producing bacteria and viruses that cause measles, pneumonia, and mad cow disease in humans. All told, Mr. Alawi estimated that Iraq had some 1,200 facilities involved in making lethal substances.[36]

Most of the U.N. inspectors agree that as soon as international monitoring ends, the Iraqis could initiate a biological warfare program the next day. The Iraqis could very well have a blueprint ready for resuming production of deadly biological agents. Documentation supporting reconstitution might reveal the locations of hidden plants, personnel and arms.[37]

---

[35] "Anthrax: Iraq's Doomsday Option?," *Washington Times* (November 9, 1997), pp. A1, A7. See also A. M. Rosenthal, "The Chosen Weapon," *New York Times* (October 17, 1997), p. A39.

[36] Jay Bushinsky, "UN Inspections Won't Harm Saddam's Bio-Warfare Ability," *Jerusalem Post* (December 7, 1997).

[37] Broad and Miller, "Iraq's Deadliest Arms," p. A11.

CHAPTER 4

Chemical Weapons

C hemical weapons in the hands of regional adversaries pose significant threats to the U.S. armed forces. Their potential use by Iraq during the Persian Gulf War against urban areas in Israel and Saudi Arabia—as well as against U.S. military forces and those of other Coalition members—drove home the point that chemical weapons remain a serious threat in regional conflicts. Chemical weapons are especially lethal against unprotected civilians and unprepared military or guerrilla forces. Well-equipped and trained armed forces, on the other hand, can defend themselves reasonably well against known chemical agents with detectors, gas masks, protective garments, decontamination, and effective casualty management. Over time, however, the friction generated by operating in a contaminated environment can be expected to reduce military effectiveness as the rigors associated with chemical warfare wear down the uniformed personnel and restrict their operations.

Among the first recorded use of chemical weapons occurred during the Peloponnesian War in 423 B.C. when allies of Sparta used a hollowed out beam to direct smoke from lighted coals, sulfur, and pitch into an Athenian fortress. Later, Kallinokos of Heliopolis, a Syrian architect, was the apparent inventor of Greek fire. He gave the secret formula for this chemical weapon—a mixture of sulfur, pitch, niter, petroleum, and possibly quicklime—to Emperor Constantine Pogonatus during a siege of Constantinople by the Saracens in 673 who outfitted his galleys to squirt the flaming liquid into enemy vessels. Greek fire burned fiercely and clung to whatever it hit.[1]

Poisoning of wells, crops and animals was employed over time, but it was not until the origin of modern organic chemistry in the late nineteenth and early twentieth centuries that interest in the use of chemicals for military purposes received greater attention. Various proposals for the use of cyanide- and chlorine-filled shells or bayonets dipped in cyanide had been made during the nineteenth century and rejected as being inhumane or against the rules of warfare.

---

[1] Bernard Brodie and Fawn M. Brodie, *From Crossbow to H-Bomb* (Bloomington: Indiana University Press, 1973), pp. 14-15.

These moral inhibitions broke down in World War One, beginning with the German release of some 150 tons of chlorine gas from 6,000 cylinders near Ypres, Belgium, on April 15, 1915. The attack killed approximately 800 soldiers and prompted the rapid retreat of some 15,000 Allied troops. The Allies prepared to respond with chlorine, phosgene, and chloropicrin which damaged the upper and lower airways; gas masks were developed to prevent inhalation injuries as well as protection against cyanide that had been developed by the French and British. The Germans presented the Allies with a new set of problems with an attack on July 12, 1917, near Ypres with artillery shells filled with a new chemical agent, sulfur mustard—20,000 Allied casualties resulted. Dispersed in the form of a nonvolatile liquid, mustard was longer lasting than previously used agents and affected not only the lungs but also the eyes and skin. Soldiers were affected by what they touched as well as inhaling the agent. Mustard had a latent period of several hours before the exposure became manifest. Soldiers now had to wear hot, bulky protective clothing in addition to masks as well as protection for their horses.[2]

The Italians used mustard gas and phosgene in attacks against the Ethiopians in 1935-36 by aerial spraying. The chemical attacks had a massive psychological impact on Ethiopian soldiers and probably hastened Italy's victory. Germany used cyanide and perhaps other chemicals in the concentration camps during World War Two. The Japanese used phosgene, mustard gas, and lewisite against the Chinese from 1937 through at least 1943. Aircraft bombing and artillery shells were the preferred delivery means. Mustard and phosgene gas were used by the Egyptians during the 1963-67 Yemen War. According to hundreds of eyewitness accounts, the Soviet Union used phosgene, tabun and VX[3] chemical agents during the 1979-88 Soviet-Afghan War. Iraq and Iran both used tabun and mustard agent during their 1980-88 conflict.[4] According to the Iranians, Iraqi chemical weapons during the Iran-Iraq War accounted for 50,000 casualties, including some 5,000 deaths. Through a swap of naval mines for chemical weapons from Iran, Libya dropped chemical agents on Chad's soldiers in 1987. Finally,

---

[2] U.S., Department of the Army, *Medical Management of Chemical Casualties,* 2d ed. (Aberdeen Proving Ground, Md.: Medical Research Institute of Chemical Defense, 1995), pp. 2-5.

[3] VX is one of the most toxic man-made chemical substances. A droplet the size of a pinhead or less on the skin will cause death within two minutes.

[4] Robert Mandel, "Chemical Warfare: Act of Intimidation or Desperation?," *Armed Forces & Society,* 19-2 (Winter 1993), pp. 194-203.

The New Face of War

the dispersal of chemical agents on Coalition forces during the Persian Gulf War—whether the result of limited attacks by the Iraqis, blowback from Coalition bombing raids against Iraq's chemical weapons industry and storage sites or post-war destruction of Iraqi chemical weapons stockpiles—remains an open question.

At least twenty-five countries are believed to either possess or to be developing chemical weapons. See Figure 4.1. Number twenty-six could be Sudan's National Islamic Front that in late 1997 was trying to gain access to chemical weapons. According to news reports, the Front has received technical assistance from Russia, Bulgaria, Iraq, and Iran.[5] The U.S. cruise missile attack in August 1998 against a key plant in Khartoum producing chemical precursors may set back Sudan's chemical weapons plans as well as those of its benefactors. Senior Iraqi scientists were reported to have been helping to produce precursors for VX at the factory in Sudan.

- **Libya,** for instance, has a suspected underground chemical weapons plant at Tarhunah, forty miles southeast of Tripoli. In a 1996 threat to bomb Libya's Rabta facility if construction was not halted, U.S. officials cited the GBU-28 5,000-pound laser-guided bomb as the weapon of choice to destroy the plant. It is believed the plant will be capable of producing 110 tons of mustard and nerve agents over three years.[6]
- **Syria**, with the reported assistance of Russian scientists, is manufacturing the highly lethal nerve agent VX and was preparing for its delivery by missile in mid-1997. The Syrians already had sarin gas, which enters the body via the respiratory system. VX is a significant qualitative improvement in its chemical weapons capabilities. According to U.S. estimates reported in September 1997, Syria was "within months" of producing chemical bomblets for Scud C ballistic missiles. Syria is believed to have sixty of the North Korean designed Scud Cs.[7]
- **Iran** possesses one of the largest stockpiles of chemical warfare agents in the non-Western world. Totaling several thousand tons of sulphur

---

[5] "Sudan Seeking Chemical Weapons," *Arabic News* (October 25, 1997).

[6] U.S., Department of Defense, *Proliferation: Threat and Response* (Washington, D.C.: Government Printing Office, April 1996), pp. 26-27, and Art Pine, "U.S. Hints It Would Bomb Libyan Weapons Facility," *Los Angeles Times* (April 11, 1996).

[7] "Israel Warns Syria on New Nerve Gas," *Washington Times* (April 30, 1997), p. A13, and "Syria to Make Chemical Bomblets for 'Scud Cs,'" *Jane's Defence Weekly* (September 3, 1997).

The New Face of War

Figure 4.1
Global Chemical Weapons Proliferation

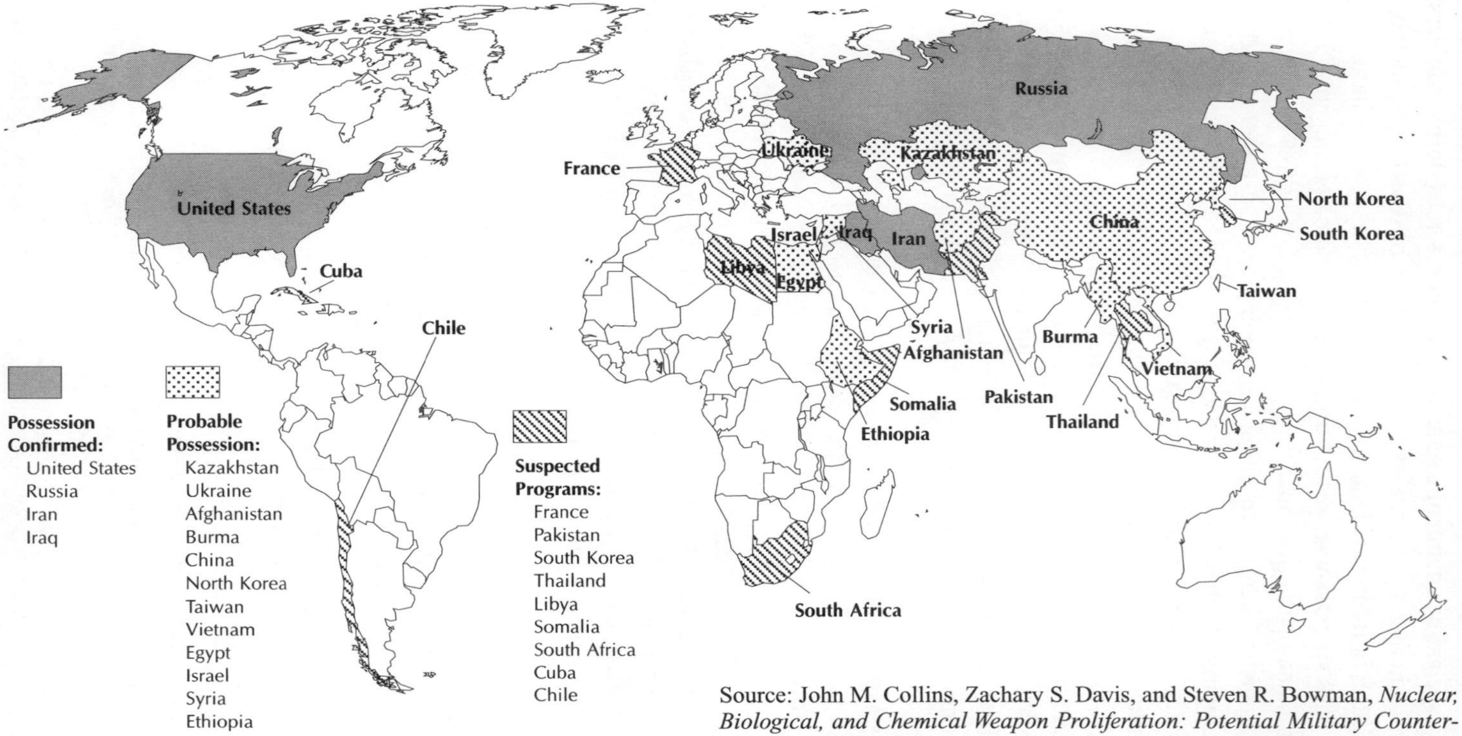

North Korea
South Korea
Taiwan
Vietnam
China
Russia
Burma
Thailand
Kazakhstan
Pakistan
Iran
Syria
Afghanistan
Somalia
Iraq
Ethiopia
Israel
Egypt
Ukraine
Libya
South Africa
France

Chile
Cuba
United States

Possession Confirmed:
United States
Russia
Iran
Iraq

Probable Possession:
Kazakhstan
Ukraine
Afghanistan
Burma
China
North Korea
Taiwan
Vietnam
Egypt
Israel
Syria
Ethiopia

Suspected Programs:
France
Pakistan
South Korea
Thailand
Libya
Somalia
South Africa
Cuba
Chile

Source: John M. Collins, Zachary S. Davis, and Steven R. Bowman, *Nuclear, Biological, and Chemical Weapon Proliferation: Potential Military Countermeasures* (Washington, D.C.: Congressional Research Service, Library of Congress, June 28, 1994), p. 2.

mustard, phosgene, and cyanide agents, the Iranians have enough materials to produce 1,000 tons of agent annually. Iran is developing a capability to produce more toxic nerve agents, and China is supplying Iran with chemical weapons precursors and key components, including anti-corrosive pipes and reaction vessels required due to the caustic nature of nerve agent manufacture.[8]

- **North Korea** has a chemical weapons program that includes mustard and blister agents. About 5,000 tons of chemical weapons were stockpiled in early 1998 or enough to bring about widespread destruction to South Korea. Pyongyang is capable of producing about 5,000 tons of chemical weapons annually.[9]

- **Iraq** could revive its chemical weapons production within weeks of the United Nations sanctions and on-site inspections being lifted. Despite the systematic destruction of the country's chemical weapons stockpiles and precursor chemicals, a significant amount of production equipment remains. In addition, the Iraqis may well have secret stockpiles of chemical agents and munitions in the ready.

The 1997 Chemical Weapons Convention bans the development, production and possession of poison gas weapons; and prohibits the use of chemical weapons or preparing to use or assisting others in the use of chemical weapons. Existing stockpiles of chemical weapons and their production facilities must be destroyed with a specific period of time. Iran might pose the Convention's first test. While Iran was one of the 164 countries that signed the Chemical Weapons Convention in 1991 and says it will ratify the treaty, it possesses a large-scale chemical weapons program partially hidden behind a veil of secrecy. Violators of the Convention can face full-scale sanctions.[10]

---

[8] Barbara Starr, "Iran Has Vast Stockpiles of CW Agents, Says CIA," *Jane's Defence Weekly* (August 14, 1996), p. 3; Rowan Scarborough, "China Helps Iran Develop Chemical Arms," *Washington Times* (April 11, 1997), pp. A1, A13; and Eric Croddy, "Putting the Lid Back On the Chemical Box," *Jane's Intelligence Review* (January 1998), p. 41.

[9] U.S., National Defense University, *1997 Strategic Assessment,* p. 138, and Kim Sang-Beom, "For the Record," *East Asian Review* (Winter 1997).

[10] U.S., Arms Control and Disarmament Agency, "Chemical Weapons Convention: A Balance Between Obligations and the Needs of States Parties," *Occasional Paper* (Washington, D.C.: January 5, 1993); David Kay, Ronald F. Lehman, and R. James Woolsey, "First the Treaty, Then the Hard Work," *Washington Post* (April 13, 1997), p. C7; and Jonathan Landay, "Iran May Pose First Test of Chemical-Arms Ban," *Christian Science Monitor* (April 28, 1997).

The Australia Group is an informal forum of twenty-nine countries that harmonizes national export controls to discourage and impede the proliferation of chemical (and biological) weapons and their precursor materials and equipment. A principal tool in this nonproliferation effort are control lists of materials used in the manufacture of chemical weapons, including dual-use chemicals or those having both commercial and military applications.

Table 4.1
Australia Group – Chemical Weapons

Control List of Dual-Use Chemicals (Selected)

Chemical	Commercial Use	Chemical Weapon
Thiodiglycol	plastics	Mustard Gas
Phosphorus Oxychloride	insecticides	Nerve Agent
Dimethyl Methylphosphonate	fire retardant	Nerve Agent
Potassium Fluoride	cleaning agent	Nerve Agent
Thionyl Chloride	plastics/pesticides	Mustard Gas
Arsenic Trichloride	ceramics	Lewisite

List of Dual-Use Chemical Equipment (Selected)

Equipment made from specific materials such as nickel or alloys with more than 40 percent by weight; tantalum or alloys; zirconium and alloys; fluoropolymers; glass or glass-lined:
* Reaction vessels, reactors or agitators
* Storage tanks, containers or receivers
* Heat exchangers or condensers
* Distillation or absorption columns
* Valves
* Multi-walled piping
* Pumps

Chemical Warfare Agents

Over the years, hundreds of thousands of toxic chemicals have been examined for military potential. Only about sixty passed the test and have been used in war or stockpiled in quantity.

Nerve agents and mustard are the two chemical agents most likely to be used on the modern battlefield. Yet, yesterday's technology in the West can be today's technology in non-Western countries. Iraq's reported use of

---

cyanide in the death of Kurds in the late 1980s, for instance, should alert us to future possibilities. Similarly, pulmonary intoxicants such as phosgene may be old hat in the West but they still pose a credible threat.

The four basic types of chemical agents are nerve agents, vesicants, cyanide, and lung-damaging agents. *Nerve agents* are the most toxic of the known chemical agents and can cause death within minutes of exposure. *Vesicants* cause blisters (vesicles) on the skin and can damage the eyes and airways by direct contact. *Cyanide* requires high concentrations to kill quickly but such concentrations can be maintained in the open air for only a few minutes. *Lung-damaging agents* include the World War One agent phosgene; other agents in this category are more hazardous materials usually associated with conventional warfare than chemical agents per se.

Nerve Agents. Nerve agents were first developed by Germany during the 1930s. Despite having stockpiles of nerve agent munitions, the Germans did not use them. Although many countries have the capacity to manufacture nerve agents, the only known battlefield usage was during the Iran-Iraq War in the 1980s.

Table 4.2
Nerve Agent Effects (Vapor Exposure)

Mild

Eyes: Excessive constriction
Dim vision
Headache
Nose: Excessive discharge of mucus
Mouth: Salivation
Lungs: Tightness of the chest
Time of onset: seconds to minutes after exposure

Severe

All of the above, plus
Severe breathing difficulty or cessation of respiration
Generalized muscular twitching, weakness or paralysis
Convulsions
Loss of consciousness
Loss of bladder, bowel control
Time of onset: seconds to minutes after exposure

Five known nerve agents include GA (tabun), GB (sarin), GD (soman), GF, and VX. Under temperate conditions nerve agents are liquid. The more volatile agents[11] present both vapor and liquid hazards when disseminated. The less volatile agents, such as GF, primarily present a liquid hazard.

Table 4.3
Nerve Agent Effects (Liquid on Skin)

Mild/Moderate

Muscle twitching at site of exposure
Sweating at site of exposure
Nausea, vomiting
Feeling of weakness
Time of onset: 10 minutes to 18 hours after exposure

Severe

All the above, plus
Severe breathing difficulty or cessation of breathing
Generalized muscular twitching, weakness, or paralysis
Convulsions
Loss of consciousness
Loss of bladder and bowel control
Time of onset: minutes to an hour after exposure

Exposure to even a small amount of nerve agent vapor causes effects in the eyes, nose and airways. Excessive constriction of the eyes is often accompanied by complaints of pain, dim vision, blurred vision, nausea, and, sometimes, vomiting. Excessive discharge of mucus from the nose might be the first indication of nerve agent vapor exposure. The affected person may feel tightness of the chest after exposure to a small amount of agent and severe distress as the result of a large amount of agent—cessation of respiration occurs within minutes after the effects are first indicated. Nausea and vomiting are the early signs of liquid exposure on the skin; diarrhea may result from large amounts of agent.

The effects from nerve agent vapor begin within seconds to several minutes after exposure. Agents with a high concentration are quick acting—

---

[11] Nerve agents are liquids under temperate conditions but they are to a certain extent volatile—they "volatilize" or evaporate, just as water and gasoline does, to form an often invisible vapor. The vapor is the gaseous form of the agent at a temperature lower than the boiling point of the agent at a given pressure.

The New Face of War

Table 4.4
Effects of Mustard Vapor

Organ	Severity	Effects	Onset of First Effects
Eye	Mild	Tearing Itchy Burning Gritty feeling	4-12 hours
	Moderate	Above, plus Reddening Swelling of lids Moderate pain	3-6 hours
	Severe	Marked swelling of lids Possible cornea damage Severe pain	1-2 hours
Airways	Mild	Runny nose Sneezing Nosebleed Hoarseness Hacking cough	12-24 hours
	Severe	Above, plus Severe productive cough Shortness of breath mild to severe	2-4 hours
Skin		Redness Blisters	2-24 hours

within one minute a loss of consciousness and seizure activity can be anticipated. A large amount of liquid on the skin causes effects within minutes, followed by a sudden onset of a cascade of events, including loss of consciousness and seizure activity.[12]

---

[12] U.S., Department of the Army, *Medical Management of Chemical Casualties,* pp. 17-37.

Vesicants. *Vesicants* cause blisters (vesicles) on the skin and can damage the eyes and airways by direct contact. Sulfur mustard (HD and H) has posed a military threat since its first use in World War One. Lewisite (L) was synthesized later during the war and has not been used on the battlefield. Phosgene oxime is a nettle agent that causes a corrosive type of skin lesion. The vapor is extremely irritating, and both the vapor and liquid cause almost immediate tissue damage.

Sulfur Mustard. Mustard poses a vapor and a liquid threat to exposed skin and mucous membranes. The effects are delayed, appearing hours after exposure. Organs most commonly affected are the eyes (inflammation of the mucous liner under the eyelid to severe eye damage), airways (mild irritation of the upper respiratory tract to severe bronchular damage), and skin (redness and blisters). Immediate decontamination is the only way to reduce damage.

Mustard is a light yellow to brown oily liquid with an odor of garlic, onion or mustard (hence, its name). Mustard evaporates slowly under temperate conditions and is mainly a liquid hazard. With increasing temperature, its vapor hazard increases. Within minutes of contact, mustard binds with tissue. Only immediate decontamination can prevent damage; later decontamination can prevent a more severe lesion.

Lewisite. This vesicant causes immediate pain or irritation, although lesions require hours to mature. Lewisite may be stockpiled by some countries and can be mixed with mustard to achieve a lower freezing point of the blend for ground dispersal or aerial spraying. It is oily, colorless liquid with the odor of geraniums. Eyes may be swollen shut an hour after contact; liquid lewisite causes severe eye damage within minutes of contact. The agent causes the same airway signs and symptoms as mustard.

Cyanide. Sometimes referred to by the antiquated term "blood agents," cyanide is a rapidly acting (six to eight minutes) lethal agent that has limited military usefulness due to its high volatility and high concentrations required. In a liquid state in munitions, cyanide rapidly vaporizes upon detonation. Large munitions are necessary to achieve the concentrations needed for effects. The French used about 4,000 tons of cyanide during World War One without notable success because they used one- and two-pound munitions that could not achieve the concentrations necessary. Cyanide smells like bitter almonds.

A moderate exposure to cyanide vapor will produce symptoms of dizziness, headache, transient increase in the rate and depth of breathing, nausea and vomiting. If the exposure continues, these reactions may progress to severe levels: 15 seconds—transient increase in the rate and depth of breathing; 30 seconds—convulsions; 2-4 minutes—cessation of respiration; and 4-8 minutes—cessation of heartbeat.

Pulmonary Agents. Phosgene is the prototype of these weapons. First synthesized in 1812, phosgene was developed as a chemical warfare agent and used by Germany at Verdun in 1917. Subsequently, both sides used phosgene, sometimes mixed with chlorine or other substances.

Following the explosion of liquid-filled shells, the phosgene vaporizes rapidly and spontaneously converts to a colorless, low-flying gas. It has the odor of sweet, newly mown hay. A latent period follows exposure and onset of worsening respiratory distress that may progress relentlessly to pulmonary edema and death. Initial symptoms may be perceived as shortness of breath and tightness of the chest. Symptoms of damaged lungs and pulmonary edema within four hours of exposure places the individual at a high risk of death.[13]

Pathways to Chemical Weapons Proliferation

Chemical weapons proliferation has become a global problem as commercial industry has responded to the needs in developing countries for fertilizers, pesticides and pharmaceuticals. The dual-use nature of much of the technology, combined with the training of thousands of organic chemists and chemical engineers from developing countries in the United States and elsewhere, has diffused competence in chemistry and chemical technology from the rich to the poor parts of the world.

The technical and production pathways for chemical weapons are well worn. Many of the basic chemicals are available for commercial purposes. The ability to manufacture some of the precursors for nerve agents is spreading. The need for organic chemists and chemical engineers is easily satisfied. Most of the process design and engineering for producing chemical agents are widely published. Much of the equipment needed has legitimate industrial applications, and conversion of chemical plants to weapons production facilities is feasible. Developing advanced chemical weapons is difficult but workable, and more common munition designs are widely published and available. Since the production pathways for nerve agents, vesicants, cyanide and pulmonary agents are well understood, non-Western countries would find few technical difficulties in developing a chemical

---

[13] *Ibid.,* pp. 38-103.

arsenal of mustard, lewisite, phosgene, tabun, and sarin. Production of the nerve agent soman ratchets the technology and expertise required upward a notch and VX production would occur a few notches higher on the technical complexity scale.

Eight basic steps are involved in producing chemical agents, designing, testing and building of suitable munitions for delivery, acquiring the right delivery systems, and fielding a workable operational capability. These steps would be necessary for a proliferating country to acquire a fully integrated chemical weapons capability. See Figure 4.2. A country might also find ways to cut corners to save time and money or opt for "old" agents, such as phosgene and lewisite.

Owing to the growing availability of chemical expertise and production equipment and the globalization of the chemical trade, more than 100 countries possess the capability, if not the intent, to produce simple chemical weapons such as phosgene, hydrogen cyanide, and sulfur mustard. Two basic pathways are open for acquiring a chemical weapons production capability. One approach is to build a plant dedicated to chemical agent production. The other path is to convert existing chemical facilities on a temporary or permanent basis to production of agents for chemical weapons. Libya and Iraq purchased entire chemical plants from German companies and then converted them to production of chemical agents. More recently, proliferating countries are purchasing the components and expertise for chemical production plants from a variety of sources and then integrating them behind closed doors.

Building a clandestine chemical weapons plant in an isolated location, such as the Rabta plant in Libya, would keep it away from the prying eyes of inspection teams conducting routine reviews under the Chemical Weapons Convention. But, like the Rabta facility, an isolated plant, even an underground one, can draw a lot of international attention. Or, a country might try to create a chemical weapons facility within the confines of a commercial industrial complex where the prohibited activities could be hidden inside the noise of the larger production processes. Alternatively, one might build small, pilot-scale chemical plants that are easy to conceal and could be used over a period of years to accumulate a sizable arsenal of chemical warfare agents and munitions.

The second pathway—converting an existing chemical plant to chemical agent production—may be best facilitated by building into the initial design the manufacturing equipment and processes necessary for a rapid conversion. In 1989, for instance, Libya's Pharm-150 plant at Rabta was

Figure 4.2
Proliferation Pathways Toward Chemical Weapons

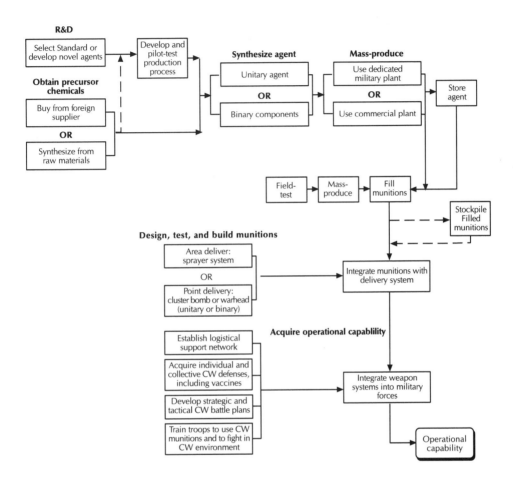

Source: U.S., Congress, Office of Technology Assessment, *Technologies Underlying Weapons of Mass Destruction*, OTA-BP-ISC-115 (Washington, D.C.: Government Printing Office, 1993), p. 20.

Table 4.5
Acquisition Steps for Chemical Weapons

1. Acquire *equipment, materials,* and the *expertise* needed for chemical weapons agent production.
2. Build a *pilot facility* that will produce small amounts of agent, work out the technical details of the synthetic process, and scale up to a production plant.
3. Design, prototype, test, and produce *suitable munitions* and *delivery systems* or purchase them from foreign sources.
4. *Fill the munitions* with agent.
5. Build *bunkers* and other *storage facilities* and establish *logistical support networks* for the stockpiling, transport, handling, and use of bulk agents and munitions.
6. *Deliver chemical munitions* to the military logistics systems for storage and transport to the battle zone.
7. Acquire *individual* and *collective protection* and *decontamination equipment* and train troops in their use.
8. Develop strategic and tactical *battle plans for chemical weapons use* and practice through operational testing and field exercises.

capable of converting from chemical agent production to commercial pharmaceuticals within *twenty-four hours.* In most cases, however, converting a chemical plant to the production of chemical warfare agents involves more than simply changing piping or valves. Conversion would be especially difficult for the production of nerve agents, especially at chemical plants that are custom-designed for the production of a single product in large quantities. Multipurpose plants would be easier to convert since they are often designed for maximum flexibility. Extra pipes can link various configurations to manufacture different chemicals over a period of time. Moreover, the equipment is usually designed to handle highly corrosive materials, such as the precursors to chemical warfare agents. Such multipurpose, flexible chemical plants might be able to switch over to chemical agent production in a few days with little chance of being detected.

Compared with the more toxic nerve agents, mustard is easy to produce and can be stored for extensive periods. Nine production processes for sulfur mustard are documented in published chemical literature. A mustard agent plant could be located at an oil refinery where sulfur could be extracted from petroleum or natural gas. The precursor of choice for large-scale production today is thiodiglycol, a sulfur-containing organic solvent. Thiodiglycol has many industrial uses in the production of inks for ballpoint pens, lubricant additives, plastics, photographic developing solutions, and textile dyes. What makes thiodiglycol so attractive is that it is just one step away from producing mustard agent: a reaction with a chlorinating agent like hydrochloric acid which is a widely used industrial chemical. In a word, sulfur mustard is relatively easy to produce and could probably be concealed rather easily.

From a production standpoint, nerve agents can be grouped in three clusters: tabun, sarin/soman, and VX. *Tabun* is the simplest to produce and was the first militarized nerve agent. It is made from four widely available precursor chemicals; two of them have commercial applications in the production of pharmaceuticals, pesticides, missile fuels, and gasoline additives. The tabun synthesis results from a two-step process that involves mixing the ingredients and a carrier solvent in a reaction vessel equipped with a scrubbing system to neutralize the gaseous byproduct. An air-tight enclosure is needed to prevent the escape of toxic vapors. Little or no distillation equipment is needed. The Iraqis produced tabun agent of about forty percent purity during the Iran-Iraq War.

Sarin/soman are both made in a batch process and have the same basic reaction steps. They have different alcohol ingredients which affects toxicity and volatility but not the difficulty of the production process. Both agents are produced by extremely corrosive compounds which requires reaction vessels and pipes made of corrosion-resistant alloys containing forty percent nickel. Hence, the Australia Group's control list for equipment with such alloys. Sarin and soman both require an alkylation reaction that is rarely used in the industrial production of pesticides, making it hard to mask the required equipment behind a shroud of commercial activity.

VX production is far less corrosive than sarin/soman but requires an alkylation step involving high temperatures and dangerous byproducts such as hot hydrochloric acid. Careful temperature control, heat exchangers based on fluids or oils rather than water, containment of highly toxic gas, and a distillation step to produce high-purity VX are among the technically challenging aspects of VX production.

Proliferation Template:
Iraq's Chemical Weapons Program

Iraq began research into the production of chemical weapons in the 1970s and by the 1980s began to batch-produce selected chemical agents. Although heavily dependent on precursor chemicals from foreign suppliers, Iraq started producing blister agent mustard (HD) in 1981. The quality of the mustard agent was only about eighty percent pure, although it could be either stored for an extensive period in bulk form or weaponized. The nerve gases tabun (GA) and sarin (GB) entered production in 1984; production modifications resolved stabilization problems that marred early efforts. Both the tabun and sarin produced were poor, having a maximum purity of sixty percent. These problems prompted Iraq to refocus its nerve agent research, development, and production to sarin (GB/GF). A binary approach was adopted to weaponization to overcome this problem: precursor chemicals for sarin were stored separately for mixing in the munitions just prior to use. This production program resulted in near-pure sarin for delivery against Iraq's enemies.[14]

The Al Muthanna State Establishment, also known as "Samarra," topped the list of the five main facilities making up Iraq's chemical warfare complex. It is located near the town of Samarra, about seventy-five miles northwest of Baghdad. Officially known as the State Enterprise for Pesticide Production (SEPP), the Al Muthanna production complex included the three intended precursor production sites at Al Fallujah and the munitions stores at Al Muhammadiyet. This huge twenty-five square kilometer facility was Iraq's primary chemical weapons research, development, and production facility. The site operated continuously from 1983 to 1991, producing thousands of tons of precursors, nerve agents and mustard gas. It included several pilot plants with state-of-the-art production facilities for both precursor chemicals and chemical weapons. Al Muthanna also included storage facilities for several dozen types of chemicals, an inhalation chamber for lethality estimation, and manufacture of aerial bomb cases. Chemical agents from this facility included mustard gas, sarin, tabun, and VX. U.N. inspectors after the war discovered more than 12,000 munitions (6,000 sarin-filled 122-millimeter rockets) and 205 tons of mustard gas.

---

[14] United Nations, Security Council, *Report of the Secretary-General on the Status of the Implementation of the Special Commission's Plan for the Ongoing Monitoring and Verification of Iraq's Compliance With Relevant Parts of Section C of Security Council Resolution 687 (1991)*, U.N. Doc. S/1995/284 (April 10, 1995), pp. 11–12.

The New Face of War

Al Fallujah I, located about thirty-seven miles northwest of Baghdad, was under construction when the Gulf War occurred and therefore had not been used for the production of chemical weapons-related items. This factory was intended to be an additional precursor facility for the chemical weapons program.

Al Fallujah II, located about forty miles northwest of Baghdad, produced chemical weapon precursors destined for the Al Muthanna site. Products included chlorine, phosphorus trichloride and oxychloride, thionyl-chloride, and, with high probability, two direct nerve agent precursors. The site was heavily bombed during the Gulf War. Remaining precursors and equipment were transferred to the Al Muthanna site for destruction under the supervision of the United Nations Chemical Destruction Group.[15]

Al Fallujah III, located some forty-three miles northwest of Baghdad, was in the late stages of construction at the time of the Gulf War. The facility, intended to support the Al Muthanna site, contained multi-purpose production plants. These production areas were extensively damaged in the 1991 bombing. The intended products of this site remain unclear, but it may have been connected with the VX program.

Muhammadiyet, located about eighty-seven miles west of Baghdad, was the primary storage area for filled chemical weapons. At the time of the Gulf War, the site contained numerous chemical warfare munitions, many of them filled with chemical agent. The site was heavily damaged during the war. The UNSCOM teams and the Chemical Destruction Group eliminated the chemical weapons that survived the bombardment.[16]

The location of Iraq's five main chemical weapons facilities and eighteen primary chemical weapons sites are shown in Figure 4.3.

The Al Muthanna State Establishment was the primary site used by UNSCOM inspectors for destruction of all chemical activities. With the exception of on-site destruction of some unsafe 122-millimeter rockets at Khamisiyah, all destruction activities occurred at Al Muthanna. Unfilled and emptied munitions, after being thoroughly decontaminated, were

---

[15] UNSCOM established the Chemical Destruction Group in June 1992, numbering twenty-three persons, including medical support, from twelve countries.

[16] United Nations, Security Council, *Report By the Executive Chairman of the Special Commission,* U.N. Doc. S/23165, pp. 26–27; U.N. Special Commission, unpublished information paper (October 16, 1995); and White, *Characterization and Historical Review of Chemical/Biological Weapons.*

Figure 4.3
Twenty-Three Iraqi Chemical Facilities

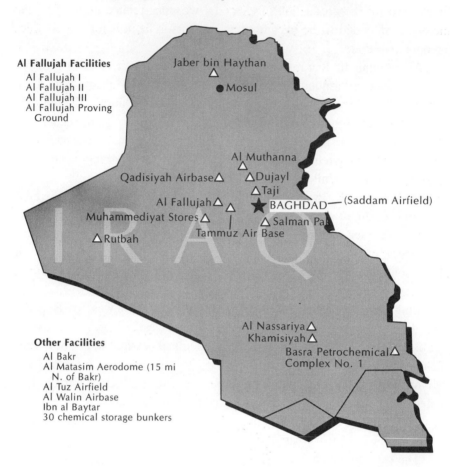

Al Fallujah Facilities
Al Fallujah I
Al Fallujah II
Al Fallujah III
Al Fallujah Proving
  Ground

Jaber bin Haythan

●Mosul

Al Muthanna

Qadisiyah Airbase△ △Dujayl
                  △Taji
Al Fallujah△ △ ★BAGHDAD——(Saddam Airfield)
Muhammediyat Stores △
△Rutbah   △Salman Pak
       Tammuz Air Base

Al Nassariya△
Khamisiyah△

Other Facilities
Al Bakr
Al Matasim Aerodome (15 mi
  N. of Bakr)
Al Tuz Airfield
Al Walin Airbase
Ibn al Baytar
30 chemical storage bunkers

Basra Petrochemical△
Complex No. 1

destroyed through crushing or cutting with an oxy-acetylene torch. Filled munitions were either drained, as in the case of aerial bombs, or destroyed by a combination of simultaneous explosive opening and high-temperature incineration. Bulk mustard agent was destroyed by incineration. The nerve agents GB and GB/GF mixtures were destroyed by controlled hydrolysis in a specially constructed plant meeting UNSCOM specifications. The aqueous wastes from the plant were allowed to partially evaporate and the remainder was cast into concrete blocks and buried on the site.[17]

The destruction activities were extensive and lasted from June 1992 to May 1994. All told, more than 480,000 liters of chemical warfare agents, nearly 40,000 chemical munitions and nearly 1,800,000 liters, more than 1,040,000 kilograms and 648 barrels, of some forty-five different precursor chemicals for the production of chemical warfare agents were destroyed.[18] See details in Table 4.6.

While these figures represent a salutary achievement by the U.N. Special Commission on Iraq, accounting for the more deadly VX nerve agent remains open. Not until November 1995 did the Iraqis acknowledge that they had produced 3.9 tons of VX (up from the 583 pounds of VX declared previously). Iraq claims to have destroyed the related weapons and feedstock in 1990 and turned instead to production of sarin and cyclosarin. Yet, at the end of the war they may have had as much as 3,800 kilograms (8,360-pounds) of VX nerve agents, plus twelve to sixteen missiles ready to deliver them against distant targets.[19] Also missing are chemical precursors that would be sufficient to produce 200 to 300 tons of VX.[20] VX works on the central nervous system. A pinprick-sized drop on the skin will result in

---

[17] United Nations, Security Council, *Fourth Report of the Executive Chairman of the Special Commission Established By the Secretary-General Pursuant to Paragraph 9 (b) (i) of Security Council Resolution 687 (1991), On the Activities of the Special Commission,* U.N. Doc. S/24984 (December 17, 1992), pp. 22–23.

[18] United Nations, Security Council, *Ninth Report of the Executive Chairman of the Special Commission Established By the Secretary-General Pursuant to Paragraph 9 (b) (i) of Security Council Resolution 687 (1991), On the Activities of the Special Commission,* U.N. Doc. S/1995/494 (June 20, 1995), p. 5, and John Barry, "Unearthing the Truth," *Newsweek* (March 2, 1998), p. 41.

[19] Cordesman, *Weapons of Mass Destruction in Iraq,* p. 4, and U.N., Security Council, *Tenth Report of the Executive Chairman,* U.N. Doc. S/1995/1038 (December 17, 1995).

[20] Philip Finnegan, "Saddam's Bio-Chem Arsenal Could Snarl U.S. Gulf Plans," *Defense News* (November 18-24, 1996), p. 58.

---

death within two minutes. In April 1996, the U.N. Special Commission concluded that it "...cannot be confident that VX production capabilities, stocks of precursors and appropriate munitions do not remain in Iraq."[21]

Table 4.6

Chemical Warfare Items Destroyed at Al Muthanna

Description	Amount
Munitions:	
Bombs, Rockets, and Artillery Shells	Nearly 40,000
Missile Warheads	30
Chemical Warfare Agents:	
Mustard agent	398,046 liters
Nerve agent (GA)	21,365
Nerve agent (GB/GF)	61,633
Total Precursor Chemicals	1,798,513 liters
Total Chemical Precursors	1,040,836 kg
Other:	
White phosphorus	648 barrels
Bulk storage containers	32

Source: United Nations, Security Council, *Seventh Report of the Executive Chairman of the Special Commission Established By the Secretary-General Pursuant to Paragraph 9 (b) (i) of Security Council Resolution 687 (1991), On the Activities of the Special Commission,* U.N. Doc. S/1994/750 (June 24, 1994), pp. 25–27, and U.S. National Security Council in John Barry, "Unearthing the Truth," *Newsweek* (March 2, 1998), p. 41.

In June 1998, despite Iraq's insistence that it never weaponized VX, U.S. Army tests of fragments of missile warheads that had been destroyed by the Iraqis showed evidence of having been filled with VX. The U.N. chief weapons inspector, Ambassador Richard Butler, emphasized that "there is absolutely no doubt that VX was present in some of those missiles. It is utterly unambiguous."[22]

Experts from nine countries in February 1998 endorsed a U.N. claim that Iraq could have a secret stockpile of as much as 100 tons of VX that

---

[21] United Nations, Security Council, *Report of the Secretary-General,* U.N. Doc. S/1996/258, pp. 16-17.

[22] John M. Goshko, "Iraq Nerve Gas Tests Confirmed," *Washington Post* (June 25, 1998), p. A30.

The New Face of War

had been produced before the 1991 Gulf War. The U.N. inspectors suspect the VX has been kept in a form that is chemically stable and usable. The expert panel—consisting of members from China, Germany, France, Russia, Switzerland, Sweden, Britain, and the United States—also concluded that Iraq probably still has the equipment, expertise, and material needed to produce 200 tons more of VX.[23]

Another outstanding problem is the dual-use and related equipment remaining in Iraq. Several pieces of dual-use equipment, which had been used in the production of chemical weapons, and analytical tools to ensure quality control of chemical warfare agents produced are still in Iraq. The U.N. chemical monitoring group in Baghdad is providing surveillance of 150 Iraqi facilities. All told, the U.N. had discovered through 1997 more than 200 pieces of undeclared dual-use equipment, such as heat exchangers, glass reactor vessels and distillation columns capable of use in proscribed chemical weapons; some 800 pieces of related equipment also have been found.[24]

The evidence now suggests that the Iraqi risk calculus in the Gulf War viewed chemical weapons as those to be used as a last resort or in response to nuclear attacks. It was equally likely at the outset of the Gulf War, and so assumed by the U.S.-led Coalition, that Iraq would use its large chemical arsenal tactically against Coalition forces in the field and strategically through attacks against populated areas. This operating premise proved wrong but that does not mean similar inhibitions to chemical weapon use will be present in future crises.

According to one assessment, Iraq's failure to use chemical weapons may have had more to do with the collapse of its command and control system and destruction of much of its delivery capability than with Baghdad being deterred or making the strategy choice to use them only as a last line of defense. If this is the case, as Dr. Andrew Rathmell argues, "Operation Desert Storm may have demonstrated to other proliferators the need to acquire a more sophisticated, flexible and decentralized CW capability."[25]

---

[23] R. Jeffrey Smith, "2 Panels Reject Iraqi Claim on Arms," *Washington Post* (February 20, 1998, p. A19.

[24] United Nations, Security Council, *Report of the Secretary-General,* U.N. Doc. S/1997/301, pp. 18-19.

[25] Dr. Andrew Rathmell, "Chemical Weapons in the Middle East: Lessons From Iraq," *Jane's Intelligence Review* (December 1995), p. 560.

Chemical Weapons

A far simpler and more direct reason may lie behind Iraq's non-use of chemical weapons. Having gambled and lost that they could seize Kuwait without a military response from the West, the Iraqi leaders could simply have chosen not to give the U.S.-led international coalition an excuse to declare and prosecute a political objective of eliminating Saddam Hussein's regime. By lying low and taking his lumps, Saddam Hussein could accept his inevitable eviction from Kuwait, although it was important psychologically to the Muslim world to give the show of a good fight. Saddam could choose when to pull his Republican Guard back to Baghdad so as to consolidate his power base while his "eviction notice" was served in Kuwait City.

CHAPTER 5

Advanced Conventional Weapons and Military Technology

The end of the Cold War triggered a virtual explosion of activity in the international arms market. Weapons of mass destruction aside, much of the 1990s activities centered on unrestricted conventional arms sales are taking place between traditional Western supplier countries and non-Western buyers. The downturn of Cold War defense industries in the United States, Western Europe and the former Soviet Union brought declining defense budgets, lesser military procurement, loss of jobs, and economic dislocation. Defense conversion, or shifting from production of military to civilian goods, which became the icon of many economists in the early 1990s, turned out to be a pipe dream. The solution for many companies in the defense industry was international sales. Through the mid- to late-1990s the bustling international arms bazaar unleashed a massive diffusion of military technology worldwide through white, grey and black markets.

The driving trend of arms sales in the 1990s has not been all push for weapons at bargain basement prices from the Western supplier side of the equation. A great deal of "pull" from non-Western countries for top-of-the-line weapons also played a strong role. The Persian Gulf War demonstrated to many countries the advantages of possessing qualitatively superior weapons and many turned to finding force multiplier technologies. The restoration of oil sales in the Middle East after the war and the economic expansion in China and Southeast Asia freed resources in many countries for purchase of new weapons.

At the same time, the international coordinating committee (COCOM)[1], which controlled the transfer of defense-related technology during the Cold War, was disbanded in March 1995. A process of free-floating national export restrictions has supplanted the stringent controls of yesteryear. The

---

[1] COCOM=Coordinating Committee for Multilateral Export Controls.

U.N. conventional arms registry, which in theory is supposed to keep track of intentional arms transfers, is shot full of holes since buyers often do not want the supplier countries to report all arms purchases since the data could tip off regional rivals of the extent of their modernization programs. France, for instance, reported only about half of its arms sales in 1996. Buyers such as Saudi Arabia, United Arab Emirates, Algeria, and Egypt do not fully participate in the U.N. Registry of Conventional Arms. In some countries, grey and black markets have evolved where actual foreign sales may be two to five times greater than legal sales.

The net result of these 1990s trends is that the sharp post-Cold War drop in foreign military sales hit bottom in 1994 and appear to have been on the increase ever since. Since the international arms market in the new era is clearly smaller, competition is ever more fierce among the arms exporters. Andrew Hull and David Markov, defense analysts at the Institute for Defense Analyses in Arlington, Virginia, examined the growing global bazaar in great detail. They conclude that this buyers market will continue to exert negotiating leverage over price and availability of advanced technology weapons. The buyers also possess leverage to dictate terms that will ensure de facto technology transfer.[2]

The developing countries have been the primary focus of arms sales since the end of the Cold War (seventy-two percent during the years 1987-1994 of all arms transfer agreements worldwide). One would think that the grey and black markets are even higher in terms of percentage of arms sales to the developing nations. The United States has been the principal arms supplier to these countries, $50.7 billion, or about forty-eight percent of all arms transfers with developing nations between 1991 and 1994. France, Britain, and Russia make up a distinct second tier of arms suppliers that compete directly with the American industry for international sales. A third tier of suppliers is made up of China and European and non-European countries that have sporadic involvement in the arms trade.[3]

Some commentators, like the Monterey Institute's William W. Keller, look at all of this international wheeling and dealing and ask: "Did the West defeat Soviet communism only to make the world safe for American and

---

[2] Andrew Hull and David Markov, "A Changing Market in the Arms Bazaar," *Jane's Intelligence Review* (March 1997), pp. 140-42.

[3] Richard F. Grimmett, *Conventional Arms Transfers to Developing Nations, 1987-1994* (Washington, D.C.: Congressional Research Service, Library of Congress, 1995), pp. 1-7.

The New Face of War

European weapons? Is this the meaning of the end of the cold war?"[4] Efforts to use export controls to regulate the bustling international trade in modern weapons and technology so far have been rather puny.

Since the United States accounts for nearly half of the world's arms transfers, it must assume the mantle of international leadership on designing effective international tools that will help to control the proliferation of advanced military weapons and technology. The United States first has to get its own house into order. The problem is that the need for effective export controls on the proliferation of advanced weapons and technologies arose at the very time that the U.S. was cashing the 1993-94 "peace dividend" resulting from the end of the Cold War. Hence, it should not be surprising that arms exports were seen by many as a means to ease the pain on American industry and workers and as a tool to assure the nation's industrial base.

It was not until February 1995 that President Clinton approved a comprehensive national policy to govern the transfer of conventional arms. The policy was designed to strike a balance between support for arms transfers that serve U.S. security interests and those of its allies and friends, and, on the other hand, restraint on arms transfers that might endanger regional peace and stability. A set of criteria was developed to assist in making informed decisions on U.S. arms exports. Importantly, the U.S. conventional arms transfer policy recognized the need to create a new international regime that would establish effective controls on arms sales and the transfer of sensitive technologies.[5]

The initial framework of the Wassenaar Arrangement, a global regime to increase transparency and responsibility of trade in conventional arms and dual-use goods and technology, was announced in December 1995. Wassenaar, initially signed by twenty-eight countries, was billed as a successor regime to COCOM. The participants agreed to control globally all items set forth on (1) a basic list of dual-use goods and technologies and (2) a munitions list. Enforcement is based on voluntary national controls similar to the Missile Technology Control Regime, Nuclear Suppliers Group, and the Australia Group (chemical and biological). After a plenary session

---

[4] William W. Keller, "The Political Economy of Conventional Arms Proliferation," *Current History* (April 1997), p. 179.

[5] U.S., Arms Control and Disarmament Agency, *World Military Expenditures and Arms Transfers 1995* (Washington, D.C.: Government Printing Office, 1996), pp. 31-34.

in April 1996 and signing up new members in July, the Wassenaar Arrangement began the practical work of developing frameworks, basic guidelines
and lists. Yet, the U.S. mantle of international leadership was quickly shred-
ded when it found itself alone among the participants in insisting upon
comprehensive information-sharing of arms transfers and prior notification
of transfers.[6]

By June 1997, the Wassenaar Arrangement was still being characterized as an "empty vessel" in search of a system to govern the international
conventional arms trade. Wassenaar, unlike COCOM before it, lacks the
authority to halt arms sales; the regime requires that participants notify each
other *after* the arms sales occur. A Russian diplomat put it simply: "This is
not an arms control agreement; it's more like an export cartel. It's a forum
for exporters to raise specific issues."[7]

The chickens have yet to come home to roost on transfers of advanced
weapons and military technologies. "What level of conflagration will be
required before effective controls are instituted?," William W. Keller asks.[8]
R. James Woolsey, former Director of Central Intelligence, warned the
Senate Select Committee in January 1995 that "the proliferation of advanced conventional weapons and technology" presents "a growing military
threat as unprecedented numbers of sophisticated weapons systems are offered on the world market." He went on to note that such weapons systems
could be used to deliver weapons of mass destruction and could "disrupt
U.S. military operations and cause significant U.S. casualties."[9]

International Arms Bazaar

Andrew Hull and David Markov best summarized the driving trends of the
global arms market in their exceptional spring 1997 study for *Jane's Intelligence Review:* "Indeed, virtually any type of weapon, apart from weapons
of mass destruction and long-range ballistic missiles, is available some-
where in the international arms market if the price is right."[10] This is a bold

---

[6] *Ibid.,* pp. 35-39.

[7] As quoted in Jeff Erlich, "Diplomats Work to Fill 'Empty' Wassenaar Arrangement," *Defense News* (June 9-15, 1997), pp. 1,76.

[8] Keller, "Political Economy of Conventional Arms Proliferation," p. 179.

[9] As quoted by Jennifer Washburn, "Unethical Arms Sales," *Washington Times* (May 14, 1997), p. A15.

[10] Andrew Hull and David Markov, "Trends in the Arms Market - Part One," *Jane's Intelligence Review* (April 1997), p. 189.

---

statement that shouts to us all: Strategic conditions have changed, regional threats are far more deadly than during the Cold War, planning assumptions may no longer be valid, and regional planning scenarios, which have become a stock-in-trade in the Pentagon, may be a mug's game because the threats to U.S. forces are increasingly diverse, versatile, and lethal.

The arms market in 1998-99 is unlike the familiar Cold War model where non-Western countries were offered stripped-down versions of top quality weapons systems. In the new, highly competitive market suppliers offer technological inducements to woo buyers away from rivals. The Russians, for example, are offering an advanced radar for MIG-29 exports even though their own Air Force is not yet equipped with the new radars; SU-35 fighters have been offered to the United Arab Emirates' (UAE) planned purchase of eighty strike fighters worth about $8 billion along with the AA-12, Russia's most advanced air-to-air missile; when Malaysia insisted on upgrading the engines and avionics as a condition of MIG-29 buys, the Russians agreed; and Russia is designing some very sophisticated weapons strictly for export, such as the highly capable TOR surface-to-air missile system. Other countries are also exporting advanced military technology and weapons. A French-German-Russian consortium will soon make an active tank defense system available to foreign buyers. The French bid for the eighty strike fighters in the UAE included its Rafale fighter which at the time was still in prototype stage, and Paris promised it would equip the aircraft with its best air-to-air missile. On the part of the United States, the UAE made it clear that it would not consider the F-16 and F-15 without the AMRAAM, the most advanced air-to-air missile in the inventory. Finally, an export-only low-observable shroud for drones or cruise missiles has been developed by South Africa—land-attack cruise missiles promise to become a favored WMD delivery platform early in the twenty-first century.

The following list consists of examples of the diverse kinds of military technologies for sale in the 1990s arms bazaar. Andrew Hull and David Markov make two key points about the technologies and systems listed. First, the items listed were among those most carefully guarded by the United States during the Cold War and, secondly, these systems can be significant force multipliers for non-Western countries, even when fielded in small numbers:

- Reactive armor (multiple versions) (Russia, Ukraine, several East European countries);
- Satellite photography (France, Russia, China, United States);
- Military surveillance satellites (France);

- Airborne early warning aircraft (Russia, United States, Israel);
- Aerial refueling aircraft (United States, Israel);
- Theater ballistic missile defense systems (Russia, France, Israel, United States);
- Countermeasures to ballistic missile defenses (Russia, perhaps China and North Korea in 1997-98);
- Low-observable technologies (France, South Africa, Russia, United States);
- Remotely piloted vehicles and unmanned aerial vehicles (Israel, France, Russia, United States);
- Counter-stealth radars for detecting low-observable aircraft (Russia, Czech Republic);
- Laser weapons (Russia and China);
- Diesel-electric submarines (Russia, Germany, Sweden, the Netherlands, France, Australia); and
- Cryptological equipment (Russia).[11]

Upgrading existing military weapons systems is being offered by consortiums from multiple supplier states as a way for buyers to obtain greater combat capability for very low costs (when compared with the capabilities of new equipment). A French-Russian consortium, for example, is upgrading from 125 to 150 Indian MIG-21s; an eight-fold increase in air-to-air capabilities and a four-fold increase in air-to-ground capabilities are anticipated from the upgrades. T-72 tank engines with twenty-five percent more power are being exported cooperatively by Belgium and the Ukraine. Meanwhile, Poland and South Africa are teaming to provide the T-72 an improved fire control radar. Not only does the new fire control system extend the operational life of the T-72 by ten to fifteen years, but it is said to dramatically improve its day and night fighting capability nearly on a par with current U.S. and British fire control systems on the M1 and Challenger main battle tanks.

The new international arms market continues to open innovative paths with unknown twists and turns as defense firms seek to share costs and reduce risks of developing, producing, and selling new and often complex military systems. One growing phenomenon is combining the best of weapons systems in the East and West into hybrid products. "The international

---

[11] *Ibid.,* pp. 190-91.

The New Face of War

market now makes it possible," Hull and Markov explain, "...to buy a Russian airframe, equip it with U.S. or British engines, then add Israeli avionics and arm it with French munitions."[12] Electronic black boxes that allow the firing of Western and Russian tactical missiles from the same aircraft during a single sortie are also on the market by a Russian firm. The potential for hybridization of military products will remain an enormous opportunity for defense firms in future years. International cooperative efforts promise a growing trend.

International arms sales are also a means for achieving access to technical know-how. In some cases, a country might directly hire foreign scientists and engineers. China, for instance, reportedly recruited some 3,000 Russian defense scientists and engineers with about 1,000 takers between 1991 and 1993. About 300 have stayed on with long-term commitments.[13]

Another technique being used to transfer military technology of the supplier states is through offset agreements where the buyer desires to co-produce portions of weapons systems. In the past, offsets were commonly used to maintain domestic employment, create a national defense industrial base, acquire modern technology, and assist in the purchaser's balance of payments position. The buyer's market and ongoing redefinition of the international military sales in the post-Cold War era is producing growing demands for greater technology transfer, higher offset percentages, and more local content in defense products. Dassault, for instance, as part of a $3.5 billion sale of Mirage fighters to Taiwan in 1995 agreed to form partnerships with Taiwanese firms, transfer technology, and manufacture equipment for civilian markets. In some countries, the offset price is not directly tied to the weapons system manufacture but to helping create local businesses and build the country's commercial infrastructure. France's Thomson-CSF, for example, started a garment manufacturing enterprise in Abu Dhabi as an offset to a contract for tactical transceivers and audio systems.[14]

The growing importance of both grey and black markets is another phenomenon of the 1990s international arms bazaar. In a good year, according to a "best guess" estimate by Andrew Hull and David Markov, illegal

---

[12] *Ibid.*

[13] Andrew Hull and David Markov, "Trends in the Arms Market - Part Two," *Jane's Intelligence Review* (May 1997), p. 233.

[14] U.S., General Accounting Office, *Military Exports: Offset Demands Continue to Grow* (Washington, D.C.: General Accounting Office, 1996), pp. 1-11.

---

sales can amount to as much as $5-$10 billion and $1-$2 billion in poor years. These markets serve buyers that might be ineligible for market sales and as a means of obtaining weapons not otherwise available. Armaments worth as much as $2 billion, for example, may have reached Bosnia in 1993. Russia has had a flourishing black market in international arms since at least 1992. Old fashioned greed has been a main driving factor for the illegal sales while some Russian officers have often been motivated to sell equipment as a means of feeding and housing their men. The widespread corruption and breakdown of military controls allows officers to sell regularly massive amounts of equipment and ammunition on the black market. When Russia's 14th Army in Moldova was inventoried by the Ministry of Defense, only thirty percent of the allocated equipment could be located. Early in 1992, 1,118 railway carriages, each carrying twenty tons of artillery ammunition, were missing. Other countries are also involved in the illegal arms transfers. Bulgarian, Portuguese, Ukrainian, and Bolivian grey and black market arms traders reportedly are also involved.[15]

A Moscow-based Russian gang, including former Soviet soldiers, has organized an international arms smuggling ring to get weapons to the Kurdistan Worker's Party or PKK in Turkey. The Russian gang is supported by high-level government officials and has encountered no problems in transferring arms across national borders. One smuggling route passes through Poland, the Slovak Republic, former Yugoslavia and Bulgaria. The weapons are probably small arms, shoulder-fired anti-aircraft missiles, and rocket-propelled grenades, perfect for the Turkish PKK's terrorist campaign against the government. PKK gunners downed two Turkish helicopters in June 1997 during a raid on the Marxist-Leninist group's positions in northern Iraq.[16]

Russia's arms sales in the open market also have been quite successful. Peddling fighter aircraft, submarines, and small arms in Southeast Asia, the Middle East, and Latin America promises to net Moscow $4 billion in sales in 1997. The Russians have made deals in fifty-one countries worldwide. As a result, the Russians now boast being in second place in global weapons sales behind the United States ($11 billion worth of arms deals in 1996). One of their best clients is China where arms sales and technology

---

[15] Hull and Markov, "Trends in the Arms Market – Part Two." pp. 236-37.

[16] Bill Gertz, "Russian Smuggling Ring Arms Kurd Rebels in Turkey," *Washington Times* (June 23, 1997), pp. A1, A5.

transfers are growing rapidly. Russia needs Chinese procurements for survival of its arms industry; the Chinese need military technology to keep pace with Taiwan and Southeast Asia. Russia sees China as a continuing customer for such products as the SU-27 combat aircraft, "Kilo" class submarines, and technical assistance to build nuclear-powered submarines and the first of three planned aircraft carriers.[17]

According to the Rosvooruzheniye company, a state-owned entity with a monopoly on arms exports, Russian weapons are highly competitive because they are "effective, simple, reliable, and at a reasonable price." At the same time, the Russians offer advanced weapons. The Yakhont ("Gem" in Russian) supersonic anti-ship cruise missile was unveiled and offered for sale in August 1997. This missile has a range of 190 miles and travels at two and one-half times the speed of sound. The missile outclasses the U.S. subsonic Tomahawk and Harpoon missiles as well as the French Exocet anti-ship missile, which has a range of forty-five miles.[18]

The "international arms bazaar" is truly the right characterization for the late 1990s where virtually all weapons, except WMD and ballistic missiles, are available to any buyer with the cash in hand. Oil revenues combined with economic growth in Asia, though tapering off in 1998, have given many more countries the wherewithal to purchase the most advanced military systems. This new market is wide open. Foreign policy concerns are often pushed aside in order to "close the deal." Military weapons and technology are simply a part of the broader international market for a wide range of goods. In the absence of workable national export controls, it is a come-as-you-are business where cash on the barrel-head is the only requirement.

Global Diffusion of Military Technology

While the market is still in the midst of radical transformation, some have begun to wonder what the world will look like when the international community sobers from its binge of unrestricted arms sales and purchases.

The case examples, illustrations, and anecdotes cobbled together in the following paragraphs throw cold water on the idea that the U.S. may have time to fully deploy its forces or reinforcements to a theater before the

---

[17] Stephen Blank, "Russia's Clearance Sale," *Jane's Intelligence Review* (November 1997), pp. 517-22, and "China Acquires Arms Technology," *Jane's Intelligence Review and Jane's Sentinel Pointer* (November 1997), p. 8.

[18] Peter Ford, "Russia Races U.S. in Military Sales," *Washington Times* (September 1, 1997), p. A17.

---

shooting starts. One of the driving forces for the proliferation of advanced conventional weapons and military technologies is to deny the United States time to deploy overseas and to deny it access to regional ports and airfields. The following sample catalogue of improving foreign military capabilities highlights some of the unique challenges to the U.S. power projection strategy.

- **Missiles.** (1) Kazakhstan is in the process of selling Russian-made SA-10 surface-to-air missiles to Iran; (2) Russian dealers are seeking to sell advanced SA-12 missiles and hand-held anti-aircraft rockets to Iran;[19] (3) Russian arms brokers are working to strike a secret arms deal with Iran for S-300 series and SA-18 anti-aircraft missiles at discount prices—the S-300 series missiles are especially good in shooting down warplanes and short-range missiles; (4) Russians deny U.S. claims that it has transferred SS-4 medium-range ballistic missile technology to Iran while the U.S. persists in trying to block any long-range missile technology transfer to Iran;[20] (5) China is reportedly helping Pakistan construct a factory to build their own ballistic missiles;[21] (6) Iran-China collaboration on a tremendous variety of technical systems, including missile guidance components and technology, rocket motors, and test equipment, is helping Tehran develop short-range missiles; (7) Iran-Russia collaboration on surface-to-surface missiles overlaps Beijing's assistance with projects on wind tunnels used in missile design, modeling missile manufacture, and development of computer software and providing guidance systems, laser equipment, and tungsten-coated graphite;[22] and (8) Belarus is assisting China's efforts to develop a new mobile intercontinental ballistic missile by providing technology important to the launcher and sup-

---

[19] Bill Gertz, "U.S. Protests Kazakh's Plans to Sell Iran Advanced Missiles," *Washington Times* (June 4, 1997), p. A4.

[20] Bill Gertz, "Russia Sells Missiles to Iran," *Washington Times* (April 16, 1997), p. A1, A7, and "Russian Missile Assurance Challenged," *Washington Times* (June 6, 1997), p. A10.

[21] "CIA Reports China Built Missile Plant in Pakistan," *Reuters* (June 24, 1997).

[22] Bill Gertz, "China Joins Forces With Iran on Short-Range Missile," *Washington Times* (June 17, 1997), p. A3; "U.S., Russia Still At Odds Over Iran," *Reuters* (January 16, 1998); and U.S., Senate, Committee of Governmental Affairs, *The Proliferation Primer,* A Majority Report of the Subcommittee on International Security, Proliferation, and Federal Services (Washington, D.C.: January 1998), p. 9.

The New Face of War

port equipment—the transfer of a Belarussian MAZ chassis supports a new Chinese mobile ICBM for use against U.S. allies and forces in the Pacific and the western United States.[23]

- **Naval Vessels and Equipment.** (1) Russia agreed early in 1997 to a secret arms deal with China to sell it two guided-missile destroyers. A part of the deal was the sale of the supersonic SS-N-22 Sunburn anti-ship missiles, an extremely fast sea-skimming missile designed to attack U.S. warships equipped with the Aegis battle management system. On June 11, 1997, the House of Representatives threatened to cut off a portion of Russia's aid package if the missile deal goes through; (2) Russia has sold China two and Iran four diesel-powered Kilo-class submarines at very low cost; and (3) China is seeking to purchase the ship-borne Helix-A anti-submarine warfare helicopter from Moscow.[24]

- **Supercomputers.** President Clinton deregulated the export of computers in 1995. In just two years China purchased forty-seven supercomputers, which can be highly useful in their nuclear program. Even very small, underground, undetectable explosions can yield useful scientific results through the huge amounts of data that can be processed by these computers. Gary Samore at the National Security Council said that "we don't have any information that these computers are being used by the Chinese for military purposes, including nuclear weapons."[25] One of the computers, however, ended up at China's Academy of Sciences which is involved in nuclear weapons research. In addition, two other supercomputers were sold without license to Russia's nuclear weapons laboratories which gave the nuclear labs a total of five of the high-speed American processors. Finally, in June 1997 the U.S. Commerce Department was investigating American supercomputers sold to Dubai that were re-exported to Iran.[26]

---

[23] Bill Gertz, "Missile-Related Technology Sold to Beijing By Belarus," *Washington Times* (June 12, 1997), p. A9.

[24] Ahmed Hashim, "New Sino-Russian Partnership," *Jane's Intelligence Review and Jane's Sentinel Pointer* (September 1997), p. 10.

[25] Jeff Gerth, "China Buying U.S. Computers, Raising Fears of Enhanced Nuclear Weapons," *New York Times* (June 19, 1997).

[26] Bill Gertz, "Supercomputer Diversion Prompts Criminal Probe, Senate Panel Told," *Washington Times* (June 12, 1997), p. A8.

- **U.S. Software Source Codes.** To increase arms sales, the U.S. reversed its longstanding policy of refusing to release software codes that determine the tactics, performance, and maintenance requirements of military systems. All software-dependent U.S. equipment, from air-to-air missile and mission control computers to electronic warfare gear and shipboard defenses, are included in the new policy. Critics, however, see the policy change as undermining U.S. military superiority since once the software is given away there is no way of controlling its subsequent uses.[27]

- **Sensitive Dual-Use Machine Tools.** China diverted to military purposes the machine tools exported from the United States to support the manufacture of commercial aircraft in a co-production arrangement with a U.S. firm. The export control violations were not formally investigated by the enforcement office of the U.S. Commerce Department until six months after the violation was first reported.[28] One U.S. government investigator concluded that China never had an intention of building commercial aircraft parts plant. "It was a fantasy plant," he said. The machines were planned for Chinese military use right from the beginning.[29]

- **Telecommunication Equipment.** Despite the knowledge that the Chinese armed forces were striving to upgrade their telecommunication equipment, which could benefit their command and control networks during the first decade of the 21st century, the U.S. Commerce Department approved dual-use telecommunication exports to China where the end user could not be identified—military applications of the equipment exported include sharing of intelligence, imagery and video between several locations, and command and control of military operations.[30]

---

[27] Barbara Opall, "DoD Lifts Code Limits in New Export Drive," *Defense News* (June 9-15, 1997), pp. 1, 74.

[28] U.S., General Accounting Office, *Export Controls: Sensitive Machine Tool Exports to China,* GAO/NSIAD-97-4 (Washington, D.C.: General Accounting Office, November 1996), pp. 1-3.

[29] John Mintz, "Sale of Aircraft Machinery Shows Perils of Exporting Technology," *Washington Post* (June 7, 1998), pp. A8, A9.

[30] U.S., General Accounting Office, *Export Controls: Sale of Telecommunications Equipment to China,* GAO/NSIAD-97-5 (Washington, D.C.: General Accounting Office, November 1996), pp. 1-11.

- **Portable Satellite Ground Station.** A Canadian firm has developed a portable ground station to receive imagery from earth-observation satellites or electro-optical sensors. The ruggedized electronics shelter weighs about four tons and is transportable by C-130, a common military transport in many air forces. The satellite terminal gathers images up to 25,000 kilometers distant from its location. The ground station can serve a wide range of current satellites, including the U.S. LANDSAT 5, French SPOT series, Japanese ADEOs and MOS, and Indian IRS-1c. Customers so far include China, Saudia Arabia, and Thailand.[31]
- **Global Positioning System.** The GPS consists of twenty-four satellites that provide accurate navigation capabilities. The core technologies of GPS—atomic clocks, computer chips, and satellites—can provide locational accuracies within a meter or less. Receivers access the signals of three or more satellites to determine their location and gain direction to other locations. The United States Air Force is responsible for maintaining the system, which has many useful military applications, including battlefield navigation, precision weapons delivery, and various command and control activities. Civilian and non-U.S. military users are employing the systems to take advantage of the locational accuracies attainable through use of low-cost receivers. In civilian mode, GPS provides accuracies on the order of fifty meters. The growing civilian demand has prompted efforts to get around the military's efforts to degrade the GPS signal (intentional errors are introduced in the unencrypted signals) and locational accuracies are attainable to ten meters.[32]
- **Long-Range Artillery Rocket.** Avibras, a Brazilian firm, developed its SS-80 long-range artillery rocket, which includes a four-tube launcher and 300-millimeter rocket with a range of fifty-five miles—for export to Iraq, Qatar, and Saudi Arabia.[33]

---

[31] "Transportable Station Receives Satellite Imagery," *Jane's International Defense Review* (February 1997), p. 18,

[32] *The Global Positioning System: Civil and Military Uses,* MIT Security Studies Conference Series (Cambridge, Mass.: Massachusetts Institute of Technology, Security Studies Program, 1997).

[33] Christopher Foss, "Latest Brazilian Rocket Revealed," *Jane's Defence Weekly* (May 14, 1997), p. 11.

- **Self-Propelled Gun-Mortar System.** Russia is selling 100 mobile 120-millimeter weapons systems, the 2S23 Nona-SVK, to China. The amphibious 2S23 systems are capable of firing laser-guided artillery projectiles as well as mortars. The precision-guided artillery shells, Kitolov-2, are guided to their targets with laser designators and have a range of up to nine miles, making them effective against the U.S. M1 tank. The laser-guided mortar shells, the Gran, would be highly effective against bunkers and other hardened facilities. Some fear that China will copy the Kitolov-2 and Gran precision-guided rounds and sell them to rogue regimes in the Middle East.[34]
- **Missile Technology Transfer.** Assistance to other countries in supporting and developing their space launch vehicle technology can be applied readily to ballistic missile programs. The only significant difference between space launch boosters and military ballistic missiles is the payload at the tip of the rocket. When U.S. firms began using China's space boosters to launch American-made satellites, with U.S. government permission, technology transfer took place, which later began showing up in improved Chinese missiles. After a launch mishap destroyed a satellite owned by Loral Space and Communications Limited, the U.S. firm assisted the Chinese evaluation of the causes for the booster explosion. In the process, according to a Pentagon report, "potentially very significant help" had been given to China's military ballistic missile program. The transfer, according to a White House memo, "involved guidance system problems and based on initial evaluations appear to be serious."[35]
- **NBC Decontamination.** China exported to Iran two tons of calcium hypochlorate which is commonly used for NBC decontamination.[36]

---

[34] Bill Gertz, "Russia Sells China High-Tech Artillery," *Washington Times* (July 3, 1997), pp. A1, A10.

[35] Walter Pincus, "Pentagon, CIA Differ on Missile Threat, *Washington Post* (June 7, 1998), p. A9; Jeff Gerth and John M. Broder, "The White House Dismissed Warnings on China Satellite Deal," *New York Times* (June 1, 1998); Bill Gertz, "Technology Transfers Detailed for Senate," *Washington Times* (May 22, 1998), p. A13; and "National Security For Sale?," *Detroit News [Editorial] (May 24, 1998).*

[36] Robert Karniol, "China Supplied Iran With Decontamination Agent," *Jane's Defence Weekly* (April 30, 1997), p. 17.

• **Illicit Arms Deliveries.** Ostensibly without formal permission or actual knowledge of the high command, Russia transferred some $1 billion of conventional weapons to Armenia beginning in 1992. A total of 139 flights by Russian transports delivered much of the equipment: eight Scud B launchers with twenty-four missiles, twenty-seven SA-4 surface-to-air missile systems with 349 missiles, forty SA-8A missiles, eighty-four T-72 tanks, fifty battlefield transports, forty SA-18s, eighteen multiple rocket launchers, 8,000 assault rifles, twenty-six mortars, 306 machine guns, twenty grenade launchers, 230,000,000 rounds of small arms ammunition, and 500,000 artillery rounds.[37]

This small sample of the proliferation of conventional weapons and military technology around the globe illustrates the sheer force of the dynamism of the international arms market as the twentieth century comes to a close. The situation is unprecedented, somewhat reckless and wholly unpredictable. Regional threats to U.S. forces may come in a variety of shapes, sizes, and military consequences as adversaries use advanced weapons in innovative ways.

International arms sales often involve the proliferation of weapons of mass destruction as well as advanced conventional weapons. China, Iran, and North Korea stand out as countries oftentimes trading, as suppliers or buyers, in the grey and black markets for weapons and technology. The Chinese, whose arms exports were once motivated by political and ideological concerns, appear to be driven increasingly by economics. Its weapons sales provide access to its buyers, advanced technology and hard currency for modernizing Beijing's own military forces. Export sales by North Korea likewise serve as a major source of funds for modernizing the country's armed forces. Iran has built a network of clandestine buying and shipping entities to take advantage of the grey and black market arms sales.[38]

At the same time, many of the 1990s entrants to the international arms buying market do not necessarily buy the latest technology. Rather, they demand weapons that are sufficiently advanced to keep pace with or give them an advantage over rivals. "Closely related, is the sub-national market, in which states sell to insurgents," explains Dr. John E. Peters of the RAND

---

[37] Nikolai Novichkov, "Russia Details Illegal Deliveries to Armenia," *Jane's Defence Weekly* (April 16, 1997), p. 15.

[38] Hull and Markov, "Trends in the Arms Market – Part Two," pp. 235-36.

Corporation. "Israel, for instance, sold arms to the Tamil Tigers, and Hungary, Romania, South Africa, and Singapore all supported the Croatian national guard."[39]

In South Asia, India has provided weapons to Sri Lankan, Bangladesh, and East Pakistan rebels while Pakistan has supplied arms to Indian and Kashmiri rebels. In the post-Cold War arms market, rebel groups often cooperate to procure light weapons jointly to reduce costs and increase security.[40] Dr. Peters explains how open market sales often dramatically improve the military capabilities of insurgents, such as the Global Positioning System, which can give greater accuracy to bombs and missiles and the Geographic Information System (GIS), which improves the resolution of imagery from commercial satellites and enhances the imagery's military usefulness.[41]

---

[39] John E. Peters, "Technology and Advances in Foreign Military Capabilities," *Fletcher Forum in World Affairs* (Winter/Spring 1995), p. 122.

[40] Rohan Gunaratna, "Illicit Weapons Trade in South Asia," *Janes Intelligence Review and Jane's Sentinel Pointer* (October 1997), p. 9.

[41] *Ibid.*

The New Face of War

CHAPTER 6

Ballistic and
Cruise Missiles

Weapons of mass destruction can be placed on their intended targets by a number of different delivery systems, including trucks, small boats, civil aircraft, rockets, artillery, ballistic and cruise missiles, and strike aircraft. No matter which means of delivery is used, WMD help to shape conflict at the strategic level of warfare. Many countries that have obtained or are in the process of developing nuclear, biological and chemical weapons are also pursuing ballistic and cruise missile programs. Combat aircraft are already spread around the world, although many WMD proliferators, as discussed in Chapter 5, are in the process of upgrading these delivery systems with more advanced technologies.

Ballistic and cruise missiles are particularly threatening to the United States and its regional allies and friends because of their capabilities to penetrate to the target with their deadly payloads. Ballistic missiles—because they have the shortest time of flight—are the most dangerous systems since they give the country under attack little warning and a brief time to react. Cruise missiles offer accurate delivery on low and slow flying platforms that are difficult to detect.[1]

More than a dozen countries, other than the five declared nuclear powers, already possess or are developing ballistic missiles with ranges from 155 to 370 miles. Cruise missiles or other unmanned aerial vehicles with ranges of thirty to 125 miles are readily available. Advances in cruise missile guidance, propulsion, and airframe technology are moving forward rapidly, and they are increasingly accessible to non-Western countries.

---

[1] Cruise missiles are essentially pilotless aircraft. Powered by turbojet or turbofan engines, cruise missiles are much smaller than aircraft and can fly close to the ground which makes detection difficult. Even when detected, intercepting aircraft may experience problems in picking the slow-flying missile out of the background clutter on the ground. Navigation aids such as the Global Positioning System (GPS) can give cruise missiles high accuracy in delivering WMD payloads.

The missile proliferating countries of particular concern to the United States include China, North Korea, India, Pakistan, Iran, Iraq, Libya, and Syria. In addition, Israel is believed to have nuclear warheads for its missiles; Iran, Iraq, North Korea, and other countries have missile and biological weapons programs; and Israel, Vietnam, Egypt, Saudi Arabia, South Korea, and Taiwan possess missiles and chemical weapons. In addition to Western countries and the republics of the former Soviet Union, twenty-one countries possess ballistic missiles. See Figure 6.1. The proliferation of the knowledge and technologies necessary for development of advanced conventional warheads, such as fuel-air explosives and cluster bombs, increases the military effectiveness of ballistic and cruise missiles.[2]

At least eight developing countries obtained Scud ballistic missiles directly from the Soviet Union in the Cold War years through the 1980s: Afghanistan, Egypt, Iraq, Libya, North Korea, Syria, and North and South Yemen (now unified). Since the Cold War, international traders in short- and long-range missiles and missile technology have become underwriters of global proliferation, especially Russia, China, and North Korea. It is not a very complex or expensive task to reverse engineer and modify short-range missiles for delivery of payloads beyond 185 miles (range limit of existing missile export controls). For missiles with ranges of up to 3,100 miles or more, those that might threaten the United States directly, two principal hurdles stand in the way: first, manufacturing the larger propulsion systems needed to achieve higher velocities required for longer range and, secondly, designing the more complex multi-stage missiles. Stable fuel combustion and flight characteristics also become more complicated. The key to developing longer range missiles is the expertise available by engineers and technicians skilled in subsystem integration, testing, production methods, and other essential skills.

Another source of missile proliferation is through foreign assistance in the development of a "peaceful" space-launch capability. Much of the technology in space-launch and sounding-rocket programs is directly applicable to surface-to-surface missiles. Some countries, such as Brazil, India, Israel, and Pakistan, have applied the knowledge gained in foreign assistance and civilian programs to design and build their own military systems. Israel's extended range Jericho II missile (more than a 1,700 mile range), for example, is widely known to be a military version of the Shavit space-launch

---

[2] Robert Shuey, *Ballistic and Cruise Missile Forces of Foreign Countries* (Washington, D.C.: Congressional Research Service, Library of Congress, updated October 25, 1996), pp. 1-2.

The New Face of War

Figure 6.1
Global Ballistic Missile Proliferation

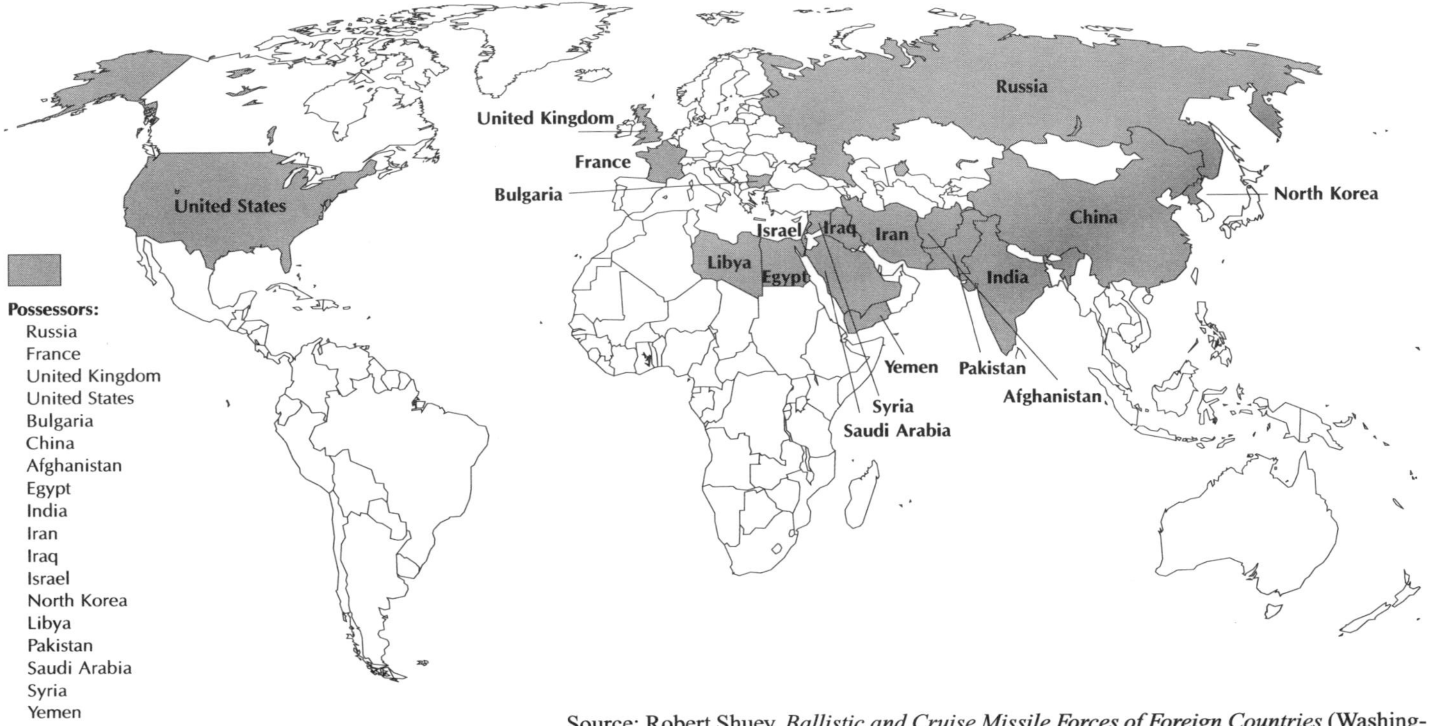
United Kingdom
France
Bulgaria
United States
Russia
China
North Korea
Israel
Iraq
Iran
Libya
Egypt
India
Yemen
Pakistan
Afghanistan
Syria
Saudi Arabia
Possessors:
Russia
France
United Kingdom
United States
Bulgaria
China
Afghanistan
Egypt
India
Iran
Iraq
Israel
North Korea
Libya
Pakistan
Saudi Arabia
Syria
Yemen

Source: Robert Shuey, *Ballistic and Cruise Missile Forces of Foreign Countries* (Washington, D.C.: Congressional Research Service, Library of Congress, October 25, 1996).

vehicle. While space-launch vehicles do not require accurate guidance and reentry technology to strike ground targets, large boosters and high-quality guidance systems required for ballistic missile programs could easily be developed and tested under the guise of the space-launch program. A country that can develop space-launch vehicles is also capable of developing ballistic missiles, including those with long ranges.

Cruise missile payloads are generally smaller than those for ballistic missiles but their ability to fly low at slow speeds makes them especially well suited for delivery of chemical and biological warheads. In the long term they could also be useful for delivery of nuclear warheads after a proliferator achieves the technical expertise necessary to produce warheads small enough for cruise missiles. The spread of new advances in satellite navigation, long-distance communications, composite materials, light weight turbojet and turbofan engines, and nuclear and blast fragmentation warheads has greatly facilitated cruise missile development in several countries.

Incorporating U.S. Global Positioning System (GPS) data into missile guidance systems could offer dramatic improvement in warhead accuracy. GPS receivers for commercial or export sales are designed to shut down if they compute that they are travelling faster than 515 meters per second or find themselves above an altitude of eighteen kilometers (eleven miles). This means that even the 185-mile range Scud missile, which reaches speeds above 1,500 meters per second and altitudes of some eighteen miles before burnout, ostensibly could not be guided by GPS receivers. This problem could be resolved, however, if a country could manufacture its own GPS receivers or obtain the critical electronic processor chips from other sources. Given the spread of knowledge and technology around the globe, one should suspect that adaptation of GPS guidance to missile warheads is within reach of several countries of concern to the United States.

Many GPS receivers approved for export could be used in cruise missiles. Even the degraded commercial signal (non-military) versions would be sufficient for a cruise missile to achieve at least a 100-meter accuracy which is sufficient to strike ports, airfields or urban areas. Any country with an aerospace industry or a modest industrial capacity should be able to produce cruise missiles with GPS receivers. This is basically bolt-on technology that integrates turbojet engines, perhaps from imported air-to-surface missiles, and home-grown composite air-frames with GPS.[3]

---

[3] U.S., Congress, Office of Technology Assessment, *Technologies Underlying Weapons of Mass Destruction,* pp. 197-255, and Amy Truesdell, "Cruise Missiles: The Discriminating Weapons of Choice?," *Jane's Intelligence Review* (February 2, 1997), p. 87.

The Missile Technology Control Regime (MTCR) was established in 1987 by the United States and its six major Western trading partners with the idea of limiting nuclear risks by controlling technology transfers relevant to their delivery. The participating states established export guidelines prohibiting the transfer to non-members of ballistic and cruise missiles with payloads of 1,100 pounds and ranges over 185 miles as well as the technologies involved in their production. The Persian Gulf War and the emergence of secondary suppliers of missiles convinced twenty-two additional countries to join the MTCR and several others to observe the regime's guidelines without becoming members.

Since many non-Western countries are unable to produce and integrate all of the components necessary for ballistic missiles, it is a good guess that the MTCR has been effective in blocking or impeding some potential indigenous programs. For cruise missiles, on the other hand, most of the components and technologies have civil purposes and are commercially available.[4]

Missile Delivery Systems

Some twenty-four countries possess ballistic missiles that can deliver an 1,100-pound warhead 185 miles or further. Over half of these are in Asia, Africa, the Middle East and South America. At least seventy-three countries possessed some type of cruise missile in mid-1997; forty of these states have anti-ship cruise missiles with ranges from fifty to hundreds of miles.[5]

Ballistic Missiles. The Soviet Scud B, based on Germany's World War Two V-2 rocket, is the most widely available ballistic missile. About twenty countries possess Scud Bs. Copies of the Scud B, in some cases with extended range and perhaps better accuracy, have been built or can be produced by North Korea, Iraq, Iran, Egypt, and probably Syria. These missiles are inaccurate relative to Western standards. With a typical circular error probable or CEP[6] of one kilometer, they are of little use against specific military targets when conventional explosive warheads are used. They can be very useful, however, as terror weapons against urban areas. In time, one can expect the copy-cats of earlier missile designs to discover new ways to

---

[4] Shuey, *Ballistic and Cruise Missile Forces of Foreign Countries,* p. 7.

[5] *Ibid.,* pp. 3-4, and Truesdell, "Cruise Missiles: The Discriminating Weapon of Choice?," p. 87.

[6] The CEP is a measure of missile accuracy that represents the radius of a circle within which half of the warheads of a particular type of missile are expected to fall.

---

acquire the technology necessary to improve accuracy, perhaps involving GPS technology.[7]

Even when firing missiles with poor accuracy the attacker can get lucky once in a while. Viet Cong gunners dropped a 122-millimeter rocket into the bomb dump at Bien Hoa Air Base [Vietnam] in August 1968 touching off a thousand 500-pound bombs in a single blast. During the Gulf War, a Scud missile was responsible for the "single worst loss of American forces" in the war when it hit a barracks in Dhahran [Saudi Arabia] killing twenty-eight soldiers and wounding ninety-seven others.[8]

North Korea. The North Koreans reverse-engineered Soviet-made Scud Bs in the early 1980s from missiles provided by Egypt and began producing their own missiles, including an extended-range Scud C version. See Figure 6.2. Iran provided financing for the North Korean missile production and used Korean-supplied Scuds against Iraq in the 1988 "War of the Cities." A follow-on program resulted in the development of a Scud variant, the Nodong-1. This single-stage, liquid-propellant missile has a range of 620 miles and was test fired in 1993. An enhanced version, the Nodong-2, has a range of about 930 miles. These mobile missiles use a Scud transporter-erector-launcher (TEL) vehicle. A new class of two-stage missile, the Taepodong, was reported in 1994 as being under development. Believed to be launched from fixed sites, the Taepodong-1 reportedly has a range of about 1,240 miles; the Taepodong-2 is said to be capable of reaching out to 2,170 miles. Because of the engineering difficulties of multi-staging and engine clustering, the C.I.A. believes the Taepodong-2 will not be deployed until the early 21st century. North Korea earns up to $1 billion a year from missile sales to Iran, Syria, Egypt, Libya, and others.

All of these missiles are believed to be capable of delivering nuclear, biological, and chemical warheads. The South Korean Defense Ministry estimates that the North can produce four to eight of the Scud C variants per month or about 100 missiles per year. Pyongyang is thought to possess about 500 Scuds.[9] According to Colonel Joo-hwai Choi, a former member

---

[7] Shuey, *Ballistic and Cruise Missile Forces of Foreign Countries,* pp. 5-6.

[8] U.S., Department of the Air Force, *Gulf War Air Power Survey: A Statistical Compendium and Chronology,* Vol. V (Washington, D.C.: Government Printing Office, 1993), p. 542.

[9] David G. Wiencek, *Dangerous Arsenals: Missile Threats In and From Asia,* Bailrigg Memorandum 22 (Lancaster, United Kingdom: Centre for Defence and International Studies, Lancaster University), pp. 21-25; Shuey, *Ballistic and Cruise Missile Forces of Foreign Countries,* pp. 8-12; Wyn Bowen and Stanley Shepard, "Living Under the Red Missile Threat," *Jane's International Defence Review* (December 1996), p. 561; and U.S., Department of Defense, *Proliferation: Threat and Response* (Washington, D.C.: Government Printing Office, November 1997), pp. 7-8.

Figure 6.2
North Korean Ballistic Missile Coverage

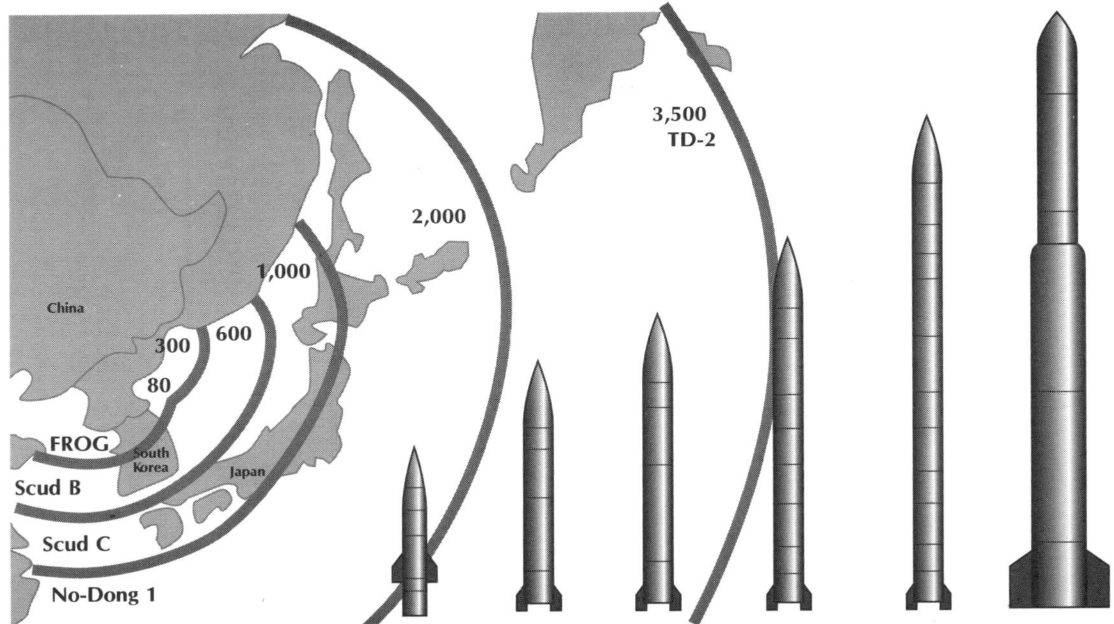

	FROG*	Scud B	Scud C	No-Dong 1	TD-1**	TD-2
Range (kilometers)	80	300	600	1,000	2,000	3,500
Inventory	100	120	180	Few	?	?

* FROG = Free Rockets Over Ground   ** TD = Taepodong

China
South Korea
Japan

FROG
Scud B
Scud C
No-Dong 1
TD-1

80
300
600
1,000
2,000
3,500
TD-2

Source: U.S.,
National Defense
University, *Strategic
Assessment 1996*
(Washington, D.C.:
Government Printing
Office, 1996), p. 200.

of North Korea's Army, the main target for Pyongyang's missiles will be "the U.S. forces based in the South and Japan." Extensive testing is not required, Colonel Choi explains, since the North "require[s] only that they impact on the target region." The strategy is to inflict more than 20,000 American casualties in the region, including those based in Japan, Okinawa, and Guam.[10] Intelligence officials predict that "North Korea will probably acquire foreign missile guidance systems that will improve the accuracy of their Scud family of missiles."[11]

North Korea is an important missile supplier for Iran. Despite denials by both countries, U.S. government officials have known at least since 1992 that substantial cooperation exists between the two countries. In February 1993, for instance, R. James Woolsey, the Director of Central Intelligence, testified before Congress that Iran had "bought some extended-range Scud missiles from North Korea."[12] Published reports suggest Iran wants to buy 150 of North Korea's medium-range missile, the Nodong-1, or Scud D, which was test-fired in May 1993 with Iranian officials present. The Nodong-1 has an estimated range of 620 miles and an extended-range version with an 800-mile range. Two new two-stage missiles are under development. The Taepodong-1 or Nodong-2 missiles may be adapted to carry nuclear or chemical warheads.[13]

China. Russia signed a five-year deal with China in the fall of 1995 for transfer of its most advanced missile technology: solid rocket fuel technology, mobile missile expertise, large liquid rocket engines, missile guidance, and multiple hardware and technology. Most of China's ballistic missiles are short- (up to 185 miles) and intermediate-range (to 3,100 miles) which makes them capable of reaching most targets of interest in the Asia-Pacific region. A small arsenal of intercontinental ballistic missiles (ICBMs) are available for delivery of nuclear weapons against targets in North America and Russia—from four to twenty DF-5/5A ICBMs with a range of more than 8,000 miles are estimated to be deployed. Two new ICBMs are under development.

China's regional missile force is growing rapidly and sending strong political messages to countries along its periphery. See Figure 6.3. In July

---

[10] Bill Gertz, "N. Korea Targets U.S. GIs," *Washington Times* (October 22, 1997), and Kevin Sullivan, "N. Korea Admits Selling Missiles," *Washington Post* (June 17, 1998), pp. A1, A21.

[11] "DIA: N. Korea Threat Declining As Economic Collapse Nears," *Defense Week* (January 12, 1998).

[12] Katzman, *North Korea: Military Relations With the Middle East*, p. 3.

[13] *Ibid.*, pp. 3-6.

The New Face of War

Figure 6.3

China's Missile Coverage in East and South Asia

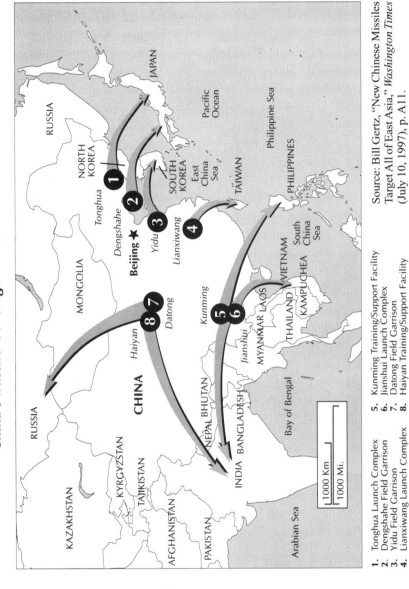

1. Tonghua Launch Complex
2. Dengshahe Field Garrison
3. Yidu Field Garrison
4. Lianxiwang Launch Complex

5. Kunming Training/Support Facility
6. Jianshui Launch Complex
7. Datong Field Garrison
8. Haiyan Training/Support Facility

Source: Bill Gertz, "New Chinese Missiles Target All of East Asia," *Washington Times* (July 10, 1997), p. A11.

1995, as if to underline its claim to sovereignty over Taiwan, China's strategic rocket force "test-launched" six Dong Feng-15 (DF-15) short-range (370 miles) and two DF-21 medium-range (1,100 miles) ballistic missiles into the East China Sea some eighty to 100 miles north of Taiwan. While Beijing played down the "tests," the political warning to Taipei was loud and clear: do not assert Taiwan's independence from China during the run-up to the country's first direct presidential election in March 1996. A second round of "missile tests" were conducted just prior to the elections when three DF-15s were fired into a declared impact zone forty-seven miles west of Taiwan's port city of Kaohsiung and another missile impacted thirty miles east of the northern port of Keelung.[14]

China's neighbors interpreted these tests as a clear signal that Beijing will not hesitate to use force to defend what it regards as its territorial possessions. Beijing's unsettled territorial disputes with India, Russia and Vietnam loom in greater importance for future conflict. The Chinese are reportedly converting some of its DF-15 and DF-21 missiles, which can carry nuclear, biological and chemical warheads, to conventional warheads for local use in regional warfare. Other ballistic missiles are also available for regional conflict. The DF-11 short-range missile (175-185 miles) can reach Taiwan, while both Taiwan and Japan are exposed to China's DF-3A (1,700 miles) and Julang-1 (JL-1) submarine launched ballistic missiles (SLBM) (1,000 miles). The DF-25, still in development, will have a range of 1,000 miles.[15]

China is replacing its older, liquid-filled CSS-2 (1,900 miles) intermediate range missiles with the newer and more accurate solid-fueled CSS-5 Mod 1 (1,330 miles). The solid fueled replacement program will be completed by 2002. The CSS-5 Mod 1 and a follow-on Mod 2 version will provide China target coverage over all of East Asia. From the launch site at Tonghua near North Korea, the CSS-5 can target all of Japan, North and South Korea, and parts of Taiwan. The CSS-5s are also being introduced to the Lianxiwang launch complex opposite Taiwan. The Jianshui launch complex near the border with Vietnam allows the CSS-5 to target all of Southeast Asia and cover the seaports as distant as the Philippines and India.

---

[14] Wiencek, *Dangerous Arsenals: Missile Threats In and From Asia,* pp. 15-19; and Bowen and Shepard, "Living Under the Red Missile Threat," pp. 560-61.

[15] Bowen and Shepard, "Living Under the Red Missile Threat," p. 561.

From an internal launch area near Mongolia, Datong, CSS-5 missiles can strike targets in India and Russia.[16]

China is also developing a new generation of ICBMs and SLBMs, including the JL-2/DF-31 (4,950 miles) and the DF-41 (7,400 miles). These missiles, according to some reports, would be tipped with multiple independently targetable re-entry vehicles (MIRV). Missile coverage would include the western United States and American allies and forces in the Pacific region.

Deployment of the DF-31, China's most advanced mobile ICBM, is expected in the year 2000. It will be armed with MIRV warheads and transported by a Chinese copy of the MAZ chassis made by the Minsk Automotive Factory in Belarus, the chassis used for mobile operations of the Soviet intermediate-range SS-20 nuclear missiles. According to newspaper reports, U.S. spy satellites photographed a MAZ chassis at a Chinese missile plant in 1996. The transporter-erector-launcher (TEL) currently used by the Chinese is limited to travel on surfaced roads. The Belarussian MAZ design will give the Chinese the opportunity to build a transporter with off-road capabilities and increase the number of deployment locations for the DF-31. Among the features that can be copied from the MAZ chassis and built into the DF-31 transporters are all-wheel independent suspension, higher ground clearance, driver-controlled central tire inflation and deflation systems, and large-diameter, wide-profile, variable inflation tires.

Although the chassis was developed as a missile launcher, Belarus officials contend that they sold the MAZ to China as an "off-road" truck for conversion to hauling jet fuel at airports and coal from mines. Under the Missile Technology Control Regime, the MAZ chassis falls under Category 2 or "launch support equipment." Past cases of MAZ exports triggered U.S. diplomatic protests but no sanctions were imposed.[17]

International concern surrounds Chinese exports of missile technology and expertise, including complete intermediate-range missiles and re-transfers of advanced Russian and Ukrainian missile technology. On-again, off-again U.S. sanctions against China since 1991 for its missile and missile-related equipment transfers to Pakistan have had little impact on Beijing's arms policies. In 1996, a seeming contradiction of the U.S. policy of non-recognition of Chinese wrongdoing occurred when the intelligence community reportedly

---

[16] "DIA: N. Korea Threat Declining As Economic Collapse Nears," *Defense Week* (January 12, 1998).

[17] Gertz, "Missile-Related Technology Sold to Beijing by Belarus," p. A9.

---

expressed the belief that more than thirty M-11 missiles (185-mile range) are stored at Pakistan's Sargogha Air Force Base and that Chinese technicians had assembled the M-11s in Pakistan for deployment.[18] Former Defense Secretary William J. Perry said it all in an April 1996 comment: "China remains Pakistan's most important supplier of missile-related technologies."[19]

China also exports missile-related technologies to Iran and Libya. Since the mid-1980s, China has supplied Iran with Silkworm and C-802 anti-ship cruise missiles. Reports of Chinese technology transfers to Iran underwrite Iran's project to produce a new version of the M-11 missile, the Tondar-68. China is believed to have helped Iran convert several dozen CSS-8 (copies of SA-2 surface-to-air missiles) to a ninety-five-mile range surface-to-surface missile. Hundreds of missile guidance systems and computerized machine tools were transferred from China to Iran in 1994-95 to support its missile program. Meanwhile, the sea-skimming C-802 anti-ship cruise missile, with a range of sixty miles and similar to the French supersonic Exocet, continued to be transferred in 1996-97 as well as the Houdong patrol craft capable of carrying the missiles. By early 1998, the Clinton Administration still had not decided to impose sanctions.[20]

India. Despite its promise to cease its assistance to India's missile program, Russia was discovered in mid-1994 to be lending India space launch integration technology designed to teach Indian scientists how to launch their rockets more precisely. The propulsion systems of the country's military missiles probably have been derived from its space program.

The Prithvi-1 (95 miles) was first test-fired in February 1988. Over the past decade, India has fielded the Prithvi-2 (155 miles), and the Prithvi-3 (215 miles) is under development. Seventy-five to eighty of the Prithvi-1s

---

[18] Chinese M-11 launchers in Pakistan triggered U.S. sanctions in June 1991, which were lifted in February 1992 after pledges to act in accordance with the guidelines in the Missile Technology Control Regime (MTCR) were obtained from Chinese officials; President Clinton extended Most Favored Nation trading privileges to China in May 1993. In August 1993, after issuing a finding that China had shipped M-11 equipment but not missiles to Pakistan, the U.S. issued category two sanctions to Pakistan's defense ministry and eleven Chinese aerospace firms which would deny then U.S. government contracts and export licenses for missile equipment and technology for two years; they were waived in October 1994, however, after the Chinese signed an agreement to transfer no more M-11 missiles. See Kan, *Chinese Proliferation of Weapons of Mass Destruction,* pp. 17-24, and Shirley A. Kan, "China's Compliance With Nonproliferation Commitments," a paper delivered at the Nonproliferation Policy Forum (Washington, D.C.: January 21, 1998).

[19] *Ibid.,* pp. 24-25.

[20] Kan, *Chinese Proliferation of Weapons of Mass Destruction,* pp. 25-27, and Bill Gertz, "China Assists Iran, Libya on Missiles," *Washington Times* (June 16, 1998), pp. A1, A14.

The New Face of War

and twenty-five Prithvi-2s were ordered in the initial production runs (Prithvi-2 finished a third test of the missile in early 1997). The system is liquid-fueled and can be fired from fixed and mobile TEL launchers. It can carry an 1,100-pound warhead, meaning it can be fitted with nuclear warheads as well as both fuel-air and conventional fragmentation explosives. The Indians are reported to have been working in late 1996 on integrating GPS updates to the Prithvi guidance systems to improve its accuracy.

In addition to the Prithvi missiles, India has also developed the Agni intermediate-range ballistic missile (1,200-1,500 mile range). This two-stage, single warhead system was tested three times between 1989 and 1994. The Indian defense minister stated in 1997 that the Agni program, after nearly a three-year testing hiatus, is "very much on." India may continue the flight test program and is already planning a follow-on to the Agni. When deployed, the Agni or a derivative follow-on missile will give India a capacity to strike targets in most of China, including Beijing, all of Pakistan, and the U.S. naval and air facilities at the island of Diego Garcia.[21]

Pakistan. With Chinese assistance, Pakistan has developed a family of short-range missiles: the Hatf-1/1A (50-60 miles), Hatf-2 (185 miles), and Hatf-3 (370 miles). The first two in the series are solid-fueled, road mobile and carry an 1,100 pound warhead suitable for nuclear, chemical and conventional weapons. Hatf-1/1A would be used on the battlefield. Hatf-2 gives Islamabad a capability to target the area of India bordering Pakistan (Moslem population is quite large) and to reach in as far as the Indian capital at New Delhi. The Hatf-3, similar to the Chinese M-9 missile, was tested in July 1997.

Pakistan announced in late 1997 that its engineers had developed a 930-mile range ballistic missile called the "Ghauri." Many U.S. analysts think the Pakistanis received technical advice from China, which had supplied Pakistan with the M-11 missile, and North Korea. The Ghauri, tested in January 1998, is believed to be Islamabad's counter to India's Agni longer-range missile program. The range of the missile lends support to the

[21] Wiencek, *Dangerous Arsenals: Missile Threats In and From Asia,* pp. 27-29; Vivek Raghunanshi, "India Denies Deployment of Prithvi Near Pakistan," *Defense News* (June 16-23, 1997), p. 74; U.S., Department of Defense, *Proliferation: Threats and Response* (1997), pp. 17-20; Ben Sheppard, "Too Close for Comfort: Ballistic Ambitions in South Asia," *Jane's Intelligence Review* (January 1998), pp. 32-35; and Shuey, *Ballistic and Cruise Missile Forces of Foreign Countries,* appendix (missile inventory).

view expressed by some analysts that the missile could be similar to the North Korean Nodong-2.[22]

Since 1990 the Chinese have supplied Islamabad with thirty to forty M-11s, production capability for the missile, and nuclear-related technology. Some believe the modern, solid-fuel M-11 missiles were renamed Hatf-2 when placed into Pakistani service. Pakistani soldiers have been seen practicing simulated launches with advice from Chinese experts.[23]

Iran. Iran has more than 200 Scud B (185 miles) and 100 Scud C (370-435 miles) ballistic missiles and is dedicated to obtaining a missile with a range of about 800 miles to cover most of the Middle East. The Nodong-2 (920 miles) would give Iran the capability to threaten most of the Arabian Peninsula, Israel, Turkey, Greece, and some parts of southern Italy. According to the Israelis, the Iranians are using Russian technology, components, and engineering assistance for two missile programs based on developing two versions of North Korea's Nodong missile. The Shahab-3, successfully flight tested in July 1998, is an upgraded version of North Korea's Nodong-1 and has a range between 800 and 930 miles with a warhead weighing up to 1,650 pounds. Project Shahab-4, still in early development, is expected to have a range of about 1,240 miles. Israel intelligence estimates the Shahab-3 will be deployed by 2001.[24] Figure 6.4 depicts the extensive coverage of Iran's growing long-range missile threat.

The Scud rocket engines were originally acquired from North Korea and upgraded on the basis of Russian technology. Hence, Iran's new missiles are based in part on the old Soviet Union's SS-4 strategic rockets. Russia, despite official denials, has been working on Iran's long-range missile projects since 1994. President Clinton is required by the Arms Export

---

[22] "Pakistan's New Danger Weapon Is 'Confirmed,'" *Jane's Defence Weekly* (December 3, 1997); Sheppard, "Too Close for Comfort," p. 32; and Amit Baruah, "Pakistan Tests 1,500 km Range Missile," *The Hindu* (India) (February 11, 1998).

[23] Wiencek, *Dangerous Arsenals: Missile Threats In and From Asia,* pp. 29-30; Raja Asghar, "Pakistan Seeks U.N. Help Over Indian Missile Threat," *Washington Times* (June 14, 1997), p. A8; U.S., Department of Defense, *Proliferation: Threats and Response* (1997), pp. 19-20; U.S., Senate, *Proliferation Primer,* p. 4; and Shuey, *Ballistic and Cruise Missile Forces of Foreign Countries,* appendix (missile inventory).

[24] Barbara Opall, "Israel Awaits NATO Summit Before Pressing Washington On Russia-Iran Missile Effort," *Defense News* (July 7-13, 1997), pp. 4, 20; Bill Gertz, "Russia, China Aid Iran's Missile Program," *Washington Times* (September 10, 1997), pp. A1, A11; and Jason Sherman, "Iranian Impact," *Armed Forces Journal International* (January 1998), pp. 10, 12.

Figure 6.4
Iran's Long-Range Missile Threat

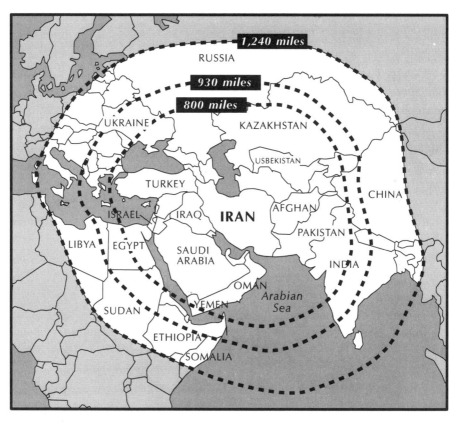

Source: Bill Gertz, "Russia, China Aid Iran's Missile Program," *Washington Times* (September 10, 1997), p. A11.

Control Act to impose sanctions on countries helping other states build ballistic missiles.[25]

Yitzak Mordechai, Israel's Defense Minister, warned in October 1997 that under certain circumstances he would favor a pre-emptive strike against Iran's long-range missiles threatening Israel. "They can cause greater harm [than Iraq's Scud attacks in 1991], particularly if they are equipped with non-conventional warheads."[26] An Iranian government spokesman responded that "those who harbor aggressive intentions against the Islamic Republic of Iran will repent their actions."[27]

Syria. North Korea delivered some sixty Scud C missiles to Syria beginning in 1991. Some missiles were transferred via Iran. In 1993, Russian aircraft are believed to have delivered additional North Korean Scud Cs to Damascus. North Korea may also be supporting Syria's attempt to build its own missile production facility for Scud Cs with Iranian funding and technical assistance. According to one report, the North Koreans in the late 1980s also helped Syria develop chemical warheads for ballistic missiles.[28] A new report suggests that Syria may have provided North Korea with an SS-21 missile to be reverse-engineered for a new version, the Tochka, or an enhanced version with a 75-mile range, the Tochka-U.[29]

Libya. Libya holds more than 240 Scud Bs, more than fifty Scud Cs, and thirty-six plus SS-21s (forty-five miles). Iran is believed to have struck a secret deal with Libya to help it develop a ballistic missile of more than 1,250 miles. Under the memorandum of understanding signed by the two countries, Iran would supply the Libyans with surface-to-surface mis-

---

[25] Kenneth R. Timmerman, "Missile Threat From Iran," *Reader's Digest* (January 1998). See also Jane Harman and Jon Kyl, "Make Russia Face Reality," *Defense News* (October 20-26, 1997), p. 21.

[26] Arieh Osullivan, "Mordechai Favors 'Pre-Emptive Strikes' Against Missiles," *Jerusalem Post* (October 28, 1997).

[27] "Tehran Warns Israel Against Attack On Its Ballistic Missiles," *Arabic News* (October 30, 1997).

[28] Katzman, *North Korea: Military Relations With the Middle East,* pp. 9-10.

[29] Wiencek, *Dangerous Arsenals: Missile Threats In and From Asia,* pp. 25-26; Shuey, *Ballistic and Cruise Missile Forces of Foreign Countries,* appendix (missile inventory); Bill Gertz, "China Sold Iran Missile Technology," *Washington Times* (November 21, 1996), p. A1; Bill Gertz, "Russia Disregards Pledge to Curb Iran Missile Output," *Washington Times* (May 22, 1997), p. A3; Harold Hough, "Iran Targets the Arabian Peninsula," *Jane's Intelligence Review* (October 1996), pp. 459-60; and U.S., Department of Defense, *Proliferation: Threat and Response* (1997), pp. 36-39.

siles and technology. In this first phase, the Libyans would develop a missile with a range in excess of 800 miles and a 1,650-pound warhead. An advanced system would follow with a range of 1,250 miles and a 2,200-pound warhead.[30]

Cruise Missiles. During an eighty-day period in June, July and August 1944, approximately 8,200 of Germany's V-1 cruise missiles or "buzz bombs" were fired against London, 2,300 V-1s were launched against other targets in Britain, and some 7,800 missiles were fired on continental targets, chiefly in Antwerp. An automatic pilot and a variety of clockwork devices controlled it in flight. It could carry a 2,000-pound bomb 150 miles at speeds of 350 to 400 miles per hour. British anti-aircraft guns and fighters shot down thousands of the V-1s—seventy-nine percent, in fact, of those launched in the final week of the eighty-day period. Nonetheless, some 2,300 got through to London and many of those shot down exploded upon hitting the ground. The death toll was about one per V-1 launched; the psychological impact was enormous. More than 200,000 houses were destroyed during the first two weeks of the aerial onslaught. The Allies launched a massive air campaign against the V-1 cruise missile and V-2 ballistic missiles. Approximately 65,000 sorties were flown and 122,000 tons of explosives were dropped in the vicinity of the well-camouflaged sites, with the cost of 450 aircraft and 2,900 airmen. The net result was that no missiles were destroyed on their launchers.[31]

Most cruise missiles since the V-1 have been designed for coastal defense in an anti-ship mode. Only a few missiles are available for land attack where digital map correlation is the key for reaching their targets. The ongoing commercial information revolution is allowing the transformation of cruise missiles into an effective land attack weapon. Guidance and navigation technologies based on GPS, new mission planning tools, and remote sensors have improved cruise missile accuracy by a factor of at least ten. At the same time, the globalization of the aircraft industry means that many are using the buyers market to obtain technology transfer that can be used in

---

[30] "Tehran Deal To Help With Libyan Missile," *The Times* (London) (November 21, 1997).

[31] Brodie and Brodie, *From Crossbow to H-Bomb,* pp. 230-32; Thomas B. Buell and others, *The Second World War: Europe and the Mediterranean* (Wayne, N.J.: Avery Publishing Group, 1984), pp. 314-15; William R. Graham and others, *Ballistic Missile Proliferation: An Emerging Threat 1992* (Arlington, Va.: Systems Planning Corporation, October 1992), pp. 5-7; and David Israel, Assistant for Theater Missile Defense, "An SDIO In TMD Counterforce" (Washington, D.C.: Strategic Defense Initiative Organization, June 1992).

---

development of cruise missiles.[32] Dennis M. Gormley and K. Scott McMahon summarize:

...relatively low cost and technically straightforward modifications can convert antiship missiles for land-attack missions. Indeed, when antiship missiles are combined with cheap guidance, navigation maps developed from commercial satellite imagery, defense penetration measures, and improved propulsion systems, they present a stark reality: antiship cruise missiles transformed into precision land-attack models could emerge with little notice to threaten Western interests.[33]

Since cruise missiles fly at slow speeds when compared to ballistic missiles and can be tracked by radar, they are generally thought to be susceptible to air defenses. A host of low-observable technologies, however, can be applied to cruise missiles to greatly reduce their radar reflectivity and in some cases make them all but invisible to conventional radar.

Cruise missiles powered by turbojets need about one-third of the fuel of rocket engines and the follow-on turbofan engine, combined with greater fuel efficiency, increases their potential range to 1,860 miles. High accuracies can be achieved by terrain-contour matching (TERCOM) and GPS systems. TERCOM stores digital terrain maps of the flight path and target area in the missile's guidance system in order to minimize in-flight drift and can achieve accuracies of thirty to 100 meters. The availability of SPOT and LANDSAT satellite imagery and computer-aided software in producing digitized terrain maps may place TERCOM within reach of far more countries today than in the recent past when the associated costs were prohibitively high for many states.

Using GPS data inputs, the Geographic Information System permits users to create very accurate digital maps with personal computers and sophisticated software. GPS provides corrected flight guidance information to cruise missiles—horizontal (latitude and longitude) and vertical (altitude) data fixes—from an array of twenty-four satellites transmitting navigation signals and receivers that translate the satellite data into precise positional

---

[32] Dennis M. Gormley, Remarks at the "Conference on Nuclear Non-Proliferation: Enhancing the Tools of the Trade," Carnegie Endowment for International Peace (Washington, D.C.: June 10, 1997).

[33] Dennis M. Gormley and K. Scott McMahon as quoted in Wiencek, *Dangerous Arsenals: Missile Threats In and From Asia,* p. 31.

The New Face of War

information. In wartime, the U.S. could degrade the commercially available GPS data to the point where the quality is reduced to 100 meters in the horizontal plane and 140 meters in the vertical; this is accurate enough for many users, especially those delivering WMD against large area targets such as airfields, ports and cities. Accurate terrain elevation can be programmed into a cruise missile, allowing it to fly at very low altitudes without an expensive terrain-avoidance radar system.[34]

Amy Truesdell provides just the right image of the implications of cruise missiles for delivering weapons of mass destruction:

> Potentially, the most frightening application of cruise-missile technology is not now known to exist, namely use as a delivery vehicle for chemical or biological warheads. There are reports, however, that Syria, Iran and China are developing this capability. The fact that cruise missiles are unmanned vehicles travelling at relatively slow speeds at low altitude would make them extremely effective vehicles for the dispersal of chemical and biological agents. Iraq is believed to have been developing an aerosol dispersal system before the Gulf War. Other states with strategic ambitions but no nuclear assets may also see the benefit of outfitting their cruise missiles with chemical or biological warheads.[35]

France, Italy, Russia and other former Soviet republics, the United Kingdom, China, and the United States are the primary suppliers of anti-ship cruise missiles to the developing world. Since most of the sales of these missiles involved short-range systems, the transfers have fallen below the 185-mile restriction imposed by the Missile Technology Control Regime. Nonetheless, with the technologies now available worldwide, these anti-ship missiles can be converted rather easily to a land-attack mode. China has

---

[34] Cruise missile users can work around the degraded GPS signal through a procedure that is known as differential GPS or DGPS. Accuracies on the order of ten meters are possible with DGPS. This simple procedure uses a second ground station at a precise location to broadcast a correctional signal on a different frequency than the first GPS receiver, improving the accuracy of the positional data. See two excellent discussions of the technologies and operational uses associated with cruise missiles in Amy Truesdell, "Cruise Missiles: The Discriminating Weapon of Choice?," *Jane's Intelligence Review* (February 2, 1997), and Dennis M. Gormley and K. Scott McMahon, "Proliferation of Land-Attack Cruise Missiles: Prospects and Policy Implications" in *Fighting Proliferation: New Concerns for the Nineties,* ed. by Henry Sokolski (Washington, D.C.: Government Printing Office, September 1996), pp. 140-45.

[35] Truesdell, "Cruise Missiles: The Discriminating Weapon of Choice?," p. 89.

Ballistic and Cruise Missiles
137

already exported anti-ship missiles widely; with Russian stealth technology now available to Beijing's land-attack cruise missiles, exports of low-observable versions are a distinct near-term possibility. The Chinese have already reverse-engineered the Russian SS-N-2 Styx to develop their own HY-2 Silkworm anti-ship cruise missile and other derivatives.[36] In early 1997, Iran possessed some 400 Silkworms imported from China and North Korea. Iran also possesses an unknown number of indigenously produced Silkworm variants and more than 200 other Chinese-built anti-ship cruise missiles. Silkworm missiles have also been exported to Pakistan, Bangladesh, and Egypt. Thailand has more than fifty of China's C-801 anti-ship cruise missiles, and Iraq had several Chinese-built CSS-C-2 Silkworm missiles (fifty-mile range) before the Gulf War—an unspecified number are still in service.[37]

Iran has about forty Chinese-supplied C-802 anti-ship missiles with a range of about seventy-five miles with a fifty-five-pound warhead. The C-802 increases Iranian military firepower and dimensions of the threat since they can be launched from Chinese-supplied Houdong patrol boats and airborne platforms. Together with Kilo-class submarines acquired from Russia, Iran has the capacity to threaten merchant shipping and naval forces, and affect passage through the Strait of Hormuz.[38]

North Korea was reported in 1994 to be developing a longer-range variant (100 miles) of its copy of the Silkworm anti-ship cruise missile. In May 1997, North Korea test-fired a new anti-ship cruise missile whose propulsion, range and radar guidance are similar to the SS-N-2 Styx and China's CSS-2 Silkworm. This new missile, the AG-1, has some unique characteristics and could be destined for export to the Middle East.[39]

While seventy-three countries possessed cruise missiles in mid-1997, only nineteen had production programs and just twelve exported cruise missiles.[40] See Figure 6.5. On the other hand, a growing number of non-Western countries are capable of producing the necessary airframes, propulsion, warheads, and guidance systems for cruise missiles. The threat to the U.S. power projection strategy will increase as more countries produce large, accurate, and stealthy cruise missiles with sufficient range to be launched from

---

[36] *Ibid.,* p. 90.

[37] Wiencek, *Dangerous Arsenals: Missile Threats In and From Asia,* pp. 31-35.

[38] U.S., Senate, *Proliferation Primer,* p. 7.

[39] *Ibid.,* p. 36; Bill Gertz, "N. Korea Fires New Cruise Missile," *Washington Times* (June 30, 1997), pp. A1, A8; and "Hyperbolic Missile," *Aviation Week & Space Technology* (July 7, 1997).

[40] Truesdell, "Cruise Missiles: The Discriminating Weapon of Choice?," p. 89.

Figure 6.5
Global Cruise Missile Proliferation

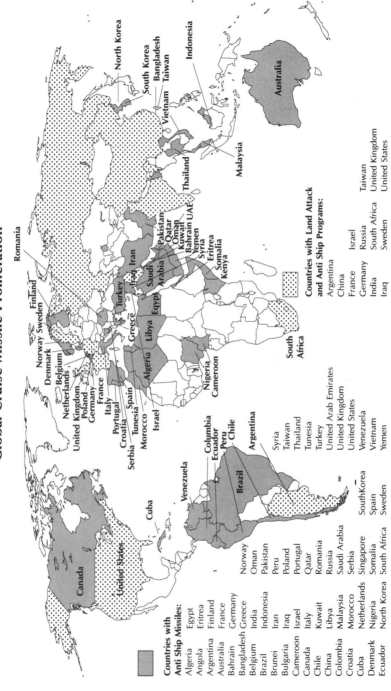

Source: Amy Truesdell, "Cruise Missiles: The Discriminating Weapon of Choice?," *Jane's Intelligence Review* (February 2, 1997), p. 90.

outside air defense envelopes. Dennis M. Gormley and K. Scott McMahon offer a balanced strategic perspective:

> An explosion in commercially available navigation, guidance, and satellite-based digital mapping technology portends the widespread proliferation of unmanned air vehicles. Due to their precision delivery, low-flight profile, and potentially low radar cross section, they threaten effective delivery not only of nuclear, biological, and chemical weapons, but conventional payloads as well. Without effective export controls or improved air defenses, a cruise missile-armed adversary could present new challenges to the ability of the United States to project military power globally.[41]

In recognition of this cruise missile threat, the Defense Department formed a team in mid-1997 to examine the dangers to the United States directly and the defenses needed against cruise missiles for military theaters overseas. The idea is to build defenses before adversaries are able to exploit U.S. vulnerabilities at home and abroad.[42]

Pathways to Missile Proliferation

Proliferating countries have several missile acquisition routes open to them. They can became importers of missiles through direct purchase; sixteen of the twenty-two non-Western countries possessing surface-to-surface missiles bought them "off-the-shelf" in other countries. For countries without the industrial infrastructure to develop and manufacture their own missiles, direct purchase is the only means of acquiring them—Saudi Arabia, Libya, and Yemen fall into this category. Off-the-shelf buys also have an advantage of the transfer taking place relatively quickly, often within a year. Yet, the MTCR places an important barrier to the transfer of whole missiles with ranges of 185 miles or more and 1,100-pound warhead capacity.

Proliferators can also import missiles and then improve them and manufacture their own copies. In some cases suppliers may provide parts and technical assistance in assembling missiles, or help the buyer produce some

---

[41] As quoted in Shuey, *Ballistic and Cruise Missile Forces of Foreign Counties,* pp. 4-5.

[42] Jeff Erlich, "U.S. Officials To Study Cruise Missile Threat," *Defense News* (June 16-22, 1997), p. 21; Eugene Fox and Stanley Orman, "Cruise Missile Threat Grows," *Defense News* (September 30-October 6, 1996), pp. 37, 52; and "War Games to Include Cruise Missile Threats," *Aviation Week & Space Technology* (July 14, 1997).

of the components or subcomponents. The buyer might persuade the supplier to agree to a full-licensed production agreement. In this case, the supplier may still provide key parts of the missile but a large percentage of the components are domestically produced. Reverse-engineering is an unauthorized form of technology transfer. It is a difficult task to disassemble missiles and duplicate their components. The processes and procedures involved in producing copied parts are also dependent on the knowledge of the techniques used in the original manufacture. The North Koreans, for instance, apparently had difficulty in reverse-engineering and copying a Scud B because the Soviets would not share certain critical production information. Pyongyang had to turn to China for assistance.

It is always possible to establish clandestine procurement networks such as those developed by Iraq before the Gulf War and Armenia (receiving Russian armaments) in 1992-94. An array of techniques can be used to circumvent export controls in supplier countries.

Another missile acquisition route is possible by countries that import, improve, copy, and become producers of missile technologies or missile systems on their own. Sounding rockets, for instance, are unguided ballistic missiles that carry small scientific payloads. Yet, the Pakistani Hatf-1 and Hatf-2 missiles are copies of sounding rockets produced in cooperation with France. North Korea, for instance, produces and markets the Scud C, an improved version of the Scud B. Iraq, which will be discussed below, wrote the book on how to build ballistic and cruise missile capabilities in a world hostile toward technology and missile transfers.[43]

In terms of ballistic missile production capabilities, non-Western countries can be placed in one of four major categories:

- **Advanced.** Able to design and produce missiles comparable to those deployed in the United States in the mid-1960s, i.e., ICBMs and space-launch rockets. Countries: India and possibly Taiwan.
- **Intermediate.** Able to reverse-engineer, modify and improve, and manufacture Scud-like missiles, and to manufacture solid-propellant short-range missiles. Countries: Brazil, North Korea, South Korea, Iraq (before the Persian Gulf War), and possibly Argentina and South Africa.

---

[43] L. Dunn and others, *Global Proliferation: Dynamics, Acquisition Strategies, and Responses,* Vol. V - Missile Proliferation (Newington, Va.: Center for Verification Research, December 1992), pp. 31-35.

- **Incipient.** Some capability to modify existing Scuds, but little else. Countries: Egypt, Pakistan, and Iran (and improving fast).
- **No Indigenous Capability.** No missile design or manufacturing capability but have imported missiles with ranges beyond sixty miles. **Countries:** Afghanistan, Libya, Saudi Arabia, Syria, Yemen, and possibly Algeria and Cuba.[44]

Since nearly all of the developed countries are members of the MTCR, non-Western countries increasingly sell or transfer missiles between themselves. Countries that have built successful missile programs owe their achievement to slow, steady expansion of their indigenous capabilities.

The proliferation of ballistic and cruise missiles in the non-Western world is a fact. Even with the possible enhancement of the Missile Technology Control Regime or other arms control treaties, it would be an illusion to believe that long-range ballistic and cruise missiles will continue to be a monopoly of the Western countries. As more scientists and engineers from non-Western countries are educated in the best universities or technical schools of advanced technology in Western countries, the knowledge of how to produce missiles will be further disseminated throughout the world. Industrial countries will continue to sell finished military products, technical assistance, equipment, and technologies to non-Western countries. Financial capability to develop missiles is increasing as the world economy expands. All of these trends are converging to the point where it is safe to say that there is a great likelihood that advanced missile technologies will soon be in the hands non-Western states, many of which are hostile toward the United States and its security objectives.

Proliferation Template: Iraq's Missile Program

An essential component of the Iraqi drive to be capable of delivering weapons of mass destruction throughout the Middle East was the effort to build a robust ballistic missile production base. The first proliferation steps involved the receipt of whole missiles from outside suppliers. The Iraqis received their first Scud Bs from the Soviet Union in the 1970s and later obtained Scud C derivatives from North Korea.[45]

---

[44] U.S., Congress, Office of Technology Assessment, *Technologies Underlying Weapons of Mass Destruction*, p. 212.

[45] The Soviet Scud As were first seen in 1957 and were probably derived in part from the German V-2. Scud Bs were deployed in the mid-1960s. The missile accompanied Soviet ground

The New Face of War

The second step toward a missile production base involved drawing on foreign technology and expertise, primarily from Brazil, Argentina, Germany, Austria, and Italy. The Iraqis achieved considerable success. Step three was a joint venture for missile development with Egypt and Argentina; both partner countries withdrew from the deal with the Iraqis in 1988 and 1989, respectively, under pressure from the United States. Nonetheless, the Iraqis continued to pursue the joint missile project on their own. When the Gulf War came, the Iraqis had made substantial progress in developing the Badr 2000 missile—a 650-mile range, two-staged, solid-fueled missile capable of carrying a warhead in excess of 1,000 pounds. This missile was intended to be Iraq's primary nuclear delivery system, with some reports claiming it to be fuel-air capable as well.[46]

The Iraqis also had an ongoing program to extend the range of the Scud Bs obtained from the Soviet Union. One of these missiles, the "Al Hussein," had been used by the Iraqis during the 1988 "War of the Cities" phase of the Iran-Iraq War. Over a period of eight weeks, the Iraqis launched 189 Al Husseins at six Iranian cities. The Iraqi modifications had doubled the range of the Scud B with the addition of more than 2,000 pounds of fuel. The tradeoff price for extending the range was paid by reducing the payload from about 1,800 to 400 pounds. This small, inaccurate warhead offered little capability against military targets unless by chance a direct hit took place. Nonetheless, the warhead was accompanied by the Al Hussein one-ton missile body, which normally slammed into the ground nearby at a terminal velocity of more than four times the speed of sound. Figure 6.6 depicts the coverage of the Scud (185 miles) and Al Hussein (400 miles) missiles from a nominal launch point in Baghdad. Twelve countries are within range.

An upgraded variant of the Al Hussein, the "Al Abbas" had a range of about 450 miles and was said to have had greater accuracy than its antecedents. Another variant, one with about the same range as the Al Hussein, was

---

forces on an eight-wheeled vehicle called a "transporter erector launcher" or TEL. The Scud B is a single-stage, liquid-fueled rocket and is believed to have a 300 kilometers (185 miles) range with a payload of 2,100-pounds and an accuracy rate on the order of 3,000 feet. See U.S., Department of the Air Force, *Gulf War Air Power Survey: Operations and Effects and Effectiveness,* Vol. II, Part 2 (Washington, D.C.: Government Printing Office, 1993), p. 317.

[46] Michael Eisenstadt, *"The Sword of the Arabs:" Iraq's Strategic Weapons,* Policy Paper No. 21, (Washington, D.C.: Washington Institute for Near East Policy, 1990), pp. 18–21, and *Like a Phoenix From the Ashes? The Future of Iraqi Military Power,* Policy Paper No. 36 (Washington, D.C.: Washington Institute for Near East Policy, 1993), p. 35. See also Kathleen C. Bailey, *The UN Inspections in Iraq: Lessons for On-Site Verification* (Boulder: Westview Press, 1995), pp. 73–74.

Figure 6.6
Iraq's Scud and Al Hussein Missile Rings

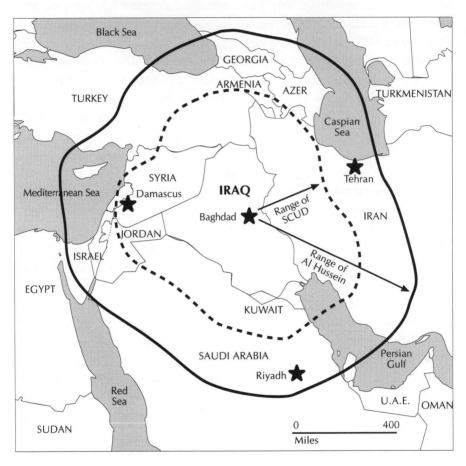

Source: R. Jeffrey Smith, "Iraq's Drive for a Biological Arsenal," *Washington Post* (November 21, 1997), p. A49.

The New Face of War

the "Al Hijarah." A few of these were fired by the Iraqis during the Persian Gulf War. In addition to these three ballistic missiles, the Iraqis were working on the "Al Abid" satellite-launch vehicle. The Al Abid consisted of a three-stage missile with a cluster of five Scud boosters strapped together to serve as the first stage, a single Scud rocket engine as the second stage, and modified surface-to-air missiles (SA-2) as the third stage. Its sole test flight in 1989 was unsuccessful. The concept for the Tammuz I was developed to produce a two-stage missile with a 1,200-mile range—an extended-range Scud booster rocket was topped by a modified SA-2 second stage. Finally, the Iraqis were in the process of converting SA-2 missiles to surface-to-surface modes in the Al Fahd 300 and Al Fahd 500 programs with ranges of 150 and 90 miles, respectively. The program was abandoned after it was clear the modified missiles would be too inaccurate to have much usefulness. (The Bosnian Serbs fired such a weapon against the town of Bihac during a 1994 offensive.) A similar effort was underway to convert the Silkworm anti-ship missile for ground targets in the "Faw" cruise missile program.[47]

Like Iraq's biological and chemical program on the eve of the Gulf War, Baghdad's ballistic missile program was well advanced and ready. The Iraqis demonstrated extraordinary technical skill and innovation in developing their weapons of mass destruction and missiles. Figure 6.7 shows the location of Iraq's most important missile facilities. With U.S. and other forces clustered at a few bases, Saudi ports jammed with ships, transport aircraft parked wingtip-to-wingtip, and the Israeli, Saudi, and other Arab peoples open to attack, the region was poised on a precipice of disaster. While the events that unfolded did not trigger the Iraqi use of these weapons, that was a result more of Iraqi strategic doctrine than of a conscious design by U.S. policy makers and military planners.

The Iraqis fired two Scud missiles with concrete-filled warheads at Israel's Dimona nuclear complex during the Gulf War. Apparently, the attempt was made in the hopes of cracking the containment dome on the Israeli reactor and spewing radioactive material across the Middle East to Jordan, Saudi Arabia, and Egypt. Both missiles crashed in the Negev Desert

---

[47] U.S., Department of the Air Force, *Gulf War Air Power Survey: Operations and Effects and Effectiveness,* Vol. II, Part 2, pp. 317–19; Bailey, *UN Inspections in Iraq,* pp. 73–74; Eisenstadt, *Like a Phoenix from the Ashes,* pp. 35–37; and Nagler and others, *Ballistic Missile Proliferation,* pp. 16–17.

Figure 6.7
Twenty-Nine Iraqi Missile Facilities

Other Facilities
Luadl ar Ratqa
Qasr Amij East
Qasr Amij West
Rasheed Campi
Wadi Al Jabaryah
Yawru Al Izim

The New Face of War

far from the intended target but close enough to gain Israel's attention. A third Scud missile was said to have contained the deadly nerve agent VX which could have killed many of the workers at Dimona.[48]

While U.N. inspectors scoffed at the Iraqis pitiful attempt to hit the Dimona rector, Saddam Hussein's intention may have been more strategic than tactical. The odds of hitting Dimona were extremely low, though a lucky hit would have been payback for Israel's surprise air raid against the Osirak reactor in 1981. Baghdad's actual objective, however, may have been aimed at triggering an Israeli response against Iraq in order to foster defections by Arab members of the anti-Iraq Coalition.

From the beginning of the post-war on-site inspections by the U.N. in 1991, the Iraqis were determined to assure themselves a residual missile force and presumably biological and chemical warheads. Missiles and their components were buried, hidden in a variety of locations, and some reportedly were placed aboard trucks that kept moving around the country. False declarations and blatant lies supplemented the Iraqi actions as a grand cat-and-mouse game was played with the UNSCOM inspectors over the next six years.

By April 1995, the Commission had put a multi-level and comprehensive monitoring system into place covering Iraq's missile research, development, testing and production facilities, as well as those related to dual-use capabilities. The Special Commission missile monitoring group located in Baghdad provides the surveillance required. The sense at UNSCOM was that it had "essentially completed the accounting of proscribed ballistic missile capabilities," although "investigation will continue until the Commission is satisfied that it has obtained as detailed a picture as possible of all aspects of Iraq's past programmes and current capabilities."[49]

The U.N. supervised the destruction of forty-eight Scud and Scud-derivative missiles, fourteen conventional warheads, and six mobile launchers. The Iraqis claimed to have unilaterally destroyed several missiles, two

---

[48] Stewart Stogel, "Iraq Fired Scuds At Israeli Reactor," *Washington Times* (January 1, 1998), pp. A1, A7.

[49] United Nations, Security Council, *Ninth Report of the Executive Chairman of the Special Commission Established By the Secretary-General Pursuant to Paragraph 9 (b) (i) of Security Council Resolution 687 (1991), On the Activities of the Special Commission,* U.N. Doc. S/1995/494 (June 20, 1995), pp. 4–5.

[50] United Nations, Security Council, *Report to the Secretary-General On Activities of the Special Commission Established By the Secretary-General Pursuant to Paragraph 9 (b) (i) of Resolution 687 (1991),* U.N. Doc. S/1996/848 (October 11, 1996), p. 7.

---

mobile launchers, and other related equipment. By 1998, the UNSCOM inspection teams were still unable to verify the unilateral destruction of these proscribed missiles and components.[50]

By mid-1995, it had become apparent that the Iraqis had resumed their acquisition of foreign equipment, technologies, supplies and material for both missile- and non-missile related activities. Iraq explained that these efforts were mostly in support of its development of its Ababil-100 program, a missile with a range of sixty to ninety-five miles.[51] At the same time, satellite pictures showed rebuilding efforts at several key missile facilities, including the Al Kinde Missile Research and Development Facility at Mosul.[52] Nonetheless, UNSCOM in 1996 discovered Iraqi projects for the acquisition and development of missile propellants, missile testing, and missile computer simulations and telemetry. The Commission also collected evidence of undisclosed acquisition of proscribed missile components from a number of suppliers.[53] The U.N. Special Commission viewed Iraq's progress on developing the Samoud missile, which has a declared range less than ninety-three miles, and corroborated the Iraqi declarations.[54]

On December 9, 1995, thirty gyroscopes that had been removed from Russian SS-N-18 submarine-launched missiles (maximum range 4,970 miles with seven nuclear warheads) found their way into a canal of the Tigris River near Baghdad. The U.N. divers retrieved these mechanisms which are essential to keep ballistic missiles on course to their targets, especially over long distances. Slightly larger than a pack of cigarettes, the gyroscopes are very light. The thirty gyroscopes in question came from a Russian-disassembling plant. Twice before U.N. inspectors had stumbled across missile gyroscopes destined for Iraq; one shipment was seized in Jordan in November 1995.[55]

---

[51] United Nations, Security Council, *Report of the Secretary-General On the Status of the Implementation of the Special Commission's Plan for the Ongoing Monitoring and Verification of Iraq's Compliance With Relevant Parts of Section C of Security Council Resolution 687 (1991)*, U.N. Doc. S/1995/864 (October 11, 1995), p. 13.

[52] James Bruce and Barbara Starr, "US Exploits Images of Military Rebirth...As Iraq Rejects UN Resolution on Oil Sales," *Jane's Defence Weekly* (May 6, 1995), pp. 4–5.

[53] United Nations, Security Council, *Report of the Secretary-General On the Activities of the Special Commission Established By the Secretary-General Pursuant to Paragraph 9 (b) (i) of Resolution 687 (1991)*, U.N. Doc. S/1996/848 (October 11, 1996), pp. 8-9.

[54] United Nations, Security Council, *Report of the Secretary-General,* U.N. Doc. S/1997/301 (April 11, 1997).

The UNSCOM inspections revealed that the Iraqi ballistic missile force was much larger than was believed during the Gulf War. Iraq's evasions throughout more than six years of inspections and supervised destruction of missiles and missile-related equipment raise the question of whether Baghdad has retained a residual force of missiles. Former C.I.A. Director Robert Gates estimated the residual force to number perhaps in the hundreds of missiles. R. James Woolsey, Gates' successor, said that the residual force numbered 100–200 missiles and twelve to twenty launchers, including Scuds and extended-range versions such as the Al Hussein.[56] In December 1996, Rolf Ekeus, then chief of the U.N. arms inspections in Iraq, said that "we believe that Iraq is still holding a significant number of operational missiles which could constitute a complete missile force, including all support equipment, rocket fuel, launchers and everything."[57] In addition, the Iraqis were quite clever in reverse-engineering Soviet Scuds to produce their own versions. Baghdad officials insist that most of the Iraqi-made missile engines were of a low quality and discarded. Yet, all documentation has disappeared.[58]

Some analysts estimate that it would take Iraq a few years to restore its missile production base after the U.N. sanctions are lifted. The "complete missile force" that the Iraqis apparently have successfully held back so far would provide them a missile capability within days, perhaps even hours. In addition, Iraq test-fired a new medium-range missile in November 1997. The Al Samoud missile has a range of ninety-three miles which is not proscribed by the 1991 U.N. Security Council resolutions.[59] When the missing Scuds, Scud-derivatives, and the new medium-range missiles are combined with biological and chemical warfare agents unaccounted for, it is quite evident that Iraq could mount a significant threat to its neighbors in a very short time.

---

[55] David Hoffman, "Russia's Missile Gyroscopes Were Sold to Iraq," *Washington Post* (September 12, 1997), pp. A1, A33.

[56] David C. Isby, "The Residual Iraqi 'Scud' Force," *Jane's Intelligence Review,* (March 1995), pp. 115–17.

[57] "Iraq Likely Has Hidden Missiles, Inspector Says," *Washington Times* (December 19, 1996), p. A13.

[58] "Interview: Rolf Ekeus," *Dallas Morning News* (December 21, 1997).

[59] "Security Council Informed of Missile Test Last Fall," *Washington Post* (February 14, 1998).

CHAPTER 7

Biological and Chemical "Blowback"

L ike peeling an onion, a reluctant Defense Department every so often pulls back another layer to reveal a little more about the possible exposure of American troops to biological and chemical toxins during the Persian Gulf War. The difficulty is that upward of some 100,000 veterans are suffering from Gulf War Syndrome; they and their families are the ones shedding tears. Officially, the veterans are suffering from ailments of unknown origin. Yet, many are convinced a part of the cause for the Syndrome is exposure to chemical agents and perhaps one particular biological agent called aflatoxin.

Two big questions remain open. Did the Iraqis launch biological and chemical attacks against the Coalition's forces? Did toxic gas, released as a result of Coalition bombing, drift southward and douse the allied troops with low-levels of toxic agents? The answers are important not only to help uncover the mystery origins of Gulf War Syndrome but also to shape U.S. strategy and military doctrine for future operations in contaminated environments.

The blowback[1] associated with Gulf War Syndrome is centered in three different areas. The first set is made up of a hardy group of truth-seekers who are simply trying to find out what happened to the veterans suffering from the syndrome since the Gulf War. Skeptical of past responses by federal agencies (e.g., the "atomic veterans" from post-war Japan and military participants in the 1945-62 atmospheric nuclear testing, the herbicide Agent Orange veterans from Vietnam), this group does not buy into the sweeping condemnations of the government typical of most of those pursuing the

---

[1] "Blowback" is common jargon referring to negative consequences resulting from particular activities directed against an adversary. This specialized phrase is especially descriptive of Gulf War Syndrome. The meaning of "blowback" includes the military, intelligence, physical (drift of toxic agents or pathogens toward friendly forces), and political consequences of combatting a biological and chemical weapons-armed enemy.

cover-up theory. Rather, they are working hard to dig out the data to give them the light of day and let the facts speak for themselves. James J. Tuite, III, author of two 1994 U.S. Senate reports on Gulf War Syndrome and director of the Gulf War Syndrome Foundation, is the oft-mentioned but more often unheralded leader of the truth-seekers who frequently have differing views among themselves.[2]

Second is the political bluster resulting from the veterans' complaints that the medical community in the Defense Department and Veterans Administration are not taking their ailments seriously. In an October 1996 survey of Gulf War veterans conducted by the Veterans of Foreign Wars, seventy-seven percent of the respondents said they were ill, and of those, sixty-seven percent said their illness had not been diagnosed.[3] In August 1995, the Presidential Advisory Committee on Gulf War Veterans' Illnesses began to examine the health concerns related to service in the Gulf War and issued a final report in January 1997; President Clinton extended the Committee's mandate through September 1997.

A third blowback area associated with Gulf War Syndrome consists of those who believe the Defense Department, Central Intelligence Agency, and Veterans Administration, as well as other federal agencies, are engaged in a monumental cover-up of the facts associated with Iraq's use of chemical and biological warfare agents. Most Americans, according to one scientific survey of 1,009 adults, seem to agree. Proposition: *Our military leaders are withholding what they know about nerve gas or germ-warfare attacks on American troops during the Persian Gulf War.* Responses: Very likely – 48%, Somewhat likely – 32%, Unlikely – 11%, and Don't know or other – 9%.[4] To put it another way, eighty percent thought it was likely the government was withholding information and eleven percent did not.

Which blowback camp is best for you, in the final analysis, depends on your belief system. The paucity of knowledge about the possible Iraqi use of biological and chemical weapons and the "undiagnosed illnesses" means

---

[2] James J. Tuite is an authentic American hero by virtue of his service as an Army medic on "Dustoff" missions during the Vietnam War. "Dustoff" was the code name for aeromedical helicopters that often flew into hot zones to retrieve American wounded and then spirit them off to waiting doctors and nurses at field hospitals. The "Dustoff" aviators and medics saved many lives.

[3] "Persian Gulf Vets Still Searching for Answers," *Checkpoint,* a publication of the Veterans of Foreign Wars (January/February 1997), pp. 1-2.

[4] Thomas Hargrove and Guido H. Stempel III, "Poll Says Americans Suspect Worst of Their Government," *Washington Times* (July 5, 1997), p. A2.

The New Face of War

that what one believes is an article of faith. The simple fact is that the *knowns* about Gulf War Syndrome are swamped by the *unknowns* and the *unknowables*. There are too many uncertainties to predict with confidence gas dispersal and resulting casualties. Different chemical types means that gas properties vary when mixing with the atmosphere. Such physical variables as quantity, density, volatility, temperature, pressure and dispensing mechanism or cause leave many unanswered questions. Environmental factors introduce many other uncertainties, including such matters as wind intensity, direction, and variations with altitude; atmospheric temperature, pressure, and humidity; terrain variations—hills, valleys, water surfaces, and vegetation; and time or the day/night cycle, sunlight, and cloud cover. The populations at risk will vary according to sensitivity to specific agents, distribution of exposure levels and times, density of people versus distance from the event, and pre-health of the population, including vaccines.[5]

Accurate exposure information to a wide range of potentially toxic substances—pesticides, vaccines, smoke from oil fires, chemical and biological warfare agents, and others—is the key to identifying the potential causes of Gulf War Syndrome and understanding the risk factors sufficiently to diagnose, treat and prevent the illnesses. Given the large number of variables that defy accurate identification six to seven years after the war, it is impossible to obtain a comprehensive understanding of exposure during the war. In the absence of the appropriate exposure data, cover-up theorists are having a field day and could distract attention from the two most pressing issues.

To the extent that the government does not know or will not acknowledge the exposure to biological and chemical agents, future U.S. strategy and military operations can be affected. Unless Pentagon planners know what happened and how to prevent similar occurrences in the future, the United States could be led down the wrong path, pursue the wrong strategy, and buy the wrong military forces. Hence, there are two issues. The first and paramount concern is taking care of today's veterans and remaining loyal to them in an unceasing effort to find the best ways to treat their illnesses. The second is understanding more fully what could happen to U.S. forces in future military operations against WMD-armed adversaries.

---

[5] W. C. Yengst and others, *Dispersal of Hazardous Gases* (McLean, Va.: Science Applications International Corporation, September 1994).

What Happened in the Gulf War?

Testifying before the Senate Armed Services Committee in June 1993, more than two years after the Persian Gulf War, several veterans spoke of several unexplained events during the war that they related to chemical warfare attacks. Many of the veterans reported symptoms consistent with mixed agent attacks. A month later, the Czech Minister of Defense reported that one of its chemical decontamination units had detected sarin, a nerve agent, in areas of northern Saudi Arabia in the opening days of the Gulf War. The Czechoslovak units attributed these detections to blowback from the Coalition's bombing of Iraq's chemical agent production facilities. In September 1993, Senator Donald W. Reigle, Jr., issued a staff report that raised the possibility of a connection between Iraq's chemical, biological and radiological warfare research and development programs and the illnesses being reported by thousands of Gulf War veterans.

In what was to become known as "Gulf War Syndrome," many believed by late 1993 that tens of thousands of veterans were suffering from muscle and joint pain, memory loss, intestinal and heart problems, fatigue, nasal congestion, urinary urgency, diarrhea, twitching, rashes, sores, and a number of other symptoms. Multiple symptoms were manifested in the veterans many months after the Gulf War; a number of the sick died and family members also began suffering these debilitating symptoms. Many Americans recognized a growing medical problem that demanded urgent efforts to find out what the veterans had been exposed to in the Gulf and how to best treat their symptoms. The Senate Banking Committee began an inquiry and uncovered a great deal of evidence of hazardous exposures and suspicious events.

Curiously, the Defense Department was less than fully supportive of the Senate inquiry and stood fast in its position that there was no evidence that U.S. forces were exposed to chemical agents. Major General Ronald Blanck, commander of the Walter Reed Army Medical Center in Washington, D.C., said in a September 1993 telephone interview that the possibility of chemical and biological warfare agent dispersal had not been explored since "military intelligence" had already staked a claim that such exposures never occurred. During a November 1993 unclassified briefing, a Pentagon official, responding to direct questioning by members of the U.S. Senate, said the Department of Defense was withholding classified information on the exposure of U.S. forces to biological materials. This same official later admitted at a conference at Los Alamos National Laboratory on May 6-7,

1994, that biological agent detection systems were not fielded with U.S. military forces anywhere in the world.[6]

Khamisiyah Ammo Depot – Southern Iraq. In a prepared statement and in testimony before the U.S. Senate Committee on Banking, Housing and Urban Affairs on May 25, 1994, Edwin Dorn, the undersecretary of defense for personnel and readiness, was emphatic that "...no chemical or biological weapons were found in the Kuwait Theater of Operations—those portions of Southern Iraq and Kuwait that constituted the battlefield—among the tons of live and spent munitions recovered following the war." He also explained that U.S. military personnel had been present in Iraq, under the supervision of the U.N. Special Commission, and involved in *each of the teams* overseeing the destruction of Iraq's chemical arsenal. "All of these [Iraqi] chemical agents and related equipment were found stored at locations a great distance from the Kuwait Theater of Operations."[7]

In October-November 1991 a U.N. Special Commission on-site inspection team visited three chemical storage sites declared by Iraq: Al Tuz, Muhammadiyat, and Khamisiyah in southern Iraq. The team found munitions at Khamisiyah too unsafe to be moved and for which drilling and draining would be too hazardous. These chemical munitions were destroyed at the site between February 21 and March 24, 1992. The Commission reported to the U.N. Security Council: "At Khamisiyah, the Special Commission has supervised the first destruction of filled chemical munitions...." All told, the U.N. Special Commission destroyed 463 122-millimeter rockets at Khamisiyah: 389 were filled with a mixture of the nerve agents GB (sarin) and GF, thirty-six were partially filled and thirty-eight were unfilled. Approximately two and one-half tons of the deadly GB/GF mixture was destroyed.[8]

---

[6] U.S., Congress, Senate, Committee on Banking, Housing and Urban Affairs, *U.S. Chemical and Biological Warfare-Related Dual Use Exports to Iraq and Their Possible Impact on the Health Consequences of the Persian Gulf War,* 103d Cong., 2d sess. (May 25, 1994), pp. 1-6.

[7] U.S., Congress, Senate, Committee on Banking, Housing, and Urban Affairs, *United States Dual-Use Exports to Iraq and Their Impact on the Health of the Persian Gulf War Veterans,* 103d Cong., 2d sess. (Washington, D.C.: Government Printing Office, 1994), p. 92.

[8] United Nations, Security Council, *Report of the Executive Chairman of the Special Commission Established By the Secretary-General Pursuant to Paragraph 9 (b) (i) of Security Council Resolution 687 (1991),* U.N. Doc. S/23268 (December 4, 1991), p. 5; United Nations, Security Council, *Report of the Status if Compliance By Iraq With the Obligation Placed Upon It Under Section C of Security Council Resolution 687 (1991) and resolutions 707 (1991) and 715 (1991),* U.N. Doc. S/23993 (May 22, 1992), p. 5; and United Nations, Security Council, *Third Report By the Executive Chairman of the Special Commission Established By the Secretary-General Pursuant to Paragraph 9 (b) (i) of Security Council Resolution 687 (1991),* U.N. Doc. S/24108 (June 16, 1992), p 21.

Not until 1996, two years after Mr. Dorn's testimony before U.S. Senate, did the story of Khamisiyah begin to unfold about Americans having been exposed to Iraqi nerve gas and other chemical agents. Members of the U.S. Army's 37th Engineer Battalion blew up thirty-three Iraqi bunkers at Khamisiyah on March 4, 1991. Twenty-seven of thirty-seven members of the battalion in the area at the time of the explosion have suffered serious health problems since the war. Chemical alarms went off after the explosion and the soldiers donned their protective gear. Pentagon officials suggested that the U.N.'s public accounts of GB/GF were overlooked "in the crush of other intelligence information."[9] There is, of course, Mr. Dorn's May 1994 testimony that U.S. military personnel had been present on each of the U.N. Special Commission inspection teams at chemical sites in Iraq. A November 1991 intelligence report also informed the top national security agencies in the U.S. government of the chemical munitions at Khamisiyah.

In a novel approach to estimating the number of persons possibly exposed to nerve agents resulting from the destruction of some bunkers at Khamisiyah in March 1991, the Pentagon issued periodic guesses. In June 1996, about 400 engineers were thought to have been exposed. In September the number was upped to 5,000 persons. In early October 1996, the figure was raised to 15,000 and three weeks later to 20,000 and then 20,800 or those believed to be within a thirty-two mile radius of the explosion. In June 1997 the number of potential exposures to nerve gas resulting from the Khamisiyah explosion six years earlier was increased to 27,000.[10] In July 1997 the number of exposures to low levels of toxic chemicals was said to be as high as 80,000. According to news accounts, Pentagon officials explained in a memorandum prepared for Defense Secretary William S. Cohen that "...there is little evidence that low-level chemical exposure causes serious health problems, but the Pentagon should expect significant costs from performing medical examinations on exposed troops." The memo also

---

[9] Philip Shenon, "Legacy of Illness for Unit That Blew Up Bunkers," *New York Times* (August 11, 1996).

[10] Philip Shenon, "Report Shows U.S. Was Told in 1991 of Chemical Arms," *New York Times* (August 28, 1996), pp. A1, A8; Dana Priest, "Poison Gas Exposure Estimate Is Growing," *Washington Post* (October 2, 1996), p. A12; Philip Shenon, "U.S. Widens Search For Gulf Veterans Near Depot Blast," *New York Times* (October 23, 1996), pp. A1, A23; "20,800 Gulf Vets Exposed To Nerve Agents," *Veterans of Foreign Wars* (December 1996), p. 11; and "U.S. Raises Estimate of Troops Near Iraqi Chemical Arms," *Washington Post* (June 27, 1997), p. A26.

The New Face of War

warns defense officials to expect "renewed questions about whether the government is telling the whole story...."[11]

In late July 1997, the Defense Department again raised the estimate of American exposures to sarin nerve gas at Khamisiyah to 98,910 based on a new C.I.A. model that ostensibly accounts for a large number of relevant variables. The precise number of exposures—98,910, not 99,000 or about 100,000—implies a degree of certainty that is unwarranted, especially in light of the previous estimates. It presupposes that the nose count of the number of Americans was accurate and represents a snapshot in time when the sarin cloud passed overhead. The model shows that the sarin cloud or plume travelled 300 miles over 98,910 troops. Defense officials explained that the sarin did not dissipate as quickly as had been believed at first. The sarin, it appears, was soaked up by the sand and wooden crates holding the rockets when they were exploded; the sarin-soaked boxes remained viable for a longer period than previously postulated.

Defense Secretary William J. Perry and the Chairman of the Joint Chiefs of Staff, General John M. Shalikashvili, signed a May 25, 1994, memorandum for Gulf War veterans, stating in part that "there is no information, classified or unclassified, that indicates that chemical or biological weapons were used in the Persian Gulf."[12]

Yet, the Senate Banking Committee cited "a growing body of evidence" in May 1994 that exposure of Gulf War veterans to chemical and biological agents may be the cause for the complex of illnesses reported. Three primary sources of exposure were cited as a result of:

- Direct attack via missile, rocket, artillery or aircraft munitions;
- Blowback of intermittent low-level exposure to fallout from Coalition bombing of Iraqi chemical and biological warfare plants and munitions storage bunkers; and
- Nerve agent pre-treatment drugs administered to some U.S. military personnel that act similar to actual nerve agent.

---

[11] Rick Maze, "Pentagon Ups Number of Troops Exposed to Toxic Weapons in Persian Gulf," *Army Times* (July 21, 1997), p. 2.

[12] U.S., Congress, Senate, Committee on Banking, Housing, and Urban Affairs, *United States Dual-Use Exports to Iraq and Their Impact on the Health of the Persian Gulf War Veterans,* p. 98.

Direct Attack Exposures. Seventeen possible direct attack exposures have been recorded by the Senate Banking Committee as reported by members of the armed forces serving in the Gulf War. While unable to verify every detail of the reports of missile and rocket attacks or aerial explosions, additional data over time strengthened the veracity of the accounts. Many veterans located at the key rearward logistic and staging areas and those areas breached during the liberation of Kuwait reported seeing large numbers of dead or dying animals in the area after the attacks. One veteran said that "all the insects were dead too." The seventeen direct attack exposure events are summarized below (see map at Figure 7.1).

Event 1 – Cement City, January 17, 1991. Willie Hicks, a non-commissioned officer in charge of arms and ammunition shipments, heard a loud explosion followed by alarms at about 2:30 a.m. His face began to burn as he dashed to a bunker. Two or three days later he started to feel ill and noticed blood in his urine. Several other in his unit also began to suffer problems with their rectums. Their commanding officer ordered the soldiers not to discuss what had happened. Of the unit's 110 members, eighty-five suffer from medical problems and one has died. At the time of the event, one soldier was seriously incapacitated. Mr. Hicks suffers from memory loss, headaches, blood in his urine, insomnia, joint and muscle pain, deteriorating vision, loss of mobility in his left arm, night sweats, and diarrhea (sometimes bloody).

Event 2 – Camp 3, six to seven miles west of Port of Jubayl, Saudi Arabia, January 19, 1991. Petty Officer Sterling Simms reported that a "real bad explosion" occurred overhead between 2:00 and 3:00 a.m., setting off the alarms. While running toward bunkers, Petty Officer Simms said there was a sharp odor of ammonia in the air, his eyes burned and his skin stung. His unit donned chemical protection gear for two hours before the all-clear was sounded. Later, his unit was advised that they had heard a sonic boom and were told not to discuss the event. Petty Officer Simms questioned the sonic boom explanation since there was a fireball associated with the explosion. He has since experienced fatigue, sore joints, running nose, a chronic severe rash, and open sores; he has been treated for streptococcus infections. Five other witnesses corroborated Simms' testimony, adding further details to the incident. One witness had written a letter to his mother: *"I know they detected a cloud of dusty mustard gas because I was there with them, but today everyone denies it. I was there when they radioed the other camps north of us and warned them of the cloud."*

Figure 7.1

Approximate Locations of Direct Chemical (Biological) Exposure Events

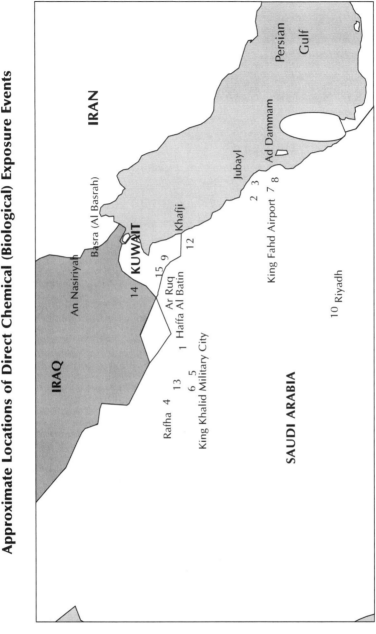

Source: U.S., Congress, Senate, Committee on Banking, Housing and Urban Affairs, *U.S. Chemical and Biological Warfare-Related Dual Use Exports to Iraq and Their Possible Impact on the Health Consequences of the Persian Gulf War*, 103d Cong., 2d sess. (May 25, 1994), p. 86.

Biological and Chemical "Blowback"

Event 3 – King Abdul Aziz Naval Air Station, three miles south of Port of Jubayl, Saudi Arabia, January 19, 1991. Four witnesses report an explosion in the early morning hours, followed by a mist. One witness reported that he began to feel a burning sensation on his arms, legs, the back of his neck, and on his ears and face. His lips felt numb.

Decontamination teams were called to respond. The next day they were told not to discuss the incident; the two explosions they heard were explained as being sonic booms. Their chemical gear was collected and replaced with new equipment. Witnesses reported sufferings in 1994 that included headaches, diarrhea, aching joints, blood-shot eyes, bloat, intestinal problems, and chronic fatigue.

Event 4 – Log Base Charlie, seven miles from the Iraqi border near Rafha. Valerie Sweatman was serving as a telecommunications specialist in the U.S. Army. One night in late February 1991 she was awakened by a sergeant and told to don her chemical gear. She put on her protective garment and mask and was putting on her gloves while walking outside. The next morning her hands were itching from the wrists down, and she developed blisters. She was treated for a skin condition. In 1994, Ms. Sweatman was suffering from headaches, exhaustion, fatigue, memory loss, nausea, muscle and joint pains, rectal and vaginal bleeding, and rashes.

Event 5 – In the desert in northern Saudi Arabia, early February 1991. Four witnesses testified that explosions at night and at least one during the day were accompanied by gas alert signals. In three cases, personnel were ordered to don chemical gear. They were told the explosion they heard was a sonic boom. Among the symptoms manifested in 1994 were headaches, joint and muscle pain, memory loss, urinary urgency, numbness, abnormal hair loss, and others. In one case, a man's wife suffers from rashes, fatigue, recurring yeast infections, menstrual irregularities, and others. One 23-year-old female soldier's child in 1994 had been getting fevers and rectal and penile discolorations.

Event 6 – Near King Khalid Military City, Saudi Arabia, February 22, 1991. Two witnesses reported that in the late afternoon or early evening an explosion occurred that triggered the chemical alarms. One witness believes the explosion was due to Patriot missiles intercepting three Scud missiles. After the explosions, her face, eyes, and throat began to burn, her nose began to run, she felt nauseous, and she had a funny taste in her mouth. A second witness located nearby reported similar symptoms, adding that he felt very tried. Among the shared symptoms are severe headaches, hair loss, insomnia, muscle and joint pain, and dizziness as well as other problems.

Event 7 – Vicinity of King Fahd International Airport, early morning January 20, 1991. A Marine lance corporal observed what he believed to be a Scud missile being shot out of the sky almost directly overhead by a Patriot missile. The explosion "blossomed like a flower" and exploded again when it hit the ground. He experienced a "very strong raunchy taste, like bitter burnt toast." When it became daylight, he noticed that his hands were tingling and looked as though they had been sunburned. Two days later while on patrol he saw several dead sheep and a couple of camels that appeared very sick. He suffers from joint pain, dental problems, muscle pains and spasms, insomnia, blurred vision, and other symptoms. Since his return from the Gulf his wife has had bladder surgery, a swollen thyroid, and other symptoms.

Event 8 – Dhahran, approximately January 20, 1991. After a Patriot missile intercepted an incoming Scud, one witness reported that her eyes began to burn, she smelled an ammonia-like odor, and she began to experience headaches, nausea, vomiting, and sensitivity to bright lights. She suffers from memory loss, joint and muscle pain, dizziness, gastrointestinal problems, and other symptoms. A second witness recalled becoming nauseous, weak, and dizzy. He suffers joint pain, memory loss, insomnia, and symptoms similar to other Gulf War Syndrome veterans.

Event 9 – During the ground war: Task Force Ripper. Three witnesses testified concerning detection of chemical agents in Kuwait. One witness, using a FOX NBC reconnaissance system, detected lewisite blister vapors around the Ahmed Al Jaber Airbase. After reporting the findings to division headquarters, he was ordered to send the print-out tape of the detection up the chain of command. A report came back that the FOX had alerted on oil smoke. A second witness reported a lewisite detection following an artillery attack up wind of his unit; the agent detected was in a concentration considered to produce casualties but not death. A mustard gas detection by three FOX vehicles at Ahmed Al Jaber Airfield was cited by a third witness.

Event 10 – Riyadh, date unknown. During the first Scud attack on Riyadh, a driver/mechanic reported three missiles had come in. The chemical alarms went off and troops donned their protective gear. The witness saw a rainbow in the sky after the attack. He immediately began to experience nausea and a sore throat, his nose began to run, and his eyes burned. These symptoms never went away, and he also suffers from memory loss, rashes, aching joints, headaches, rectal bleeding, nausea, and others.

Event 11 – Log Base Alpha, around midnight, January 18, 1991. A non-commissioned officer was awakened when a Scud intercepted by a

Patriot missile set off a large explosion, triggered chemical alarms, and positive readings by chemical detectors. Headquarters told them that they had heard a sonic boom. A few days later, he was too sick to work. He experienced burning eyes and lungs, diarrhea, sores, nausea and a runny nose. Three years later he was suffering from headaches, chronic fatigue, joint and muscle pain, rashes, insomnia, gastrointestinal problems, and other symptoms.

Event 12 – Near Ras Al Khafji, January 1991. A Marine Corp staff sergeant said that four or five days into the air war chemical alarms sounded and also those at his unit's supply area twenty miles away. The following night his platoon began falling ill. He suffered from headaches, nausea, and diarrhea for a day; others were sick longer. In 1994, he still suffered from headaches, joint pain, memory loss, insomnia, dizziness, and other symptoms. His wife suffers from fatigue, joint and muscle pain, menstrual irregularities, and chest pain.

Event 13 – West of Log Base Echo, January 19 or 20, 1991. A military police staff sergeant said that his unit NBC non-commissioned officer reported that they were under chemical attack. Afterward everyone in the unit had runny noses. He suffers from headaches, fatigue, joint and muscle pain, rashes, insomnia, gastrointestinal problems, dizziness, and others. His wife experiences fatigue, menstrual irregularities, joint pain, hair loss, and other symptoms.

Event 14 – In Iraq near the Kuwait border, February 25, 1991. An Army mechanic smelled a sweet, almond-like taste and smell, accompanied by a burning in his throat and lungs, watering eyes, blurry vision, nausea, dizziness, and diarrhea. No one else seemed affected. He has been sick ever since, including fatigue, joint and muscle pain, memory loss, rashes, insomnia, gastrointestinal problems, and other symptoms.

Event 15 – February 24, 1991. A Marine unit's FOX vehicle confirmed positive readings for a nerve agent and for mustard gas after an encounter with chemical mines. A second detecting device gave the same positive reading. General Schwartzkopf told reporters that he considered the chemical agent detection event to be "bogus."

Event 16 – During the ground war. British troops discovered Iraqi chemical mines on the Gulf battlefield; an official said that the incident was reported to the Prime Minister's war cabinet.

Event 17 – Taif, Saudi Arabia, January 21, 1991. A sergeant's unit of U.S. Air Force F-111 fighter bombed thirty-two chemical targets, 113 bunkers, eleven missile sites, and four mine entrances. The aircraft were washed down with water rather than special decontamination solution. On January 21, after decontaminating several aircraft after a bombing raid, an airman's face began to burn and swell; he noticed a pungent odor and began to experience headaches, nausea, vomiting and diarrhea. In 1994, he suffered from headaches, fatigue, joint and muscle pain, memory loss, insomnia and other symptoms. His wife suffers from similar symptoms.[13]

The Senate Committee on Banking, Housing and Urban Affairs drew several conclusions from these seventeen incidents of possible direct attacks against Coalition forces with chemical and/or biological warfare agents.

- Chemical or mixed agent attacks, from multiple witnesses, appear to have occurred. Symptoms were manifested simultaneously with chemical alarms going off, Patriot anti-missile missiles intercepting Scuds, and alert klaxons sounding.
- The smells, tastes, burning, stinging, and numbness reported by witnesses are consistent with chemical or mixed agents.
- Chemical gear is removed and replaced when contaminated or when their prescribed useful life has expired.
- Sonic booms are not accompanied by fireballs; ordinarily a commander would not prohibit troops from discussing sonic booms.
- Rates of illness in the exposed units are said to be high.
- Commanding officers did not give credible explanations for the events to service men and women.
- "The Department of Defense has consistently denied that there is evidence to exposure to chemical and biological warfare agents by U.S. forces, altering its position on specific aspects of this issue only when challenged with evidence that is difficult to dispute."[14]

News accounts in December 1996 reported that Iraq had developed and may have used the biological agent aflatoxin, a long-term cancer-causing agent, that would have been impossible to detect. The near-term effects of aflatoxin are similar to those reported by veterans suffering from Gulf War Syndrome.[15]

---

[13] U.S., Congress, Senate, Committee on Banking, Housing and Urban Affairs, *U.S. Chemical and Biological Warfare-Related Dual Use Exports,* pp. 58-84.

[14] *Ibid.,* pp. 84-85.

[15] Hanchette and Brewer, "U.N., Intelligence Reports Show Iraq Could Have Spread Deadly Aflatoxin."

Blowback Exposures From Coalition Bombing. Serious concerns were expressed during the war of possible exposure of Coalition forces resulting from fallout of the bombings of Iraqi chemical, biological and nuclear facilities and storage depots and bunkers.

The Lawrence Livermore National Laboratory provided a report to the Air Force three months before the start of the Gulf War about the possibility of blowback of deadly nerve agents that could endanger American troops from bombing Iraq's chemical weapons facilities. The study predicted dispersal over an area ten times greater than that estimated later by Pentagon and C.I.A. studies.[16] In a widely circulated April 1996 report on proliferation released by the Office of the Secretary of Defense, a quotation from a report to Congress is included and set apart from the text in a box to give it prominence:

During December [1990], a team was formed in...the United States...to determine the most effective way to attack Iraq's arsenal of CW/BW [chemical warfare/biological warfare] weapons. Several experiments were conducted.... Finally, through the timing of attacks and choice of munitions, planners were able to minimize the chance for toxins to spread. *No chemical or biological agents were detected after the attacks and no CW/BW collateral damage was experienced.* [emphasis added][17]

Like other hazardous substances, chemical agent dispersal is influenced by wind direction and speed, temperature, precipitation, topography, and humidity. Satellite imagery confirmed that debris from the Coalition bombing of chemical and biological plants and storage areas was dispersed upwardly and caused chemical and/or biological agents to be carried by upper atmosphere currents, distributing "trace amounts" of chemical fallout over down-wind locations. The French Ministry of Defense reported on February 4, 1991, that blowback from the Coalition bombing of Iraqi chemical plants had been detected in small quantities and that there was "a little bit everywhere."

A Czechoslovak anti-chemical defense unit provided continuous chemical intelligence and surveillance in the headquarters of the northern region troops located in King Khalid Military City and 4th and 20th brigades of

---

[16] "Chemical Risk to Gulf Troops Was Forecast," *USA Today* (August 14, 1997), p. 1.

[17] U.S., Department of Defense, *Proliferation: Threat and Response* (1996), p. A-12.

Saudi Arabia. The unit was equipped with the most modern chemical surveillance and control technology. The Commander's Report for January 1-February 28, 1991, contained the following:

- Borderline, life-threatening concentrations of distilled mustard (HD) and sarin (GB) nerve agent were identified several times.
- The source was identified as "probably the result of the Allies' air attacks on the [chemical] storage facilities...."

One U.S. soldier reported that a Czech colonel, the commanding officer, told him that Iraq "did hit us with chemicals." After a Scud attack, the Czech unit detected traces of sarin and another agent. When reported to the U.S. command officials, the Czech colonel was asked not to say anything about it.

According to a French report, two chemical weapons alarms were triggered in the vicinity of King Khalid Military City when a storm blew wind from Iraq. Mustard and nerve agents were detected on January 24 and 25.

At another location some forty miles east of King Khalid Military City, more than thirty chemical alarms went off at once. The unit received word via radio that the Coalition had bombed a nerve agent plant about 150 miles away. The soldiers were told to take no action.

The evidence strongly suggests that Coalition forces were exposed to mixed chemical agents as a result of the blowback from the bombing of Iraq's facilities and that the resulting fallout may be contributing to the health problems associated with Gulf War Syndrome. The U.S. Senate report also concluded:

The combination of prevailing wind directions, the open terrain, the lack of structural impediments, and other factors...indicate that chemical and possibly nuclear and biological agents from allied bombings became airborne and were being blown and carried across coalition forces emplacements along the Saudi-Iraqi and Saudi-Kuwait border.

Chemical nerve agents, such as Sarin and others, are known to have a cumulative effect, i.e., they have a slow rate of detoxification. Little is known about the long-term effects of continuous low levels of exposure. Many of the veterans claiming to be suffering from Gulf War Syndrome are exhibiting symptoms of neurophysical disorders.[18]

Inoculations. "Military intelligence reports indicated there was a real possibility that Iraqi forces would employ biological and chemical weapons," Major General Ronald Blanck, commander of the Walter Reed Army Medical Center, explained. "In response to that threat, anthrax vaccine and botulinum vaccine were administered." The anthrax vaccine was administered to 150,000 soldiers and 8,000 were given the botulinum vaccine. Soldiers were also given a course of medication used for neuro-muscular disorders called pyridostigmine bromide (PB). Several soldiers reported side effects from PB, such as uncontrollable twitching eyes, runny nose, excessive frothing from the mouth, and neck and shoulder pain.[19]

Drawing on the results of a 1996 survey of Gulf War veterans, researchers for the Veterans of Foreign Wars found a potential linkage between those troops receiving the vaccinations and those afflicted with Gulf War Syndrome. See Table 7.1. The director of the VFW's Action Corps, Dennis Cullinan, says that "...there appears to be a correlation between various vaccinations given to troops as precautionary measures and the illnesses from which they now suffer."[20] The percentage reporting illness increases substantially when insect repellents used in the Gulf were combined with vaccinations. The 1996 survey also showed that some spouses and/or children of veterans who took the vaccinations developed the same symptoms.

The mystery surrounding the origins of Gulf War Syndrome deepened in 1997 when blood tests revealed the presence of a synthetic version of squalene in blood samples of hundreds of veterans. Squalene is an experimental adjuvant that is mixed with medicine to help the body respond more quickly in creating protective antibodies against disease or infection. The test results were similar to those from test subjects in experimental HIV virus and sexually transmitted disease studies being conducted at the National Institutes of Health. The Walter Reed Army Medical Center also has been experimenting with immunizations that could be effective against the HIV virus, which causes AIDS, using squalene as an adjuvant. The Defense

---

[18] *Ibid.,* pp. 132-33.

[19] *Ibid.,* pp. 134-38.

[20] "Persian Gulf Vets Still Searching for Answers," p. 2.

Table 7.1
Inoculation Syndrome?

Percentage of veterans who received a vaccination then reported illness:

Anthrax	68%
Pyridostigmine Bromide (CB)	48
Botulism	35
Anthrax and Botulism	31
Botulism and PB	28
PB and Anthrax	39
Anthrax, Botulism and PB	25

Source: "Persian Gulf Vets Still Searching for Answers," *Checkpoint* (January/February 1997), p. 2.

Department denies the use of squalene. Yet, 400 ill soldiers showing antibodies to this synthetic squalene adjuvant stand in direct contradiction to the Pentagon denials. One immunologist who has conducted some of the laboratory tests on the blood of Gulf War veterans responds: "He can say they never used squalene all he wants. You can't escape facts that the antibodies are showing up."[21]

The Pentagon maintained that "there is no reliable scientific data that shows that a one-time, low-level exposure to sarin would create the sleepiness, memory loss, joint pains and other illnesses affecting some veterans."[22] The flip-side of this pseudo-scientific statement is left unstated: *There is no reliable scientific data showing that one-time, low-level exposure to sarin would not create the sleepiness, memory loss, joint pains and other illnesses affecting some veterans.* Fortunately, skeptics like Senator John D. Rockefeller, III, help to place the July 1997 revelations into an appropriate perspective: "I have very real concerns that the exposure was, in fact, greater than the Pentagon is now reporting. And I continue to be worried that there were 'other Khamisiyahs' that we still don't know about."[23]

---

[21] Paul M. Rodriguez, "Pentagon Denies Use of Compounds," *Washington Times* (August 15, 1997), p. A3, and "Anti-HIV Mix Found in Gulf Veterans," *Washington Times* (August 1, 1997), pp. A1, A8.

[22] Dana Priest, "Gas Exposure in Gulf War Revised," *Washington Post* (July 24, 1997), p. A28.

[23] *Ibid.,* and "U.S. Tells Gulf Veterans of Exposure During War," *Washington Times* (July 25, 1997), p. A4.

Why Are Numerous Gulf War Veterans Ill?

About 697,000 American men and women served in Operations Desert Shield and Desert Storm from August 1990 to June 1991. American fatalities included 148 combat deaths and 145 deaths due to disease or accidents; wounded Americans numbered 467. Upon their return from the Persian Gulf, some began to experience debilitating illnesses. The most common symptoms included fatigue, muscle and joint pain, memory loss, and severe headaches. In early 1992, the Defense Department conducted an epidemiologic study of one unit reporting several ill members but found no evidence of disease. The Veterans' Administration established a health registry where Gulf War veterans could report their symptoms.

Reports continued to mount and medical programs were established to identify and treat Gulf War illnesses. "By early 1995," says the Presidential Advisory Committee on Gulf War Veterans' Illnesses, "the clinical evaluation programs had enrolled more than 49,000 veterans and the research portfolio included more than 30 studies. Many medical and scientific experts—from inside and outside the government—had reviewed the government's efforts.... Still, a substantial number of Gulf War veterans did not have the answers they sought about what kind of illnesses they had, about exposures in the Gulf region that might have made them sick, or about the strength of the country's commitment to veterans."[24]

It is no wonder many veterans are still looking for answers. Members of the 24th Naval Mobile Construction Battalion, for instance, explain that something exploded over their camps in northern Saudi Arabia early in the morning of January 19, 1991, the third day of the war. Chemical alarms sounded as a dense cloud of gas floated over their camps. Within minutes many experienced burning sensations on their skin, their lips turned numb and their throats began to tighten. They washed down for decontamination but some members of the unit began to manifest blisters. Commanders insisted the noise was a sonic boom and there was no need for alarm. Of the 152 members serving in the battalion, 114 were sick with illnesses attributed to the war in September 1996. Many had been hospitalized several times, and adverse job and career choices were forced on them.

In response to Philip Shenon's investigative report for the *New York Times* in September 1996, a statement from the Pentagon was issued: "Reports confirm that a Scud missile aimed toward Dhahran was intercepted at

---

[24] U.S., *Presidential Advisory Committee on Gulf War Veterans' Illnesses: Final Report* (Washington, D.C.: Government Printing Office, December 1996), pp. 1-2.

high altitude in the area [of the 24th Naval Mobile Construction Battalion] around the time of the reported incident." The statement also said that the ailments reported by members of the unit were not consistent with a chemical attack and that rocket propellant probably was the cause of the symptoms they experienced.

Newly declassified logs made available to the Gulf War Veterans of Georgia show that U.S. forces were alerted in the early morning of January 19 to a chemical attack near the port of Jubayl, or the area where the 24th Battalion was located. A British soldier in the region reported a positive reading of mustard gas.[25]

Charles Jackson, a Department of Veterans Affairs physician at Tuskegee, Alabama, who has cared for many members of the 24th Battalion, said both his department and the Pentagon were ignoring evidence that these veterans had become ill from their service in the Gulf, possibly through exposure to chemical or biological agents. "There's something going down," he said. "I don't know what they're hiding."[26]

The Presidential Advisory Committee went to some lengths to find that Americans were not exposed to chemical and biological agents during the Gulf War. The Committee's Final Report appears concerned about ratifying government denials of such exposures.

- "...the best evidence available to the Committee indicates U.S. personnel were not exposed to biological warfare agents during the Gulf War. This conclusion is based on imperfect information."
- "Based on information compiled to date, there is no persuasive evidence of intentional Iraqi use of CW agents during the war. Again, the best available information is less than ideal."
- "The best evidence available indicates theaterwide contamination with CW agent fallout from the air is highly unlikely."[27]

The Committee's December 1996 *Final Report* also confirmed the Czech detections of nerve agent at two locations northeast of Hafir al Batin, Saudi Arabia, on January 19, 1991, and mustard agent at a site six miles north of King Khalid Military City. Noting that the Defense Department cannot

---

[25] Philip Shenon, "Many Veterans of the Gulf War Detail Illnesses From Chemicals," *New York Times* (September 20, 1996), pp. A1, A24.

[26] *Ibid.*

[27] U.S., *Presidential Advisory Committee...Final Report,* pp. 38-40.

---

identify the source of the chemical agents for any of the detections, the Committee says that "low-level exposure—at the detection sites—must be presumed."[28]

The causes for the illnesses suffered by the approximately 100,000 veterans and many family members remain a mystery. Presumptive conclusions, even when tagged with pseudo-scientific labels as "imperfect information," "information...less than ideal," and "best evidence available," are not at all conclusive. What is wrong with simply stating: "the Committee does not have enough information to make a reasoned judgment?" The Committee does say that "many of the health concerns of Gulf War veterans may never be resolved fully because of the lack of data," but that lack of data dressed up as "imperfect information" and "less than ideal" did not prevent the Committee from making very carefully hedged preemptive conclusions.[29]

By August 1997 almost half of the Committee members were back-pedalling from their earlier conclusions since, as one panel member put it, "...we now know that chemicals were scattered across the battlefield." Another Committee member, Rolando Rios, said that "we have to make some changes. I personally think that it was inappropriate for us to say that it was unlikely that chemical weapons were responsible for the health problems. How can we say it's unlikely if we haven't done the homework?"[30]

The Committee's November 1997 *Special Report* recommended a new panel, one that would be independent of the Department of Defense, to oversee the Department's investigation into possible chemical weapons exposures. "The legacy of the Gulf War should be a recognition by all Americans that the government acknowledges and honors its obligations to care for Gulf War veterans," the advisory committee concluded, "not the perception the government cannot be trusted to candidly address their health concerns." The *Special Report* goes on to say that "time after time over the past 10 months, the Committee has battled with DOD [Department of Defense] about its fact finding and interpretation related to possible CW agent incidents—an approach we believe serves to exacerbate DOD's credibility problems."[31]

---

[28] *Ibid.*, p. 41.

[29] *Ibid.*, executive summary.

[30] Philip Shenon, "Half of Gulf-Illness Panel Now Calls Gas a Possible Factor," *New York Times* (August 19, 1997).

[31] U.S., *Presidential Advisory Committee on Gulf War Veterans' Illnesses: Special Report* (Washington, D.C.: Government Printing Office, October 1997), pp. 1,19.

Most of the principal critics of the Pentagon's handling of the Gulf War Syndrome greeted the creation of the new panel with alacrity. Former Senator Warren B. Rudman will head the five-person oversight panel whose purpose is to ensure that the Pentagon's investigations "meet the highest standards."[32]

Gag Warfare?

Many believe the Pentagon is engaged in a massive cover-up of the actual circumstances leading to the exposure of thousand of veterans to chemical and biological agents. A *Washington Post* editorial in April 1997 opines that "it is clear that the CIA as well as the Defense Department has been complicit in a stonewall, if not a coverup."[33] Congressman Christopher Shays, whose staff has been investigating the health problems of Gulf War veterans, said: "I believe with all my heart and soul that both the Department of Defense and Department of Veterans Affairs are covering up the fact that our troops were exposed to chemicals and maybe biological agents."[34]

As if to validate these judgments, the Defense Department withdrew intelligence documents relating to the Khamisiyah ammunition depot from its Internet site, GulfLINK, in February 1996, four months before it was disclosed that some U.S. personnel may have been exposed to chemicals there after the war in March 1991. One of those withdrawn reports said that thirty-seven storage buildings and 10,000 tons of ammunition at the depot were destroyed by air attacks on February 3, 1991. The United Nations and Defense Department insist that the nerve gas at Khamisiyah was stored in a single bunker and in a dirt pit on the outer edge of the depot—they insist neither was damaged in the air war. Yet, U.N. inspectors, in reference to Al Tuz, Khamisiyah, and Muhammadiyat, in October-November 1991 reported that "in a few cases, due to extensive destruction by coalition bombing, it was not possible to observe and count all munitions...."[35]

James Tuite, the principal investigator of Gulf War illnesses for the U.S. Senate in 1993-94, said, "I find it disturbing that all of the documents

---

[32] David Brown, "Independent Panel Recommended To Oversee Probe of Gulf War Illness," *Washington Post* (November 9, 1997), p. A4.

[33] "Sloppily and Unreliable," *Washington Post* [Editorial] (April 11, 1997), p. A26.

[34] Shenon, "Legacy of Illness for Unit That Blew Up Bunkers."

[35] United Nations, Security Council, *Report of the Executive Chairman of the Special Commission Established By the Secretary-General Pursuant to Paragraph 9 (b) (i) of Security Council Resolution 687 (1991)*, U.N. Doc. S/23268 (December 4, 1991), p. 5.

---

regarding Khamisiyah were withdrawn, including those that showed that 37 bunkers had been destroyed by the bombing. The whole appearance that we see emerging here is one of political or bureaucratic damage limitation, admitting only what they absolutely have to admit."[36] Two months later, Matthew Puglisi, director of the American Legion's Persian Gulf task force, called for a criminal investigation when he was informed that the Pentagon cannot locate computer logs from the Gulf War headquarters in Saudi Arabia for an eight-day period that coincides with the destruction of the chemical weapons bunker at Khamisiyah.[37]

Two persons in particular have alleged a massive government cover-up regarding the exposure of veterans and their families to chemical and biological agents. Joyce Riley, a seasoned nurse and Air Force captain in the reserve, formed the American Gulf War Veterans Association. Its purpose is to notify the American public that U.S. service men and women were knowingly placed in harms way, biological and chemical warfare was used [by Iraq], many have become sick from the immunizations that were required, the disease is communicable, the Veterans' Administration hospitals and the Department of Defense are not telling the truth, and many Desert Stormers are sick and dying.[38] The Association offers an information packet, video tapes, and audio cassettes that make the case for certain points of view on Gulf War Syndrome, its sources, and the governments attempts to hide the full story.

Captain Riley includes reports, newspaper articles, and government documents that support the purpose statement of the Association. Riley offers ten reasons for the alleged cover-up of Gulf War Syndrome:

- U.S. officials chose not to acknowledge Iraq's use of chemical and biological agents.
- Cost of medical care for afflicted veterans would be prohibitive.
- American chemical suits and detection alarms were ineffective.
- To keep from soldiers that their leaders sent them into battle with worthless protection against chemical and biological warfare.

---

[36] Philip Shenon, "U.S. Jets Pounded Iraqi Arms Depot Storing Nerve Gas," *New York Times* (October 3, 1996), pp. A1, A18.

[37] "Defense & Diplomacy – Gulf War Logs," *Washington Post* (December 14, 1996), p. A8.

[38] Joyce Riley, R.N., B.S.N., Letter to "Dear Gulf War Veteran and/or Supporter" (Sugarland, Tex.: American Gulf War Veterans Association, 1996).

- Cover the secret that the U.S. provided Iraq with chemical weapons and technology and materials to manufacture their own for use against Iran (1980-88 war).
- The U.S. used chemical weapons in the Gulf.
- The U.S. struck a deal with Israel after Iraq attacked Israel with nerve gas, killing at least three Israeli citizens, to keep them from retaliating in order to save the Middle East peace process.
- American soldiers were not allowed to refuse the unapproved, experimental, and investigational botulinum toxoid vaccine.
- Admitting the Iraqi use of chemical and biological weapons would embarrass the Bush [and Clinton] presidencies.
- Admission would seriously embarrass General Colin L. Powell.[39]

Another government cover-up theorist is Patrick G. Eddington. Both Mr. Eddington and his wife, Robin, resigned from the Central Intelligence Agency in 1996. They insist that the C.I.A. has documents showing tens of thousands of Americans may have been exposed to chemical weapons during the Gulf War. They allege that their research inside the C.I.A. turned up sixty incidents in which nerve gas and other chemicals were released near American troops. "The evidence of chemical exposure among our troops is overwhelming," Mr. Eddington contends, "but the Government won't deal with it." Mrs. Eddington said that the C.I.A's attitude over the possibility of chemical exposures was one of "cowardice and conformity."[40]

Mr. Eddington wrote a very peculiar book after his departure from the C.I.A. which is difficult to track. In essence the book is really three books in one. While telling the "true story" of what happened in the Gulf War, it mixes what are presented as facts with hyperbole that body-slams everyone, in Mr. Eddington's eyes, that may have one time or another wronged him. The third aspect of the book is monologue mixed with discourse on how the C.I.A. and the Defense Department put pressure on him to resign. Mr. Eddington's heart is in the right place in terms of doing whatever is necessary to help those suffering from Gulf War Syndrome. In the end, however, his book is filled more with his pain than his logic.[41]

---

[39] Joyce Riley, R.N., B.S.N.,"Reasons for the Cover-Up of 'Gulf War Syndrome,'" *Gulf War Syndrome,* information packet (Sugarland, Tex.: American Gulf War Veterans Association, 1996).

[40] Philip Shenon, "Ex-C.I.A. Analysts Assert Cover-Up," *New York Times* (October 30, 1996), pp. A1, A14.

[41] Patrick G. Eddington, *Gassed in the Gulf: The Inside Story of the Pentagon-CIA Cover-Up of the Gulf War Syndrome* (Washington, D.C.: Insignia Publishing Company, 1997).

The cross-fire between the mainline truth-seekers, federal officials, veterans organizations, sick veterans and their families, the Presidential Advisory Committee, and cover-up theorists make any judgment about Gulf War Syndrome extremely difficult and encourages a human tendency to hedge when all of the facts are not on the table. Suffice it to say the single most important fact is the illnesses suffered by some 100,000 Gulf War veterans and many of their families. The objective of making judgments about what is known must be driven by two factors. What happened to the veterans in the Gulf? And, how do we avoid similar consequences in future conflicts? All other matters are so much excess baggage that should be left behind, including bureaucratic gamesmanship, rearranging facts to be consistent with what the boss or the agency, department, office or whatever has already said, and the all-too-human "get even" score settling. The facts that we know should speak for themselves. Since we do not have all the facts and our efforts are swamped by the unknowns and unknowables, we must extend our reach ever so carefully to make reasoned judgments of events.

The evidence and eyewitness accounts contained in the 1994 U.S. Senate Committee on Banking, Housing and Urban Affairs are very persuasive. This writer knows how nervous, uncertain people in wartime can leap to conclusions that may not be valid. On the other hand, 14,000 chemical alarms during the Gulf War are hard to swallow as all being "false."

Three conclusions seem warranted as a rational extension of what we know:

- Saddam Hussein probably used chemical weapons with incapacitating doses of mustard and nerve agents against Coalition forces in the areas of the Port of Jubayl and King Khalid Military City. His objective was probably political: to break up the Coalition.
- Given the first conclusion, the report of a nerve agent attack against Tel Aviv might also be correct. First reported on CNN at the time, the events were later corrected and explained as persons who had manifested psychosomatic symptoms.
- The blowback of trace amounts of chemical agents and fallout on Coalition forces is very probable. Chemical and biological weapons specialists are generally very good at what they do. They know what happens at the point of attack and the immediately surrounding area. The chemical or biological cloud, however, resembles an elongated plume. Where the plume is narrowest and furthest from the impact or dispersal point, we know very little about the effects on humans and,

importantly, the cumulative effects of exposure to low levels of multiple agents and other environmental disturbances. Beyond the plume, we know nothing. Trace amounts of nerve agent are assumed to be inconsequential. Maybe. Maybe not.

James Tuite draws just the right conclusion: "There is plentiful and significant causal and medical evidence to support the claim that their illnesses are the result of either the immediate or delayed toxic effects of exposure to chemical, and possibly biological, warfare agents."[42] In June 1997, Donna Heivilin of the U.S. General Accounting Office arrived at the right conclusions during testimony before the Senate Committee on Veterans Affairs.

While the government found no evidence that biological weapons were deployed during the Gulf War, the United States lacked the capability to promptly detect biological agents, and the effects of one agent, aflatoxin, would not be observed for many years.

Evidence from various sources indicates that chemical agents were present at Khamisiyah, Iraq, and elsewhere on the battlefield. The magnitude of the exposure to chemical agents has not been fully resolved. As we recently reported, 16 of 21 sites categorized by Gulf War planners as nuclear, biological, and chemical (NBC) facilities were destroyed. However, the United Nations Special Commission found after the war that not all the possible NBC targets had been identified by U.S. planners.... Regarding those the Commission has not yet inspected, we determined that each was attacked by coalition aircraft during the Gulf War. *One of these sites is located within the Kuwait theater of operations in close proximity to the border, where coalition ground forces were located.*[43] [emphasis added]

---

[42] James J. Tuite, III, "Persian Gulf Syndrome and the Delayed Toxic Effects of Chemical Agent Exposure" (March 1995), p. 1. Photocopy.

[43] Donna Heivilin, *Gulf War Illnesses: Reexamination of Research Emphasis and Improved Monitoring of Clinical Progress Needed,* testimony before the Senate Committee on Veterans Affairs, GAO/T-NSIAD-97-191 (Washington, D.C.: General Accounting Office, June 25, 1997), pp. 17-18. See also Philip Shenon, "Study Links Chemicals to Sick Veterans," *New York Times* (June 15, 1997), and "GAO Ties Gulf War Illness to Nerve Gas," *Washington Times* (June 15, 1997), p. A4.

A General Accounting Office (GAO) report released in June 1997 recognized that "six years after the war, little is conclusively known about the causes of Gulf War veteran's illnesses." Offering a critique of the Presidential Advisory Committee report that was endorsed by the Defense Department, the GAO report notes that several questions remain open. One is the Committee's conclusion that stress is likely an important contributing factor to the broad range of illnesses reported. The GAO found that the link between stress and the veterans physical symptoms was not well established by the evidence. Secondly, the GAO believes the Committee was too quick to discount a virulent parasite (leishmania tropica) as a potential risk factor. Thirdly, the Committee, in the face of substantial evidence that mustard chemical warfare agents might be associated with delayed or long-term health effects similar to those experienced by Gulf War veterans, concluded that the illnesses reported were not due to exposure to these agents. Finally, the GAO cited unresolved questions concerning the possible exposure of veterans to (1) the fallout of chemical agents resulting from the bombing of Iraq's suspected chemical weapons storage sites, and (2) the biological agent aflatoxin whose health effects may not be manifested for months or years after exposure.[44]

Fourteen federal and private organizations were examining potential exposure of U.S. military personnel to chemical agents. In addition, the Department of Defense Inspector General's Defense Criminal Investigation Service was investigating the missing 200 pages (of 237 pages total) of log entries on nuclear, biological, and chemical events during the Gulf War. The logs, which might provide assistance in identifying potential exposures to toxic agents, mysteriously disappeared.[45]

It is important that this work be done well. Something happened to poison U.S. troops in the Gulf War—we need to understand these events before we send young Americans again into potentially contaminated environments.

---

[44] U.S., General Accounting Office, *Gulf War Illnesses' Improved Monitoring of Clinical Progress and Reexamination of Research Emphases Are Needed,* GAO/NSIAD-97-163 (Washington, D.C.: General Accounting Office, June 1997), pp. 1-5.

[45] U.S., General Accounting Office, *Gulf War Illnesses: Public and Private Efforts Relating to Exposures of U.S. Personnel to Chemical Attacks* (Washington, D.C.: General Accounting Office, October 1997), p. 2.

CHAPTER 8

Super-Terrorism

At exactly 12:18 p.m., Friday, February 26, 1993, a massive explosion ripped through the B-2 level of the parking garage of the World Trade Center in New York City. The force of this blast (2,000 pounds of TNT) moved at a velocity of more than 15,000 feet per second, creating a crater 150 feet in diameter and five stories deep. Vehicles parked four stories below and 600 hundred feet away from the center of the detonation were destroyed. The forty cars closest to the blast were reduced to scraps of metal no larger than footballs. Fortunately, the toll in human lives was contained. Of the 50,000 people in the World Trade Center at the time of the explosion, six were killed and fifteen were injured by the blast itself. An additional 985 people suffered smoke inhalation injuries when power generators and exhaust systems within the World Trade Center and the adjacent Vista Hotel were knocked off-line and smoke from the explosion traveled up the elevator shafts of the two buildings.

The World Trade Center blast marked a new threshold for terrorism in the United States. Heretofore, international terrorist incidents in America usually had been constrained, low-level attacks. The World Trade Center was unique both in the magnitude of the explosion and the fact that it was carried out by individuals directly connected to overseas terrorist organizations for avowedly international purposes. This single incident served most clearly to demonstrate America's vulnerability inside the United States. The bombing scarred the American psyche and left the public with an unsettling sense of insecurity.[1] According to a poll conducted four years after the bombing of the World Trade Center, more than three out of four believed there was a chance that terrorists could use nuclear, biological or chemical weapons against an American city.[2]

Shortly after 10 p.m. on June 25, 1996, Air Force sentries on the roof of the Khobar Towers high-rise apartment complex in Dhahran, Saudi Arabia,

---

[1] Frank G. Wickersham, III, "Technology Fault Lines" (McLean, Va.: Strategic Planning International, Inc., November 9, 1994), pp. 8-11.

[2] "Americans Unmoved By Washington's Big Stories," *Pew Research Center* (April 11, 1997).

---

saw two men park a tanker truck adjacent to a fence just eighty feet away. Many of the 2,900 U.S. airmen present were sleeping. Recognizing the possibility of a truck bomb, the sentries successfully evacuated the first three floors of Building 131 when an estimated 5,000 pounds of TNT exploded. The face of the apartment building was ripped away by the blast and four other buildings were damaged. Nineteen Americans were killed and another 547 were wounded. See Figure 8.1.

The event marked another new threshold for terrorist incidents against Americans outside of the United States since the blast was significantly greater than the next largest explosion used by terrorists in Saudia Arabia. The force of the blast left a crater eighty-five feet wide and thirty-five feet deep.[3] This unprecedented explosion, initially estimated by the Pentagon to have been a 20,000-pound TNT bomb, was described as a "weapon of mass destruction" by General John M. Shalikashvili, then-Chairman of the Joint Chiefs of Staff.[4]

The bombing offered just a glimpse of super-terrorism's destructive— and strategically eviscerating—potential. Defense Secretary William J. Perry was clear that the Khobar Towers bombing "dramatically underscored that for U.S. forces deployed overseas terrorism is a fact of life." He continued that "...the Khobar Towers attack should be seen as a watershed event pointing the way to a radically new mind set and dramatic changes in the way we protect our forces deployed overseas from this growing threat."[5] The Force Protection Initiative announced by Secretary Perry would be modeled on the assumption that terrorists would soon turn to weapons of mass destruction.

The greater availability of weapons of mass destruction, combined with a growing fanaticism of religious and ethnic extremist groups, is the root cause of the emergence on to the world stage of "super-terrorism"—the

---

[3] John T. Correll, "Fallout From Khobar Towers," *Air Force Magazine* (September 1997), p. 3; Bill Gertz, "Terrorism and the Force," *Air Force Magazine* (February 1997); and Jack Kelley, "Warning Plentiful in Saudi Bombing," *USA Today* (August 26, 1996), p. 16A.

[4] Pat Cooper and Robert Holzer, "Shalikashvili: Plan for Terror," *Defense News* (August 12-18, 1996), pp. 1, 35.

[5] William J. Perry, Secretary of Defense, "Report to the President on the Protection of U.S. Forces Deployed Abroad" in *Defense Issues,* 11-80 (Washington, D.C.: Office of the Assistant Secretary of Defense for Public Affairs, September 16, 1996), p. 1.

The New Face of War

Figure 8.1
Khobar Towers

terrorist threat and use of nuclear, biological, and chemical weapons.[6] This specter of WMD terrorism is entirely too real since bombings already are the preferred method of terrorist attack. Terrorists can be expected to transition comfortably, especially those with connections to state-sponsors, from their familiar incendiary and conventional bombs to those containing chemical, biological or nuclear components—super-terrorism.

Second, significantly less chemical, biological, and nuclear materials are necessary to achieve equal or greater results than with conventional explosions. Mere grams of WMD materials are sufficient to conduct the "warfighting" tasks assigned to terrorism. Consider the potential effects if the approximately 2,000 pounds of explosives used at the World Trade Center could have been replaced by a sixty pound nuclear device, ten pounds of chemical toxins or twelve grams of biological agent. These minor amounts of nuclear, biological, and chemical materials would have increased casualties tenfold or more and caused the paralysis of one of the world's major cities.

As depicted in Figure 8.2, three emerging trends in the future of war, proliferation of WMD, and the utility of terrorism are on a path that will converge and, if not countered, will increase from possible to probable the likelihood that a terrorist incident involving WMD will occur in the United States or against U.S. forces overseas some time during the coming decade.[7]

The emergence of the WMD terrorism threat is a result of the convergence of the United States and terrorist groups. Both the "rogues" and terrorists want to constrain the U.S. capability and will to intervene in the region. Their pact is based on (1) the desire of the rogue regimes to attack forward deployed U.S. forces in peacetime under the conditions of plausible deniability, and (2) the need of the terrorists for the rogue's resources and expertise to enable them to penetrate and overcome the increasingly sophisticated U.S. anti-terrorism capabilities. The threat and actual use of super-terrorism attacks allows the rogue regimes to raise, perhaps prohibitiveiy, the perceived cost of stationing Americans abroad in peacetime, and use of WMD to deter U.S. intervention and/or disrupt U.S. military deployments and operations with deniability during wartime. Super-terrorism blurs

---

[6] The phrase "super-terrorism" was used to characterize a terrorist act involving WMD at an international conference in Holon, Israel, in March 1997. See Ron Purver, *Report on Conference, "Preventing Super-Terrorism: Threats and Responses," at Tel Aviv University and the Center for Technological Education, Holon, Israel, 11-13 March 1997* (Ottawa: Canadian Security Intelligence Service, 1997).

[7] Wickersham, "Technology Fault Lines," p. 10.

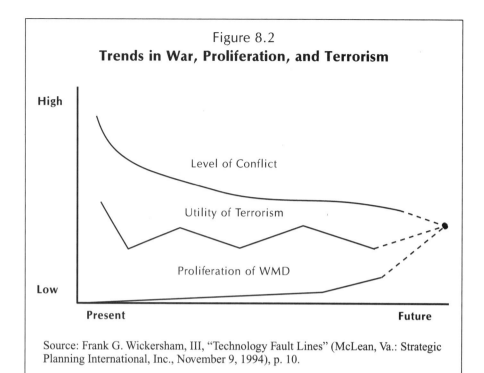

Figure 8.2
Trends in War, Proliferation, and Terrorism

High

Level of Conflict

Utility of Terrorism

Proliferation of WMD

Low

Present　　　　　　　　　　　　　　　　　　**Future**

Source: Frank G. Wickersham, III, "Technology Fault Lines" (McLean, Va.: Strategic Planning International, Inc., November 9, 1994), p. 10.

the distinction between not only terrorists and enemy armed forces, but also peace and war, allowing adversaries to attack the U.S. transoceanic power projection strategy across the spectrum of conflict.

The U.S. policy on counterterrorism is very clear about deterring, defeating and responding to terrorist attacks occurring in the United States or abroad:

> The United States shall give the highest priority to developing effective capabilities to detect, prevent, defeat and manage the consequences of nuclear, biological or chemical (NBC) materials or weapons use by terrorists. The acquisition of weapons of mass destruction by a terrorist group, through theft or manufacture, is unacceptable. There is no higher priority than preventing the acquisition of this capability or removing this capability from terrorist groups potentially opposed to the U.S.[8]

---

[8] U.S., White House, "U.S. Policy on Counterterrorism," Presidential Decision Directive 39, partially declassified and released on January 1, 1997 (Washington, D.C.: June 21, 1995). See also U.S., Department of Justice, Federal Bureau of Investigation, *Terrorism in the United States: 1995* (Washington, D.C.: Government Printing Office, 1997), p. 17.

Despite the strong policy words in the presidential directive, the reality of the situation is that terrorism can be countered but it cannot be prevented. Super-terrorism will increasingly impact the lives of Americans as countries hostile toward the United States apply terrorism as a tool of warfare. "Acts of terrorism will prove even more devastating as terrorists develop and use chemical, biological and nuclear weapons," Congressman Curt Weldon warns. "Currently, the United States is woefully unprepared to deal with such a disaster."[9]

Despite many significant improvements in the Defense Department's anti-terrorism program, a year after Khobar Towers, according to the General Accounting Office, the Pentagon still had not formed a "comprehensive, consistent approach to antiterrorism." The protection of American forces overseas was weakened by a lack of common standards for assessment of vulnerabilities, an absence of prescriptive criteria for a minimum level of protection for U.S. military forces, lack of consistency in the security countermeasures to be taken in response to threats, and unclear security responsibilities for all Department of Defense personnel overseas.[10]

The stakes for American troops overseas will remain high and weaknesses in the Defense Department's anti-terrorism program could end up encouraging super-terrorism rather than dissuade it. "Some...enemies feel our greatest vulnerability is our intolerance for casualties," retired Army General Wayne A. Downing explains. "If we prove ourselves incapable of responding to terrorism, the terrorists will continue to represent a significant threat to us, especially to our service men and women deployed overseas."[11]

The Ostrich Factor

The terrorist bombing of the Khobar Towers complex in Dhahran, Saudia Arabia, was a watershed event. This huge blast not only killed nineteen Americans and injured more than 500 others serving their country, but its reverberations spread throughout the U.S. defense establishment. Two types of feedback were drawn from the incident. The first set of lessons learned centered on actions necessary to reduce the risks of further attacks of this

---

[9] Curt Weldon, Representative, "Word For Word," *Defense News* (August 5-11, 1996), p. 12.

[10] U.S., General Accounting Office, *Combatting Terrorism: Status of DOD Efforts to Protect Its Forces Overseas,* GAO/NSIAD-97-207 (Washington, D.C.: General Accounting Office, July 1997), p. 9.

[11] As quoted in Gertz, "Terrorism and the Force," p. 71.

The New Face of War

kind. A second set of lessons that should have been learned from the bombing concerns the broader threat to the U.S. strategy of rapidly deploying military forces overseas in a crisis or conflict. This set of lessons has been largely ignored.

The basic source of terrorism is the extreme hostility to the American presence in Saudia Arabia by Islamic militants who see the presence of "infidels" on Saudi soil as a defilement of Islam. Once planning and final preparations were completed, the attack was reported to have been given approval at a major terrorist summit convened in Tehran. Terrorist leaders from around the world attended the meeting and took on the name "International Hezbollah." They have many sympathizers around the world and among many Saudis who view the royal family as guilty of excess, corruption, and permitting the slow contamination of Islamic society by Western culture. The terrorists that carried out the attack against Khobar Towers were trained and financed by the "International Hezbollah." According to one report, a Saudi group calling itself the "Legions of the Martyr Abdallah al-Huzuyfi" claimed responsibility for the attack. Further action was threatened by the Legions, if all U.S. and other foreign troops "occupying the holy Saudi land" are not removed.[12] General John M. Shalikashvili, then-Chairman of the Joint Chiefs of Staff, warned that similar attacks will occur and that the risk of terrorism cannot be eliminated. "The question," as he put it, "is not whether another Khobar Towers will occur but when another Khobar Towers will occur."[13]

Still reeling from blistering Congressional criticism of the military and civilian chains-of-command that permitted weaknesses in defensive preparations to persist at Khobar Towers, Defense Secretary William J. Perry moved quickly to stop the political bleeding by personally accepting responsibility for the loss of life. Just three weeks after the bombing, Secretary Perry announced the "force protection initiative," a sweeping plan to protect U.S. troops worldwide from huge truck bombs and biological and chemical weapons.

---

[12] Chris Lozlow, "The Bombing of Khobar Towers: Who Did It, and Who Funded It," *Jane's Intelligence Review* (December 1997), p. 557.

[13] As quoted in Gertz, "Terrorism and the Force," p. 68; David M. Gosoroski, "Sentry Duty in Saudi," *Veterans of Foreign Wars* (September 1996), pp 18-20; John Mintz and R. Jeffrey Smith, "Military Underestimated Terrorists, Perry Says," *Washington Post* (July 10, 1996), pp. A1, A14; and Youssef M. Ibrahim, "Saudi Exile Warns More Attacks Planned," *New York Times* (July 11, 1996), p. A6.

The Defense Department's initiatives to better protect U.S. forces included improved physical security for U.S. forces based overseas, increased training and intelligence analysis, and greater protection resources for forces in the Persian Gulf region. The U.S. moved about two-thirds of the Air Force operation at Khobar Towers (about 4,200 personnel and seventy-eight aircraft) to the Al Kharj airfield some fifty miles away. Now called Prince Sultan Air Base, the installation has ten guard towers and a series of barriers (walls, razor wire, ditches, berms) that extend out into the desert. The Saudi government financed the $114 million project to ensure it was well protected. The compound, according to one Air Force officer, "sort of gives the impression of a prison." The move achieved two things. Surrounded by desert, Prince Sultan Air Base can afford the Air Force operations far more security than the urban environment in Dhahran. Secondly, separating much of the U.S. presence from the Saudi people will presumably lessen the influence of Western culture and dampen resentment against the Americans.[14]

The hasty move out of the Dhahran area testifies that security at Khobar Towers was inherently insufficient and that no amount of barbed wire or fences could have immunized the Americans from attack. The blame for the Khobar Towers bombing should lay squarely on the terrorists and their sponsors whose attack should be considered an act of war against the United States.[15] Another victory of sorts was handed to the terrorists on a silver platter when the hapless on-scene Air Force commander was cited by Defense Department officials as being at fault for weaknesses in the physical and procedural defenses.[16]

The "lessons learned" from the Khobar Towers attack led to separating the U.S. forces from the very people they were sent to defend. The foolhardiness of placing Americans at isolated, heavily defended garrisons away from the local populace was "learned" in Vietnam and then "unlearned" with bloody consequences. The "force protection initiative" in Vietnam

---

[14] John Diamond, "U.S. Housing to Be Safer At Saudi Desert Air Base," *Washington Times* (December 30, 1997), p. A11, and Douglas Jehl, "U.S. Military in Saudi Arabia Digs Into the Sand," *New York Times* (November 9, 1996), p. 3.

[15] John Shaud, "The Other Side of Khobar Towers," *Washington Times* (August 26, 1997), p. A13, and Correll, "Fallout From Khobar Towers," p. 3.

[16] More than 130 enhancements had been taken at Khobar Towers to protect the forces before the June 25th terrorist attack. Barriers were raised and moved out, fences strengthened, entrances restricted, and guard forces increased. The on-scene commander had put in place a wide variety of new security measures. See Perry, "Protection of U.S. Forces Deployed Abroad."

ceded territory to the enemy and separated U.S. forces from the Vietnamese people for whom the battle for hearts and minds was all about. American fire bases built in the jungles of Vietnam made them inviting targets for the Communist forces and allowed the populace to opt out of the struggle.

Similarly, moving U.S. forces into the desert at Prince Sultan Air Base concentrates the Americans and so separates them from the Saudi people that super-terrorists can now tee off on them at will with biological and chemical weapons, and soon perhaps even nuclear weapons, without involving the local populace. The expected payoff for Islamic militants in these circumstances is high—maximum U.S. casualties with few, if any, collateral deaths and injuries.[17] The next terrorist attack in Saudi Arabia is likely to come over the fence in the form of rockets, unmanned aircraft, or perhaps in the form of anthrax spores spreading silently with the wind in the darkness of night from an aerosol dispersal line some miles away.

Another lesson that should have been learned from the Khobar Towers bombing is that the real target under attack by Islamic militants was the U.S. transoceanic power projection strategy that consists of forward-based forces in peacetime and rapid deployment in times of crisis or conflict. By characterizing the threat as limited to terrorist attacks against small-scale American outposts, the Defense Department obscures the real problem: If 5,000 U.S. troops in Dhahran make lucrative targets in peacetime, what about 500,000 troops in wartime? With so few ports and airfields usable by arriving U.S. forces it becomes plausible for WMD-armed terrorists to launch commando-like raids against the arriving troops and equipment.

The WMD "threat" favored by the Pentagon also ignores the history of Iraq's nearly successful nuclear program and focuses on biological and chemical weapons. Yet, exploding crude nuclear devices aboard ships in Saudi ports could shut down U.S. reinforcing actions. The Pentagon's "force protection initiative" simply ignores the future nuclear threat.

Forward-based forces in the Cold War were sometimes labelled as "tripwires" for deterring escalation to nuclear conflict. This was one of the functions of the U.S. troop strength in NATO and South Korea. But in the Persian Gulf region, deterring Islamic militants is wide open to question. Rather than serve as "tripwires," forward-garrisoned American forces can serve as "mortar magnets" like they did in the fire bases in Vietnam. The difference this time is that the undeterred Islamic super-terrorist can now be

---

[17] Robert Holzer, "Antiterror Plans May Endanger U.S. Forces," *Defense News* (September 2-8, 1996), p. 3.

armed with weapons of mass destruction. Wartime attacks against these forward-based forces could kill thousands of Americans and stop U.S. deployments or combat operations in their tracks. WMD-armed terrorists should be recognized as being paramilitary forces that can be used to plant truck or ship bombs in coordination with wider WMD and conventional military attacks.

One of the main lessons from the Khobar Towers bombing is that Islamic militants and their state-sponsors regard terrorism as a strategic tool in both peace and war. Their joint goal is to disrupt the American transoceanic power projection strategy and break the U.S. will to continue the fight or, for that matter, to fight at all. Peacetime terrorism is the psychological stage-setting for the cutting-edge of the super-terrorist in war. "I feel that we're being stalked...," explained Marine Corps General Anthony Zinni who heads the military command responsible for the Gulf region. "We sense that we're being watched."[18]

A New Catalog of Terror

Terrorism by Islamic radicals "is the greatest threat coming to us domestically in the United States," the chief of the FBI's counter-terrorism section explains. "No longer is it just the fear of being attacked by international terrorist organizations—attacks against Americans and American interests overseas.... A lot of these groups now have the capability and the support infrastructure in the United States to attack us here if they choose to." These trans-national terrorist groups, bound not by their country or nation but by religious conviction, are engaged in several "theaters of war": Afghanistan, Sudan, Egypt, Algeria, Bosnia, Chechnya, Kashmir, and Mindanao. Nearly every one of these very fluid and dynamic groups has a presence in the United States.[19]

"Islam is a revolutionary ideology and programme which seeks to alter the social order of the whole world," explains S. Abdul A'la Maududi—a leading theologian of the Fundamentalist Islam movement, "and rebuild it in conformity with its own tenets and ideals."[20] The leaders of the move-

---

[18] Ed Blanche, "Reports Show Gaps in U.S. Security," *Jane's Intelligence Review and Jane's Intelligence Pointer* (October 1997), p. 6.

[19] Don Harvey, "Intelligence Notebook: Terrorism," *Periscope,* Newsletter of the Association of Former Intelligence Officers (July 1996), p. 8.

[20] As quoted in Francis Spranza, "The Will of Allah?," *Aviation Security International,* 2-2 (1997), p. 15.

---

ment in Tehran have made it clear that, if necessary, they will continue their worldwide campaign by violent means. The very real fear exists in Iran that the United States will ultimately find a way to launch attacks against it in the same way that Washington crippled Iraq. In order to build momentum and support overseas for the movement's goals, Tehran is working through a global network of 150 radical organizations.[21]

Private financial sources from wealthy individuals in Saudi Arabia and other Gulf states aligned with the United States are guaranteed for terrorists who attack Americans, Israelis, and their sympathizers in the West. Afghanistan-based Osama bin Laden, for example, supports terrorist groups operating in northern Africa, Europe, and the Middle East. Stripped of his Saudi citizenship, bin Laden, whose personal fortune is estimated to be $250 million, is widely suspected of bankrolling a range of terrorist operations by Islamic militants, including the August 1998 attacks against the U.S. embassies in Kenya and Tanzania.[22]

The growing availability of biological and chemical agents opens new doors for the militant Islamic terrorist. In order to gauge the likelihood of future attacks, it helps to understand what characteristics might be most attractive to the super-terrorist, and what expertise would be needed to manufacture, transport, and deliver WMD safely (for the terrorists). First, for instance, they would allow a few individuals to inflict a large number of casualties quickly. Secondly, even if only a few casualties occur, they could be sufficient to produce panic and social and economic dislocation, at least for a limited period. If used against sea and aerial ports of embarkation and debarkation, the military forces present and moving through those facilities could suffer high casualties and become disorganized, at least for some length of time. The ports and airfields themselves could be reduced significantly in throughput capacity, if not shut down completely.

Use of radiological weapons to contaminate small areas and nuclear use by terrorists cannot be fully discounted. Saddam Hussein's nuclear program proves that the expertise is available, and the questions about Russian controls over its nuclear weapons and fissile material injects a degree of uncertainty about future terrorist actions.

---

[21] Cuba, Iran, Iraq, Libya, North Korea, Sudan, and Syria are on the official U.S. list of countries that support international terrorism. See U.S., Department of State, *Patterns of Global Terrorism: 1996* (Washington, D.C.: April 1997). See also Al J. Venter, "Iran Still Exporting Terrorism to Spread Its Islamic Vision," *Jane's Intelligence Review* (November 1997), pp. 511-16.

[22] Jeff Gerth and Judith Miller, "Funds for Terrorists Traced To Persian Gulf Businessmen," *New York Times* (August 14, 1996), pp. A1, A14.

Biological Terrorism. The menu of lethal agents deemed by a variety of experts as most likely to be used by super-terrorists includes botulinal toxin, anthrax, and ricin in the biological area and mustard and cyanide gases and nerve agents (tabun, sarin, and VX) in the chemical realm. Nuclear and radiological weapons also are on the main menu.[23]

Extreme toxicity could make biological agents very attractive to terrorists wishing to inflict mass casualties. Some types of botulinal toxin have a mean lethal dose that could run as low as a few tenths of a microgram. Saddam Hussein apparently placed a great deal of importance on botulinum since he reportedly had 19,000 liters, more than twice the amount of anthrax, and nearly 10,000 liters loaded into bombs and Scud warheads at the war's end.

Anthrax, if its spores are dispersed appropriately, also has high toxicity. When used against an unprotected urban or military base population, for instance, the fatalities resulting from anthrax are on the order of those expected from the use of nuclear weapons. Other biological agents or chemical agents do not come close to the operational effectiveness of anthrax. Iraq possessed 8,500 liters of anthrax, 6,000 of which had been filled into bombs and Scud warheads.

A third common biological agent is ricin. This agent poisons the blood, causing circulatory collapse. About 800 grams would be needed to inflict heavy casualties over a one square-mile area as compared to eighty grams for botulinum and eight grams for anthrax for the same area.[24]

Terrorists are said to be attracted to biological agents, too, because of the smaller quantities of agent that would be required. This means that a lesser infrastructure is needed, and there is a reduced chance of discovery by foreign intelligence services. Costs are also lower. In addition, biological agents are undetectable to traditional anti-terrorist sensor systems, which makes it difficult for the defenders to be certain they are under assault, especially in the early stages of attack. The time-lag between the release of the agent and its effects on the human body offers a bonus value to the

---

[23] Sam Nunn, "Terrorism Meets Proliferation: A Post-Cold War Convergence of Threats," *The Monitor,* 3-2, Center for International Trade and Security at the University of Georgia (Spring 1997), p. 4.

[24] Ron Purver, *Chemical and Biological Terrorism: The Threat According to Open Literature* (Ottawa: Canadian Security Intelligence Service, June 1995), pp. 3-6; Bruce W. Nelan, "The Price of Fanaticism," *Time* (April 3, 1995), p. 40; and Jonathan B. Tucker, "Chemical/Biological Terrorism: Coping with a New Threat," *Politics and the Life Sciences* (September 1996), pp. 173-74.

The New Face of War

super-terrorist by reducing significantly the chances of being apprehended. Finally, the disruption of military and civilian activities from biological attacks can be significant.

Virtually no technical knowledge is needed to use or produce biological agents. Simple brewery equipment may be all that is needed to produce some agents (such as anthrax). The "how-to" aspects of producing the deadly agents is available in the open literature, including detailed steps to be taken in their production. Similarly, aerosol equipment for dispersal is easy to obtain from the open literature and ready commercial sources.

For botulinum, anyone with a background in microbiology or a related discipline could produce several hundred thousand human doses in a short period of time. Ricin can be extracted from castor beans through a well-documented, two-step procedure involving solvent extraction of the protein albuminoid toxin. Yet, there are questions whether its lower toxicity as compared with other agents is sufficient for it to qualify as a weapon of mass destruction.

Super-terrorists presumably would choose a bacteriological agent due to a combination of toxicity, ease of manufacture, hardiness, speed of effect, and contagiousness. Anthrax tops most lists of likely agents. Biological agents such as glanders, Q-fever, and others, for a variety of reasons, do not fit the terrorist context because of such difficulties as cultivation, self-protection, and similar troubles.

Acquiring operational quantities of biological agents can be satisfied by beginning with seed culture, stealing the agent from a legitimate source such as public health or pharmaceutical research laboratories, buying it on the black market, or extracting it from the natural environment. Maximum security could be attained by acquiring a seed culture from the natural environment and then sampling, isolating and identifying the organism. All of these variegated functions probably could not be conducted by a layman, but the process would be most secure. Super-terrorists could also obtain biological agents from friendly governments desiring to sponsor their activities.

Contrary to fictionalized accounts, effective delivery of biological agents is somewhat more difficult than producing them. Among the possible delivery methods are dispersal via aerosol inside a building, tunnel, or metropolitian subway; contamination of foodstuffs or liquids at the source or in the production and distribution processes; dispersal via aerosol in an open area such as a port, airfield or city (or portions thereof); indirect transmission through infected fleas, ticks, rats, other animals, or via parcels

---

and letters; and direct human contact such as ricin-tipped umbrellas to puncture a particular target's skin. One would think that super-terrorists might be especially attracted to aerosol dissemination of such agents as anthrax because of the wide-area coverage possible and high lethality. Even then the super-terrorist can face problems in ensuring survival of the agent long enough to infect the intended target. Aerosolization itself may kill a large proportion of the pathogenic agent. Environmental influences such as sunlight and temperature changes also can reduce the potency of the agents.

One oft-described delivery method is dispersal of anthrax spores that can be carried safely and conveniently in light bulbs. By leaving the bulbs on the subway track for breakage with arrival of the next train, the super-terrorist has time to flee from the scene. Once the light bulb is broken, the anthrax can spread throughout the subway system by the natural air flows and those induced by the trains.

One legitimately may ask why, if biological agents are so lethal and offer so much killing power to the terrorist, have these deadly weapons not been more widely used. The answer might be quite simple since biological weapons represent unexplored territory for most terrorists. The terrorists may have troubling uncertainties about the agent effectiveness, fear for their own safety, concern about unwanted collateral damage to non-targets, moral qualms injuring large numbers of innocent people, and fear of retaliation by the targeted group or government.

Strategic conditions are changing rapidly in regions around the world. The increasing availability of biotechnology for legitimate purposes in the non-Western countries, the spread of knowledge in how to create biological warfare capabilities, the sense of instability in many regions, and the well-known U.S. dependence on regional bases, ports, and airfields to deploy or reinforce its forces overseas all encourage the potential use of biological weapons in the coming decade.[25]

Chemical Terrorism. The toxicity of chemical weapons falls at the lower end of the scale for weapons of mass destruction. With substantially lower toxicity than biological agents, chemical weapons are closer to the lethality of conventional weapons. Moreover, chemical weapons vary considerably in their own lethality.

For the super-terrorist, the characteristics of the target is more important than the availability of chemical agents. Since effective delivery and dissemination is required for all chemical weapons, the likelihood of

---

[25] Purver, *Chemical and Biological Terrorism,* pp. 14-57.

---

terrorists being able to inflict thousands of casualties against military operations is minuscule. Even using VX, which is ten times more toxic than sarin when inhaled and 300 times greater when absorbed through the skin, a terrorist attack would be limited to inflicting casualties on a few thousand people at a time.

It would be quite easy for terrorists to obtain all that they need to know about producing chemical agents from the open literature. Both Britain and the United States, for instance, declassified the formula for making the potent nerve agent VX in 1971. The formulas for other deadly nerve gases are reported to be available at the British Library. The ink in ballpoint pens is only one step removed from sarin, a potent nerve agent. Production of chemical agents, however, could be quite hazardous. Hence, the likely alternative courses include theft of chemical weapons from military facilities, their purchase on the black market, or rogue regimes supplying the weapons.

Delivering chemical weapons can be more difficult than manufacturing them. Much of the problem is the target itself. If dissemination over large areas is required, such as at a port or airfield, the small quantity of chemical agent that can be delivered by a terrorist may be insufficient to inflict the desired level of casualties. The quantity of agent is relevant only in terms of the size and environmental conditions of the intended target. On the other hand, dispersing lethal vapor concentrations from volatile agents within enclosed spaces, such as hotels or office buildings, can be expected to inflict high casualties.[26] The first true terrorist chemical assault on civilians occurred in the Tokyo subway attack. On the morning of March 20, 1995, eleven plastic pouches containing liquid sarin (nerve agent) were left on five separate subway trains that were due to arrive four minutes apart at the Kasumigaseki station in the heart of Japan's government district at the height of the morning rush hour, between 8:09 and 8:13 a.m. Twelve persons died and more than 5,500 people were injured by the attack.

Police raided the facilities used by the Aum Shinrikyo religious sect and seized precursor chemicals for making sarin. Several hundred tons of forty different chemicals were found. The members of Aum Shinrikyo also had the capacity to produce tabun, a nerve agent far deadlier than sarin. They were found to have been experimenting with production of biological warfare agents and investigating nuclear weapons through the enrichment of uranium. Police confiscated solutions used to cultivate bacteria and other microorganisms as well as some quantity of clostridium botulinum.

---

[26] *Ibid.*, pp. 57-80.

Japanese police believe the sect was also successful in cultivating cholera and other bacilli. It also experimented with laser beam equipment that could be used to enrich uranium. Among the Aum Shinrikyo's members were several highly trained graduates from Japan's most prestigious universities in the fields of medicine, biochemistry, architecture, biology, and genetic engineering.

The attack on the Tokyo subway produced a national crisis. The Japanese government came under attack for not moving sooner against the Aum Shinrikyo and for failing to solve earlier evidence of sarin poisoning by the sect. A slow-down in the Japanese economy was triggered when people avoided being in public places for fear of sarin gas attacks.

Police raids at 130 Aum Shinrikyo locations in May and June 1995 yielded the arrest of the sect's leader and forty of his followers. Notebooks seized at the cult facilities, combined with the testimony by members of the sect, revealed that the Aum Shinrikyo was planning a full-scale urban guerrilla attack against the Japanese government in November 1995. The dispersal of sarin over several Japanese cities was planned through the use of remote-controlled helicopters; 530 pounds were to be spread across Tokyo alone.[27]

Nuclear Terrorism. Until September 1997, it was generally believed that it would be very difficult for a terrorist group to make, steal or buy nuclear weapons. Although many are skeptical, former Russian General Alexander Lebed said in an interview on the CBS program *60 Minutes* that the Russian military had lost track of as many as 100 suitcase-sized, one-kiloton bombs. "A nuclear explosive with a yield of a kiloton," Theodore B. Taylor explained in 1973, "detonated in the center of the New York City financial district during a work day would kill more than 100,000 people. Would any extremist political or terrorist organization be willing to carry out such mass destruction? Would responsible government officials or the public in the target area take such [a] threat seriously? There are no firm

---

[27] *Ibid.,* pp. 153-79, and "The Threat of Chemical/Biological Terrorism," *Commentary,* No. 60 (Ottowa, Canada: Canadian Security Intelligence Service, August 1995). The writer wishes to thank Ron Purver and the Canadian Security Intelligence Service for making its unclassified open-source research available to better understand the strengths and weaknesses of the threat of chemical and biological terrorism. A combination of informed publics and well-honed counter-terrorism programs inside the intelligence services are two key components in defense against the super-terrorists.

answers to these questions."[28] "Terrorists would love to have [suitcase bombs]," Congressman Curt Weldon said on the *60 Minutes* program, "we know they have been trying to buy long-range offensive weapons and nuclear capability from Russia. That's a fact."[29]

So far nuclear terrorism has been limited to hundreds of false alarms. But the first nuclear contingency, Uwe Nerlich points out, will be a major surprise. The target country and the international community will almost certainly be unprepared for the doctrinal and strategy shifts that will be required. Albert Einstein warned President Roosevelt in a 1939 letter that a "single bomb of this type [atomic bomb], carried by boat and exploded in a port, might very well destroy the whole port altogether with some of the surrounding territories. However, such bombs might very well prove to be too heavy for transportation by air."[30] The aerial delivery problem was solved quite readily, but the potential for a terrorist nuclear bomb detonation on a ship in a port in the United States or a receiving port in an overseas region still looms as a latent threat and one that in reality may well be looming larger.

The problem, Uwe Nerlich explains, is that nuclear terrorism does not fit the strategic context usually associated with nuclear deterrence, including coercive efforts to convince an opponent to give up its nuclear option, preventive strikes before hostilities begin (e.g., Israeli strike against the Iraqi Osirik reactor on June 7, 1981), dissuasion to control escalation where remote nuclear options could be contemplated, deterrence of possible attacks by actors with a cost-risk-benefit strategic calculus, and accidents and other nuclear risks. "In particular, it is fairly obvious that nuclear deterrence which may itself increasingly face problems of proportionality and legitimacy is not providing workable answers to the range of options that may be open to nuclear terrorists."[31]

Examining the super-terrorist's menu of possible attack options across the board, it is evident that the danger is growing in several dimensions inside the United States and against American forces based overseas as well

---

[28] As quoted in Uwe Nerlich, *Nuclear Non-State Actors: Lessons from the RAF-GDR Connection?* (Ebenhausen, Germany: Stiftung Wissenschaft und Politk (SW), Forsdhungsinstitut fur Internationale Politik und Sicherheit, August 1993), p. 7.

[29] General Alexander Lebed and Congressman Curt Weldon, remarks on *60 Minutes,* CBS Television (September 7, 1997).

[30] As quoted in Nerlich, *Nuclear Non-State Actors,* p. 7.

[31] *Ibid.,* pp. 9-10.

as reinforcements or expeditionary forces in times of crisis. The basic materials, know-how and technologies are increasingly available to terrorist groups and rogue regimes that might sponsor their activities against the United States. Another factor behind the convergence of terrorism and WMD are the changing motivations of some terrorist organizations.[32] Professor Ved Marwah at the Center for Policy Research in New Delhi, for instance, thinks that the previous supposed moral inhibitions of terrorists to eschew mass casualties is being overridden by the "hate factor." He also believes that it would be very difficult to prove state sponsorship of a super-terrorist event.[33] Professor Amazia Baram of Haifa University believes use of biological agents by terrorists would be "frighteningly easy" and says that sponsoring states could quite easily disclaim responsibility for super-terrorist attacks.[34] Yet, terrorists seem to prefer conventional chemistry. Several constraints come into play: (1) political backlash by financial backers, (2) manufacture of chemical and biological agents is not easy, (3) chemical weapons are dangerous to store and handle, and (4) the goal of terrorism as the twentieth century comes to a close is still the political act of violence rather than the number of people killed.[35]

Americans Are the Target

The clock is ticking on the potential terrorist use of weapons of mass destruction as a weapon of war. WMD terrorism can be used to deny the U.S. access to overseas seaports and airfields, as well as to block U.S. military operations from foreign soil and close-in littoral waters. The primary goal is to weaken the will of the American people to support the overseas deployment of U.S. military forces. Peacetime terrorism prepares the mental groundwork for evoking perceptions of numerous American casualties in event of war. Super-terrorism is changing the rules for combatting terrorism and needs to be recognized for what it is: an act of war that kills and maims for political ends.[36]

As underlined by the August 1998 terrorist bombings at the U.S. embassies in Kenya and Tanzania, *Americans Are the Target.*

---

[32] Zachary S. Davis, "Weapons of Mass Destruction: New Terrorist Threat?," *The Monitor,* 3-2, Center for International Trade and Security at the University of Georgia (Spring 1997), p. 11.

[33] As reported in Purver, *Report of Conference, "Preventing Super-Terrorism,"* p. 5.

[34] *Ibid.,* p. 8.

[35] Croddy, "Putting the Lid Back On the Chemical Box," p. 43.

[36] Caleb Carr, "Terrorism as Warfare: The Lessons of History," *World Policy Journal,* 13-4 (Winter 1996/97), pp. 1-12.

A New Power Projection Risk Calculus

INTRODUCTION: PART III

Will America's transoceanic power projection strategy work against the new challenges of WMD proliferation, widespread availability of advanced conventional weapons and technologies, and the portent for state-sponsored terrorism in peace and war?

Chapter 9 traces the American buildup in the Persian Gulf from August 1990 to the air war that began on January 16, 1991. Two deep water ports and a major airfield were the primary reception centers in Saudi Arabia. The war revealed America's dependence on time to project its military power across the oceans and the dependence on unhindered and unobstructed access to seaports and airfields.

A second aspect is the enormity of Iraq's WMD programs, which were far greater in scope and complexity than was believed before the war. It was only after the war that the United Nations and the International Atomic Energy Agency discovered the broad scope of the nuclear, biological, and chemical weapons and ballistic missile programs.

These two sets of findings converge in considerations of future warfare. The Persian Gulf War demonstrated the dependence of U.S. strategy on time to build up forces and unfettered access to ports and airfields. The discoveries about the details of Saddam Hussein's WMD after the war demonstrated that future proliferators could use biological and chemical weapons in the near-term, perhaps nuclear as well, and missiles to impose delays on U.S. force deployments and deny access to regional reception facilities.

Chapter 10 presents a clarion call that America's strategy is under attack by WMD proliferators who can use these weapons in innovative ways to challenge the two main weight-bearing assumptions of U.S. strategy: time and access. New challenges, often posed against U.S. forces in innovative ways, undermine these two main pillars or weight-bearing assumptions of American strategy. These new challenges introduce severe risks to U.S. strategy. The reader is taken step-by-step through the logic of how WMD proliferation, advanced conventional weapons, and state-sponsored terrorism make execution of the current U.S. military strategy highly risky and perhaps even unworkable.

Chapter 11 asks what approach has been taken by the Clinton Administration for dealing with the new challenges and increasing military risks. The Administration's efforts to redefine force structure criteria are reviewed and military options—nuclear deterrence, theater defense, and counterforce—favored by the Administration are evaluated. These strategy options, though each boasts many positive elements, are insufficient in themselves or all three together to mitigate the risks facing the U.S. strategy. A part of the problem is that the Administration may not even realize just how bad are the military risks mushrooming ahead. By using budget-based planning instead of the proven objectives-based planning approach, the Administration has put blinders on policy makers and planners alike, leaving them without a compass to understand, let alone reduce, military risks. How self-serving planning assumptions are used by the military services and the Defense Department to push severe military risks out of sight are also discussed. The situation in the Pentagon is not unlike the course adopted by the French government and armed forces during the 1930s.

Part Three concludes that U.S. military strategy is broken. It is susceptible to asymmetric attacks by WMD-armed adversaries against the weight-bearing assumptions of America's military strategy: time and access. A new strategy is needed. Or, as the National Defense Panel said in its December 1997 final report: "In short, we must radically alter the way in which we project power."

CHAPTER 9

Lessons From the
Persian Gulf War

A country's last war is always the most crucial one for sifting the experiences of man and machine for insights to guide tomorrow's military doctrine and strategy. The Persian Gulf War is no different. Drawing the right lessons from the Gulf War, however, can be a bit tricky. It was after all an oddly prolonged and set-piece affair with the ultimate outcome a well-recognized given once the United States and its Coalition partners had moved their counter-offensive forces into the theater. Americans seem to have too easily come to believe in the unchallenged military superiority of the United States. Furthermore, many of the Gulf War's most crucial lessons may not be self-evident by a simple reading of the course of events.

Recognizing that the unique circumstances of the Persian Gulf War does not give a wholesale validation to America's transoceanic power projection strategy is one of the most significant lessons. In the final analysis, the United States dispatched a highly complex armada of air, ground, and maritime forces to the Persian Gulf region under absolutely ideal conditions, and Saddam Hussein, whatever might have been his motivations, did not interfere with the armed buildup and allowed the Coalition all the time it needed to fully deploy military forces into the theater of operations.

A second important lesson is that weapons of mass destruction in the hands of regional adversaries undermine key assumptions of the U.S. military strategy. Americans and their Coalition partners for the first time faced an adversary armed with biological and chemical weapons and ballistic missiles to deliver them (and just a few months away from a workable nuclear device). The fact that Iraq did not use its biological and chemical weapons (at least in widespread and deadly ways) against the U.S.-led Coalition should not distract us from this growing threat to America's military strategy and forces. Thanks to the United Nations inspections of Iraq's weapons-making complex following the Gulf War, Americans are offered a rare glimpse into an unfolding future filled with deadly new threats and grave risks as the up-gunning of non-Western nations continues worldwide.

For the countries in search of chemical, biological, and nuclear weapons, Iraq's successful development of weapons of mass destruction and missiles offers a virtual "how-to" book on alternative proliferation pathways.

Force Buildup in the Gulf

The Gulf War serves as a useful basis for understanding the fundamental military challenges to the longstanding U.S. transoceanic power projection strategy. Most of the variables relevant to future warfare were present during the Gulf War: a short warning time, the large size of the deploying forces, the lack of an adequate amount of prepositioned equipment, and the great distance from the United States.[1] Still, the U.S. and other Coalition members enjoyed an impressive array of assets to facilitate their buildup: unhindered access to two of the most modern and well-equipped seaports in the world, full access to several modern airfields for support of logistics and air combat operations, total political support by the regional host countries, absence of any Iraqi efforts to hinder the Coalition's force buildup, and plenty of training time to prepare military personnel for the upcoming battle. The buildup phase of the war, five-and-a-half months of uninterrupted operations, was a Pentagon dream scenario. In the process, however, the ease of the force buildup overstated key strengths of the U.S. power projection strategy while understating its weaknesses.

The two first-rate Saudi ports at Al Jubayl and Ad Dammam (Figure 9.1) on the Persian Gulf just a few miles from Iraq's army in Kuwait were great luxuries. The throughput capacity of these ports are among the best in the world. The modern port at Ad Dammam, for instance, can berth and off-load thirty-nine ships simultaneously, including very large sealift vessels. Equally impressive are the airports at Dhahran, Riyadh, King Fahd, and King Khalid Military City. In terms of the projection of U.S. forces, these facilities were vital. Most of the reception facilities in the world could not have handled the types and numbers of ships and aircraft that provided the backbone of the force buildup. The U.S. and allied force deployment took place under ideal conditions.[2]

The distance from the United States to Saudi Arabia greatly complicated the deployment of the military forces: 7,000 miles for air transport

---

[1] Scott W. Conrad, *Moving the Force: Desert Storm and Beyond,* McNair Paper 32, Institute For National Strategic Studies, National Defense University (Washington, D.C.: Government Printing Office, December 1994), p. 3.

[2] *Ibid.,* p. 38.

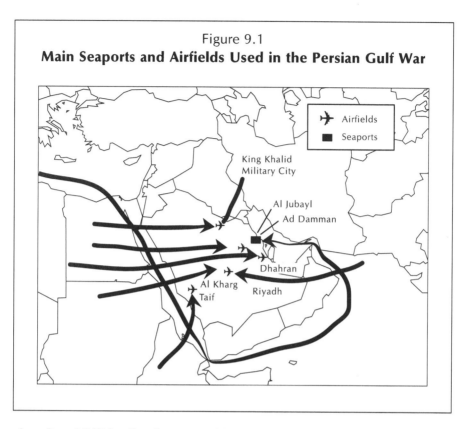

Figure 9.1
Main Seaports and Airfields Used in the Persian Gulf War

aircraft and 8,700 miles for cargo ships and tankers departing from ports on the eastern seaboard. Given the access to fully equipped seaports and airfields available and the advanced technology offloading equipment at the Saudi ports, it was hardly surprising that the force buildup was uninterrupted for the entire seven-month operation. During the first three months, for example, beginning from a standing start, the U.S. moved about 1,000 aircraft, sixty ships, 250,000 tons of supplies and equipment, and some 240,000 troops to the Gulf. The intensity and size of this accelerated strategic movement swamps all comparisons with Vietnam and Korea. Yet, even as impressive as the numbers are, it took more than six weeks to get the first heavy division into place. And, it took several months to insert a sustainable armored force capable of offensive operations.

Furthermore, early arriving units were lightly armed. The 82nd Airborne Division was positioned between Iraqi forces in Kuwait and Saudi Arabia in an attempt to deter the Iraqis. If Saddam Hussein had chosen to move against the Saudi oil fields near Dhahran, the U.S. would have had no way to block Iraqi armored assaults other than very limited air strikes and

---

ground-fired anti-armor missiles. This "speed bump" strategy, as soldiers of the 82nd Airborne called it, would simply have temporarily slowed an Iraqi drive into Saudi Arabia. The U.S. anti-armor capabilities where increased on August 25 when two Marine brigades received 123 M-60 tanks from storage ships that had been pre-positioned near the Persian Gulf. It took another month before the first Army armored division was in place.[3]

Fifty to sixty-five of the large Air Force transport aircraft—C-141 and C-5 aircraft—arrived in the Persian Gulf theater each day in August 1990 during the initial surge of deploying troops and equipment. All told, the Air Force committed ninety-four percent of its C-5s (118 aircraft) and seventy-three percent of its C-141s (195 aircraft) to full-time support of Operation Desert Shield. The daily number of arrivals began to taper off to about forty-four by mid-September, mostly for supply sustainment of forces already in the theater. Fifty to sixty additional airlift missions were carried out daily by commercial airliners discharging troops and cargo, KC-10 tanker aircraft, and C-130 cargo planes used for transport of troops and supplies inside the theater of operations.

The civilian airline industry played a critical role in satisfying the airlift requirement. Civil air carriers provided eighteen passenger and twenty-one cargo aircraft to the air transport fleet supporting Operation Desert Shield. These operations peaked at some twenty-five missions a day. An additional fifty-nine passenger and seventeen cargo aircraft were made available in January 1991 for sustainment of the wartime operations.

When the air war began on January 16, 1991, after 165 days of air transport operations, the airlift effort had completed more than 10,500 missions to move 355,000 tons of cargo from the United States, Europe, and elsewhere to the Persian Gulf region. Ten thousand tons more were hauled by KC-10 aerial tankers whose dual configuration allows movement of cargo and passengers as well as fuel.[4]

The airlift operation was a stunning display of U.S. military reach and dedication of its armed forces. Yet, early coordination problems were troublesome and common. First, air transports were made available before the deploying units were ready to move, causing delays and clogging airfields.

---

[3] U.S., Congressional Budget Office, *Moving U.S. Forces: Options for Strategic Mobility* (Washington, D.C.: Government Printing Office, February 1997), p. 33.

[4] U.S., Department of Defense, *Conduct of the Persian Gulf War* (Washington, D.C.: Government Printing Office, April 1992), pp. 412-13.

The New Face of War

When an F-15 squadron was deploying from Langley Air Force Base, Virginia, for example, nine C-141s and three C-5s showed up in the first six hours. Over the next day and a half nationwide, eighteen of twenty-two airlift missions were late because of the loading delays. Similar experiences occurred elsewhere when units could not generate unit equipment fast enough to satisfy the available airlift.

Airfields en route to the Persian Gulf also were saturated. Eighty-four percent of the approximately 8,000 C-5 and C-141 missions refueled and changed aircrews at just four European bases, two in Germany and two in Spain. Rhein Main Air Base outside of Frankfurt, Germany, supported 138 arrivals and departures on August 15, 1990. For a time, sixty-eight aircraft were on the ground where only fifty-six parking spaces were available.

From August through November 1990, eighty-two percent of all airlift operations were off-loaded at four airfields in Saudi Arabia: Dhahran (sixty-one percent), Riyadh (eleven percent), Jubayl (seven percent), and King Fahd (three percent). More than thirty transport aircraft per day were handled at Dhahran through November. Difficulties were experienced in moving fuel from storage to the aircraft; insufficient fuel pits, fuel trucks, and drivers were available. Dhahran became saturated with cargo, especially since a sizable amount of the early air freight shipments were marked only "Desert Shield" since the unit movements were classified.

The U.S. Navy's sealift vessels were supplemented by large numbers of chartered domestic and foreign ships to satisfy the initial surge and sustainment requirements in the Persian Gulf. During the entire period, 385 ships delivered unit equipment, support equipment and supplies, and petroleum products. During the defensive phase of Desert Shield from August through November 1990, sealift moved the equipment for more than four Army divisions along with the supplies necessary for sustainment of the more than 100,000 troops in the theater. More than 180 ships were assigned or under charter during this period and delivered nearly 1.2 million tons of cargo and 3.5 million tons of fuel. By the time the war was over in March 1991, sealift had provided an average of 4,200 tons of cargo per day.[5]

The U.S. sealift operation experienced several difficulties. First, the easy to load roll-on/roll-off fast sealift vessels were in short supply. This meant that the heavy armored forces were delayed. The slow buildup continued in September and October. After all, Saddam Hussein's armored forces were not going anywhere; they had already seized Kuwait.

---

[5] *Ibid.*, pp. 416-18.

Secondly, some 212 of the 359 ships available in the Persian Gulf were chartered; 180 of these vessels (or about half) flew foreign flags. This dependence on foreign flag carriers could cause problems in the future in meeting U.S. force projection requirements. If adversaries threaten or use weapons of mass destruction to deny access to regional ports, for instance, owners of foreign merchant ships could balk at putting their vessels and crews into harms way.

The deployment was slowed further by the glut of arriving cargo piled high at ports and marshalling areas. As illustrated in Figure 9.2, a Scud attack against the port of Al Jubayl came close to striking a devastating blow against the Coalition on February 16, 1991, when a missile warhead impacted just 130 yards away from the U.S.S. *Tarawa* as it approached a pier to unload AV-8 Harrier aircraft. The missile warhead did not detonate. Eight other ships were tied at the pier, which was jammed with ammunition and equipment.[6]

And, fourth, the glut at the ports had a domino effect that was magnified by the shortage of storage space, cargo handling equipment, and skilled equipment operators. In the end, military units lost confidence in the system and submitted multiple supply requirements for the same items in the hope one of them would wind its way through the logistics system. The result was a further choking of the system by duplicate supply items, and a further slowing of the delivery of critical items.[7]

During the 1980s, the United States had prepositioned equipment and supplies aboard ships for early arriving units in the Persian Gulf. The Army operated twelve prepositioning ships, eight dry cargo and four tankers. The first vessel arrived in Saudi Arabia on August 17 and discharged its cargo of packaged food, general supplies and equipment, packaged fuel, construction and barrier equipment, ammunition, and medical supplies. Another vessel carried essential port operating equipment, including floating cranes, tugboats, rough terrain forklifts, and other support equipment. The Air Force had about $1 billion worth of fuel, ammunition, and equipment in Oman and Bahrain in addition to three prepositioning ships. These assets were designed for bare base operations that would include 1,200 personnel at each of fourteen aircraft beddown locations.

---

[6] Gordon and Trainor, *The Generals' War,* p. 239.

[7] Conrad, *Moving the Force,* pp. 35-36.

The New Face of War

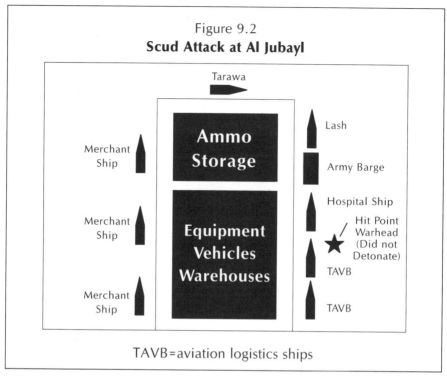

Figure 9.2
Scud Attack at Al Jubayl

Tarawa

Merchant
Ship

**Ammo
Storage**

Lash

Army Barge

Hospital Ship

Merchant
Ship

**Equipment
Vehicles
Warehouses**

Hit Point
Warhead
(Did not
Detonate)

TAVB

Merchant
Ship

TAVB

TAVB=aviation logistics ships

The Marine Corps prepositioning included thirteen ships organized in three squadrons. Each squadron carried enough equipment for a Marine Expeditionary Brigade and supply sustainment for at least thirty days. All three brigades required about 250 airlift sorties to deploy and either met or surpassed the goal of unloading the ships and marrying up with equipment within ten days.[8]

Trucks became a limiting factor during the Gulf War. The Army deployed seventy-five percent of its truck companies to support about a quarter of its combat divisions and still came up short of the mark. Lieutenant General William G. Pagonis, the principal architect of the logistics support, presents the sheer magnitude of the effort of supporting a quickly moving force:

> Simply put, the two Army corps and all their equipment had to be trucked westward and northward to their jumping-off points for the assault. VII Corps was trucked 330 miles across the desert, and XVII Airborne Corps leapfrogged more than 500 miles west and north. This required us to assemble a fleet of nearly 4,000 heavy

---

[8] U.S., Department of Defense, *Conduct of the Persian Gulf War,* pp. 379-81.

Lessons From the Persian Gulf War

205

vehicles of all types, many of which had to be contracted for. Just before the ground assault began, peak traffic at a checkpoint on the northernmost of these supply routes approached 18 vehicles per minute, seven days a week, 24-hours a day. This volume of traffic was sustained for almost six weeks.[9]

During the defensive phase of Desert Shield, each mechanized division's daily requirement included 345 gallons of diesel fuel, 50,000 gallons of aviation fuel, 213,000 gallons of water, and 208 40-foot truck trailers for other supplies ranging from barrier materials to ammunition. When the ground offensive got underway, a single division consumed 2.4 million gallons of fuel transported on 475 5,000-gallon tankers (this is about eight times larger than monthly sales by an average gas station in the United States).[10]

If the ground war had gone on much longer than 100 hours, it is likely that combat units would have out-run their logistics tail requiring combat operations to come to a grinding halt until resupply was completed. Providing adequate fuel and ammunition to sustain heavy armored forces remains a limiting factor of maneuver warfare.

There is a long litany of problems plaguing the move to the Gulf. Units being sent to the Gulf were sometimes confused about where or when they should meet their air transport or where they should marry-up equipment with departing ships. As a result, aircraft often flew partially empty or with low priority cargo, and a unit's equipment would be shipped on more than one vessel. This sometimes left units milling around in Saudi Arabia waiting for their equipment. One of the most potentially dangerous situations occurred when 30,000 VII Corps soldiers were left standing at the ports waiting for their equipment when the air war started. These soldiers bunched at ports provided a very lucrative target for an adversary inclined to strike them, especially one armed with biological and chemical weapons, or even nuclear weapons.[11]

All told, the Army accounted for about forty-three percent (by weight) of all equipment for early deploying units, including airlift (forty-six percent of all available airlift in the first month), fast sealift, and prepositioning. The Marine Corps had about thirty-five percent and the Air Force twenty-two

---

[9] As quoted in Conrad, *Moving the Force,* p. 46.

[10] *Ibid.,* p. 15.

[11] *Ibid.,* pp. 24-25.

The New Face of War

percent of the early deploying capability. The Army's armored and mechanized infantry divisions demanded the bulk of the sealift in the Gulf War. The M1 Abrams Main Battle Tank, for example, weighs sixty-seven tons, while its partner, the M2 Bradley Fighting Vehicle, weighs in at thirty-three tons. In the future, the Army is expected to claim seventy-seven percent of the workload of strategic airlift aircraft.[12] With these trends, *National Defense* reporter Sandra I. Meadows observes, "U.S. ground fighting forces two or three decades from now will be beaten by their own weight, unless leaders can find a way to lighten the load troops take to battle."[13]

The basic trouble with the buildup in the Gulf War was not, as is often assumed, insufficient cargo aircraft and ships to meet the power projection requirements. Rather, the real problem was a strategy that takes much too long to buildup tactical air, land, and maritime forces in the theater. Even with prepositioned and unlimited airlift and sealift *and* access, equipment shortages were exacerbated by procedural snafus and human-generated friction throughout the deployment.

Second, ground combat units are simply too heavy to participate in fast-moving crises. This constraint places into greater question the utility of the land force components in modern expeditionary strategies. Unless we can be assured of a set-piece Napoleonic battle similar to the Gulf War, an unlikely event, armored forces are likely to arrive too late to have an impact on military operations. During the critical early days of the conflict, after swallowing Kuwait in a sudden nine-hour assault, Iraq could have taken Riyadh, the capital of Saudi Arabia, in just four days. Third, the logistics needed to support extensive air and ground operations are immense. It is open to question whether the logistics task of modern warfare can keep up with the expenditure rates of rapid-fire weapons or the fuel consumption of tactical air forces on land and at sea and of land warfare units. Finally, the Persian Gulf War reveals an American power projection strategy that is very complex and highly susceptible to slow-downs generated by the simple friction of trying to harmonize all of its parts. This means that the U.S. strategy is extremely fragile and open to enemy actions that could delay and disrupt the deployment of U.S. forces.

---

[12] U.S., Congressional Budget Office, *Moving U.S. Forces,* pp. 7-8.

[13] Sandra I. Meadows, "Logistics Load Makes Land Force Too Slow for 21st Century Warfare," *National Defense* (September 1997), p. 18.

New Threats and Risks

When Saddam Hussein invaded Kuwait in August 1990, the U.S. intelligence community had no idea of the extent or maturity of Iraq's biological and nuclear weapons programs. Slightly better intelligence pictures of Saddam Hussein's chemical weapons and ballistic missiles were available, but even then there were gaping holes in the information base. For example, despite the fact that most of the 970 Coalition air strikes against the nuclear, biological, and chemical weapons target set hit chemical weapons facilities, 40,000 of these weapons were discovered and had to be destroyed by U.N. inspectors after the war. Coalition air forces also spent a considerable amount of time and resources, roughly 1,460 air strikes, against Iraq's ballistic missile capabilities. Nearly half of these sorties were dedicated to chasing mobile Scud missile launchers; not even a single Scud missile or launcher was destroyed.[14]

A careful reading of the Gulf War informs us about the ominous impact of facing regional adversaries armed with WMD. In the face of WMD-armed adversaries, everything of importance to projecting power is more vulnerable, including the regional seaports and airfields, urban areas and militaries of prospective host countries, and the U.S. military forces themselves at home, en route overseas, and in the theater of operations. It is increasingly difficult to justify the longstanding assumption that the United States will be able to project military power easily to wherever it is needed in the world.

Nuclear Weapons. The debate over when Iraq may have had nuclear weapons continues to intensify among Western experts as additional evidence of its clandestine program comes to light. For instance, Paul Leventhal of the Nuclear Control Institute thinks "the Iraqi nuclear program is far from dead." He points out that when the Iraqis claimed they were only three months away from a nuclear weapons capability, they must have had the components ready to assemble the device once they had sufficient fissile material. Yet, the International Atomic Energy Agency (IAEA) did not find the components after the war. If the Iraqis have the essential parts of nuclear devices hidden, does it mean they are still three months away from a nuclear

---

[14] U.S., Department of the Air Force, *Gulf War Air Power Survey: Summary Report* (Washington, D.C.: Government Printing Office, 1993), pp. 80-81, 85-86, and *Gulf War Air Power Survey: Operations and Effects and Effectiveness* (Washington, D.C.: Government Printing Office, 1993), Vol. II, Part 2, pp. 330-32.

The New Face of War

explosive? Some believe the Iraqis may be shopping for fissile material on the international black market as well as for the nuclear expertise necessary to hurdle technical difficulties.[15]

The Western countries were very fortunate that Saddam Hussein acted before he had a few nuclear weapons readied for delivery. As discussed in Chapter 2, the Iraqi nuclear weapons program illustrates some alternative pathways that nuclear proliferators may take in the future. Tomorrow's proliferators have also been informed by the Coalition bombing during the Gulf War and post-war IAEA inspections of what the telltale signatures of a nuclear program might be—they are likely to make Western detection of their nuclear weapons programs far more difficult than was the case in Iraq.

Future nuclear proliferators are likely to adopt defensive techniques similar to those used so successfully by the Germans in World War Two. Michael Eisenstadt of the Washington Policy Institute, for instance, believes that the facilities supporting nuclear programs are likely to be widely dispersed, camouflaged and concealed in a variety of ways. Buildings will be located and constructed to minimize vulnerability to U.S. air attack, including the use of blast walls, underground facilities, and versatile structures that permit rapid removal of key machinery and equipment and their dispersal to secure areas. Whenever possible, one should expect weapons design, development and testing to be conducted in small, inconspicuous buildings. In some cases, the nuclear facility may be hidden within the activities of much larger manufacturing structures. A host of measures will be taken to eliminate or lower the "signatures" of nuclear facilities through control of emissions, including discharge of heat, radiation and isotope effluents. Other functions, such as electronic communications elements and vehicular and pedestrian traffic, would be altered to mask the actual activities.[16]

The Iraqis demonstrated that plutonium is not necessary to produce nuclear weapons—highly enriched uranium is "good enough." Moreover, nuclear expertise is readily available. According to some reports, nuclear scientists and engineers from the former Soviet Union are willing to cross borders to assist foreign programs, if the price is right. Much of the equipment necessary to produce nuclear weapons falls into the dual-use, civilian and military category, opening the door to plausible denial of the actual end

---

[15] As quoted in Barbara Crossette, "Experts Doubt Iraq's Claims On A-Bomb," *New York Times* (August 30, 1995), p. A6.

[16] Eisenstadt, *Like Phoenix From the Ashes?*, pp. 26-27, and Kenneth R. Timmerman, "A Nuclear Iraq—Again," *Wall Street Journal* (November 12, 1993).

---

uses. Furthermore, the international black market of fissile material—the quintessential core of making nuclear weapons—from gangs or other illegal activities in countries of the former Soviet Union could provide viable alternatives to indigenous production of highly enriched uranium. With trained scientists and engineers, and a sufficient amount of fissile material, all that is required to build a nuclear bomb is a little ingenuity.

The Iraqis spent $6 to $12 billion to duplicate the U.S. programs that produced the first atomic bombs. An elaborate complex of nuclear research and development facilities was established in various parts of the country. This effort was supported by thousands of foreign-trained scientists and engineers; numerous Jordanian front companies were used to obtain needed materials from abroad. Undetected by Western intelligence, Iraq was within eighteen months of producing its first nuclear device.

In the final analysis, and with the advantage of U.N. on-site inspections after the war, the world learned that Iraq had fifty-six nuclear facilities (nineteen primary facilities) scattered throughout the country rather than the four to eight nuclear targets attacked by the Coalition during the war. Evidence of these activities in Western intelligence was fragmentary. After the war, the Defense Intelligence Agency concluded that "prior to Desert Storm, little was known about Iraq's highly compartmented nuclear weapons program."[17] With Western intelligence agencies thrown totally off track by Iraq's deception measures about the nuclear program, the Coalition's military planners operated on the basis of what were proven to be faulty assumptions. These inaccurate operating premises led to the Coalition's counter-nuclear operations being conducted in the blind.

Why is intelligence on a regional adversary's nuclear activities so important? Nuclear weapons, even a small arsenal of some five to ten weapons, offer high leverage to the proliferator. The U.S. would be hard pressed to neutralize regional nuclear threats against the proliferator's neighbors. It is open to question whether a regional ally or friendly country would shrug off nuclear coercion to grant the American armed forces unrestricted access to seaports, airfields, and other facilities. The RAND Corporation's Marc Dean Millot, Roger Mollander and Peter Wilson, for example, found from their penetrating political-military simulations examining key aspects of

---

[17] As quoted by Gordon and Trainor, *The Generals' War,* pp. 181–82, 457.

nuclear proliferation that "...even a very small number of nuclear weapons can wreak havoc on U.S. power projection operations."[18]

Biological Weapons. The speed with which Iraq was able to start a biological weapons program and produce militarily significant deliverable quantities of anthrax, botulinum toxin and aflatoxin is quite remarkable. The lesson for the non-Western countries interested in posing asymmetrical responses to U.S. conventional military superiority is that biological weapons can be produced secretly. As discussed in Chapter 3, the Iraqi proliferation pathway shows how to do it and not be discovered. Another contemporary lesson can be drawn from the rapid conversion of Iraqi biotechnology facilities to support wartime requirements following the August 1990 seizure of Kuwait. The dual-use capabilities inherent in legitimate programs for civil purposes—such as the production of vaccines—provides a ready standby biological warfare capability; all that is needed is a cadre of trained scientists and technicians and a plan of action for quick conversion to the production of biological warfare agents.

Dr. Richard Spertzel, a U.S. member of the U.N. inspection team, believes Iraq's biological weapons would have been effective if they had been used during the Gulf War. Deployed in bombs and warheads for the extended-range Al Hussein missiles, Iraq's arsenal was designed for strategic purposes, not tactical situations. Although the weapons were armed with impact-fuze detonators, a less than ideal way to disseminate biological agents, Dr. Spertzel believes it is clear that they would have produced casualties. Iraq's program should be seen as an indicator of the pathways that may be taken by future proliferators. "There may be some that already have done that," he says.[19] In just five years of rapid progress, the Iraqi program demonstrated how easy it is for a rogue regime to develop these types of weapons and to keep the details away from very intrusive U.N. inspections.

The U.N. Special Commission convened a panel of international experts in March 1997 to review and assess Iraq's declarations on the biological weapons program. The expert assessment concluded that Iraq had (1) failed to report all imports of equipment and materials, in particular growth media; (2) under-reported the production of bulk biological warfare agents; (3) given an inaccurate account of production of aflatoxin; (4) provided

---

[18] Marc Dean Millot, Roger Mollander, and Peter A. Wilson, *"The Day After..." Study: Nuclear Proliferation in the Post-Cold War World,* Vol. I - Summary Report (Santa Monica, Calif.: RAND Corporation, 1993), p. 17.

[19] Gertz, "Horror Weapons," p. 47.

---

false declarations on its biological warfare programs; and (5) failed to give a full accounting of procurement activities associated with the biological weapons program.[20]

Iraq, having already built a successful biological program and with the necessary expertise available, could rebuild its biological weapons capability within six to twelve months after termination of U.N. inspections. A resumption of Iraq's biological program could have serious consequences in the region. Among the most vulnerable neighboring cities, owing to their layout and prevailing wind patterns, are Ankara, Riyadh, Cairo, Esfahan, Tehran, and Damascus.[21] Moreover, Rolf Ekeus, the former head of the U.N. Special Commission on Iraq, thinks it is highly likely that Iraq retains an operational Scud missile force and biological warheads to go with them.[22] According to Iraq, it produced, stored and, after the war, destroyed 158 gallons of anthrax in concentrated form or enough to be packed into forty or fifty bombs and warheads. Each could kill thousands of people, perhaps even tens of thousands.[23] David Kay, the former chief nuclear inspector for the U.N. Special Commission on Iraq, estimated that 2,000 tons of the anthrax that is unaccounted for or enough to kill forty-five to sixty million people under optimal distribution in urban areas. Anthrax, after being dried, can last for decades.[24] Among the scenarios of greatest concern, given Iraq's stockpiles of anthrax and other biological agents as well as technical expertise, include trucks driving along the Iraq-Kuwait border spraying biological agents during a period of high winds, killing much of the Kuwaiti population, or agricultural sprayers used to hit American allies or U.S. military facilities in the theater.[25] According to one report, the Iraqis used biological weapons in conjunction with chemical weapons in 1984 against Iranian troops. Bombs filled with trichothecene mycotoxins—the trauma from the toxins simultaneously affect multiple organ systems in the body and can have catastrophic results—were delivered by Iraqi fighter aircraft.

---

[20] United Nations, Security Council, *Report of the Secretary-General,* U.N. Doc. S/1997/301, pp. 16-17.

[21] Philip Finnegan, "U.N. Woes May Allow Bio-Chem Revival in Iraq," *Defense News* (November 18-24, 1996), p. 30.

[22] Martin Sieff, "Albright Oks Saddam's Ouster," *Washington Times* (March 27, 1997), p. A13.

[23] Smith, "Iraq Had Program for Germ Warfare," pp. A1, A17.

[24] Philip Finnegan, "Saddam's Bio-Chem Arsenal Could Snarl U.S. Gulf Plans," *Defense News* (September 30-October 6, 1996), pp. 1, 58.

[25] Finnegan, "Limited U.S. Action May Boost Iraqi Biological Threats," pp. 3, 42.

The bombs "exploded silently in mid-air, giving no indication of their lethal content."[26]

America's defenses against biological weapons were inadequate during the Persian Gulf War. While gas masks can be effective in filtering the microscopic particles in biological warfare aerosols, the U.S. armed forces lacked reliable detectors that could have alerted troops in time to don their gas masks before they were exposed.[27]

Since defenses against biological weapons were questionable at best, the Coalition's commanders placed a top priority on eliminating Iraq's presumed biological weapons. Intelligence sources knew that Iraq's biological weapons program began sometime in the late 1970s, but the exact nature and current status of the program were unknown. As a consequence of the intelligence failure to provide an accurate picture of Iraq's biological weapons, Coalition planners considered the prospect of their use to be a remote possibility. Later, the Defense Intelligence Agency reversed itself and concluded that Iraq had an ongoing anthrax program. By October 1990, the assessment included botulinum toxin—a single Scud warhead filled with the toxin and the right dispersal capabilities and tactics could contaminate 3,700 square kilometers and allied casualties would begin four hours after exposure. For six weeks the debate raged inside the Bush Administration over what to do about Iraq's biological weapons, including macabre questions about how to handle contaminated corpses. Some advocated seeding known storage areas with mines to keep the Iraqis away from the weapons. Others argued, including Lieutenant General Charles A. Horner, commander of the Air Force component assigned to the U.S. Central Command, that just-before-dawn strikes by stealth fighters could crack the bunkers open and F-111s could follow with specialized munitions that would fuel a conflagration. Any escaping anthrax spores should be burned off by the sun's ultraviolet rays. "If there's collateral damage in Iraq," Horner said, "perhaps that's not all bad. There has to be some penalty for building and storing these weapons." General H. Norman Schwartzkopf added during the briefing to Defense Secretary Dick Cheney that "CENTCOM's position is that we attack these targets."[28]

---

[26] Al J. Venter, "Biological Warfare Atrocities Revealed," *Jane's Intelligence Review and Jane's Sentinel Pointer* (March 1998), p. 1.

[27] Tucker, "Biological Weapons Threat," p. 171.

[28] Rick Atkinson, *Crusade: The Untold Story of the Persian Gulf War* (Boston: Houghton Mifflin, 1993), pp. 87-89, and U.S., Department of the Air Force, *Gulf War Air Power Survey: Operations and Effects and Effectiveness,* Vol. II, Part 2, p. 322.

The Coalition was successful in identifying five suspected research and production facilities. Iraq also had scattered throughout the country twenty-one specially designed, refrigerated bunkers that were suspected of containing biological or other special weapons. Eighteen of these had been identified before the war. It was believed that Iraq had produced anthrax spores and botulinum toxin as agents and that it was pursuing other agents as well. Baghdad's supposed lack of operational experience with biological weapons made U.S. early intelligence estimates very tenuous. Analysts "could only speculate that Saddam might resort to biological weapons to preempt a coalition offensive, achieve certain battlefield objectives, or save himself and his regime from destruction."[29]

The biological targets in Iraq also created new operational problems for planners. Given the virulent microorganisms and toxins that might be widely dispersed as a result of bombing, "they feared high-explosive bombs striking these buildings might produce clouds of aerosolized agents that could travel long distances, contaminate large areas, and poison thousands or even millions of people within and outside Iraq."[30] The air commander, General Charles A. Horner, believed that the risk of bombing the biological bunkers could be managed, and he argued that "if there was a small outbreak of disease as result, that would be a lesson to third world nations about the risks of producing biological weapons."[31]

Chemical Weapons. Despite Iraq's lack of widespread use of chemical weapons against Coalition forces in the Persian Gulf War, they were used extensively during the 1980-88 Iran-Iraq War, providing an experience base for development of operational doctrine by proliferating countries. The Iraqis began using mustard gas in December 1982 as a means of dealing with Iran's human-wave and night attacks. Use of mustard and possibly the nerve agent tabun continued through 1983 and 1984. After their ground barriers would delay or halt the Iranians and result in a bunching of their forces, Iraq used fighter-bombers and helicopters to deliver the chemical munitions against the massed Iranians. In March 1984, Iran charged that Iraq had used mustard and sarin nerve agent in an attack on Majnoon Island.

---

[29] U.S., Department of the Air Force, *Gulf War Air Power Survey: Planning and Command and Control,* Vol. I, Part 1 (Washington, D.C.: Government Printing Office, 1993), pp. 160–61.

[30] *Ibid.*

[31] As quoted in Gordon and Trainor, *The Generals' War,* p. 192.

As discussed previously, the Iraqis may have also used the chemical attacks to cover their use of biological weapons. On three occasions, the Iraqis suffered losses from their own chemical attacks due to their inability to compensate for unfavorable winds. After nearly a two-year hiatus on the use of chemical weapons, Iraq began using them again in 1987, including against noncombatants in Kurdish villages that resulted in more than one hundred casualties. On February 28, 1988, in an effort to repel an Iranian attack on the Kurdish town of Halabjah (population: 70,000), Iraqi fighter-bombers dropped 100-liter containers of mustard that vaporized on impact and formed a white gas cloud. When the civilians began to flee, the Iranians, thinking they were Iraqis, fired hydrogen cyanide gas into the region. Casualties numbered between 4,000 and 5,000.[32] The effects of the attack lingered ten years later. Kurdish villagers showed a variety of nervous system disorders, birth deformities, and changes in individuals' DNA that will result in abnormal births for generations to come.[33] Overall, out of the approximately 50,000 casualties resulting from chemical weapons during the Iran-Iraq War, about 5,000 resulted in death.

Iraq had the largest chemical agent production capability in the Third World when it entered Kuwait in 1990. As examined in Chapter 4, each year it produced thousands of tons of mustard gas, and nerve agents sarin (GB) and GF. A nonpersistent agent, sarin is relatively easy to produce from readily available precursors. GF is a semi-persistent nerve agent similar to soman (GD) that was produced by Iraq after Western nations began to restrict shipments of the precursors for soman. Iraqi chemical agents were to be delivered by aircraft spray tanks as well as rockets, bombs, mortars, artillery shells, and missile warheads.[34]

Unlike the nuclear and biological weapons programs, the Iraqi chemical weapons effort was difficult to hide. By the time of its invasion of Kuwait, Iraq was well along the way to producing indigenously all of the essential precursors of mustard, tabun, sarin, and VX. "I recommend that we send a demarche to Baghdad," General Schwartzkopf told General Powell. "We'll say, 'if you use chemicals, we're going to use nuclear weapons on you.' We may never do that but...it would not hurt one bit to send that signal to Baghdad."[35]

---

[32] White, *Characterization and Historical Review of Chemical/Biological Weapons.*

[33] Dr. Christine Gosden, remarks on *60 Minutes,* CBS Television (February 28, 1998).

[34] U.S., Department of Defense, *Conduct of the Persian Gulf War,* p. 15.

[35] As quoted in Atkinson, *Crusade,* p. 86.

The U.S. commanders assumed from the beginning that Iraq would use chemical weapons. President George Bush, Secretary of Defense Dick Cheney, and Chairman of the Joint Chiefs of Staff General Colin L. Powell were all told by General H. Norman Schwartzkopf and his commanders that "Iraqi forces will use chemical weapons" in the event of war. Hence, planners were told "to destroy Iraqi capability to produce and [deliver] weapons of mass destruction" and to do so "as early as possible."[36] Since chemical weapons were considered the most probable threat, this was the exclusive focus of the target set defined in August 1990. Later, nuclear and biological targets were added, broadening the target set. In the meantime, the chemical target list had grown from eight targets in August 1990 to twenty-five targets by December 1990, and leveled off to twenty-three targets by mid-January 1991. The percentage of targets in the nuclear-biological-chemical (NBC) category remained constant at about ten percent of the overall target planning.[37]

The bulk of the 970 strikes against NBC targets was against the Iraqi chemical warfare capabilities. Three primary targets were the three chemical precursor production facilities near Al Fallujah, research centers at Salman Pak (also associated with production of biological warfare toxins), and the Al Muthanna chemical munitions production facilities near Samarra. At peak production, U.N. inspectors estimated that Al Muthanna could have produced five tons of mustard agent and 2.5 tons of sarin per day. Iraq had nineteen primary chemical installations. Also listed for attack were suspected storage bunkers for chemical weapons throughout the country.

The Air Force's judgment of the effectiveness of the air campaign was that Iraq did not use chemical weapons during the war for fear of the Coalition's ability to retaliate with nuclear weapons. Moreover, the attacks against Iraq's research, development, and production facilities began the process of taking away Baghdad's ability to threaten its neighbors. Finally, the attrition of artillery among Iraqi front line units made it very difficult to coordinate a systematic use of chemical munitions. In sum, "even though air attacks against Iraq's chemical-warfare capabilities fell well short of destroying them completely, it by no means follows that these attacks were militarily futile or served no purpose."[38] After the war, the United Nations

---

[36] U.S., Department of Defense, *Conduct of the Persian Gulf War,* p. 161.

[37] *Ibid.,* p. 185.

[38] U.S., Department of the Air Force, *Gulf War Air Power Survey: Summary Report,* p. 81.

The New Face of War

supervised the destruction of nearly 40,000 chemical-filled missile warheads, bombs, artillery shells, and 122-millimeter rockets, plus 481,000 liters of chemical warfare agents and 1.8 million liters of precursor chemicals.

An issue of continuing concern to U.S. military planners is Iraq's missing stockpile of VX-hydrochloride and VX-salt, both of which can be stored for many years, plus the up to 300 tons of chemical precursors for VX. Since VX is an oily liquid that can remain lethal for several weeks or longer after an attack, it could be used to contaminate ports, airfields, and equipment prepositioned in the Persian Gulf region. For example, U.S. equipment is stored at discrete locations in Saudi Arabia, Kuwait, Qatar, Bahrain, and Oman that could be open to chemical strikes, VX, through the use of missiles, bombs or terrorist attacks.[39]

Ballistic and Cruise Missiles. As non-Western countries continue to arm themselves with ballistic and cruise missiles of varying ranges, including long-range versions, the United States will need to find ways to conduct effective offensive and defensive anti-missile operations. The missile threat will be manifested against the U.S. and its allies in different ways. Short-range missiles or those with a range up to 100 miles will pose direct threats to military forces in the field. Medium- and intermediate-range missiles pose strategic threats against in-theater ports and airfields to disrupt and block U.S. power projection operations.

The Iraqis launched eighty-eight modified Scud missiles at targets in Israel, Saudi Arabia and Bahrain during the forty-three-day Persian Gulf War. Some of their warheads were swatted down by Patriot anti-missile missiles, others slammed into residential areas in Tel Aviv and Riyadh, and a few turned and twisted on an uncertain trajectory before tumbling harmlessly into uninhabited areas. According to official U.S. assessments, none of the missiles was armed with biological or chemical warheads. Except for the warhead that hit the American barracks in Dhahran that killed twenty-eight Americans and injured ninety-seven others, the Iraqi ballistic missile attacks served little, if any, military usefulness vis-à-vis the United States.[40] Politically, however, the attacks were significant since they compelled the Coalition air forces to divert a substantial number of intelligence and attack resources from the broad counter-military air campaign against Iraq to

---

[39] Finnegan, "Saddam's Bio-Chem Arsenal Could Snarl U.S. Gulf Plans," p. 49.

[40] U.S., Department of the Air Force, *Gulf War Air Power Survey: A Statistical Compendium and Chronology,* p. 542.

---

counter-Scud operations. In this regard, the Scud attacks were among the most militarily effective actions taken by the Iraqis.

An essential component of the Iraqi drive to be capable of delivering weapons of mass destruction throughout the Middle East, as explained in Chapter 6, was the effort to build a robust ballistic missile production base. Like their WMD programs, the Iraqi missile development infrastructure was extensive. The Iraqis received their first Scud Bs from the Soviet Union in the 1970s and later Scud C derivatives from North Korea.[41] During the 1980s, the Iraqis built a modern missile development and production infrastructure by drawing on foreign technology and expertise, primarily from Brazil, Argentina, Germany, Austria, and Italy.

The promise of missile proliferation in the future is grounded solidly on the increasing spread of the knowledge and technology necessary to underwrite national and joint venture programs involving two or more countries. Moreover, it is only a matter of time until non-Western countries overcome the technical and production barriers to intermediate- and long-range ballistic and cruise missiles. Advances in in-flight navigation and precision location makes accuracy "good enough" for many targets, especially those seaports and airfields so vital to U.S. power projection. Warhead designs for nuclear, biological, chemical and conventional attacks offer non-Western countries a new versatility in confronting the United States and other Western countries.

Like Iraq's biological and chemical program on the eve of the Gulf War, Baghdad's ballistic missile program was well advanced and ready. While nuclear warheads were not yet available, radioactive debris could have been scattered by the missiles. The Iraqis demonstrated extraordinary technical skill and innovation in developing their weapons of mass destruction and missiles. With U.S. and other forces clustered at a few bases, Saudi ports jammed with ships, transport aircraft parked wingtip-to-wingtip, and the Israeli, Saudi, and other Arab peoples open to attack, the region was braced for disaster. While the events that unfolded may not have triggered the Iraqi use of these weapons, Baghdad's non-use of these weapons were

---

[41] The Soviet Scud As were first seen in 1957 and were probably derived in part from the German V-2. Scud Bs were deployed in the mid-1960s. The missile accompanied Soviet ground forces on an eight-wheeled vehicle called a "transporter erector launcher" or TEL. The Scud B is a single-stage, liquid-fueled rocket and is believed to have a 300 kilometers (164 miles) range with a payload of 2,100-pounds and an accuracy rate on the order of 3,000 feet. See U.S., Department of the Air Force, *Gulf War Air Power Survey: Operations and Effects and Effectiveness,* Vol. II, Part 2, p. 317.

more a result of Iraqi strategic decisions than of any design by U.S. policy makers and military planners.

The totality of Iraq's WMD infrastructure was enormous. The comparison of the differences in the WMD and missile facilities on the Coalition's target list during the Gulf War with the number of facilities discovered by the U.N. on-site inspectors after the war finds a target base at least two-and-a-half times larger. The 252 targets shown in Figure 9.3 understates the actual number, which is probably more on the order of 400 targets when all of the dual-use, civil and military facilities are counted. Four main conclusions can be drawn from this analysis.

Regional WMD Proliferation Is Today's Problem. Before Desert Storm, U.S. policy makers generally believed that regional WMD proliferation could be stopped. "A combination of wishful thinking and narrow legalistic analysis had persuaded most policy makers that allegations that Iraq was acquiring weapons of mass destruction were little more than anti-Arab propaganda intended to block U.S.-Iraqi reconciliation," Howard Teischer, National Security Council staff member during the Reagan Administration explains. "Iraq's signature on various non-proliferation treaties bolstered this belief."[42] The stunning series of post-Gulf War revelations about the size, scope, sophistication and maturity of Iraq's nuclear, chemical and biological weapons and ballistic missile programs have changed all that.

Regional WMD Proliferation Is Likely To Continue Unabated. Three observations drive this conclusion. First, regional states have powerful incentives to acquire WMD. The Cold War's end has lifted the restraining influence of superpower competition and unleashed long-standing tensions that remain unchecked. Rogue regimes in search of regional hegemony seek WMD to intimidate and/or defeat their neighbors and to deter and, if necessary, disrupt and block U.S. intervention. Indeed, having witnessed the U.S.-led Coalition's aerial campaign to systematically destroy the powerful Iraqi military in 1991, potential U.S. adversaries are now scrambling to acquire strategic "equalizers."

Meanwhile, as more and more states proliferate, even non-aggressor states will feel compelled to follow suit to deter WMD-armed aggression. "I think we're going to see the number of nuclear weapons states grow exponentially over the next 10 to 25 years," said Dr. John Hassard, a British nuclear

---

[42] Howard Teischer, "The Naive Hope That Allowed Hussein to Weigh Mass Murder," *Los Angeles Times* (September 10, 1995).

Figure 9.3
Iraq's WMD-Related Facilities

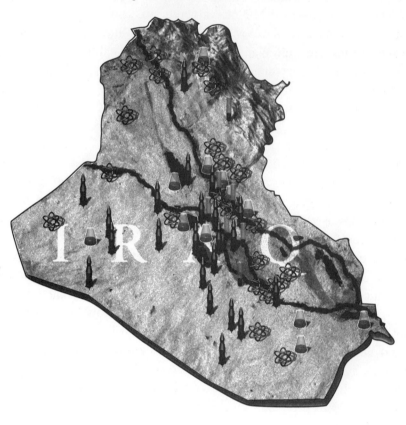

🕸	Nuclear	56
🝯	Chemical	23
⬇	Biological	93
🚀	Missiles	29
		_____
		252

Source: Robert W. Chandler, *Tomorrow's War, Today's Decisions,* (McLean, Va.: AMCODA Press, 1996)

physicist at the University of London. Hassard said that, as one country goes nuclear, "its five or six neighbours will feel much greater pressure to acquire nuclear weapons."[43]

The Iraqi case also shows that proliferation is all but impossible to prevent. And, while our experience with Iraq may provide a useful sketch of future regional WMD threats, that same information can also aid aspiring proliferators who now know more about how to develop and conceal a WMD program (and protect it from attack).[44]

Finally, nuclear, chemical and biological weapons and missiles (ballistic and cruise) are getting easier to develop and acquire. In today's world, the flow of information simply cannot be controlled and the transfer and dispersal of WMD technology is inevitable.[45] Indeed, many of yesterday's "customers"—the early proliferators—are now suppliers.

Monitoring Regional WMD Proliferation Will Be Extraordinarily Difficult, Particularly During Crises And Conflict. One of the first lessons the Coalition partners learned after the smoke cleared in the Gulf was that their pre-war WMD-related intelligence had been woefully inadequate. L. Britt Snider, a senior defense official, is reported as having put it most poignantly: "It was apparent the intelligence community didn't know squatola about the Iraqi military."[46] Obviously, these facts suggest that far more resources should now be devoted to WMD-related intelligence gathering and that substantial innovation in intelligence collection and analysis is required. James Schlesinger, a former secretary of defense, told the National Security Committee at the House of Representatives, that "we must be alert to which countries have access to what technologies—and how we might counter them.... That will pose an immense challenge for intelligence.... More broadly, the range of opportunities now available to other states to exploit modern sensors and modern electronics will pose a deep and fundamental challenge to our intelligence gathering and assessment."[47]

---

[43] "Nuclear Watchdog Unleashes New Powers to Stall Evaders," *Jane's Defence Weekly* (April 8, 1995), p. 23.

[44] For an interesting look at the Iraqi deception, see David A. Kay, "Denial and Deception Practices of WMD Proliferators: Iraq and Beyond" in *Weapons Proliferation in the 1990s,* ed. by Brad Roberts (Cambridge, Mass.: MIT Press, 1995), pp. 303–25.

[45] For a good discussion of this phenomenon, see Michael Moodie, "Beyond Proliferation: The Challenge of Technology Diffusion," *Washington Quarterly* (Spring 1995), pp. 183–205.

[46] Ernest Blazer, "Inside the Ring," *Washington Times* (November 6, 1997), p. A8.

[47] James Schlesinger, "Statement Before the National Security Committee, House of Representatives" (February 12, 1997). Photocopy.

The Distinct WMD Target Set Presents a Daunting Military Challenge. Using the Iraqi WMD program (January 1991) as a baseline target set for future counterforce operations, one is immediately struck by the sheer scale of the projected effort. Planners would have to target more than 252 "fixed" facilities (e.g., research, development and production sites), not to mention hundreds of other dispersed (e.g., weapons stocks) and/or mobile assets (e.g., missile launchers). A review of nuclear, biological, and chemical weapons and missile targets struck during the Gulf War yields a ratio of eight aimpoints for each installation. Eight aimpoints on the average is consistent with the number of precision weapons employed against the WMD target set and is in accord with other studies based on a Desert Storm target base.[48] This means that the range of total aimpoints for the entire Iraqi WMD target set actually numbered from about 2,000 (250 targets) to 2,650 (330 targets) to perhaps as high as 3,200 (400 targets). Literally thousands of separate aimpoints, each requiring one or more precision weapons, would need to be attacked—far more than were struck in the first twenty-four hours of Desert Storm.

If one assumes that the objective of any U.S. counterforce operation would be to neutralize a proliferator's WMD capabilities, the Gulf War air campaign sets a rather weak precedent. By the Air Force's own admission, the forty-three-day assault—conducted with impunity and under optimal conditions—merely "inconvenienced" the Iraqi nuclear effort.[49] Meanwhile, Iraq's chemical and biological programs had fully matured prior to Desert Storm, and large quantities of weaponized biological and chemical assets survived the allied onslaught. Indeed, the real setbacks to the Iraqi WMD program occurred only *after the fact,* when U.N. and IAEA inspectors uncovered the full extent of Iraq's WMD programs (albeit with many details hidden forever by the Iraqis).

In short, Americans can expect future WMD target sets to be large, extremely difficult to find, hardened, well-protected, and located next to things or people we do not want to damage or injure. Counter-WMD operations therefore could likely be large in scale, extraordinarily challenging from both operational and logistical standpoints, politically controversial, and very risky. Prudence demands that the U.S. strategy for countering the regional WMD threat not rest solely on our ability to eliminate it militarily.

---

[48] U.S., Department of the Air Force, *Gulf War Air Power Survey: Summary Report,* p. 82.

[49] U.S., Department of the Air Force, *Gulf War Air Power Survey: Operations and Effects and Effectiveness,* Vol. II, Part 2, p. 329.

New Challenges for Future Warfare

The current U.S. military strategy for protecting global interests is based largely on the Desert Storm experience. That is, the U.S. plans to respond to aggression abroad by rapidly deploying large numbers of short-range forces (ships, planes, and troops) to the theater of conflict, halting the invasion, and then launching a massive counter-offensive to evict the aggressor from seized territory. Since the current defense modernization plan is designed to support this strategy, tomorrow's military forces will look much like today's.

Stunned by the extraordinary success of America's deployed conventional military power in vanquishing the Iraqi army, rogue regimes and other governments hostile toward the United States have been looking for exploitable weaknesses in the American strategy. The dependence on time and access offers these adversaries opportunities for attacks against these two main pillars that support the transoceanic power projection strategy. If U.S. forces cannot readily use regional seaports, airfields, and other facilities, and aircraft carriers and other vessels are kept at a distance by mines, submarines, closure of maritime chokepoints, and other obstructions, access can be denied at least for the time needed to defeat U.S. friends and allies.

Proliferation of weapons of mass destruction in key regions around the world has much to do with attacking the U.S. military strategy by eroding the strength of its main supports or weight-bearing assumptions: time and access. WMD-armed states, some with supporting terrorist arms, have moved the world onto a higher operational stage. Saddam Hussein blazed a new trail for proliferators to follow. In the final analysis, the principal lessons to be learned from the Persian Gulf War are founded more on the strategic purposes behind Iraq's WMD programs than on the course of the conflict. The Gulf War was the last of its kind. Tomorrow, Americans will face enemies with WMD and an operational challenge that could find that the side that shoots first is twice armed.

CHAPTER 10

America's Strategy Under Attack

The Chinese military philosopher Sun Tzu wrote *The Art of War* in the fourth century B.C., and across the centuries it profoundly influenced Chinese history and Japanese military thought. Popularized in the West during the twentieth century, Sun Tzu's writings have spread around the world. After the astounding American-led victory over Iraq in the 1991 Persian Gulf War, several countries have been searching for U.S. military vulnerabilities that might be effectively exploited in future conflicts. Their approach is the one recommended by Sun Tzu: "To subdue the enemy without fighting is the acme of skill. Thus, what is of supreme importance in war is to attack the enemy's strategy."[1]

With the aim of defeating America's "big, mean war machine,"[2] regional antagonists are arming themselves with weapons of mass destruction, ballistic and cruise missiles, and advanced conventional weapons and technologies. Drawing upon lessons learned from the Gulf War and taking advantage of the bustling international arms market, these weapons offer new opportunities for posing severe asymmetric threats against the U.S. military posture. Unable to challenge the American armed forces directly, regional adversaries may attempt to counter the U.S. power projection strategy through asymmetric means by confronting the United States in ways that it cannot match, circumventing American strengths through inexpensive and unconventional approaches, or carefully exploiting military vulnerabilities associated with the deployment and operations of American expeditionary forces.

North Korea, Iran, and Iraq possess the means and the motivation to engage the United States militarily as the twentieth century comes to a

---

[1] Sun Tzu, *The Art of War,* trans. by Samuel B. Griffith (New York: Oxford University Press, 1977), p. 77.

[2] "The Big, Mean War Machine," *U.S. News & World Report* (February 28, 1994).

close. Russia and China, suppliers to some proliferators, could also be on a collision course—post-Cold War political relations leaves several questions open in the military realm. Meanwhile, several other regional powers are growing in wealth, technology, and information, which will give them greater military capabilities and more influence.

The objectives of a WMD-armed adversary vis-à-vis the United States could include (1) *deterring* the U.S. by raising to prohibitive levels the perceived cost of intervention with the threat of mass U.S. and host nation casualties; (2) *disrupting* U.S. military deployments and combat operations with WMD attacks against theater seaports, airfields, bases, and aircraft carriers in littoral waters; (3) *coercing* U.S. regional allies by means of WMD threats into denying the U.S. access to their seaports, airfields, and other reception facilities; and (4) *compelling* a limitation of U.S. war aims by threatening use of WMD as a means of ensuring survival of the regime in power. Regional WMD delivery systems could range from ballistic missiles, cruise missiles, and strike aircraft to terrorists and paramilitary forces using trucks, boats, and similar vehicles.[3]

For the United States to maintain its dominant global position and protect the nation's interests, the armed forces must be able to project decisive power anywhere, anytime, and at acceptable cost. In order to defeat the enemy, the armed forces must ensure that no region critical to national interests will be dominated by a hostile power. These objectives mean that "in event of armed conflict, US Armed Forces will render an adversary incapable of armed resistance through destruction of his capacity to threaten our interests or by breaking his will to do so."[4]

Satisfying these power projection objectives will be increasingly more difficult as WMD proliferation continues around the world. A campaign to disarm a WMD-armed adversary would be highly complex and very risky, especially since the proliferator will undoubtedly be aware that America views the development of nuclear, biological, and chemical weapons as a burgeoning threat. Preemptive strikes could resolve some of these problems, but such attacks are highly problematical politically and militarily. Offensive action by the United States would likely come only after a pro-

---

[3] Dean Wilkening and Kenneth Watman, *Nuclear Deterrence In a Regional Context* (Santa Monica, Calif.: RAND Corporation, 1995), pp. 31-38.

[4] U.S., Joint Chiefs of Staff, *National Military Strategy of the United States of America 1997* (Washington, D.C.: Government Printing Office, 1997).

　　　　　　　　　　　　　　　　　　　　　　　　　　The New Face of War

longed period of rising political tensions, during which the suspected WMD program can be expected to receive intense international scrutiny. Fearing military action, the proliferator would likely step up defensive preparations, such as concealing and dispersing critical WMD assets and placing air defenses in a much higher state of readiness.[5] Many of the most critical facilities could very well be located in hardened and/or deeply buried bunkers resistant to all but the most advanced penetrating weapons and virtually invulnerable to current-generation cruise missiles. Many facilities would probably be guarded by an overlapping system of sophisticated local-area and terminal air defenses. Moreover, many could be located in, or indeed relocated to, heavily populated urban areas. "Hugging" civilians with WMD plays against the well-known Western aversion to collateral damage, especially when played back by the Cable News Network (CNN) to the court of world opinion.

In Desert Storm, Americans and potential future adversaries learned just how very long it takes to deploy large numbers of short-range forces (ships, planes, and troops) to the theater of conflict. The Gulf War also pointed out how dependent the nation's military strategy is upon just a few seaports and airfields for the buildup of force and conduct of combat operations. Yet, the current U.S. strategy appears curiously oblivious to the military risks mounted against it by the proliferation of WMD and advanced conventional weapons and technologies.

Weight-Bearing Assumptions of U.S. Strategy

The implications are clear that America's military strategy for the twenty-first century is critically dependent on two main pillars for success: adequate *time* to deploy U.S. forces overseas, and unhindered and unobstructed *access* to theater seaports and airfields. These two weight-bearing factors are pre-conditions that enable U.S. forces to possess the strategic agility, overseas presence, power projection, and decisive force capabilities essential to defeating aggression in two overlapping major theater wars. If either or both of these weight-bearing pillars is seriously eroded or denied by a WMD proliferator's asymmetric capabilities, the existing U.S. national military

---

[5] See Philip Zelikow, "Offensive Military Options" in *New Nuclear Nations: Consequences for U.S. Policy,* ed. by Robert D. Blackwill and Albert Carnesale (New York: Council on Foreign Relations, 1993), p. 170.

---

strategy, seemingly validated by the Persian Gulf War experience, simply will not work.[6]

The new challenges posed by WMD and advanced conventional weapons introduce severe risks to America's ability to project military power across the oceans in a timely way. These weapons enable an adversary to prosecute military operations using different operational concepts than in the past. Attacks against seaports and airfields, for example, could bring U.S. deployments to an overseas theater to a screeching halt. Strikes against air bases could significantly limit U.S. air operations. On the Korean peninsula the North could challenge the air superiority enjoyed by South Korea and the United States in several ways. Air-to-air engagements between the North's interceptors and the combined South Korea-U.S. tactical fighters could produce a few losses for the South and their American ally. A few more North Korean kills could be achieved through direct attack using surface-to-air missiles and anti-aircraft guns. On the other hand, North Korean asymmetric attacks using biological and chemical warfare munitions against air bases in South Korea could cause major disruptions. They could result in South Korea conducting less than optimal air attacks which, in turn, could result in greater losses against the North's interceptors and air defenses. When these weapons are used (or perhaps just threatened) to deny air operations from Japanese air bases, the American capacity for aerial attack on the Korean peninsula could be reduced significantly.[7]

---

[6] According to the national military strategy, the armed forces must be able to employ "the right mix of forces and capabilities" to deter and, if necessary, defeat nearly simultaneous, large-scale, cross-border attacks in two distant theaters (Persian Gulf and Korean peninsula) in overlapping time frames, preferably in conjunction with regional allies. Four strategic concepts will govern the use of American forces in these two scenarios: (1) *Strategic Agility* – The timely concentration, employment and sustainment of U.S. military forces anywhere in the world and at our own initiative—the speed and tempo of operations will be conducted at a pace that cannot be matched by regional antagonists; (2) *Overseas Presence* – The visible posture of U.S. forces positioned in or near key regions—these forces can be permanently stationed or temporarily deployed forces on a rotational basis, and they offer substance to U.S. security commitments and ensure continued access to military installations in the region; (3) *Power Projection* – The ability to deploy U.S. forces rapidly and to sustain them in multiple, dispersed locations—"if necessary, it means fighting our way into a denied theater or creating and protecting forward operating bases;" and (4) *Decisive Force* – The commitment of sufficient military forces to overwhelm all armed resistance—the idea is to create new military conditions by committing superior warfighting capabilities in order to deter aggression and, if necessary, defeat a regional antagonist. See U.S., Joint Chiefs of Staff, *National Military Strategy of the United States of America 1997.*

[7] Bruce Bennett, "Implications of Proliferation of New Weapons on Regional Security," 11th Conference on Korea-U.S. Security Studies on "The Search for Peace and Security in Northeast Asia Toward the 21st Century," Seoul, Korea: October 24-25, 1996 (Santa Monica, Calif.: RAND Corporation).

The more the United States prepares for a particular asymmetric enemy action that is aimed at weakening one or both of the weight-bearing assumptions of U.S. strategy, the less will be the strategic impact of the adversary's enemy attacks—therefore, the enemy will be less likely to take that action or to pursue the military capabilities to do so. On the other hand, the less prepared the United States is for an aggressor's action, the greater will be the strategic impact and the more likely the enemy will be to take the action and pursue the capabilities to make such an attack plausible. The United States is least prepared to fight under conditions of surprise (when the assumption of sufficient time to deploy U.S. forces is denied) or when the use of regional seaports, airfields, and other facilities are limited (when the assumption of ready access is denied or severely restricted).

Time. In a strategy based on deployment of forces overseas, time is a scarcity. The longer it takes the United States to deploy the right kinds and numbers of forces, the more onerous the defensive task of allies and friends and the greater the adversary's opportunities for satisfying his military objectives before the U.S. can respond. Strategic warning is essential for timely deployment. On the other hand, high costs can be incurred when false alarms trigger the movement of military forces overseas unnecessarily. These potential costs place pressure on decision-makers to stand pat until they are sure an attack is imminent. Regional WMD-armed regimes can exploit this Western reluctance to commit forces too quickly by making their attack readying activities as ambiguous as possible. A number of political and military deception measures can be taken to mask the coming attack and encourage American decision-makers to delay the deployment of their military forces.[8]

One way of gauging the importance of time in the U.S. military strategy is to compare its force deployment assumptions with the actual buildup rate overseas. The planned-for rates of deployment for the first fourteen days of a crisis are depicted in Figure 10.1. About 800 tactical aircraft and 100 bombers are depicted as rapidly deploying overseas. The U.S. would also have two aircraft carrier battle groups present in the theater at the start of hostilities. The deployment averages 1.8 fighter squadrons per day for fourteen consecutive days. This is quite an impressive buildup pace, particularly if it was achievable. These aircraft deployments, including land- and sea-based

---

[8] Richard Brody, "The 1973 War—Summary" in *Responding to Ambiguous Warning Signals of Soviet Imminent or Future Power Projection,* Vol. II – Case Studies (Marina del Rey, Calif.: Pan Heuristics, Inc., May 1982).

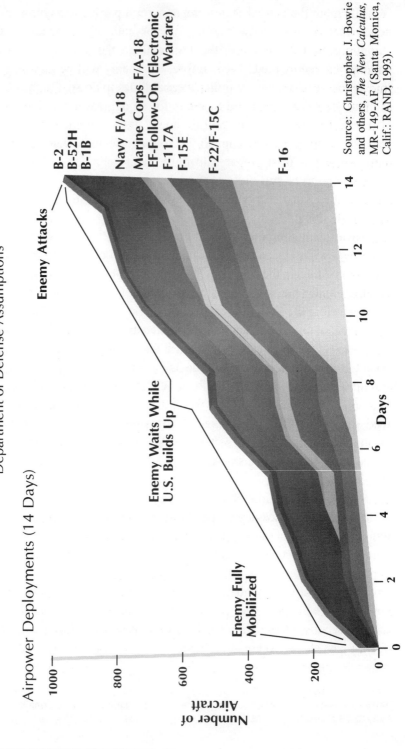

Figure 10.1
Actionable Warning and U.S. Airpower Deployment Rates
Department of Defense Assumptions

Airpower Deployments (14 Days)

Source: Christopher J. Bowie and others, *The New Calculus*, MR-149-AF (Santa Monica, Calif.: RAND, 1993).

The New Face of War

tactical fighters and long-range bombers, are common analytical assumptions in Department of Defense analyses of the military strategy and force structure. The 1995 *Heavy Bomber Force Study,* for instance, assumed the buildup rate for tactical aircraft and bombers depicted in Figure 10.1. This study resulted in an unequivocal recommendation to terminate production of the B-2 bomber at twenty aircraft. To cite Kurt Guthe's excellent critique of the badly flawed *Heavy Bomber Force Study,* this analysis, directed by the Defense Department, was an example of "planning for tomorrow's wars with yesterday's adversaries."[9]

Since the adversary invariably has the advantage of proximity to the point of dispute and is often rewarded by giving ambiguous warning signals, a United States military deployment should be expected to lag the aggressor's buildup of forces. The assumed rate of aircraft deployment neutralizes an adversary's geographical advantage. The chart also shows that the Defense Department inexplicably assumes the enemy will withhold attacks against U.S. forces until they are fully deployed.

According to a host of Department of Defense studies, U.S. forces must have at least two weeks of *actionable* warning and uninterrupted deployment time. If the warning and deployment time is less than two weeks, or if the adversary should start shooting before U.S. forces are fully deployed and in place, significant military risks could result. As illustrated in Figure 10.2, the United States has a deplorable record of recognizing and acting upon warning. As a consequence, Americans have been frequently taken by surprise, from Pearl Harbor in 1941 to Iraq's invasion of Kurdistan in 1996. Hence, it would be a rare occasion that the two weeks' time for deployment of U.S. forces would be actually available. The two case studies below illustrate the point.

Iraqi Armored Buildup on the Kuwaiti Border (1994). The Iraqi mobilization on Kuwait's border in 1994 provides a reality check between the assumptions used in Defense Department analyses (1,000 aircraft in fourteen days). The reality is that the U.S. can deploy some twenty percent or less of the 1,000 aircraft indicated in the baseline Pentagon assumption. The potential operational impact of this false assumption is depicted clearly in the U.S. response to Saddam Hussein's rather peculiar military buildup near Kuwait's border in October 1994. Beginning on October 5, the Iraqis positioned 70,000 to 75,000 troops, 1,090 tanks, 970 armored fighting vehicles,

---

[9] Kurt Guthe, *A Precisely Guided Analytic Bomb: The Defense Department's Heavy Bomber Force Study* (Fairfax, Va.: National Institute for Public Policy, September 1996), p. 13.

Figure 10.2

Actionable Warning? — Military Surprises, 1941–Present

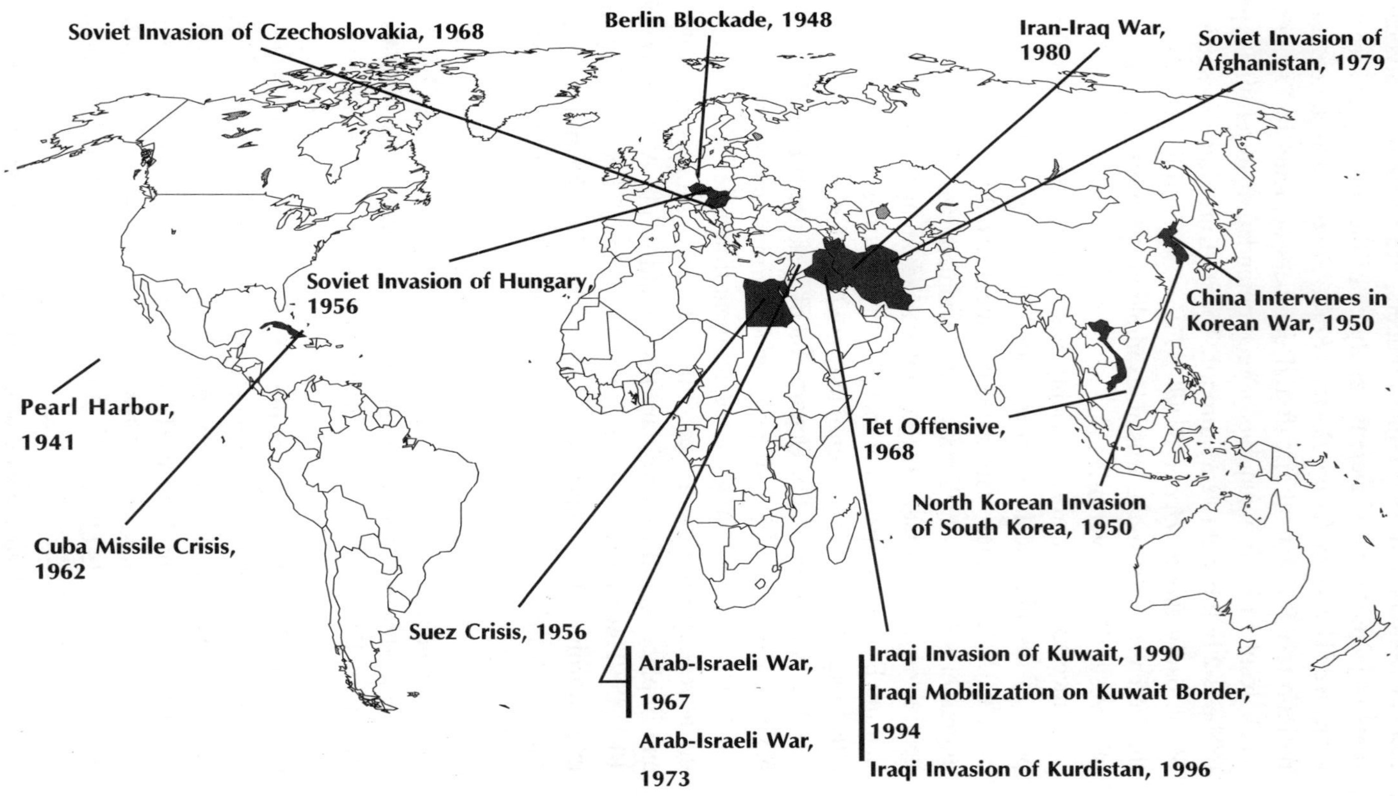

Soviet Invasion of Afghanistan, 1979

China Intervenes in Korean War, 1950

Iran-Iraq War, 1980

North Korean Invasion of South Korea, 1950

Tet Offensive, 1968

Iraqi Invasion of Kuwait, 1990

Iraqi Mobilization on Kuwait Border, 1994

Iraqi Invasion of Kurdistan, 1996

Berlin Blockade, 1948

Arab-Israeli War, 1967

Arab-Israeli War, 1973

Soviet Invasion of Czechoslovakia, 1968

Soviet Invasion of Hungary, 1956

Suez Crisis, 1956

Pearl Harbor, 1941

Cuba Missile Crisis, 1962

and 670 artillery pieces within fifteen miles of Kuwait. Included in the buildup were two of Iraq's elite Republican Guard armored divisions. The Iraqi deployment was completed on October 9. Kuwait's 16,000-man army would have been no match for the Iraqis, if they had chosen to advance.

Only a small number of U.S. forces were forward positioned in the region at the time, including sixty aircraft in Turkey, seventy tactical fighters in Saudi Arabia (twenty of them were support aircraft), and 2,000 U.S. Marines that were fortuitously conducting an amphibious exercise in the Persian Gulf off of the United Arab Emirates. While posing an early striking capability, these U.S. forces were clearly inadequate in the face of the massed Iraqi armor.

On October 6, the Pentagon sent orders to a number of units to deploy or to prepare for deployment. The 2,000 Marines present in the Gulf were ordered to positions off the coast of Kuwait, arriving on October 7. A day after Baghdad completed its military deployment and was readied for a possible seizure of Kuwait, the first arrivals of fighter aircraft, elements of an Army brigade, and transit of an aircraft carrier to the Red Sea occurred on October 10. Meanwhile, other force elements were moving or readying for transport to Kuwait in order to counterpoise the Iraqi buildup.

Figure 10.3 depicts the open window of vulnerability faced by Kuwait and other U.S. allies in the region. Another way to look at this is as a window open to adversaries to exploit time, or the time-distance lag in U.S. power projection. American allies, for instance, could be coerced into denying Washington access to their facilities before U.S. forces arrive. The regional aggressor could take advantage of America's delayed response by simply seizing objectives to present a fait accompli. Another option would be to stage lethal anti-access attacks against regional debarkation ports and airfields ahead of the arriving U.S. forces to further delay their intervention.

Inexplicably, the Iraqis began to pull back on October 13. The U.S. buildup moved forward nonetheless. By October 19, a full ten days *after* Baghdad had completed its buildup at the Kuwaiti border, the United States had deployed 14,000 personnel to join the roughly 12,000 Americans already present in the theater on October 5. A U.S. Navy carrier battle group reached the Persian Gulf on October 15 (another carrier could have been on station by October 22). The Air Force had about 100 fighters and 100 support aircraft in position by October 19. The Army, however, had managed to insert only about 5,000 troops.

The sluggish U.S. response, according to those reading the strategic tea leaves at the time, deterred Saddam Hussein's invasion. Yet, there was

Figure 10.3
Window of Vulnerability
October 1994 Iraqi Mobilization on Kuwait Border

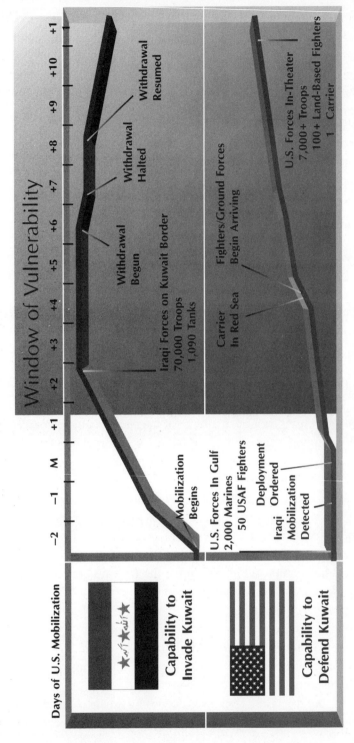

Source: Charles M. Perry, Lawrence E. Rothenberg, and Jacquelyn K. Davis, *Airpower Synergies in the New Strategic Era: The Complementary Roles of Long-Range Bombers & Carrier-Based Aircraft* (McLean, Va.: Brassey's, 1997), p. 41.

The New Face of War

something very peculiar about the Iraqi buildup followed by the rapid withdrawal from the Kuwaiti border after U.S. forces began to arrive. The quick claim of American success had a rather tin ring to the ear. What was Saddam really up to?

Saddam Hussein's strategic purpose in 1994 did not become evident to many Western analysts until the 1996 Irbil crisis when Iraq moved with impunity against the Kurds in the northern part of the country. According to some readings of the course of events, the evidence suggests that Saddam, with malice of forethought in 1994, had tweaked the American nose with a quick buildup on the Kuwait border. As the United States rushed its military forces to the region, Saddam, stopwatch in hand, determined just how long it would take the United States to deploy sufficient force to counter an armored thrust from Iraq. He learned that the United States had a serious "window of vulnerability" until it could deploy sufficient forces to disrupt or blunt Iraq's military moves in areas within reach of its armored forces—Iraq, it seems, had a "window of opportunity" before the Americans could respond. In a future crisis Saddam knew that he would have to deny the United States strategic warning, strike quickly to achieve his goals, and then withdraw speedily to position his armored forces back to their garrisons before the United States could counter them.

Figure 10.4 shows the actual U.S. aircraft deployment rates in Operation Desert Shield in August 1990 and in October 1994 when Iraq built up its armored strike forces on the Kuwaiti border. The effects of being taken by surprise are evident in both cases, especially Baghdad's unopposed seizure of Kuwait. In 1990, it was not until six days after the Iraqis were in Kuwait that the first U.S. carrier-based aircraft were available. In the October 1994 crisis, fifty aircraft were already on station in Saudi Arabia but it took two weeks to move just 100 more aircraft into position.

In both crises the U.S. enjoyed unhindered access to seaports, airfields, and other facilities. The two buildups were races against time during which a window of opportunity was wide open for Saddam Hussein.

Figure 10.5 depicts the actual U.S. airpower deployment rates as compared to analytical assumptions that underwrite the Defense Department's strategy and force structure planning. In the critical first fourteen days of Iraq's seizure of Kuwait in August 1990, some 250 U.S. aircraft were deployed or about a quarter of the assumed deployment rate. In 1994, the U.S. aircraft dispatched overseas numbered less than 200 in the first fourteen days. The difference between the assumed and actual aircraft buildup rates are disturbing. One would think that the real-life tests of aircraft

---

Figure 10.4
The Real World—U.S. Air Power Deployment Rates

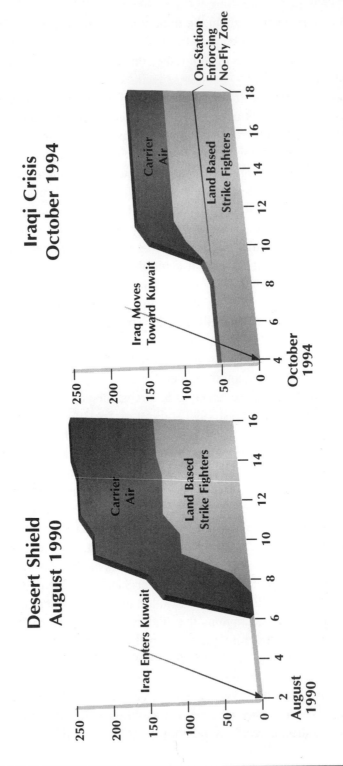

Source: U.S., Department of the Air Force, *Gulf War Air Power Strategy: A Statistical Compendium and Chronology, Vol. V* (Washington, D.C.: Government Printing Office, 1993), pp. 53-55, and Kurt Guthe, *A Precisely Guided Analytic Bomb: The Defense Department's Heavy Bomber Force Study* (Fairfax, Va.: National Institute for Public Policy, September 1996), p. 30.

The New Face of War

Figure 10.5

U.S. Airpower Deployment Rates Versus Department of Defense Assumptions

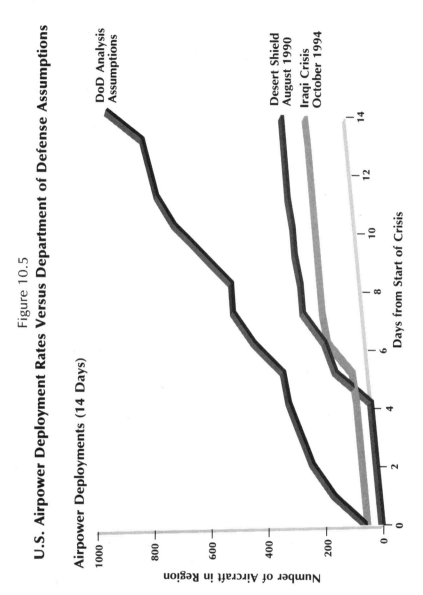

Airpower Deployments (14 Days)

Source: Kurt Guthe, *A Precisely Guided Analytic Bomb: The Defense Department's Heavy Bomber Force Study* (Fairfax, Va.: National Institute for Public Policy, September, 1996), p. 30.

deployment rates, one of the Pentagon's most important analytical assumptions, would have prompted an adjustment to reflect the actual pace of the overseas buildup. As will be discussed in Chapter 11, the assumptions of force deployment rates are so far divorced from reality conditions that the strategy may be dysfunctional unless the leisurely buildup rate experienced in the Gulf War can be repeated.

Access. Conflict scenarios conducted by the Pentagon are invariably limited to the littoral regions (where military targets can be reached by short-range carrier-based aircraft). The U.S. forces are assumed to have unlimited and unobstructed access to theater ports, bases, airfields, and coastal waters. The ideal conditions of the Persian Gulf War seem to have validated the Defense Department's assumptions. Yet, future adversaries are unlikely to surrender months of uninterrupted time to deploy U.S. forces, and their missiles should be expected to more accurate than Iraq's Scuds. "In the future," warns Andrew Marshall, the director of the Pentagon's Office of Net Assessment, "'we can't create large, juicy targets'"[10] such as those presented to Saddam Hussein during the Gulf War.

The dependence of U.S. military strategy on unlimited and unobstructed access to regional seaports, airfields, other facilities, and the littoral waters is being exploited by significant political, geographic, and military-technical anti-access threats. Political cooperation by potential overseas host countries is one prerequisite. Figure 10.6, for instance, reflects the politically-driven denials of and constraints on theater access for land-based air forces. Over the four decades of the Cold War, the U.S. faced the loss of basing rights (from eighty-one bases in 1960 to fourteen in 1996), access to foreign bases, denial of overflight rights, and operational restrictions on the use of bases. These geographic shifts were emphasized recently by the dramatic 1998 denial by Arab states of regional bases to support U.S. and British air strikes against Iraq in the crisis over U.N. inspection teams, revealing the weakness of assuming access to regional bases during crisis. In the absence of regional bases, except in Kuwait, the Anglo-American force would have been compelled to operate from aircraft carriers and fire long-range cruise missiles at Iraqi targets. Sea-mines, submarines, and a range of direct attack weapons can be used at critical chokepoints in the sea lanes, outside key harbors, or against the seaports themselves to hinder access. Two recent

---

[10] Thomas E. Ricks, "How Wars Are Fought Will Change Radically, Pentagon Planner Says," *Wall Street Journal* (July 5, 1994), p. A1.

Figure 10.6

Politics — Denials of, Constraints on Theater Access for Land-Based Air Forces, 1947-98 (Selected)

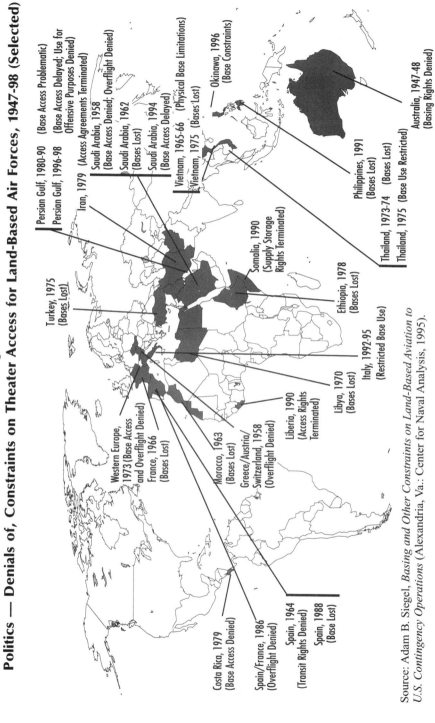

Persian Gulf, 1980-90   (Base Access Problematic)
Persian Gulf, 1996-98   (Base Access Delayed; Use for Offensive Purposes Denied)
Iran, 1979   (Access Agreements Terminated)
Saudi Arabia, 1958   (Base Access Denied; Overflight Denied)
Saudi Arabia, 1962   (Bases Lost)
Saudi Arabia, 1994   (Base Access Delayed)
Vietnam, 1965-66   (Physical Base Limitations)
Vietnam, 1975   (Bases Lost)
Okinawa, 1996   (Base Constraints)
Australia, 1947-48   (Basing Rights Denied)
Philippines, 1991   (Bases Lost)
Thailand, 1973-74   (Bases Lost)
Thailand, 1975   (Base Use Restricted)
Somalia, 1990   (Supply Storage Rights Terminated)
Ethiopia, 1978   (Bases Lost)
Turkey, 1975   (Bases Lost)
Italy, 1992-95   (Restricted Base Use)
Libya, 1970   (Bases Lost)
Liberia, 1990   (Access Rights Terminated)
Greece/Austria/Switzerland, 1958   (Overflight Denied)
Morocco, 1963   (Bases Lost)
Western Europe, 1973 (Base Access and Overflight Denied)
France, 1966   (Bases Lost)
Spain, 1964   (Transit Rights Denied)
Spain, 1988   (Base Lost)
Spain/France, 1986   (Overflight Denied)
Costa Rica, 1979   (Base Access Denied)

Source: Adam B. Siegel, *Basing and Other Constraints on Land-Based Aviation to U.S. Contingency Operations* (Alexandria, Va.: Center for Naval Analysis, 1995).

crises illustrate many of the access problems likely to challenge Americans in the future.

Irbil Crisis in the Fall of 1996. More insight between the real world of U.S. airpower deployment rates and the analytical assumptions used by the Defense Department in making military strategy and force structure decisions is shown in Figure 10.7. It shows how politics and geography can work together in denying the United States access critical to force deployment.

When two Kurdish factions, the Patriotic Union of Kurdistan and the Kurdistan Democratic Party, renewed fighting in August, Iran moved troops to its northern region. Flouting U.N. restrictions and ignoring American warnings, Iraq responded on August 31, 1996, by sending three divisions of the elite Republican Guard into the Kurdish city of Irbil about 200 miles north of Baghdad, which was inside the declared U.N. "safe haven" that was being protected by U.S.-led forces.[11] Some 40,000 troops, 450 tanks and other equipment made up the Iraqi invasion force. Readying activities for a force of this size would have been extensive—it is safe to assume that the pre-invasion preparations were conducted in secret and probably stretched out over time to deny the United States strategic warning. The number of American air sorties over the protected area of northern Iraq were doubled, and President Clinton placed U.S. forces in the region on a high alert status.[12]

The United States soon found itself unable to respond militarily. When Turkey, Jordan, and Saudi Arabia signalled Washington that they would not permit air strikes against Iraq to be launched from their territories, U.S. options were narrowed significantly. Without close-in airfields, the use of land-based fighters was made impossible. Although an aircraft carrier (USS *Carl Vinson*) was able to move into position in the Persian Gulf, targets near the city of Irbil were beyond the range of carrier-based fighters. Days passed before Kuwait accepted a limited U.S. deployment. The B-1 and B-52 bombers had the range to stage operations from outside the region, but they would be vulnerable to Iraqi air defenses, and neither non-stealth air-

[11] The Western allies imposed a no-fly zone at the 38th parallel and above in April 1991 to protect the Kurds. The area was patrolled by U.S. Air Force fighters based in Turkey and more than forty French, British and Turkish aircraft.

[12] Steven Lee Meyers, "Pentagon Sees A New Threat By Iraq Forces," *New York Times* (August 31, 1996), pp. 1,2; Waiel Faleh, "Saddam Attacks Kurds in Safe Haven," *Washington Times* (September 1, 1996), pp. 1, 12; Steven Lee Myers, "U.S. Calls Alert As Iraqis Strike a Kurd Enclave," *New York Times* (September 1, 1996), pp. 1,8; and Waiel Faleh, "Iraqis Remain in Kurd City Despite Order," *Washington Times* (September 2, 1996), pp. A1, A10.

The New Face of War

Figure 10.7
1996 Irbil Crisis—Access Constraints

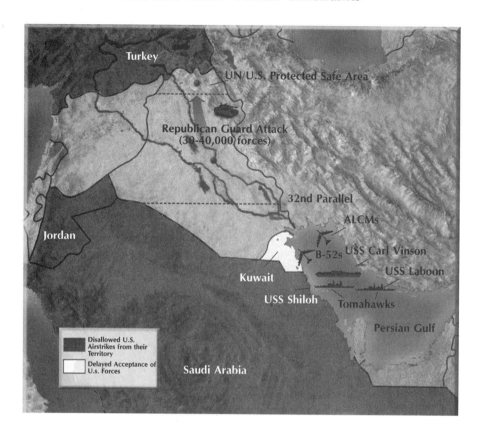

craft had the capability to deliver precision weapons. The B-2 stealth bomber has the range and can fly safely into the teeth of Iraqi air defenses, but the force was not yet operational. Cruise missiles could not be targeted against the Republican Guard's armored elements, and the missiles lacked the punch to destroy hardened command and control facilities inside Baghdad.

Unable to strike the offending forces in the north, the United States had to settle for strikes against Iraqi air defense facilities south of Baghdad. Twenty-seven cruise missiles were launched on September 3 and seventeen more the next day from ships and B-52s coming all the way from Guam in the Pacific Ocean. The southern no-fly zone in Iraq also was expanded to within thirty miles of Baghdad.[13]

Iraq began withdrawing many of the 40,000 troops rushed to the Kurdish enclaves, leaving behind a group of secret agents to reassert Saddam Hussein's control. Despite Washington's claims of having "punished" Saddam for his aggression against the Kurds, it was clear to many strategic analysts that the feeble cruise missile strikes in the south, more than 200 miles from Iraq's offending forces mopping up the Kurds, were a poor substitute for direct attacks. When the city of Sulaimaniya fell on September 10 without a shot being fired, Massoud Barzani's Kurdistan Democratic Party, which was backed by Saddam, took control of all the big cities in Iraq's Kurdish region.[14] Laurie Mylroie of the Foreign Policy Institute in Philadelphia summed up the events rather poignantly: "Saddam has used his chance to butcher off his opponents while the United States sat and watched. It's disgusting."[15]

1997-98 U.N. On-Site Inspection Crisis. In October 1997, Iraq imposed new restrictions on U.N. weapons inspectors and blocked their access to presidential palaces suspected of housing prohibited weapons and materials. On October 29, Saddam Hussein escalated the brewing crisis by ordering U.S. members of the U.N. Special Commission (UNSCOM) weapons

---

[13] Alison Mitchell, "U.S. Prepares Further Action Against Iraq As Clinton Vows He Will Extract 'a Price,'" *New York Times* (September 4, 1996), pp. A1, A8, and Warren P. Strobel, "U.S. Launches Second Attack on Iraq," *Washington Times* (September 4, 1996), pp. A1, A9.

[14] Eric Schmitt, "Clinton, Claiming Success, Asserts Most Iraqi Troops Have Left Kurds' Enclave," *New York Times* (September 5, 1996), pp. A1, A10; Tim Weiner, "Iraq Pulling Out, But Leaving Spies Behind, U.S. Says," *New York Times* (September 6, 1996), pp. A1, A16; Douglas Jehl, "Faction of Kurds Supported By Iraq Takes Rival's City," *New York Times* (September 10, 1996), pp. A1, A8; and "Iraq-Backed Kurds Celebrate Triumph," *Washington Times* (September 11, 1996), pp. A1, A10.

[15] As quoted in Martin Sieff and Refet Kaplan, "Experts: U.S. Should've Seen Attack Coming," *Washington Times* (September 3, 1996), pp. A1, A16.

The New Face of War

inspection teams out of Iraq and threatened to shoot down American U-2 surveillance aircraft flying missions in support of the United States. In protest, the U.N. pulled all of its inspectors out of Iraq in November, except for a small skeleton crew at its monitoring facility in Baghdad. After a brief suspension, the U.N. ordered the U-2 flights to continue, and they did so without incident. Some observers believed that the U.N. on-site inspectors, before being tossed out of the country, had been homing in on Iraq's hidden stocks of VX, anthrax, and other chemical and biological agents. The crisis, highlighted by a U.N. walkout, offered Saddam Hussein several weeks of unhindered activity to squirrel away his toxic agents at new locations.

As diplomatic efforts to resolve the crisis moved forward, the United States beefed up its regional presence in preparation for possible air strikes. By February 1998, the United States, joined only by Britain, prepared to conduct air strikes against Iraq to punish Saddam Hussein for repeatedly blocking the weapons inspectors from the United Nations. According to news accounts the bombing campaign would last three days and concentrate on known and suspected weapons facilities, air defenses, command bunkers, and presidential palaces suspected of concealing weapons of mass destruction, including stores of VX chemical agent and anthrax and other biological agents.[16]

Turkey and Saudi Arabia and other Arab countries refused to allow the U.S. to strike Iraq from bases on their soil. Only Kuwait would permit U.S. stealth fighters and fighter-bombers use of its airfields. (See Figure 10.8). Other strike fighters would come from two U.S. aircraft carriers and one British carrier. Fourteen B-52 bombers armed with cruise missiles were positioned at the island of Diego Garcia in the Indian Ocean; surface ships and submarines in the Persian Gulf rounded out the cruise missile strike assets. American aircraft in Bahrain could have joined the air campaign, including three B-1 bombers, but late equivocation by the host government opened their use to question. Finally, F-15 fighter bombers would have been compelled to make long flights across the Mediterranean from bases in Italy, Portugal, Spain, England, and Germany.[17] In the end, however, last minute diplomatic maneuvers revived the U.N. inspections and the air strikes were called off.

---

[16] Rowan Scarborough, "Iraq 'Show' Riles Joint Chiefs," *Washington Times* (February 4, 1998), pp. A1, A12, and Philip Finnegan and Robert Holzer, "Politics Foul Strike Plans Against Iraq," *Defense News* (February 23-March 1, 1998), pp. 1, 50.

[17] Bruce W. Nelan, "How the Attack On Iraq Is Planned," *Time* (February 23, 1998), pp. 40-43.

Figure 10.8

Forces Positioned for Air Strikes Against Iraq, February 1998

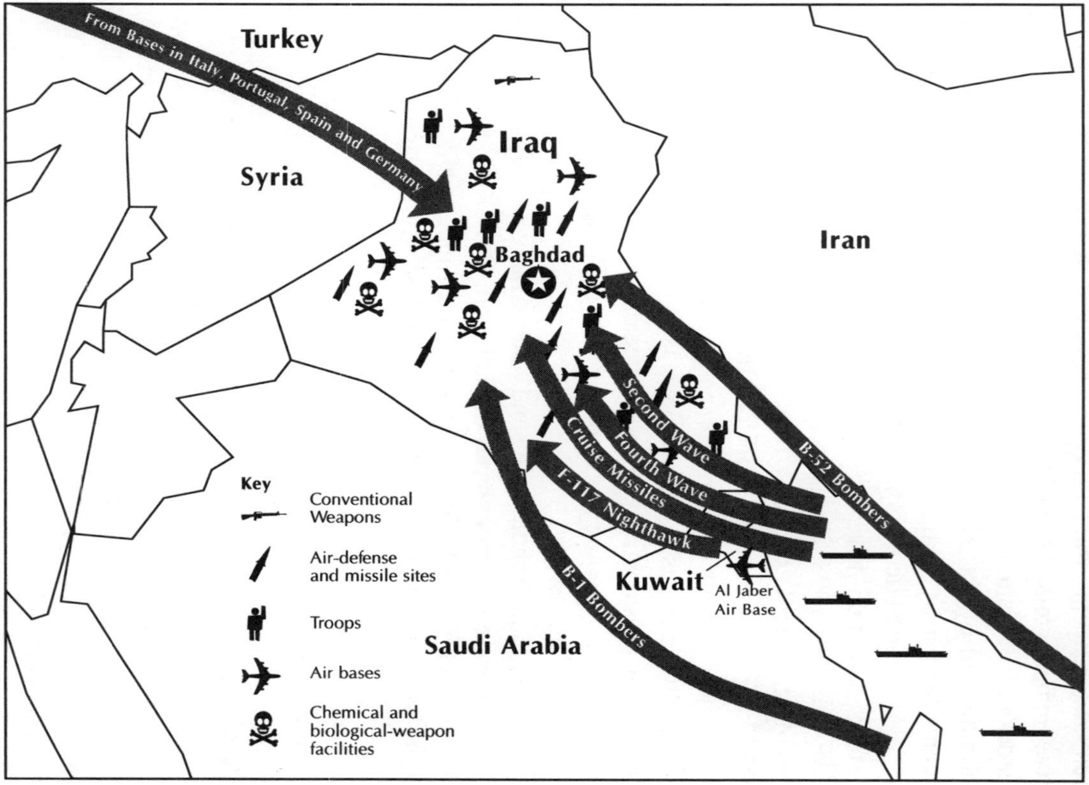

Source: Derived from Bruce W. Nelan, "How the Attack in Iraq Is Planned," *Time* (February 23, 1998), pp. 40-41.

Iran

Turkey

Syria

Iraq

Baghdad

Kuwait

Al Jaber Air Base

Saudi Arabia

B-52 Bombers

Second Wave

Fourth Wave

Cruise Missiles

F-117 Nighthawk

B-1 Bombers

From Bases in Italy, Portugal, Spain and Germany

Key
Conventional Weapons
Air-defense and missile sites
Troops
Air bases
Chemical and biological-weapon facilities

The New Face of War

The key point of both the Irbil and U.N. on-site inspection crises is the U.S. dependence on foreign air bases and, in the case of Baghdad's grab of the Kurdish areas in northern Iraq, on the lack of strategic warning as well. These events raise serious questions about the current U.S. military strategy and whether it is viable in light of the new challenges. Given the inability to respond rapidly, and the large numbers of lives put at risk, why are short-range, foreign-base dependent air and ground forces still the main focus of U.S. power projection strategy? Will operational constraints be placed on the U.S. use of foreign bases in the future as they have in the recent past?

Military-Technical Anti-Access Threats

The ability of the United States to project combat power rapidly to overseas theaters is the key to regional stability in many parts of the world. Unhindered access to overseas ports and airfields in a variety of regions is a prerequisite to effective exercise of America's global military strategy. This access must be timely and broad enough to ensure the United States can deploy the right kinds and numbers of forces to the right places in time to be relevant to the forces inimical to U.S. interests.

Having witnessed American prowess in the use of precision conventional weapons on CNN during the Gulf War, adversaries have strong incentives to delay, disrupt, block, and destroy U.S. forces before they are fully deployed. Countries granting the United States access to its seaports, airfields, and other military facilities could be asked to pay a heavy price, if an adversary elects to launch punishing strikes against them. The potential for nuclear, biological and chemical missile strikes looms in particular importance because of the danger they pose to host nations and U.S. forces during deployment. Advanced conventional weapons and technologies and state-sponsored terrorism are other means for attacking the two weight-bearing assumptions of the U.S. power projection strategy.

Weapons of Mass Destruction. Only one case history is available of the actual contamination of a seaport from chemical warfare agents. In a bizarre twist of events, an American merchant ship was the source of a massive contamination of a port essential to Allied operations during World War Two. A 1943 German air strike against the Allied ships in the harbor of Bari, Italy, demonstrates the potential effects of WMD attacks against seaports. The SS *John Harvey* was loaded with 2,000 chemical bombs (each contained sixty to seventy pounds of mustard gas). More than thirty Allied ships had choked the harbor and the *John Harvey* was awaiting its turn to unload. On December 2, 105 JU-88 German bombers attacked this main Allied supply port in the Italian theater. The twenty-minute bombing attack sank seventeen ships and caused several fuel ships to explode. When the *John Harvey* was hit, some of its cargo of mustard gas began to burn, some sank to the bottom, and much of the remainder spread through the harbor mixing with hundreds of tons of oil.

As illustrated in Figure 10.9, a mustard gas cloud formed. The resulting military and civilian death toll numbered about 1,000. The port was closed for three weeks and its operational capacity was not resumed for two months. In the absence of the mustard gas contamination from the *John Harvey,* repairs to the harbor and port probably could have taken a week or less. The disruption of Bari caused supply shortages and adversely affected the Allied landing at Anzio. Allied logistic shortages contributed to the Germans containing the Anzio beachhead and holding northern Italy through the winter of 1943-44.[18]

Access to the regional ports, airfields, and other facilities necessary to support U.S. power projection is today's problem and the trends in WMD and missile proliferation promise to make the situation worse over time. During the Gulf War, Iraq was just twelve to eighteen months away from having its first nuclear device and it was armed with biological and chemical weapons, many of which were deliverable by aerial bombs and missile warheads. Other countries are similarly armed or are actively pursuing these capabilities today, including North Korea, China, India, Pakistan, Iran, Iraq, and Libya.

A regional antagonist has two main attack options for using WMD to exploit U.S. time and access vulnerabilities in anti-access operations. The first alternative would involve incapacitating, non-lethal attacks to *delay* and *disrupt* the American deployment, buy more time for achieving its conventional military forces to achieve their objectives, and minimize the chances of a large-scale, regime-threatening response from the United States. The second option would execute lethal attacks against seaports, airfields, and already deployed air forces to *block* U.S. power projection operations, *destroy* U.S. capacity wage war from regional bases or close-in littoral waters, and *raise the blood price* Americans would have to pay to counter armed aggression.

Delay and Disrupt. In order to minimize the possibility of a massive U.S. conventional or nuclear retaliation, a WMD-armed adversary could

---

[18] Glen B. Infield, *Disaster At Bari* (New York: Macmillan, 1971).

The New Face of War

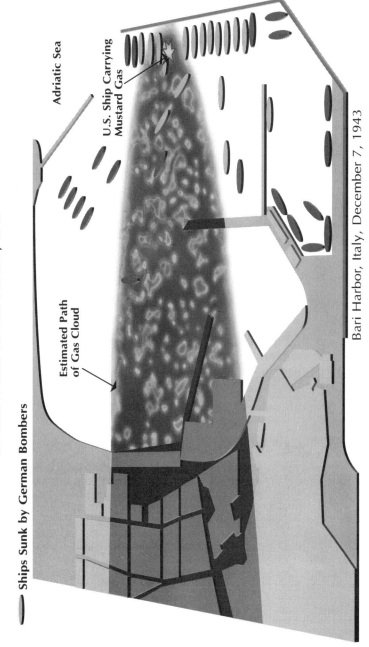

Figure 10.9
**Unlimited, Unobstructed Access?
German Attack on Bari Harbor, 1943**

Adriatic Sea

U.S. Ship Carrying
Mustard Gas

Estimated Path
of Gas Cloud

Ships Sunk by German Bombers

Bari Harbor, Italy, December 7, 1943

Source: Glen B. Infield, *Disaster At Bari* (New York: Macmillan, 1971).

constrain its use of biological and chemical weapons to non-lethal but debilitating attacks. Terrorists could be used to strike seaports and airfields inside the United States that are supporting the dispatch of forces overseas—the aim of such super-terrorism attacks would be disrupting and delaying the U.S. deployment while minimizing fatalities. With the right preparations, perhaps as many as nine or ten deployment seaports and airfields could be hit by small quantities of mustard gas or cholera and other biological agents. Hypothetically, at roughly the same time, prepositioned military equipment and supplies aboard ships and on land in or near the Persian Gulf could be struck with non-lethal concentrations of biological and chemical agents.[19] In the meantime, biological and chemical weapons could be dispersed by air-delivered bombs, cruise missiles, and ballistic missiles against the ports and airfields in Kuwait and Saudi Arabia that would receive the American deployments.[20]

No advancement over current technology is needed to produce non-lethal biological and chemical warfare agents including those longer lasting, oily compounds that are difficult to decontaminate. A variety of usable agents already exist.

Coining the phrase "weapons of mass disruption" to characterize non-lethal, small-scale biological and chemical attacks on key elements of the power projection infrastructure, Amoretta Hoeber and her study panel of respected military leaders revealed several distinct vulnerabilities in the U.S. capability to respond rapidly to crises. "We are not talking about terrorist

---

[19] The key to the American power projection strategy, especially for the critical opening days of a crisis, is the prepositioning program combined with a budget-constrained procurement of new air transports and fast sealift ships. Six Army brigade sets of equipment are stored (on land) in Europe (3), Korea (1), and Southwest Asia (2) and a Marine Corps brigade set in Norway. The Army also has armored brigade equipment afloat in fourteen ships, which can be sent to either Southwest or Northeast Asia from their stations in the Indian and Pacific Oceans. Thirteen ships containing equipment and supplies are also available in the Pacific and Indian Oceans and Mediterranean Sea to support deployment of three Marine Expeditionary Forces. Finally, the Air Force has three ammunition ships for early support of theater operations. See William S. Cohen, Secretary of Defense, *Annual Report to the President and the Congress* (Washington, D.C.: Government Printing Office, 1997), pp. 22-23.

[20] This is basically the postulated enemy planning scenario in 2010 that was used in an analysis of the effects of biological and chemical attacks on U.S. power projection. Prepared for the Office of the Secretary of Defense under the guidance of project leader Amoretta M. Hoeber, nineteen retired generals and admirals from each of the military services and two civilian experts participated in the interactive political-military simulation used in the analysis. See *Assessment of the Impact of Chemical and Biological Weapons on Joint Operations in 2010 (The CB 2010 Study): A Summary Report* (McLean, Va.: Booz, Allen & Hamilton, October 1997), p. 11.

---

attacks," former Army Undersecretary Hoeber said. "We are talking about... small attacks on power projection nodes...where few people get killed."[21] Such attacks would cause a great deal of disruption and delay a sustained U.S. response against the enemy's invasion forces. The disruption would give the aggressor's invading forces more time to achieve their objectives and the opportunity to present the United States with a fait accompli after Washington unscrambles its flow plans for overseas deployments.

Nineteen retired generals and admirals examined the evidence in 1997 and concluded that the U.S. operational concept of "fighting through" the massive battlefield use of biological and chemical weapons to enable U.S. conventional military forces to prevail is "no longer the most likely threat." Rather, U.S. forces must be prepared to both "fight through" the biological and chemical threat *and* to detect and decontaminate non-lethal doses (of diluted concentration) of deadly agents or casualty-producing agents at points of embarkation inside the United States and debarkation in the overseas theater.

Biological and chemical attacks can have a wide range of impacts on U.S. military operations. Air expeditionary and command and control forces could be diverted from their primary in-theater operating bases, separating them from their essential ground support, ranging from maintenance to air-delivered munitions, and disrupt their ability to sustain operations aimed at halting the aggressor's invading ground forces. Disruption of the arrival or ready usage of prepositioned equipment could also impose critical delays. Adding to the delay and disruption is the fact that the armed forces of friends and allies may be less than well-equipped to operate in contaminated environments. The U.S. dependence on the use of civilian personnel at the seaports and airports of host countries is a particular vulnerability for further delay and disruption. It is impossible to predict whether the work force would return after non-lethal biological and chemical attacks were cleaned up at overseas ports and airfields.[22]

Block and Destroy. A regional aggressor would face significant risks in launching lethal nuclear, biological, and chemical attacks against U.S. forces at home or overseas. Even with its regional air forces neutralized, the United States could still respond with devastating nuclear strikes against the enemy's invading conventional forces, weapons of mass destruction, and a range of

---

[21] As quoted in "A Future Look At 'Weapons of Mass Disruption,'" *Defense Week* (November 24, 1997).

[22] *Ibid.*, pp. 28-34.

---

targets associated with keeping the regime in power. Questions remain open regarding the credibility of the U.S. nuclear deterrent to WMD attacks. Nevertheless, it is important to recognize that regional powers dissatisfied with the status quo may be willing to run great risks, including the chancing of an American nuclear retaliation, to achieve their political aims.

Any number of scenarios and options for an enemy's WMD attacks against seaports, airfields, and tactical fighter operating bases can be created to illustrate the potential impact on U.S. operations. Two sample threats in particular are helpful in gaining a picture of the new strategic conditions in overseas theaters: (1) nuclear attacks—twenty-kiloton weapons delivered by Scud missiles were within Saddam Hussein's grasp during the Gulf War, perhaps only twelve to eighteen months away, and (2) chemical attacks— Scud missile-delivered VX persistent nerve agent was also included in Iraq's arsenal. Two hypothetical case studies involving nuclear and chemical attacks against the port of Ad Dammam and the airfield at Dhahran in Saudi Arabia provide keen insights into the anti-access operations that can be marshalled against deploying U.S. forces.[23]

Ad Dammam. This huge Saudi port on the Persian Gulf covers about seventeen square kilometers and has thirty-nine berths at four piers capable of handling ocean-going cargo vessels. Twenty-six of the berths can handle general cargo, seven are reserved for container ships, and six are designed to handle a variety of different vessels. The port is fully equipped with a large floating crane, eight gantry cranes, and other essential equipment. It is an ideal port for U.S. power projection.

VX could be the chemical agent of choice because it offers the best combination of high lethality and persistence of effects. The consistency of VX is like oil and adheres to equipment and other surfaces, complicating decontamination. VX evaporates over days or even weeks depending on the ambient air temperature. The agent is very lethal if inhaled or absorbed through the skin; it kills by asphyxiation, paralyzing the diaphragm muscles, and making it impossible to breathe. Non-lethal doses can cause lengthy incapacitation.

A salvo of five Scud missiles (Al Hussein version) with 1,000-meter accuracy would result in four of five warheads impacting within the port area. Figure 10.10 depicts four VX deposition patterns, each with three

---

[23] The analysis that follows is based on another of the books on weapons of mass destruction published by AMCODA Press: Greg Weaver and J. David Glaes, *Inviting Disaster: How Weapons of Mass Destruction Undermine U.S. Strategy for Projecting Military Power* (McLean, Va.: AMCODA Press, 1997).

The New Face of War

Figure 10.10
Hypothetical Scud VX Attack on Ad Dammam
Five Al Hussein Missiles—VX Deposition

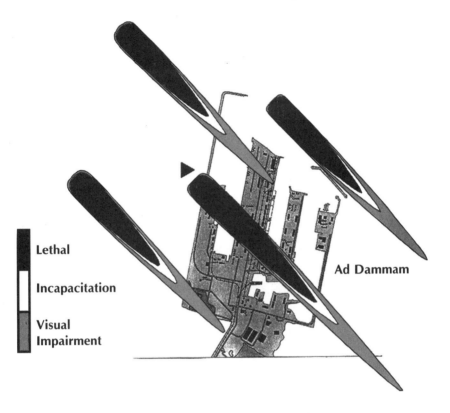

Note: Depicts 5-Missile Iraqi Scud (Al Hussein) Attack; Missile Accuracy: 1km CEP (One Scud Falls Outside of Target Area)

Source: Greg Weaver and J. David Glaes, *Inviting Disaster: How Weapons of Mass Destruction Undermine U.S. Strategy for Projecting Military Power* (McLean, Va.: AMCODA Press, 1997), p. 23.

levels of concentration: lethal, incapacitation, and visual impairment. In this case, a single Scud warhead spread tiny lethal droplets of VX across all four piers and the large cargo area. Some of the ships at berths would have been contaminated.

Casualties could include hard-to-replace skilled workers, such as local harbor pilots and cargo and container handling equipment operators. Contaminated equipment and cargo could be extensive depending on the phase of the U.S. buildup. Vigorous decontamination of equipment may take as long as cleansing through natural weathering. If that is the case, there would be little need to rush with decontamination. On the other hand, additional strikes every twenty-four hours could keep the contamination levels high.

Nuclear attacks against a seaport offer an adversary two basic options. The first alternative includes a nuclear airburst attack designed to maximize damage to the port facilities. The second option, perhaps less feasible technically, is an underwater burst in the waters near Ad Dammam designed to damage the port facilities by inundating them with massive waves and/or a radioactive steam cloud.

The consequences of the nuclear strikes would be severe. One or two twenty-kiloton airbursts would inflict severe damage to the port, although some of the critical facilities would be resistant to the attack. Table 10.1 shows the effects of nuclear airbursts over Ad Dammam. The underwater burst, on the other hand, would trigger thousands of tons of water in massive quick-moving waves. See Figure 10.11. The probable consequences include sinking or severely damaging ships near the harbor entrance, water and airblast damage to the port and equipment, and a massive radioactive steam cloud that would contaminate surviving vessels and supplies. The radiation resulting from the steam cloud would preclude access to the port for three to four days, while decontamination of ships and port facilities could takes months. Both attacks would kill or incapacitate nearly all port personnel.

If the Iraqis had attacked the ports of Ad Dammam and Al Jubayl in the first month after the U.S. began to deploy to Saudi Arabia and combined those attacks with an assault against Saudi oil fields, the U.S. would not have had sufficient forces to assist in repelling the Iraqis. On the other hand, if the Iraqis attacked later in the Coalition's force build-up phase, the air and ground counter-offensive would have been delayed.

Dhahran. The major airfields accepting U.S. strategic airlift aircraft were high priority targets due to their leading role in the power projection

---

Table 10.1

Effects on Nuclear Airbursts Over the Port of Ad Dammam

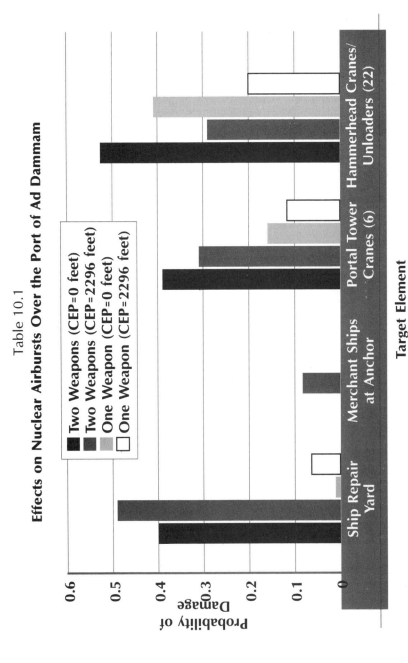

Legend:
- Two Weapons (CEP=0 feet)
- Two Weapons (CEP=2296 feet)
- One Weapon (CEP=0 feet)
- One Weapon (CEP=2296 feet)

Y-axis: Probability of Damage

X-axis (Target Element): Ship Repair Yard, Merchant Ships at Anchor, Portal Tower Cranes (6), Hammerhead Cranes/ Unloaders (22)

Source: Greg Weaver and J. David Glaes, *Inviting Disaster: How Weapons of Mass Destruction Undermine U.S. Strategy for Projecting Military Power* (McLean, Va.: AMCODA Press, 1997), p. 29.

Figure 10.11

Probable Consequences of Underwater Twenty-Kiloton Nuclear Blast at Port Ad Dammam

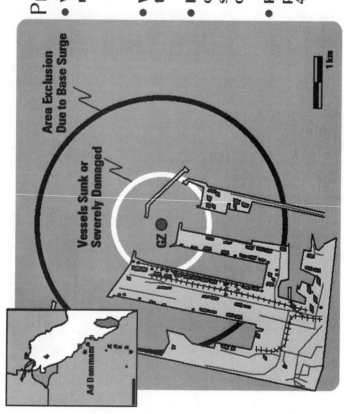

Probable Consequences:

- Vessels sunk/severe damage near harbor entrance
  - Extensive clearing/salvage operations

- Water and airblast damage to port facilities/equipment

- Base surge radioactive contamination to ships and supplies in port – months to decontaminate

- Radiation environments preclude area access for 3 to 4 days
  - Eight hour exposure after 4 days

Source: Greg Weaver and J. David Glaes, *Inviting Disaster: How Weapons of Mass Destruction Undermine U.S. Strategy for Projecting Military Power* (McLean, Va.: AMCODA Press, 1997), p. 31.

effort. Persistent chemicals have the potential to slow and otherwise disrupt such operations. Figure 10.12 depicts the VX agent deposition patterns from attacks with five ballistic missiles, less one of which failed to detonate or fell outside the range of effectiveness. Large areas of the airfield are contaminated with lethal VX concentrations, including those elements critical to air operations (runways, open ramp areas, air operations centers, logistical support functions maintenance, refueling), and cargo storage areas. The results of the hypothetical attacks suggest that persistent chemical attacks against aerial ports of debarkation could severely impact cargo throughput capacity in a matter of days. While military casualties would be low, the enemy's capability to restrike in order to keep contamination levels high will gradually grind air operations down to a halt. Continuous operations cannot be guaranteed by personal protection alone in a contaminated environment. Over time, as casualties increase and efficiency plummets, cargo throughput will be minimal. Nuclear weapons, even small arsenals of five to ten weapons, offer high leverage to the proliferator.

Critical facilities at air bases are very susceptible to nuclear blasts. In a one or two twenty-kiloton nuclear weapon airburst attack against Dhahran, for example, fifty percent of the critical facilities would be severely damaged. About ninety percent of the personnel at the base would be killed. Most aircraft present would be destroyed. Prompt and residual radiation effects, fires, and electromagnetic pulse effects on electronic equipment would further damage the airfield capabilities. Figure 10.13 and Table 10.2 illustrate the potential effects.[24]

Advanced Conventional Weapons. Several military technologies that were highly restricted during the Cold War are now available to anyone in the international market with enough cash in hand. In the absence of an effective export control regime for conventional weapons, buyers can purchase just about anything they want. Precise conventional weapons can be used to deny the U.S. access to key ports and airfields. Except for missiles and WMD, there are no restrictions on the technology levels of international arms transfers. Threats to U.S. forces can come in a variety of guises. The existence of clandestine grey and black markets open questions about transfers of WMD and missiles as well as the technologies associated with their production. The recipient of new technology weapons systems has two choices. One is to improve the battlefield performance of current military capabilities. The second is to create entirely new military concepts that

---

[24] Weaver and Glaes, *Inviting Disaster,* pp. 9-50.

Figure 10.12
Hypothetical Scud VX Attack
on Dhahran International Airfield

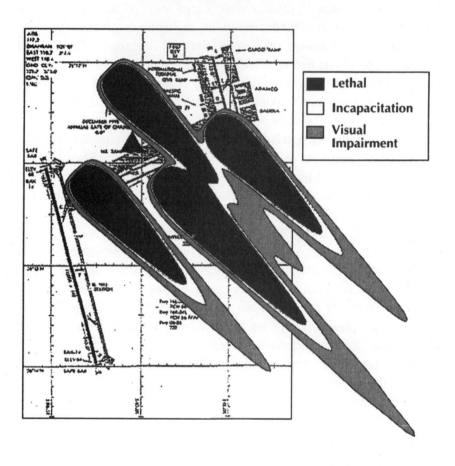

Note: Depicts 4-Missile Iraqi Scud (Al Hussein) Attack; Missile Accuracy: 1 km CEP (One Scud Falls Outside of Target Area)

Source: Greg Weaver and J. David Glaes, *Inviting Disaster: How Weapons of Mass Destruction Undermine U.S. Strategy for Projecting Military Power* (McLean, Va.: AMCODA Press, 1997), p. 37.

Figure 10.13

Potential Effects of a Twenty-Kiloton Nuclear Attack on Dhahran

Dhahran International Airfield

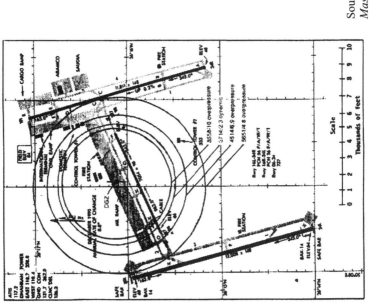

Target	R50 (ft)/psi
• Control Towers	3558/10 Overpressure
• Aircraft and Storage/Sunshades	3714/2.3 Dynamic
• Terminal	4514/6.9 Overprpessure
• Fire Station	5651/4.8 Overpressure

Source: Greg Weaver and J. David Glaes, *Inviting Disaster: How Weapons of Mass Destruction Undermine U.S. Strategy for Projecting Military Power* (McLean, Va.: AMCODA Press, 1997), p. 46.

Table 10.2
Effects of Nuclear Airbursts Over Dhahran Airfield

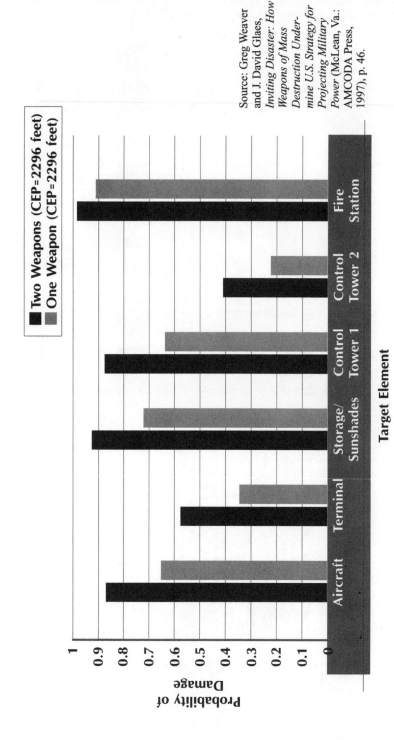

Source: Greg Weaver and J. David Glaes, *Inviting Disaster: How Weapons of Mass Destruction Undermine U.S. Strategy for Projecting Military Power* (McLean, Va.: AMCODA Press, 1997), p. 46.

The New Face of War

incorporate the new technologies. Both approaches increase U.S. military risks, especially the latter. One example cited in testimony before Congress is how a $50,000 laser no longer under export restriction can be used by any adversary to blind U.S. pilots and neutralize a $20 million airplane.[25]

An adversary armed with advanced conventional weapons and WMD might be best positioned to significantly increase the risks faced by U.S. forces. The greater number of casualties that can be inflicted by biological and chemical attacks, not to mention nuclear strikes, might be sufficient to deter any military action by the U.S. and its allies. Meanwhile, advanced conventional weapons could be used to create protective buffer zones and blackmail neighboring countries to deny the U.S. access to their bases and ports, and even overflight rights. Figure 10.14 depicts some of the modern weapons now available on the open market that could be used to deny the U.S. entry to regional ports and airfields. Defenses against an American high-technology aerial onslaught might prove to be possible even if advanced defensive systems and attack capabilities are available. In some cases, it may be possible to block access to seaports by interdicting chokepoints. As shown in Figure 10.15, the Strait of Hormuz at the entry/exit to the Persian Gulf and Arabian Sea is susceptible to closure to international shipping and war ships. Closing the Strait of Hormuz could be a bit tricky due to narrow channels and strong currents but even threats against vessels during a conflict involving Iraq or Iran could be effective. Closure of the Persian Gulf would complicate U.S. military deployments significantly. It could compel the use of the port of Jeddah, Saudi Arabia, on the Red Sea. Such a action would quadruple the truck transport distance to the engaged forces. See Figure 10.16.

A similar impact would be experienced in Northeast Asia where narrow straits are vulnerable to obstruction, at least temporarily. A delay in arrival of U.S. reinforcement and resupply materials may be sufficient to give Pyongyang an edge during crucial periods of combat. When combined with attacks designed to slow the arrival of U.S. forces, the adversary may have all of the components to turn the conflict into a prolonged slug-fest where its advanced conventional weapons, though based on technology of the 1970s and 1980s, could do quite well against the military forces of the United States and its allies. "The danger to the US is not that we will face a peer competitor in the foreseeable future," David Blair explains, "but that

---

[25] Bill Gertz, "Export Controls Need Checking, Expert Says," *Washington Times* (June 18, 1997), p. A8.

Figure 10.14

Regional Adversaries—Twenty-First Century Conventional Anti-Access Arsenals

Source: U.S., Defense Science Board, *Investments for 21st Century Military Superiority* (Washington, D.C.: Office of the Under Secretary of Defense, Acquisition and Technology, November 1995), and Michael G. Vickers, *Warfare in 2020: A Primer* (Washington, D.C.: Center for Strategic and Budgetary Assessments, October 1996).

The New Face of War

Figure 10.15
Conventional Anti-Access Threat
Straight of Hormuz Chokepoint

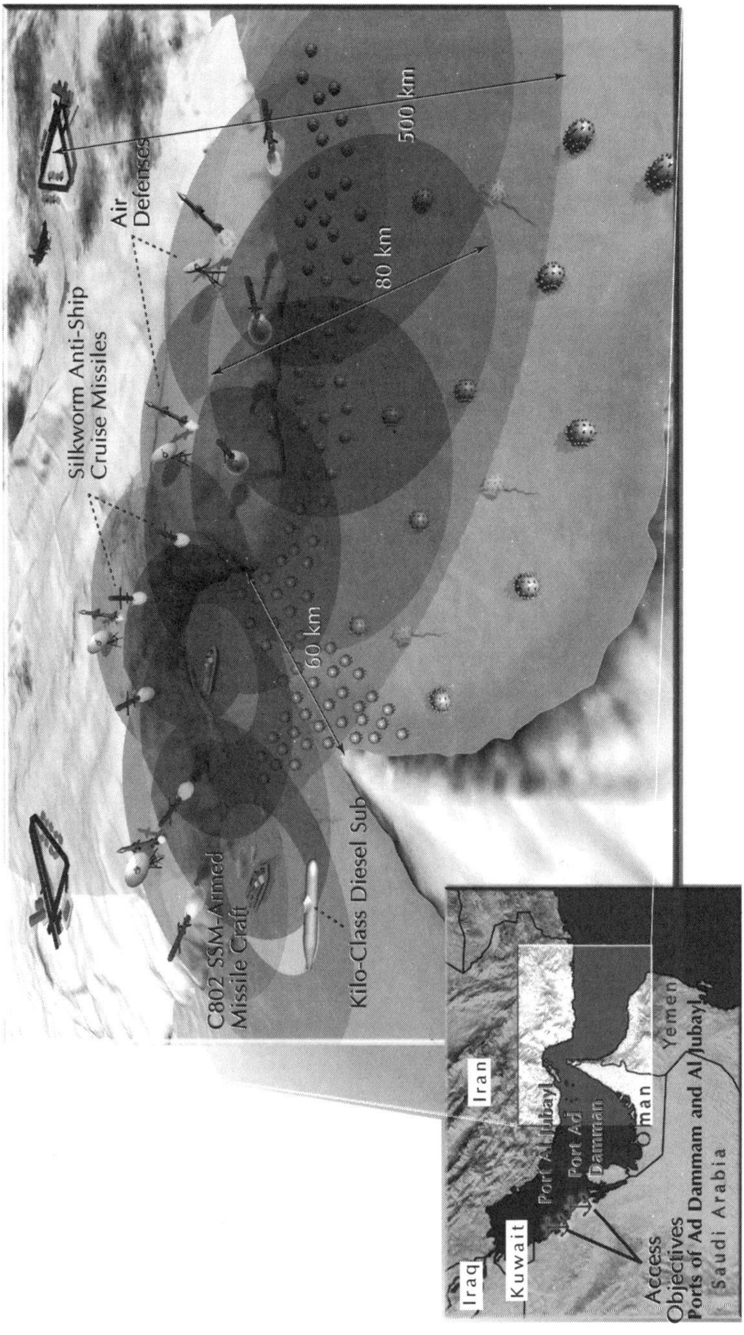

Figure 10.16

Implications of WMD Damage to Saudi Ports

Impact of Loss of Ad Dammam and Al Jubayl

- 90% of sealift used in Desert Shield forced to Red Sea ports (85.5% of all lift used)

- Quadruples truck transport distance
  - Lack of trucks was our single worst logistics problem
  - Sent 75% of Army's trucks to support 25% of force structure and still had to lease 3,000 more

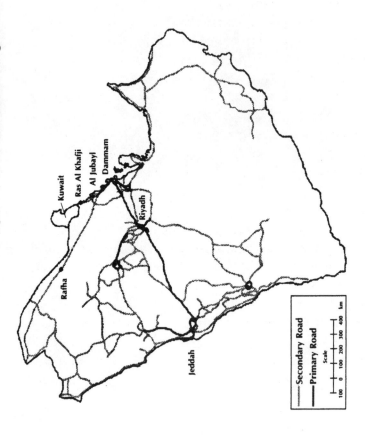

Secondary Road
Primary Road

Scale
100 0 100 200 300 400 km

Kuwait
Ras Al Khafji
Al Jubayl
Dammam
Riyadh
Rafha
Jeddah

Source: Greg Weaver and J. David Glaes, *Inviting Disaster: How Weapons of Mass Destruction Undermine U.S. Strategy for Projecting Military Power* (McLean, Va.: AMCODA Press, 1997), p. 32.

we will face regional powers that are able to keep our military from projecting power into their regions."[26]

State-Sponsored Terrorism. WMD in the hands of rogue regimes manifesting an implacable hostility toward the United States is magnified when they join forces and terrorists. For the terrorists and their state sponsors, WMD is a strategic device to counter the U.S. power projection strategy. The rogue regimes want the cover of plausible deniability offered by the terrorists while the latter need resources, expertise, and training that can be provided by states. The Khobar Towers bombing in June 1996 offers a glimpse of the growing potential to use terrorism as a means of challenging the U.S. power projection strategy.

Using terrorism as a strategic weapon, rogue regimes have a tool to blur the distinction between the actions by terrorists and those by their armed forces in peace and war. This convergence of terrorists and state sponsors allows adversaries to attack the U.S. power projection strategy continuously. Terrorism in peace, for example, can be used to raise the price of American overseas presence. Peacetime terrorism drives home the point of how American forces are placed at risk when positioned abroad. In wartime, the blood price exacted by terrorists can assist in deterring U.S. intervention or at least delaying and disrupting deployments overseas.[27]

Super-terrorism, the use of WMD by terrorists, transforms the threat of terrorism into a strategic weapon. Terrorists can become a preferred mode for delivering a nuclear, biological, or chemical weapon against Americans overseas, including U.S. embassies and commercial interests.

Implications for the U.S. Military Posture

America's strategy is under sharp attack by several countries in various parts of the globe. The strategic risks summarized in the following paragraphs show how WMD proliferators are going after the two weight-bearing assumptions of American strategy. In light of these efforts to undermine the two principal pillars of U.S. strategy, how plausible are the American assumptions of having available sufficient actionable time and unhindered access to overseas bases?

In the past, forward-based and positioned forces, whether stationed there permanently or temporarily deployed, were judged to deter adversaries while

---

[26] Blair, "How to Defeat the United States," p. 75.

[27] Carr, "Terrorism as Warfare," pp. 1-2.

---

reassuring allies and friends. The future, however, will behold an entirely new picture since forward positioned U.S. forces will be at risk of destruction by long-range strike systems. Even with air and missile defenses, in-theater air bases will be highly vulnerable to determined nuclear, biological, and chemical weapons attacks, especially during the critical early stages of a conflict. The strategic concept of "fighting our way into a denied theater or creating and protecting forward operating bases" promises to become more onerous over time as adversaries build arsenals of WMD, missiles, and advanced conventional capabilities.[28]

There are two sides to the Achilles heel in the U.S. transoceanic power projection strategy. One side of the coin is the American dependence on in-theater air bases and other military facilities as well as close-in waters for launch of carrier-based tactical fighters. The other side of the strategy coin is the prospect of enemy operations to delay, disrupt, and block U.S. forces deploying to the theater and destroying those already present in the region. The problem of the U.S. dependence on foreign bases and waters and potential enemy anti-access operations will only increase in the coming decade. The proliferation of WMD, missiles, and advanced conventional weapons will make the U.S. dependence on regional access more important at the very time the spread of advanced arms will make them more vulnerable.

Regional adversaries could inflict high casualties against American forces to raise the blood price and deter further U.S. involvement. Terrorism against forward-based forces in peacetime could be used to demonstrate the vulnerability of U.S. forces when positioned within the adversary's operational reach. Follow-up attacks in crisis could divert U.S. assets to protect fixed installations and the armed forces. While terrorism provides the adversary plausible deniability of participating in the attacks, the adversary's advanced conventional forces could include modern air defense weapons that might prove effective against disrupted and perhaps disjointed U.S. air strikes from damaged in-theater bases. Aircraft carriers could be pushed outside of the operational reach of their strike aircraft by the enemy's seeding the sea with mines, and submarines could be positioned at critical chokepoints. Meanwhile, the adversary's arsenal of WMD could compel a limitation of U.S. war aims to avoid triggering attacks against urban areas of regional partners or the United States itself.

The entire regional military strategy of the United States as the twentieth century comes to a close is based on the experience of the Persian Gulf

---

[28] U.S., Joint Chiefs of Staff, *National Military Strategy of the United States of America 1997.*

War. This strategy is centered on the timely deployment and unhindered access and use of regional bases by large numbers of tactical fighters and ground forces. Hence, the projected buys of Air Force, Marine Corps and Navy tactical fighters over the first two decades of the twenty-first century exceed 4,000 aircraft at a cost of more than $350 billion. The Army continues to field new helicopters, tactical missiles, medium tactical vehicles, and howitzers, as well as upgrades to the M1 Abrams tank and Bradley fighting vehicle. The nation's ground forces need to be leaner and more mobile. Cutting divisions and adopting a readiness posture to match the military threats may free up the resources needed to give the Army greater mobility. The trouble is that the force structure of the four military services will dictate how the United States will fight in the future, and the future promises WMD-adversaries posing far more complex and threatening challenges than can be answered by theater-based fighters or land warfare forces muscle-bound with heavy armor.

Not only do these range-limited tactical fighters require forward bases or aircraft carrier launch locations within range of their targets, but forward air operations consume large amounts of fuel, bombs and other munitions, and general supplies that must pass through regional seaports and airfields. Ready, unrestricted access to the forward bases—a key implicit assumption in the U.S. strategy—may not be forthcoming. Political decisions by regional allies can delay the granting of the U.S. access to forward air bases and impose restrictions as to whether military operations can be launched from these installations, particularly when U.S. friends remain exposed to the coercive threats of regional antagonists. Future adversaries, learning from the Gulf War, will likely take advantage of these vulnerabilities by adapting their strategies and exploiting emerging technologies.

Brent Scowcroft and the other members of the Independent Bomber Force Review Commission asked several questions about the American "capability gap" in their July 1997 report to Congress. Noting that "...we currently cannot halt a large-scale armored assault without tactical air forces in-theater prior to the outbreak of hostilities," the Commission asked several pertinent questions:

- How do we plan to...[halt a large-scale armored assault] in the case of surprise attack?
- How do we plan on deploying forces in the face of chemical and biological attack—something the QDR [Quadrennial Defense Review] says should be assumed?

- How do we plan on conducting a large-scale pre-emptive strike against an adversary's facilities for producing weapons of mass destruction?
- How do we plan on striking facilities that lie outside fighter range, such as terrorist camps in northwestern Iran?[29]

Are Chinese military officers right when they say that "U.S. military forces...are vulnerable, even deeply flawed, and can be defeated with the right strategy"?[30]

---

[29] Brent Scowcroft and others, *Final Report of the Independent Bomber Force Review Commission,* presented to The Honorable Duncan Hunter, Chairman, Military Procurement Subcommittee of the Committee on National Security, House of Representatives (July 23, 1997), p. 22. Other Commission members included Lieutenant General Richard Burpee, U.S. Air Force (retired); Jim Courter; William Hoehn; John Lenczowski; and Donald Rice.

[30] Michael Pillsbury as quoted in "Gulf War Provided Ample Information for Chinese Military Thinkers," *Inside Missile Defense* (March 12, 1997), p. 13.

The New Face of War

CHAPTER 11

The Anti-Strategy

S trategy, derived from the Greek *strategos* meaning the art or skill of the general, is no longer the sole province of the soldier. Today, *strategos* means the nation's strategy and includes the planning for, coordination of, and concerted use of resources to achieve national security objectives in peace and war.[1] Strategy links the military objectives defined by political leaders with the forces necessary to achieve them. When the resources to field the right kinds and numbers of forces are insufficient, the strategy cannot be executed without incurring severe military risks. Decision-makers have a number of risk management tools available to relieve the stress imparted on the strategy, including adding additional resources for upgrading force structure, reducing the political objectives and thereby lessen the number of forces required to satisfy them, changing the strategy to achieve a better offense-defense alignment with the threats to U.S. security interests, or accepting the current risks and asking the armed forces to do the best they can.

The previous chapter documented severe risks being introduced to U.S. military strategy as a result of the new challenges posed by the proliferation of WMD and advanced conventional weapons. These challenges are undermining the strategy's two main pillars: timely deployment of U.S. forces and unhindered and unobstructed access to regional seaports, airfields, bases, and littoral waters. Two critical questions need to be answered: Is the Clinton Administration's approach to counterproliferation adequate for dealing with the new challenges to the nation's military strategy? And, secondly, does this approach mitigate the severe military risks facing the power projection strategy?

---

[1] John I. Alger, *Definitions and Doctrine of the Military Art: Past and Present,* U.S. Military Academy History Series, edited by Thomas E. Griess (Wayne, N.J.: Avery Publishing Group, 1985), p. 5.

Clinton Administration—
Changing Military Force Structure

The late Secretary of Defense Les Aspin announced the "Counterproliferation Initiative" in December 1993.[2] Secretary Aspin had no illusions about the motivations of countries trying to field nuclear, biological and chemical weapons as offsets to unmatched American conventional military power. As compared with the days of the Cold War, when the United States and its allies in Europe used nuclear weapons as an equalizer against the numerically superior Warsaw Pact conventional forces, in the new era, Aspin said, "we're the ones who could wind up being the equalizee."[3]

A senior defense official made it clear at the outset that the Counterproliferation Initiative would be a non-nuclear program: "We, like many signatories of the Non-Proliferation Treaty, have undertaken not to use nuclear weapons against countries that don't have nuclear weapons or aren't allied with a power that is using nuclear weapons against us...our preference in dealing with special weapons is not to use special weapons back. We would like to be able, by conventional means, to defeat an opponent armed with special weapons."[4]

The Clinton Administration's approach to the growing threat of WMD and missiles is divided into three categories: nuclear deterrence, theater defense, and counterforce.[5] Although these military strategy options are

---

[2] The U.S. government usage of key concepts was defined by the National Security Council in early 1994: *Proliferation* - "...the spread of nuclear, biological and chemical capabilities and the missiles to deliver them;" *Nonproliferation* - "...the use of the full range of political, economic and military tools to prevent proliferation, reverse it diplomatically or protect our interests against an opponent armed with weapons of mass destruction or missiles, should that prove necessary. Nonproliferation tools include: intelligence, global nonproliferation norms and agreements, diplomacy, export controls, security assurances, defenses and the application of military force;" and *Counterproliferation* - "...the activities of the Department of Defense across the full range of U.S. efforts to combat proliferation, including diplomacy, arms control, export controls, and intelligence collection and analysis, with particular responsibility for assuring that U.S. forces and interests can be protected should they confront an adversary armed with weapons of mass destruction or missiles." See Daniel Poneman, Special Assistant to the President, letter to Robert Gallucci, Department of State, and Ashton Carter, Department of Defense, subject: "Agreed Definitions" (Washington, D.C.: National Security Council, February 18, 1994).

[3] Les Aspin, Secretary of Defense, remarks before the Committee on International Security and Arms Control, National Academy of Sciences (Washington, D.C.: December 7, 1993). Photocopy.

[4] U.S., Department of Defense, Background Briefing on the Counterproliferation Initiative, attributable to a "Senior Defense Official," Transcript ID No. 1020543 (Washington, D.C.: Department of Defense, December 7, 1993).

The New Face of War

based largely on the U.S. experience in the Persian Gulf War, there is no widely shared view among policy makers and military planners of how these elements come together, and their potential synergies have not been fully explored.

The Defense Department has made four attempts since the end of the Cold War to restructure the armed forces for countering future threats to U.S. security.

Base Force. Military forces were cut by about a quarter in an effort to define the "minimum force structure for enduring needs." This 1990-91 force structure plan was tailored to satisfy U.S. regional interests, be credible to friends and foes alike, and avoid the development of a "hollow force" that was experienced in the late 1970s. The Base Force anticipated the prospect of smaller forces and served as a floor of military capabilities below which the country would encounter considerable military risk.[6] The end of the Cold War "...will allow a reduction in our defense effort, but, as forces decrease in size," Congressman Les Aspin warned in February 1992, "it becomes increasingly important that the residual forces are the right forces for the future. There's less margin for error."[7]

Bottom-Up Review. A new force structure was designed to address the concerns expressed in the press and on Capitol Hill about the military risks associated with defense budget reductions. The October 1993 Bottom-Up Review promulgated the military requirement to be able to fight two "major regional contingencies" at roughly the same time (a conflict in the Middle East against an adversary of about the size of Iraq's pre-Gulf War military and war in Northeast Asia against a North Korea-like enemy).[8] The Bottom-Up Review was underfunded right from the beginning.

---

[5] R. Jeffrey Smith, "Clinton Changes Nuclear Strategy," *Washington Post* (December 7, 1997); U.S., Office of the Secretary of Defense, *Proliferation: Threat and Response* (1997), pp. 60-63; William S. Cohen, Secretary of Defense, *Annual Report to the President and the Congress* (1997), pp. 12-13. See also James Kitfield, "Counterproliferation," *Air Force Magazine* (October 1995), p. 57.

[6] Colin L. Powell, General, U.S. Army, Chairman, Joint Chiefs of Staff, "The Base Force - A Total Force," a briefing for presentation to the Senate Appropriations Sub-Committee on Defense, (1991). Photocopy.

[7] Les Aspin, Representative, Chairman, House Armed Services Committee, "An Approach to Sizing American Conventional Forces For the Post-Soviet Era - Four Illustrative Options," February 25, 1992), p. 2. Photocopy.

[8] John T. Correll, "Backing Up On Strategy," *Air Force Magazine* (June 1996), p. 5, and Les Aspin, Secretary of Defense, *Force Structure Excerpts - Bottom-Up Review* (Washington, D.C.: Office of the Secretary of Defense (Public Affairs), News Release No. 403-93, September 1, 1993).

In 1994, Congress, increasingly alarmed at the defense budget cuts, prodded General John M. Shalikashvili, then-Chairman of the Joint Chiefs of Staff, to explain whether defense resources were sufficient to support the two major regional contingencies called for by the national military strategy. In response, General Shalikashvili authorized a Pentagon exercise dubbed "Nimble Dancer" to assess the capability of the Bottom-Up Review forces to fight and win two nearly simultaneous major contingencies. Conducted between November 1994 and July 1995, Nimble Dancer from the beginning was fatally flawed. As documented by the General Accounting Office, Nimble Dancer's testing of key assumptions was limited; favorable assumptions were used concerning reserve mobilization and activation of emergency airline support for military operations; the amount of time between activation of the two contingencies was advantageous to "proving" the Bottom-Up Review strategy was viable; warning times of the number of days before an enemy attacks were more favorable that those used by the actual combatant commands; nuclear and biological warfare were ignored; chemical warfare was not fully examined; combat support forces were not analyzed; and many other glaring deficiencies plagued the analysis. In a word, Nimble Dancer was aimed at depicting the Bottom-Up Review as being viable when, in fact, it was underfunded by more than $100 billion over a five-year period, which by any measure made it unworkable and downright dangerous.[9]

Quadrennial Defense Review (QDR). The Pentagon's third try at devising a force structure for the emerging threats and demands of the new era was mandated by Congress. The May 1997 report was intended to be a comprehensive examination of military strategy and force structure through the year 2005. Right from the beginning, however, the QDR was transformed into a budget exercise of how many of what forces had to be cut to meet dollar-constrained goals. The trouble is the sharp focus on the dollar cost blinded analysts from considering shifts in strategy to meet the new threats confronting the United States. On the positive side, the QDR document called for expanding U.S. forces to better handle peace operations, combat terrorism, defend against chemical and biological weapons, and respond to small-scale contingencies. Yet, the defense review did not begin to come to grips with the single greatest threat to America's transoceanic

---

[9] U.S., General Accounting Office, *Bottom-Up Review: Analysis of DOD War Game to Test Key Assumptions*, GAO/NSIAD-96-170 (Washington, D.C.: General Accounting Office, 1996), pp. 5-13.

military strategy: anti-access operations by adversaries armed with WMD and missiles who have the will to block U.S. military deployments through attacks against the receiving seaports, airfields, and other theater facilities.

Congressman Floyd Spence, chairman of the House National Security Committee, correctly called the Administration's QDR "gamesmanship": "Another budget-first, strategy-second Bottom-Up Review.... If the QDR once again compels a smaller, under-resourced force to execute an expanding strategy, then the readiness, quality-of-life, and modernization problems we see today will quickly worsen."[10]

The QDR did little to make up the resource shortfalls of some $15 to $20 billion annually. Calling for exploitation of revolutionary military technologies in sensors, information processing, stealth, and precision-strike weapons, the QDR proposes to pay for these programs by further personnel cuts and military base closures. Yet, the resources released by these actions would provide little more than a down payment on the systems required to transform the current military strategy.[11]

In the final analysis, the QDR was based on the optimistic assumption that the United States will find itself in a "strategic pause" or "lull" over the next ten to fifteen years during which few large-scale threats will be manifested against U.S. interests. "One certainly hopes that's the case," the editors at the *Washington Times* opined, "but it's a heck of an assumption on which to base your entire military review."[12]

Advertising the QDR as a search for the "right mix of strategy, programs, and resources," the Defense Department denied that it was a "budget-driven exercise." Yet, a clear operating assumption was present right from the start: the defense budget would remain at about $245-$250 billion in real terms for some number of years. Once this glass ceiling was in place, military planners could pare and reshape service force structures through minor adjustments to their preferred courses of action. Weapons systems that did not fit the preconceptions of the armed services were swept off the table.

National Defense Panel. The fourth force structure review was completed by the nine-member National Defense Panel (NDP) in December

---

[10] "Congressional News," *Air Force Magazine* (June 1997), p. 14.

[11] Jeff Erlich, "Storm Brews As Congress Awaits QDR," *Defense News* (May 12-18, 1997), pp. 3, 43, and Michael Vickers, "QDR Fails to Boldly Confront Future," *Defense News* (June 16-22, 1997), pp. 49-50.

[12] "The Pentagon's Quadrennial Riddle," *Washington Times* [Editorial] (June 2, 1997), p. A16.

1997. This study, conducted in parallel with the Pentagon's in-house QDR completed in May, focused on the security challenges in 2010 to 2020. The report landed in Washington with a resounding "thud." Though it was not without its faults, many in the Defense Department and on Capitol Hill were too quick to brush off its strengths.

In a simple and direct statement, the NDP report provides the baseline for assessing military risk to the nation's longstanding transoceanic military strategy: "The cornerstone of America's continued military preeminence is our ability to project combat power rapidly and virtually unimpeded to widespread areas of the globe."[13] The report cites several theater access obstacles and force vulnerabilities threatening the U.S. power projection strategy:

- "Allies might be coerced not to grant the United States access to their sovereign territory."
- "As oil and gas fields in Central Asia gain in strategic value, we may need to project power greater distances, further from littorals or established bases."
- "Even if we retain the necessary bases and port infrastructure to support forward deployed forces, they will be vulnerable to strikes that could reduce or neutralize their utility."[14]
- "In short, we must radically alter the way in which we project power."[15]

Buying into the Defense Department's questionable perspective that the United States is in a "strategic lull" since it currently does not face a global peer nor is one likely to emerge before 2015,[16] the panel provided its own grand design to reduce military risks. According to the National Defense Panel, the capability of adversaries to threaten U.S. vital interests is far below that supposed by the Quadrennial Defense Review, especially if the United States would drop the requirement for overlapping theater wars in the Middle East and the Pacific. This two-war concept is a "force-sizing function and not a strategy," the panel members argued.[17]

---

[13] U.S., National Defense Panel, *Transforming Defense,* p. 12.

[14] *Ibid.,* pp. 12-13.

[15] *Ibid.,* p. 33.

[16] U.S., National Defense University, *1997 Strategic Assessment,* p. 241.

[17] John A Tirpak, "The NDP and the Transformation Strategy," *Air Force Magazine* (March 1998), p. 21.

The New Face of War

The panel is wrong. The two-war concept is an essential strategy element that has been used to great benefit in helping to preserve stability simultaneously in the Middle East and Pacific. Drop to a one-war strategy, and the world will witness frantic efforts by those designated as second-string allies as they scramble to find new ways to ensure their security. Arms races could be triggered. Some countries probably already have standby plans for an American desertion, and they may have standby WMD breakout capabilities. Regardless of the actual circumstances, the U.S. would be guaranteed less influence and security than it has today.

The "underbelly," or bulge under the QDR budget line shown in Figure 11.1 is the proposed amount to be saved by personnel cuts and base closings to help pay for advanced weapons, plus the amount available from the NDP's proposed shift from a two to a one-war strategy. The NDP proposes to tap these freed-up defense resources to the tune of a $5 to $10 billion slice of the "underbelly" annually in order to transform U.S. strategy to meet the risks of the period 2015 and beyond. See Figure 11.2.

The problem is that this entire approach is based on an assumption of "no peer competitor" until at least 2015. Adversaries are already "transforming" their strategy to exploit the U.S. dependencies on time and access for the projection of military forces overseas. The effect of the "strategic lull," if it exists at all, is negligible. The proliferation of WMD, missiles, and advanced conventional weapons and technologies, and super-terrorism belies any sense of lull. As documented in previous chapters, the United States already faces considerable military risks and these are likely to grow significantly between 2005 and 2010 when WMD proliferators and those armed with advanced conventional weapons and technologies will be capable of conducting regional anti-access operations to keep Americans out. Figure 11.3 shows the resources "underbelly" that is supposed to fund both the QDR and NDP programs to be a chimera. With military risks already growing at an alarming rate, such clinical approaches as suggested by the QDR and NDP should be taken with a large grain of salt. The level of military risk depicted is less than a decade away, meaning that the forces now in the U.S. inventory will be the ones needed to mitigate those risks. The challenge is an asymmetric one aimed directly at the dependence of the current U.S. military strategy on time and access.

Figure 11.1
National Defense Panel Strategic Risk Assessment

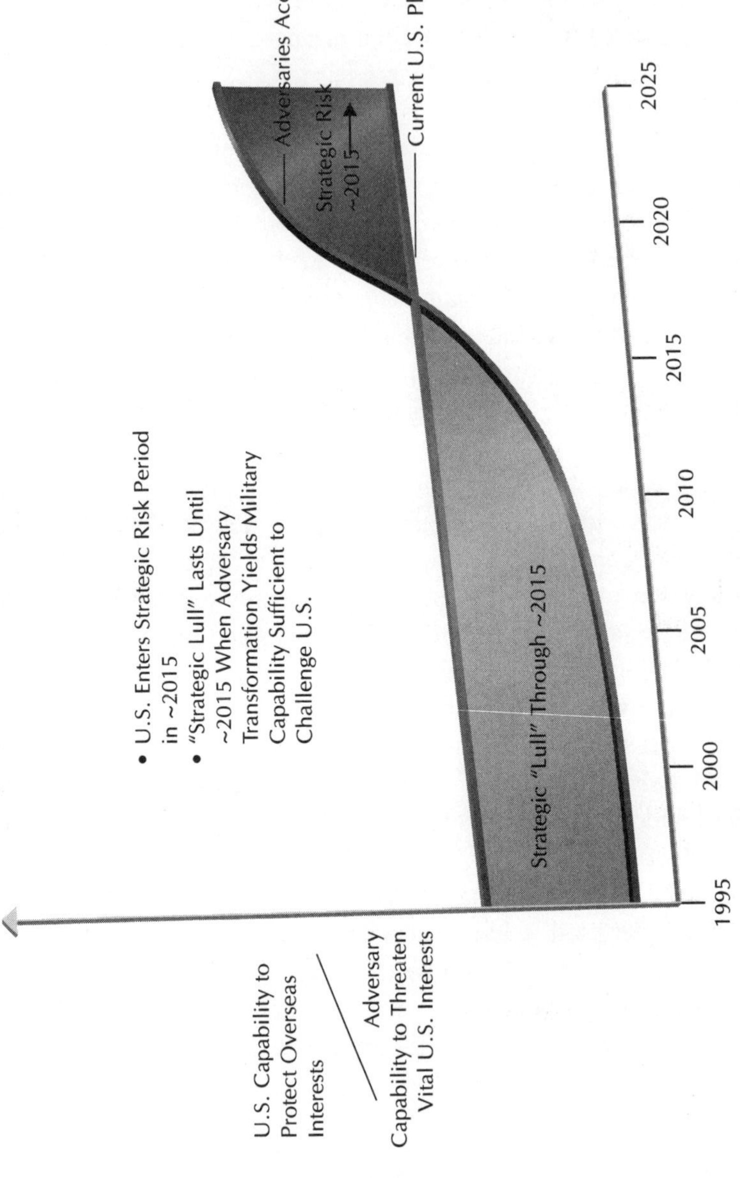

- U.S. Enters Strategic Risk Period in ~2015
- "Strategic Lull" Lasts Until ~2015 When Adversary Transformation Yields Military Capability Sufficient to Challenge U.S.

Adversaries According to NDP

Strategic Risk ~2015

Current U.S. Plan (QDR)

Strategic "Lull" Through ~2015

U.S. Capability to Protect Overseas Interests

Adversary Capability to Threaten Vital U.S. Interests

1995 2000 2005 2010 2015 2020 2025

NDP = National Defense Panel   **QDR = Quadrennial Defense Review**

Figure 11.2
National Defense Panel "Transformation Strategy"

- U.S. Exploits "Strategic Lull" to Begin Aggressive Implementation of "Transformation Strategy"
- Assumes U.S. Must Accept — and Can Afford — Near-Term Risk to "Pay" for Transformation

NDP Transformation Strategy

Adversaries According to NDP

Current U.S. Plan (QDR)

Near-Term "Cost" of U.S. Transformation

U.S. Capability to Protect Overseas Interests

Adversary Capability to Threaten U.S. Interests

1995   2000   2005   2010   2015   2020   2025

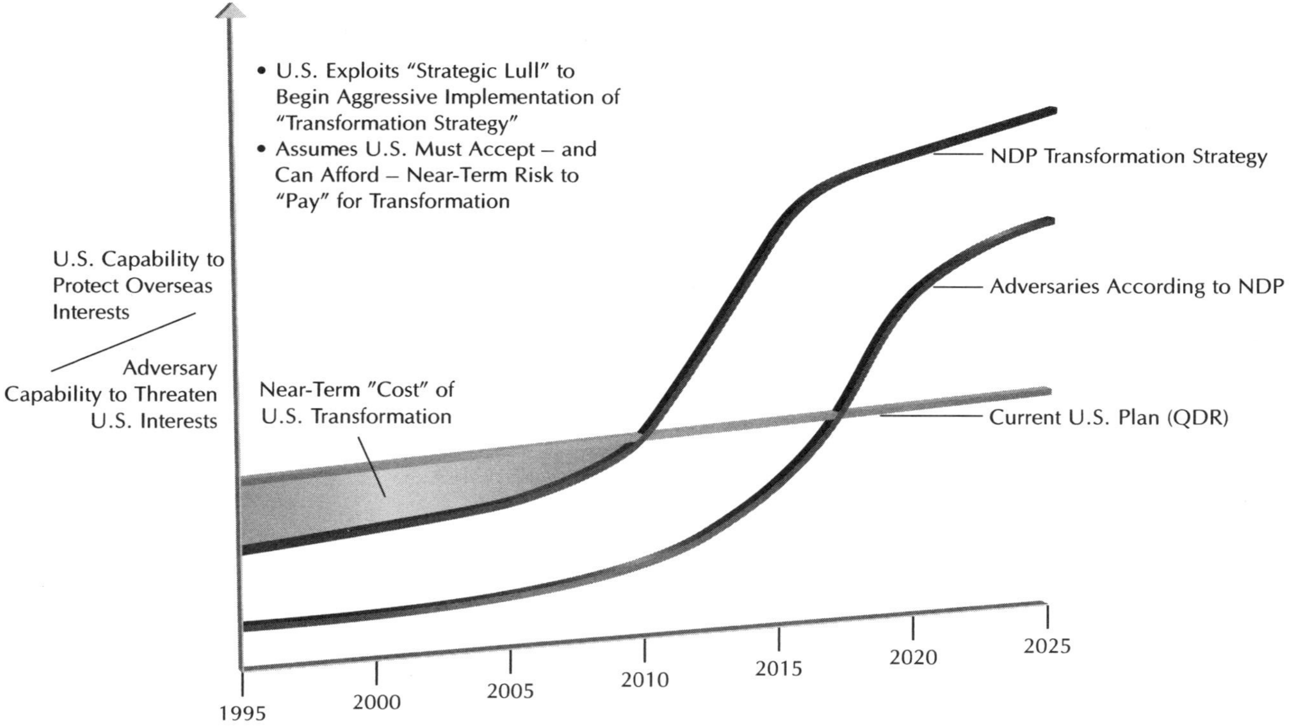

NDP = National Defense Panel   **QDR = Quadrennial Defense Review**

Figure 11.3
Military Risk Assessment

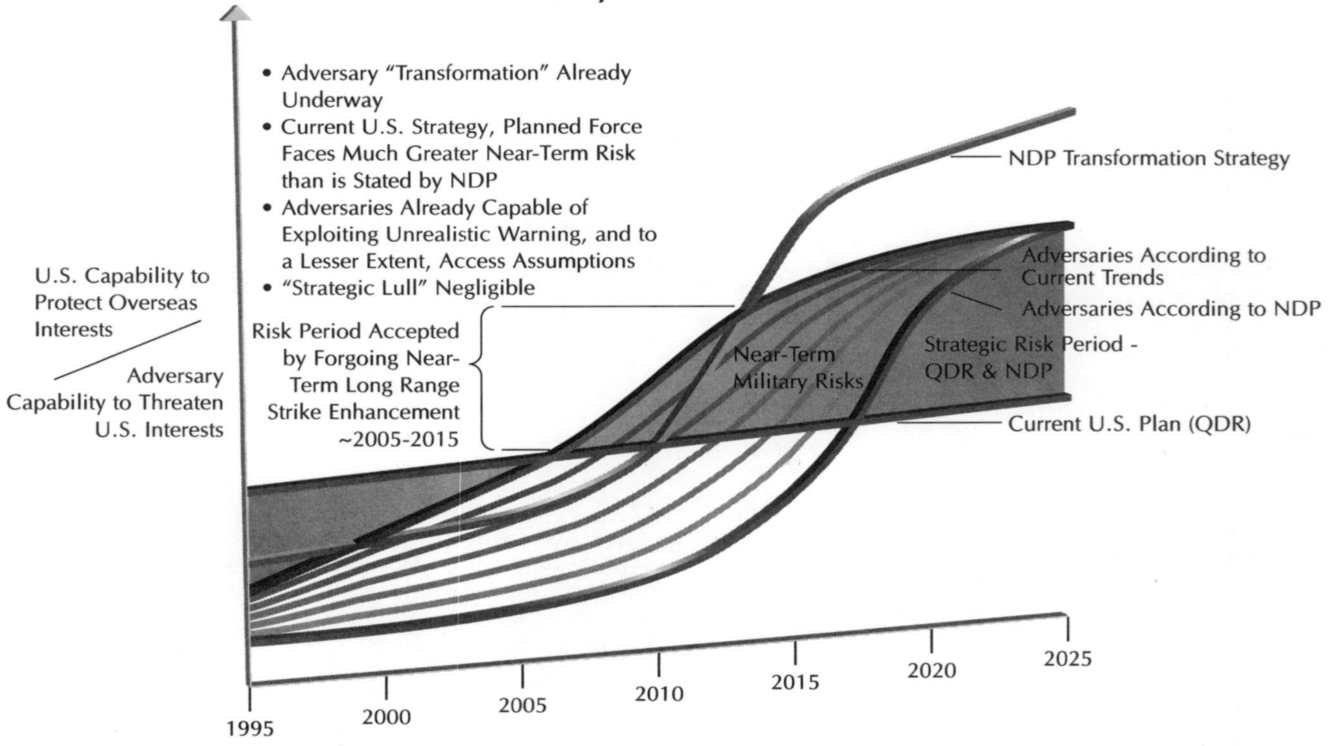

- Adversary "Transformation" Already Underway
- Current U.S. Strategy, Planned Force Faces Much Greater Near-Term Risk than is Stated by NDP
- Adversaries Already Capable of Exploiting Unrealistic Warning, and to a Lesser Extent, Access Assumptions
- "Strategic Lull" Negligible

Risk Period Accepted by Forgoing Near-Term Long Range Strike Enhancement ~2005-2015

NDP Transformation Strategy

Adversaries According to Current Trends

Adversaries According to NDP

Strategic Risk Period - QDR & NDP

Near-Term Military Risks

Current U.S. Plan (QDR)

U.S. Capability to Protect Overseas Interests

Adversary Capability to Threaten U.S. Interests

1995 2000 2005 2010 2015 2020 2025

NDP = National Defense Panel   **QDR = Quadrennial Defense Review**

Clinton Administration—Assessing Military Options

The second path taken by the Clinton Administration has been to find the right blend of counterproliferation military options among three key elements: nuclear deterrence, theater defense, and counterforce. Defense Secretary William S. Cohen's annual report to the president and the Congress continues the concentrated focus on these three military options. A great deal of effort is underway in these areas to improve U.S. military capabilities to carry out the national power projection strategy. Innovative battlefield operational concepts are being examined for new organizations and force employment approaches. Yet, while these seem to be steps in the right direction of mitigating near-terms risks, Secretary Cohen offers a word of caution: "However, it is essential that before significant portions of the defense budget are committed to programming for revised organizational arrangements or the procurement of new technologies, new operational concepts must be fully developed in joint and Service battle labs and validated in warfighting experiments."[18] Risk aversion can sometimes sound an "uncertain trumpet."

Nuclear Deterrence. During the Gulf War, many believed deterrence of biological and chemical attacks was simply a matter of making thinly veiled threats about potential use of American nuclear weapons. Secretary of State James Baker, for instance, flatly told Iraq's Foreign Minister Tariq Aziz in Geneva a week before the war started on January 16, 1991, that "before we cross to the other side—that is, if the conflict starts, God forbid, and chemical or biological weapons are used against our forces—the American people would demand revenge, and we have the means to implement this."[19] President George Bush and Defense Secretary Dick Cheney also delivered messages to Baghdad on the prospective use of nuclear weapons, if Iraq used weapons of mass destruction.

After the war, Foreign Minister Aziz and a senior Iraqi military defector, General Wafic Al Sammarai, gushed that Iraq was deterred from using WMD because of the threat of American nuclear retaliation.[20] But did the

---

[18] William S. Cohen, Secretary of Defense, *Annual Report to the President and the Congress* (Washington, D.C.: Government Printing Office, 1998), pp. 123-38.

[19] As quoted in Keith B. Payne, *Deterrence in the Second Nuclear Age* (Lexington: University of Kentucky Press, 1996), p. 83.

[20] *Ibid.*, p. 85. Brent Scowcroft, President Bush's national security advisor, admitted in 1995 that the United States had decided not to use nuclear weapons in the event of WMD use by the Iraqis. The U.S. response would have been stepped-up conventional bombing in both intensity and scope of the targets attacked.

Iraqis really believe the U.S. threat to use nuclear weapons? To have struck the Iraqis with nuclear weapons could have destroyed the carefully constructed anti-Iraq Coalition. The enmity of millions of Muslims worldwide toward the United States would have been assured for decades. Despite the commonly shared perceptions in the United States, it is quite possible that the Iraqis had no intention of using biological and chemical agents, especially after the Battle of Al Khafji when three of their best divisions were mauled by U.S. air power and other Coalition air forces. This battle rocked the Iraqi leadership. The Iraqis recognized that Coalition air strikes would deny them the prospect of fighting their preferred style of World War One trench warfare and that the continued pounding from the air would sap the Iraqi Army of strength until the final ground attack would exploit aerial victory.

The Iraqi leadership chose not to stand and fight against the Coalition ground offensive. Until the Battle of Al Khafji, the Iraqis may have planned on employing similar tactics against U.S. forces that they had used so effectively during the 1980s Iran-Iraq War: physical barriers to block forward movement of enemy forces and then strike them with chemical weapons (and biological) while they are stopped. Rather, Baghdad's grand tactic after Al Khafji turn out to be to save as much of the elite Republican Guard units as possible. "Shoot quickly and dash for Baghdad" were orders of the day. Under these conditions, there was no need for the Iraqis to use biological and chemical weapons. Had the Coalition chased the Republican Guard out of Kuwait and pursued them into the streets of Baghdad, it could have been a different situation. It is quite possible that Iraq's WMD would have been used to save the regime or serve like a dying sting of a scorpion as Saddam Hussein and his cronies passed from this world.

New theoretical concepts are necessary to provide the logical underpinnings of a workable U.S. regional deterrence concept for dealing with the emerging WMD-armed adversaries. The post-Cold War order reflects a partial return to *classical balance of power* considerations, at least with regard to the emerging WMD actors. Released from the *classical deterrence* of the Cold War, new regional balances of power are based primarily on conventional military forces—the armed capacity necessary for seizing and holding territory. Without the nuclear guarantees of the superpowers, new conditions of regional equilibrium are emerging at different rates of change in Europe, the Middle East, South Asia, and Southeast Asia. Northeast Asia, too, is evolving, but several wild cards question which direction trends may take the region (e.g., what will Japan's reaction be to the evolution of a peacefully unified, nuclear-armed Korea?).

The U.S. regional deterrence position was ostensibly strengthened in November 1997, when President Bill Clinton signed in a landmark decision directive. This new policy would target non-nuclear states for potential U.S. nuclear strikes in retaliation for biological and chemical attacks. "It's not difficult to define a scenario," Robert Bell of the U.S. National Security Council explained, "in which a rogue state would use chemical weapons and biological weapons and not be afforded protection under our negative security assurance."[21] Any country using weapons of mass destruction against the United States may "forfeit" its protection from U.S. nuclear attack afforded in the 1995 Nuclear Non-Proliferation Treaty by Russia, China, France, Britain, and the United States.[22]

Some analysts viewed the new policy as "misguided and potentially dangerous." Thomas Graham, president of the Lawyers Alliance for World Security, argues that the Nuclear Non-Proliferation Treaty contains no exceptions to support the "use of nuclear weapons to counter chemical or biological weapons." Many countries will perceive the new U.S. position as "an act of bad faith." Mr. Graham predicts that if the U.S. does not live up to the negative security assurance bargain then "the half dozen nuclear proliferation threats could become many more tomorrow."[23]

Perhaps the former chief of staff of the Indian Army, General K. Sundarji, was right in 1993 when he said the lesson he learned from the Gulf War was "don't mess with the United States without nuclear weapons."[24] "The way to deal with chemical and biological threats is with conventional power....," Thomas Graham says. "If nuclear deterrence is somewhat under-employed, let it remain so."[25]

Another nettlesome problem is what to do about small, discrete uses of biological and chemical weapons. What happens if the adversary uses small

---

[21] Negative security assurance: non-nuclear members of the Non-Proliferation Treaty not seeking to develop or obtain their own weapons nor that are allied with nuclear countries will not be the targets of U.S. nuclear reprisals. See Jeff Erlich, "New U.S. Nuclear Policy Maintains Ambiguity," *Defense News* (January 5-11, 1998), pp. 4, 19.

[22] Smith, "Clinton Changes Nuclear Strategy." See also David Ochmanek and Richard Sokolsky, "Employ Nuclear Deterrence," *Defense News* (January 12-18, 1998), p. 21.

[23] Thomas Graham, "Conventional Response," *Defense News* (February 23-March 1, 1998), p. 31.

[24] General K. Sundarji's interjection at a U.S. government-sponsored conference in Richmond, Virginia (June 7-10, 1993). Taken from the writer's notes and later reaffirmed by General Sundarji.

[25] Graham, "Conventional Response," p. 31.

---

amounts of lethal agent, inflicting only a few deaths?[26] How many biological or chemical attacks against discrete military targets have to occur before a nuclear retaliation is called for? One? Ten? More? Perhaps the threshold for U.S. nuclear use is in terms of the number of American and/or allied casualties suffered. How many dead are needed to trigger a U.S. nuclear response?[27]

The trouble for the United States is that many of these discrete below-the-presumed-threshold uses of biological and chemical agents may delay, disrupt, and even break America's transoceanic power projection strategy.

Theater Defense. A second military option adopted by the Clinton Administration is theater defense, which includes a wide-range of military capabilities: ballistic and cruise missile defense, air defense, passive defense, defense against terrorism, and counter-sea mine operations. The objective of defensive measures is to mitigate the effects of enemy attacks by providing U.S. forces some level of protection.

Theater Ballistic and Cruise Missile and Air Defense. Given the realities of worldwide WMD and missile proliferation, the United States must be able to defend against ballistic missiles from the Scud (185 miles) through the Taepodong-2 (2,170 miles) that may be armed with nuclear or bulk chemical and biological warheads or with biological or chemical (and perhaps radiological) submunitions. WMD-armed cruise missiles and unmanned aerial vehicles provide another challenge.

The United States needs defenses that provide low leakage in terms of the number of warheads that get through the defensive shield, high lethality, multiple shot engagements, wide geographic coverage, and rapid deployment. These are important counterproliferation capabilities since they protect the armed forces of the United States, its allies, and coalition partners as well as noncombatants from nuclear, biological, and chemical weapons by intercepting and destroying them in flight.[28]

---

[26] *Assessment of the Impact of Chemical and Biological Weapons on Joint Operations in 2010: Summary Report*, p. 27.

[27] Theresa Hitchens, "U.S. Must Spell Out Bio War Response," *Defense News* (September 11-17, 1995), pp. 1, 50.

[28] U.S., Department of Defense, *Report of Activities and Programs for Countering Proliferation and NBC Terrorism* (Washington, D.C.: Department of Defense, May 1997), p. 5-29, and U.S., Department of Defense, *Compendium of the Defense Counterproliferation Initiative Conference*, held at the Los Alamos National Laboratory, New Mexico (Washington, D.C.: Department of Defense, May 6-7, 1994), p. 164.

The New Face of War

Three interrelated missile defense missions must be satisfied, including defense of the battlefield where numerous company-sized targets are susceptible to nuclear, biological, and chemical attacks; theater protection to include rearward ports, airfields, and logistics facilities; and theater-wide protection against long-range missiles targeted outside the region and missiles outside the theater aimed at targets inside.

The United States has to be aware of three new kinds of strategic threats to its military operations. See Figure 11.4. As longer range missiles become available to adversaries, the U.S. will have to take measures to isolate the region from *inside-out* and *outside-in* attacks. The possibility of *inside-out* attacks or strikes against U.S. allies at some distance from the theater in rearward areas is a very real threat. This strategic threat can be extrapolated from events leading to the Arab promise to punish any country assisting the U.S. resupply of Israel during the 1973 Arab-Israeli War, including a cut-off of oil supplies. The U.S. resupply effort was denied landing, refueling and overflight rights by a number of its closest NATO European allies. Another example of "inside-out" strategic attacks, albeit at shorter range, is Saddam Hussein's Scud attacks on Tel Aviv during the Gulf War in a fruitless attempt to trigger an Israeli response so as to break up the Arab-Western coalition formed to reverse Baghdad's seizure of Kuwait. Threatening to raise the blood price through "inside-out" attacks against Western countries may be sufficient in some instances to prompt a reassessment of the risks of intervening in a regional conflict.

A second strategic missile threat that could confront the United States will be the possibility of *outside-in* attacks. When longer range missiles are available to non-Western countries, regional adversaries could be assisted by their friends and allies from outside the theater. Examples include long-range missile strikes against regional seaports and airfields or American forces in the theater, including cruise missile attacks launched from land, sea or air platforms that are moved to forward locations.

A third new category of missile threats could come in the form of *outside-out* threats or strikes by non-Western states supporting regional antagonists against Western countries, particularly those providing en route support for deploying U.S. forces.

The growing missile threat to U.S. forces and the territories of regional friends and allies from ballistic missiles has prompted seven major missile development projects: five to protect troops in the field and maritime forces, one to destroy missiles in their boost phase, and another to protect the United

States from long-range missiles.[29] The Pentagon's approach is to build on current systems by fielding near-term capabilities while developing longer term defenses to intercept enemy missile systems at higher altitudes and greater distances. The objective is to build a "family of systems" that will destroy WMD-tipped missiles as far as possible from U.S. and allied forces.

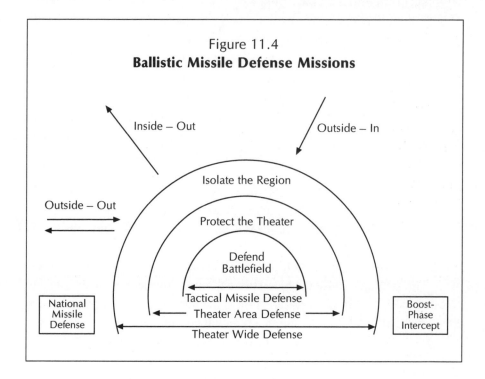

Figure 11.4
Ballistic Missile Defense Missions

Under the current U.S. military strategy theater missile defenses will be critical in future transoceanic deployments of American military power. With adversaries armed with WMD and the missiles to deliver them with sufficient accuracy at locations where U.S. and allied forces concentrate, effective missile defenses will be key capabilities essential to America's projection of power into overseas theaters. Theater missile defenses will be needed to protect U.S. forces deployed to the crisis area; reassure coalition allies of the American capability and will to protect them through early engagement and defense-in-depth; enable reinforcements through protected

---

[29] Jeff Erlich, "Ballistic Threats Trigger Interest in Missile Defense," *Defense News* (April 22-28, 1996), p. 12.

ports, airfields and staging areas; and assure timely air and sea transport to the crisis zone.

The Airborne Laser or ABL is designed to destroy enemy ballistic missiles in seconds after ignition and lift off. The high energy laser and adaptive optics that compensate for atmospheric distortion will be mounted on board a Boeing 747-400 aircraft. The ABL focuses heat on the body of the missile causing it to disintegrate or explode. Missile kills are possible up to 150 miles; with the adaptive optics, the range will increase to more than 250 miles.[30] In a simulated scenario called "Roving Sands 97," the ABL shot down sixteen of seventeen targets. The Space-Based Infrared System (SBIRS) will provide cuing for the ABL as well as other missile systems.[31]

The 1997 Quadrennial Defense Review restructured the theater area defense program when technical failures brought into question the ability to meet the system's 2004 target date. Between 1988 and 1998, just seventeen tests of anti-missile interceptors were conducted, and thirteen of these failed. Since the early 1980s, some $44 billion has been spent on various ballistic missile programs without any major new weapons systems being fielded.[32] Five theater missile defense systems were funded with the first unit of Patriot PAC-3 due in 1999, Navy area system in 2002, THAAD in 2005, Navy theater-wide system in 2006, MEADS production after 2005, airborne laser initial capability after 2005, and continued development of cruise missile defenses.[33] These time-phased milestones came only after extraordinary pressure from Congress after repeated slippage in fielding missile defenses through the 1990s. See Table 11.1.

Former Secretary of Defense Dick Cheney in a 1992 letter to Senator Sam Nunn expressed a sense of urgency that has been clearly absent in the Clinton Administration.

> As I have stated on previous occasions, it is essential that we develop now the capacity to defend the United States, our troops

---

[30] Loren Thompson, "Airborne Laser Makes Sense for Missile Defense," *Defense Week* (February 17, 1998).

[31] F. Whitten Peters, Acting Secretary of the Air Force, and General Michael E. Ryan, Chief of Staff of the Air Force, Statements Before the Senate Armed Services Committee (February 12, 1998). Photocopy.

[32] Jonathan S. Landay, "U.S. Defense Drifting Off Target," *Christian Science Monitor* (March 26, 1998).

[33] U.S., Department of Defense, *Report on Activities and Programs for Countering Proliferation and NBC Terrorism*, p. 5-36.

Table 11.1
A Family of U.S. Missile Defense Systems

Mission	Weapons System	Characteristics
Defend Battlefield	Medium Extended Air Defense System (MEADS)	A joint U.S.-European cooperative program for use against short and medium-range ballistic missiles, cruise missiles, unmanned aerial vehicles, and aircraft and helicopters.
Defend Battlefield	Patriot PAC-3	The Army's PAC-3 system is being modified with upgraded guidance and hardware and software improvements to enhance its capabilities against ballistic and cruise missiles.
Protect the Theater	Theater High Area Defense (THAAD)	Army 185-mile radius, single-stage hit-to-kill system with an exo-/endoatmospheric intercept capability. THAAD will make it possible to protect broad assets, and population centers.
Protect the Theater	Navy Area Theater Ballistic Missile Defense System	60-125 miles radius SM-2 Block IV and upgraded SPY-1 radar carried aboard Aegis ships.
Isolate the Region	Navy Theater-Wide Ballistic Missile Defense	370-620 mile radius upper-tier exoatmospheric system that leverages the Aegis weapon system, Standard Missile, and Vertical Launch System; carried aboard Aegis ships.
Destroy in Boost Phase	Boost Phase Intercept	Air Force Airborne Laser system destroys missiles as they ascend; range 150-250 miles.
Homeland Defense	National Missile Defense	Protects the continental United States, Alaska, and Hawaii from limited attack; designed to be deployable in three years.

The New Face of War

overseas, and our friends and allies against a growing ballistic missile threat. Today over 15 nations have ballistic missiles. By the year 2000, perhaps 20 nations may have them and some will be armed with chemical, biological and possibly even nuclear warheads. The threat to the U.S. homeland from accidental or unauthorized launch is present today, and the technology exists that would enable third world countries to threaten the United States in the future. As the Gulf War demonstrated, our forward deployed forces and friends and allies face a direct threat today. And the Gulf War also foreshadows the possible consequences of a dictatorially-governed regime that gains the capability to threaten the United States with long range missile attack. That is why it is absolutely urgent that we develop a system of defense against ballistic missiles *before* we are threatened by those missiles.[34] [emphasis added]

Suffice it to say, American troops will be vulnerable to enemy WMD-tipped missiles well into the first decade of the twenty-first century and perhaps longer. Given the extraordinary technical difficulties experienced by the theater missile defense program, it is questionable whether active defense will deliver a high order of protection any time soon.

Passive Defense. The 1993 Bottom-Up Review called for enhanced passive defenses, including "better individual protective gear and better antidotes and vaccines for our forces in the event they are exposed to chemical or biological attacks."[35] Through the mid-1990s aggressive actions were taken by the military services for technologies to help them deal with the chemical-biological defense: point and early warning biological detection, point and stand-off chemical detection, nuclear-biological-chemical reconnaissance, protective masks, protective clothing, chemical-biological collective shelters, decontamination, and vaccines.

According to Major General George Friel of the U.S. Army's Chemical and Biological Defense Command, the driving force behind the improved passive defenses was the weaknesses experienced during the Persian Gulf War. "We did not have the capability to adequately provide early warning

---

[34] Richard Cheney, Secretary of Defense, Transmittal Letter to Senator Sam Nunn for a Report Outlining the Defense Department's *Plan for Deployment of Theater and National Ballistic Missile Defenses* (Washington, D.C.: July 2, 1992). Photocopy.

[35] Les Aspin, Secretary of Defense, *Report of the Bottom-Up Review* (Washington, D.C.: Department of Defense, October 1993), p. 7. Photocopy.

or even adequate warning for biological attack," General Friel explains. "The first indication that a biological attack had occurred would probably have been when casualties or symptoms began to occur." Despite the large number of chemical detectors in Operation Desert Storm, commanders had no ability to get early warning, which is essential to give U.S. troops time to don their protective gear. As far as decontamination to reconstitute forces is concerned, General Friel says that "we have 1950s technology for decontamination." Lacking technology to decontaminate fixed sites such as ports and airfields, military planners worry about vulnerabilities in South Korea.[36]

The goal is to equip the armed forces with realistic training and defensive equipment that will allow them to avoid contamination, and, when a poisoning cannot be avoided, they must be able to protect themselves, decontaminate and sustain operations in overseas theaters. Several programs address these needs: systems to detect, identify, characterize, and provide warning of chemical and biological agents; protective gear for individuals and groups; methods to increase the speed and efficiency of decontamination; a broad array of chemical-biological medical defense research and development; improved casualty management and treatment; increased production and larger stockpiles of vaccines against biological warfare agents; new and improved biological vaccines; and better medical countermeasures for chemical and biological agents.[37]

The Defense Department's spending plan for 1998-2003 contains about $3.345 billion for chemical-biological defense or about forty-one percent of the $8 billion counterproliferation program during this period.[38] Despite the recent emphasis, nettlesome shortfalls plague the best efforts of all the military services through their integrated budget submissions in chemical and biological weapons defense. Funding shortfalls and delayed procurement for 1998 through 2003 are in four main areas:

- **Warning:** The Defense Science Board, examining the Pentagon's passive defense efforts, found "notable shortfalls" in capabilities to detect biological attack. In the crisis with Iraq in early 1998, the biological agent detectors still relied on a forty-five minute process of

[36] Barbara Starr, "Interview," *Jane's Defence Weekly* (August 14, 1996), p. 32.

[37] U.S., Department of Defense, *Report on Activities and Programs for Countering Proliferation and NBC Terrorism,* pp. 5-37 through 5-45.

[38] Sandra I. Meadows, "U.S. Forces Prepare for Future Chemical, Biological Blitzkrieg," *National Defense* (September 1997), p. 40.

placing air samples with wet solutions. An electronic system that can give immediate warning of germ warfare has not yet been perfected.[39]

- **Avoidance:** standoff chemical detector of nerve and blister agents; the Joint Warning and Reporting Network that analyzes detection, identification, and warning information, plots hazards and sends messages to affected units, and downlinks warnings of theater ballistic missile attacks is not fully automated.

- **Protection:** an advanced battledress overgarment for protection of the individual service men and women in contaminated environments are in short supply; stockpiles are insufficient to handle one major theater war, let alone two overlapping wars and will remain so through at least 2003; another shortage is insufficient numbers of a shelter system that will provide integrated collective protection on the battlefield.

- **Decontamination:** with insufficient funding to equip the force, the armed forces will remain unable through at least 2003 to conduct large area decontamination of theater ports and airfields; equipment is based on 1950s technology and is dependent on water for wash-down operations.[40]

While President Clinton and other officials have been proclaiming the dangers of biological weapons, by the end of 1997 they had only taken the initial steps necessary to develop the equipment, medical response, and organization needed to respond to the germ arsenals. One top Defense official said that the government deserved "a D or a C minus" for its efforts to date, adding that "we have a long way to go."[41]

The 1997 Quadrennial Defense Review warns that "the threat or use of chemical and biological weapons...is a likely condition of future warfare" and says that it is important that U.S. doctrine, operational concepts, training, and exercises take full account of the threat of chemical and biological weapons. Secretary Cohen increased counterproliferation spending by $1 billion ($200 million per year for five years)—three quarters of this sum will go to the chemical and biological defense programs.[42]

---

[39] Bradley Graham, "U.S. Forces Better Equipped for Chemical, Biological Warfare," *Washington Post* (February 8, 1998), p. A29.

[40] U.S., Department of the Army, Vice Chief of Staff, "Chemical Functional Area Assessment" (Washington, D.C.: The Pentagon, May 23, 1997). Photocopy.

[41] Paul Richter, "U.S. Germ War Defenses Porous, Officials Warn Pentagon," *Los Angeles Times* (December 28, 1997).

[42] Cohen, *Report of the Quadrennial Defense Review*, p. 13.

In the absence of a sound risk assessment of unfunded passive defense requirements, the Army vice chief of staff offers a single tenet to serve as a guide to modernizing chemical and biological defenses: *"The threat will change, doctrine will change, technologies will change, but one thing will never change...NBC [nuclear, biological, and chemical] casualties don't win wars."*[43]

It is also open to question whether troops wearing protective clothing and gas masks will "win wars." When donned in protective gear, work speed is reduced by fifty percent in wintry conditions and by seventy to eighty percent under summer conditions. Some doubt whether troops can work longer than fifteen minutes before tiring and requiring rest in a summer climate. This means that tasks such as runway repair, aircraft and vehicle maintenance, trench digging, and firing heavy weapons will be severely inhibited, if not curtailed altogether.[44]

Gas masks, protective clothing, decontamination, and collective protection shelters are no panacea. These are interim protective measures to avoid losing battles. The friction involved in operating in a contaminated environment simply grinds down personnel and equipment over time. The idea of prolonged military operations in a poisoned environment against a determined adversary is a dangerous pipedream.

The tempo of combat operations may be slowed significantly when the threat or use of WMD compels U.S. forces to don protective clothing and gas masks. The physical and mental demands of military operations can reduce individual and unit performance. Operating in protective clothing decreases sensory awareness, making it harder to stay awake. The individual's capacity to recognize and communicate efficiently can be sharply reduced when feelings of isolation and confusion increase the individual's vulnerability to combat stress. Realistic training may mitigate these operational effects to some extent by building confidence and cohesion. Yet, according to joint doctrine, U.S. forces anticipate that operations tempo may be profoundly affected by the introduction of WMD.

Operational Stress. Physical and mental demands of military operations can have profound effects on the performance of individual Service members

---

[43] U.S., Department of the Army, Vice Chief of Staff, *"Chemical Functional Area Assessment."*

[44] Maurice Eisenstein, *Early Entry Forces: An Annotated Briefing on the Question of New and Nonconventional Threats* (Santa Monica, Calif.: RAND Corporation, undated).

---

and units. This is particularly true when the stress of combat is intensified by heat, continuous operations, and NBC [nuclear, biological, and chemical] protective clothing worn as part of a unit's MOPP [Mission-Oriented Protective Posture].[45]

Joint Mine Countermeasures. Mines at sea can pose serious obstacles to U.S. power projection and military operations. Mines can be used in combination with other obstacles to restrict maneuver, disrupt operating tempo, deny flexibility, and increase friendly casualties at sea and during amphibious landings. The Defense Department is evaluating the capabilities of U.S. forces to conduct integrated mine countermeasure operations from deep water, through shallow water, very shallow water, and the surf zone. A host of new technologies and systems are being tested to automatically detect minefields, manually detect obstacles and fortifications, and display the locations in near real time from the surf zone inland. The capabilities will allow rapid command assessment and mission planning.[46]

Force Protection Initiative. To its credit, the Clinton Administration quickly recognized the strategic implications of the bombing of Khobar Towers in the outskirts of Dhahran, Saudi Arabia, in June 1996. "We have to be prepared for a chemical attack, a biological weapon attack, bombs even bigger than 3,000 pounds—bombs in the 10,000 to 20,000 pound category—mortar attacks," Secretary of Defense William J. Perry explained a month after the bombing in Saudi Arabia. "This is an initiative to provide adequate protection for our forces in the face of what I consider to be a threat of weapons of mass destruction in the hands of terrorists." He went on to say that "we are modeling our force protection on the assumption that such attacks will occur. Some people will say this is worst case planning, but I believe we have to be prepared for more attacks on our forces, not just in Saudi Arabia but all over the Gulf region...."[47]

Recognizing that the situation for forward-based forces is different in each country in terms of numbers of service families, the threat of terrorism, and exposure of security measures, Secretary Perry asked each of the major

---

[45] U.S., Joint Chiefs of Staff, *Joint Doctrine for Nuclear, Biological, and Chemical (NBC) Defense,* Joint Pub. 3-11 (Washington, D.C.: Joint Staff, April 15, 1994), p. II-6.

[46] Cohen, *Annual Report* (1998), pp. 129-31, and Robert Holzer, "Dangerous Waters: Submarines, New Mines Imperil Ill-Prepared U.S. Navy Fleet," *Defense News* (May 4-10, 1998), pp. 1, 14-15.

[47] *Reuters* (July 17, 1996).

---

combatant commanders for the overseas theaters to evaluate force protection in their respective areas of responsibility.[48]

Local commanders have been given operational control with regard to force protection. Other force protection measures put into place include improving the use of available intelligence and beefing up intelligence collection capabilities to permit seeking out terrorist groups and disrupting their activities. In Secretary Perry's report to President Clinton on force protection he concluded by saying:

> When terrorists aim their attacks at U.S. forces overseas, they are attacking our ability to protect and defend our vital interests in the world.... But terrorists cannot win unless we let them.... We cannot be a great power and live in a risk-free world. Therefore we must gird ourselves for a relentless struggle in which there will be many silent victories and some noisy defeats.[49]

At first glance, Secretary Perry's plan, which has been carried forward by his successor, seems unusually forward-looking for such a tactically minded Administration. Nothing could be further from the truth. This defensive initiative, along with the hyped estimates of the effectiveness of U.S. anti-missile and air defenses against an enemy's delivery of WMD, and the supposed efficiency of passive defense to allow continued military operations, obscures the main strategic problem. Should war breakout, the attractiveness of 5,000 Americans in Saudi Arabia as candidate targets for super-terrorist attacks is multiplied a hundred-fold when another 500,000 troops are introduced to the theater. All of the wishful thinking and analytical manipulations in the world regarding the ostensible effectiveness of theater missile and passive defenses will not hide the fact that American forces will suffer significant and perhaps war-stopping casualties.

Secretary Cohen's modernization plan outlined in the 1997 Quadrennial Defense Review will only worsen the American situation. Inexplicably, the

---

[48] Secretary Perry asked the commanders to answer six fundamental questions: (1) Should our troops remain in all present locations?, (2) Should they be removed from urban areas?, (3) Is an adjustment required in dependent status?, (4) How much should force protection interfere with the mission?, (5) Is intelligence focused to deal with the terrorist threat?, and (6) How can we work more effectively with host nations on force protection measures?

[49] William J. Perry, Secretary of Defense, *Defense Issues: DoD's Re-evaluation of the Force Protection Posture,* 11-80 (Washington, D.C.: Office of the Assistant Secretary of Defense (Public Affairs), September 16, 1996).

The New Face of War

Administration has made no plans to bolster America's long-range attack capabilities or alter U.S. warfighting strategy to reduce our dependence upon forces requiring highly vulnerable forward basing. In short, the Clinton Administration has cemented America's vulnerability to weapons of mass destruction, thus encouraging the proliferation of nuclear, biological, and chemical weapons to terrorists and rogue regimes.

Counterforce. The third military strategy option is to locate and destroy the enemy's weapons of mass destruction, "preferably before they can be used."[50] This is a difficult task, one that can never be expected to reach 100 percent effectiveness. Nonetheless, after more than four decades of building targeting plans for nuclear warfare against the Soviet Union and Communist China, the United States has already developed many of the requisite targeting and campaign planning tools to conduct very effective counter-WMD operations when combined with modern sensors, communications, and target acquisition systems.

Planning attack operations against WMD and ballistic and cruise missiles requires an adaptive targeting process that leans heavily on intelligence preparation in peacetime and a workable concept of operations. The interface between intelligence analysts and military operations specialists needs to be close and continuing across the pre-war, war, and post-war spectrum.

The peacetime collection and processing of intelligence greatly improves the possibility of identification of high-priority WMD targets and their detection and acquisition for strike operations during crisis and conflict. Intelligence about WMD targets offers clues about the enemy's intentions, provides vital input for attack planning, helps determine when and where to attack, facilitates precision strike operations, assists in minimizing collateral damage, and permits initiation of rapid counter-WMD operations. There is much WMD-armed adversaries can do to frustrate and complicate peacetime intelligence preparation. Iraq, for instance, learned from the Soviets how to deny locational cuing for their missile launchers. Some of the Iraqi practices included preparation of ready-hide positions near launch points, rapid deployment, false targets, decoys, camouflage and deception practices, and good operations security, especially radio silence.

The timelines associated with each target set define the attack operations problems for both the intelligence analysts and the operators. The timelines associated with the enemy's committed assets and their relocating

---

[50] Cohen, *Report of the Quadrennial Defense Review,* p. 13.

to forward sites are one of the most stressful for U.S. attack operations planners. Enemy WMD and missile assets must emerge from concealment or forward storage depots prior to launch. This dwell time of the weapons at their launch sites could require only minutes to accomplish, or perhaps hours in some instances.

In addition to the target timelines, an ability to relate the target sets to the distances from friendly assets greatly assists the battle managers in determining which of the available attack assets would be most effective against specific targets. When all of these factors, target sets, timelines, available attack assets, and distances are combined, a potentially effective concept of operations begins to emerge.

A final variable is distance of the target from the shoreline or political borders of its neighbors. The distance over land that must be covered is very important in selecting the right platform to strike a specific target.

In a May 1994 report to Congress, the Defense Department listed sixteen priority non/counterproliferation areas for progress. Most dealt with intelligence capabilities for detection and warning of WMD use, support for international arms control regimes, and passive defense capabilities to enable military operations in contaminated environments. Similarly, precision-strike munitions to destroy WMD targets were ignored, except for an "affordable standoff capability."[51]

In light of a Defense Department counterproliferation conference held at the Los Alamos National Laboratory, New Mexico, in early May 1994, the relative lack of emphasis on counterforce operations is not surprising. Counterforce targeting objectives at this high profile session were focused on WMD infrastructure, hardened facilities, deeply buried facilities, and mobile missile launchers. Military objectives were deemed to require high reliability and effectiveness, prompt kill, and minimal collateral effect. Unsatisfied counterforce needs were identified as being target planning aids, minimization of the spread of toxic agents from targets attacked, detection and identification of WMD and missile targets, defeat of hard and buried facilities, prompt mobile target kill, and support for special operations forces. Curiously, the prompt target kill capability assessment left unaddressed force structure or defense suppression requirements, although among the mission needs statements cited in the conference supporting documents

---

[51] John M. Deutch, Deputy Secretary of Defense, *Report on Nonproliferation and Counterproliferation Activities and Programs* (Washington, D.C.: Department of Defense, May 1994).

The New Face of War

included "Global Quick Reaction Strike Capability" and "Adverse Weather Precision Strike Capability."[52]

In 1995, a year later, fourteen counterproliferation needs included three in the counterforce mission area: defeating underground targets (priority 3), prompt mobile target kill (priority 12), and support for special operations forces (priority 13). The other eleven unsatisfied needs included intelligence and active and passive defense programs.[53]

The Counterproliferation Initiative, molded by Pentagon officials with deep roots in the scientific and engineering communities at the national laboratories and specialized defense agencies, supported a huge, well-funded research program with little operationally usable capability. Major counterforce strike platforms and munitions were left out of the picture since they would compete with the research community for resources. Defense officials explained that they would leverage counterforce programs that already were being pursued by the military services. Yet, the force modernization programs of the military services were designed to support the two major regional conflicts called for by the Bottom-Up Review, not counter-WMD operations. Moreover, the fact that the Bottom-Up Review was underfunded something to the tune of $100 billion over five years— more than $60 billion in procurement—raises questions as to whether in 1998 the United States possesses the right kinds and numbers of global strike platforms and the munitions for counter-WMD operations. Suffice it to say, the counterproliferation approach taken by the Defense Department stunted the development of counterforce programs and forces.

The de-emphasis of counterforce capabilities continued into 1997. Defense Secretary William J. Perry explained that the Department had set three lines of defense against WMD proliferation. "We are placing a heavy reliance on...[the] first line of defense—preventing the proliferation threat from emerging," he said. Regarding the second line of defense defined by Secretary Perry, "deterrence relies on having strong forces, both conventional and nuclear, and the demonstrated willpower to use them to protect our country, our forces and our allies." Finally, Secretary Perry defined the third line of defense as including (1) "active defenses, in particular ballistic

---

[52] U.S., Department of Defense, *Compendium of the Defense Counterproliferation Initiative Conference,* pp. 74-76, 145, 153-54.

[53] U.S., Department of Defense, *Compendium of the Second Annual Counterproliferation Conference,* National Defense University (Washington, D.C.: Department of Defense, October 26-27, 1995).

missile defense to shoot down missiles fired at our nation or our allies" and (2) passive defenses designed "to help protect our troops in case of attacks by nuclear, chemical or biological weapons."[54]

The May 1997 Quadrennial Defense Review, as if to recognize the previous shortcomings of the Counterproliferation Initiative, reports that "the Department must institutionalize counterproliferation as an organizing principle in every facet of military activity, from logistics to maneuver and strike warfare.... To advance the institutionalization of counterproliferation concepts, the Joint Staff and CINCs will develop an integrated counter-NBC weapons strategy that includes both offensive and defensive measures."[55] Counterforce, stunted for five years, could finally come out of the closet to be examined in balanced offensive-defensive analyses that includes active and passive defenses.

Coming on board in 1997, Defense Secretary William S. Cohen found a counterproliferation program dedicated more to obtaining research dollars for the pet projects of former colleagues of key defense officials than to developing "an integrated counter-NBC weapons strategy" as called for by the Quadrennial Defense Review. Serious gaps in counterforce capabilities, including the inability to fight for very long in an environment contaminated by biological and chemical agents, plagued the program. Tinkering at the margins to obtain the right sensors, targeting tools, and suppression of biological and chemical agent dispersal contributes to counterproliferation objectives, but these combat support capabilities will be of little use until harnessed with the right strike platforms and munitions necessary to execute a combatant commander's concept of operations.

Forward bases and littoral waters are under the threat of WMD/missile attack, which raises questions about pouring billions of dollars into short-range tactical fighters. Perhaps it makes more sense to counter an enemy's WMD and other military capabilities from the safety of bases outside the striking range of his missiles and aircraft. Yet, a third squadron of B-2 bombers (nine aircraft) was killed in 1997, in spite of the fact that it is the preeminent counter-WMD and counter-missile platform in the U.S. arsenal.

---

[54] William J. Perry, Secretary of Defense, Remarks on Weapons of Mass Destruction at the Georgetown University (Washington, D.C.: Department of Defense, April 18, 1996). See also William J. Perry, Secretary of Defense, Preface to *Proliferation: Threat and Response* (1996), and William Perry, Secretary of Defense, "Preventive Defense," *Washington Times* (November 10, 1996), p. B3.

[55] Cohen, *Report of the Quadrennial Defense Review*, p. 49.

The New Face of War

The Clinton Administration went out of its way from the very beginning to de-emphasize counterforce operations as a legitimate tool of its Counterproliferation Initiative. Rhetorical support, combined with needed technology programs involving certain munitions, distracted efforts from a realistic counterforce program. While technologists in the Department of Defense successfully deflected efforts to build strong counterforce capabilities, a peculiar mind-set evolved that viewed missile defense in competition with counterforce programs. Since research dollars were available for missile defense, studies used counterforce as so much cannon fodder to show a higher payoff by defensive systems.

The result is a patchwork of missile defense systems that do not meet expectations and short-range tactical fighters for precision strike that do not bode well for future counterforce operations. The U.S. would quickly tip its hand by deploying hundreds of fighters and multiple carrier battle groups into a region. Surprise would be lost and the adversary could disperse many critical WMD assets, reducing the chances of success. Regional allies, facing the reality of being within range of the enemy's WMD, could be persuaded to deny the United States access to their seaports and airfields. If these countries nevertheless agree to cooperate, the United States would be under tremendous pressure to succeed and to do so quickly. Yet, the land-based tactical fighters and those aboard carriers within striking range of their WMD targets would be highly vulnerable to the very WMD they were sent to destroy.

The point here is that counterforce operations can no longer be considered in a vacuum, and treated as something separate from the mainstream of U.S. strategy. The size, scale, and potential political effects of any future counterforce operation are likely to resemble more the opening days of the 1991 Gulf War than the 1986 bombing raid on Libya. If counterforce operations are to be considered a viable option for countering the WMD threat under the condition of less-than-effective theater ballistic missile and air defenses, the United States must reduce its in-theater footprint dramatically. The "theater of operations" for counter-WMD and other counterforce attacks must be extended beyond the effective range of the enemy's WMD. Such an extension should be carried out without compromising operational effectiveness or timeliness.

Clinton Administration—Shadowing Military Risks

When the writer explained these military risks to a tough-minded former governor of Pennsylvania, he was skeptical and asked why the Pentagon had not taken corrective actions, adding that the uniformed military have lots of very smart people. Here's one explanation. It is not a pretty story.

In political-military simulations designed for individuals to make choices between nuclear deterrence, theater defense, or counterforce, participants often find themselves at the end of the day to be restless and anxious with a sense that somehow the game players had missed the point. The hypothetical scenarios of WMD threats are usually plausible enough. That was not the problem, especially since they are sometimes focused on one or two weight-bearing assumptions of U.S. military strategy: time and access.

The source of personal disquietude after the fact is the inherent weakness of the two major assumptions most always present in the political-military simulations: (1) current U.S. strategy founded on the Persian Gulf War, and (2) today's military forces and those planned for over the next five years are all based on short-range capabilities (ground forces, tactical fighters, and ships). These assumptions ensured "inside-the-box" thinking and shut down even the slightest innovation. The political-military simulation players are usually given an opportunity to find the best mix of nuclear strikes, theater defense, or counterforce operations.

Since it becomes clear rather quickly in such simulations that conventional counterforce operations will not be able to disarm a WMD-armed enemy, the participants find themselves falling back on theater defenses whose uncertainties are enormous. Bizarre discussions of prolonged military operations in areas contaminated by biological and chemical warfare agents, though wholly unrealistic, are discussed with great intensity. Side discussions might address how to deal with a fully contaminated C-141 air transport loaded with 100 or more aircrews and dependent families donned in protective clothing and gas masks. Where should it land? What are the hazards? How do we go about decontaminating the people and aircraft inside and out? Experiences in such political-military simulations are surreal.

The logic around the simulation table sooner or later comes to the conclusion that counterforce and theater defense, even when working together, are not up to the task of protecting deploying U.S. forces in a biologically and chemically contaminated environment. Thus, it is not surprising that discussion turns to the potential use of nuclear weapons and elimination of the regime in power. Deep exchanges of thought follow between those advocating the use of nuclear weapons and those opposed. Disagreement usually stands unresolved since mercilessly the simulation will come to a close before all of the ramifications of using nuclear weapons can be explored.

Most in the room know in their hearts that the current U.S. military strategy cannot work against an adversary willing to use biological and chemical warfare agents to deny the U.S. access to the region. One can read it in their eyes and sense the sick feeling in their stomachs that the current U.S. strategy simply will not work.

Lies, Damn Lies, and Analytical Assumptions. The same kind of disjointed reality was evident in the Nimble Dancer wargame completed in 1995, which had the objective of assessing the ability of programmed U.S. forces to fight and win two nearly simultaneous major region conflicts. Using favorable assumptions to mask existing military risks, the analysis was able to "prove" that the two-war strategy was achievable. Among the favorable assumptions used to support the report to Congress were the following:

- Extremely quick national decisions on mobilizing reserves and activating civilian airline support
- No access problems at overseas bases
- Unambiguous warning times in strategic warning
- Favorable separation time between the two regional conflicts
- All units deployed as scheduled with no delays at ports or airfields
- U.S. forces prepared to operate in an environment contaminated with biological and chemical warfare agents

By use of such assumptions, the Pentagon study was able to prove a positive result of being able to fight and win two regional conflicts at roughly the same time. Yet, the results are untrue. The assumptions were made in a way to shroud military risks behind a veil of analytical doublespeak. "We continue to believe that certain game assumptions were favorable," the General Accounting Office examiners state, "because they set conditions that were mostly advantageous to U.S. forces, thereby minimizing risk."[56]

Sometimes the analytical tools are used in a negative way to disprove a certain scenario or weapon system. Once again cutting the cloth to match predetermined conclusions, assumptions in the hands of skillful analysts can paint a picture in direct contrast to the facts. One of the most successful negative analytical efforts were the false assumptions used in the killing of

---

[56] U.S., General Accounting Office, *Bottom-Up Review: Analysis of DOD War Game to Test Key Assumptions*, pp. 13, 16-19.

---

the initiative to expand the B-2 stealth bomber fleet. Since high Administration officials had already expressed reservations about buying twenty more aircraft, the Air Force chief-of-staff, facing a decision already made, gave the aircraft tepid support. The B-2's days were clearly numbered. Two force planning studies in particular were associated with the Pentagon's concerted effort to ensure a premature burial of the B-2 beyond the twenty-one aircraft already approved. The first study, the 1995 congressionally mandated *Heavy Bomber Force Study,* was conducted by the Institute for Defense Analyses with the stated goal of comparing alternative bomber forces needed to satisfy the Bottom-Up Review's major regional contingencies and to estimate whether procuring an additional twenty B-2 aircraft would be justified. To be sure the outcome would be the one desired, the Department of Defense gave the Institute for Defense Analyses detailed guidance and supplied scenarios, threat projections, warning times, force arrival information, aircraft apportionment and sortie allocation data. Kurt Guthe, one of the country's top civilian defense analysts, concluded from his review of the *Heavy Bomber Force Study* "that the effort flopped as a sound basis for deciding the future bomber force structure can be traced, to a large extent, to the direction set by DoD."[57]

Guthe points out in his blistering critique that the *Study* (1) concentrates on just two adversaries and one type of war while excluding other types of enemies and warfare, (2) discounts surprise attack, (3) assumes the U.S. can deploy forces into a theater with impunity even in the face of a WMD-armed adversary, (4) postulates that half to two-thirds of the bomber fleet can break off the fight in one scenario and redeploy to another with hardly a break in operational tempo, (5) compares effectiveness among bombers, fighters, and precision-strike aircraft on the basis of questionable methods, (6) fails to address tradeoffs between bombers and other forces, and (7) fails to account for peacetime attrition. In addition, the Defense Department postulated a deployment of forces so large that it was guaranteed ahead of time that the addition of twenty B-2s would have little "measurable" impact in the prescribed analysis.[58]

Glenn Buchan, a highly experienced and respected bomber analyst at the RAND Corporation, put the case rather succinctly in 1996 testimony before the House National Security Committee: "The fundamental problem with the heavy bomber study is...whoever framed the study cooked the

---

[57] Guthe, *A Precisely Guided Analytic Bomb,* p. 41.

[58] *Ibid.,* p. 13.

books. They allowed a set of assumptions that led to a preordained outcome by essentially ruling out all the things that would have led them to other result."[59]

Citing the analytically flawed *Heavy Bomber Force Study,* senior National Security Council staffer Robert Bell explained President Clinton's February 1996 decision not to buy more than twenty-one B-2s: "The President concluded that the B-2 is a highly capable, long-range and stealthy bomber that will make important strategic and conventional contributions well into the next century. But additional B-2s would be too costly, particularly relative to other defense procurement priorities."[60]

More analytical double-talk was developed in the Deep Attack Weapons Mix Study (DAWMS). Originally structured to examine mixes of munitions for deep attack, the Clinton Administration expanded the study to include tradeoffs between heavy bombers, tactical strike aircraft, and theater-based missiles. The "fix" was in from the start. The study focused on costs rather than value, it failed to fully and fairly assess the contributions of modern military forces, and the modeling and simulation methods used were misleading and biased in favor of ground forces. Jim Courter and Loren Thompson of The Alexis de Tocqueville Institution, put the issue plainly: "...the DAWMS, like the Heavy Bomber Study before it, has the potential to hide behind a cloak of mystery and obfuscation."[61] After a few fits and starts, much of the DAWMS agenda became rolled into the Pentagon's 1997 Quadrennial Defense Review.

This time the Pentagon was directed by the president, at the behest of Congress, to compare the B-2's cost effectiveness to that of other deep attack weapons systems. The same analytical group that ran the *Heavy Bomber Force Study* ran the computer model, only this time without assumptions designed to kill the B-2 program. The results set off alarms bells, Brent Scowcroft explains, since they "showed that the B-2s were more cost-effective than any other force element.... What the analysis showed in general was that very small numbers of B-2s could potentially replace large groups of planned—and thus preferred—forces." This was the wrong answer. The analysis was buried in some anonymous black hole in the Pentagon, and

---

[59] As quoted in Brent Scowcroft and others, *Final Report of the Independent Bomber Force Review Commission,* p. 17.

[60] As quoted by Kurt Guthe in *A Precisely Guided Analytic Bomb,* p. 11.

[61] Jim Courter and Loren Thompson, *Deep-Attack Weapons Mix Study: Bias May Produce Flawed B-2 Analysis* (Arlington, Va.: Alexis de Tocqueville Institution, 1996), p. 7.

---

a new analytical tactic was developed. Capability charts were developed to show contribution of the various weapons systems included in the analysis; not a single chart was dedicated to showing capabilities that would be generated by expanding the B-2 fleet.[62]

In this case, military risks were hidden deeply behind the analytical assumptions or simply ignoring superior capabilities. The back-alley killing of the B-2 bomber is another example of the anti-strategy at work inside the Clinton Administration. There are many ways to lie to Congress and the American people—one of them is to use assumptions and manipulate them in a way to present a false picture of a strategy or a force structure decision. But the problems do not stop there.

Zalmay Khalilzad and David Ochmanek of the RAND Corporation, for example, find many of the Pentagon's own canonical assumptions, scenarios and assessment tools as "validating the existing order of things and inhibiting innovation."

Scenarios are designed to accommodate the major force structure concerns of the participants. The Army will press for longer warning and deployment times to ensure its slow buildup rate overseas fits the scenario. The Navy, which has manifested a reluctance to invest in mine countermeasures, will downplay the threat to its ships. Meanwhile, the Air Force, Army, and Marine Corps will insist that they can operate from bases that have been attacked repeatedly by chemical (and perhaps biological) weapons. Defense Department senior officials tolerate "shading" of scenario assumptions toward the optimistic since usually some degree of factual basis is present in the assumption, few want to burn the political capital necessary to challenge the Services, and an assumption is, after all, a supposition with some amount of factual content.[63]

The Administration's anti-strategy and budget-based military planning can be preserved only as long as the progressive "hollowing" of the armed services and the increasing military risks can be hidden from view. "The $245 billion that America spends annually on defense is not enough to sustain current force structure for two wars while at the same time equipping that force with modern weapons, and carrying out the large number of peacekeeping operations in which we are currently involved...," Khalilzad

---

[62] *Ibid.*, pp. 19-22.

[63] Zalmay Khalilzad and David Ochmanek, "Rethinking US Defence Planning," *Survival*, 39-1 (Spring 1997), pp. 43-44, 48. See also Bradley Graham, "Pentagon's Plan for Future Draws Heavily From Cold War Past," *Washington Post* (May 11, 1997), p. A19.

and Ochmanek warn, "a gap between strategy and capability could lead us to make security commitments that we could not complete. Indeed, a force of any size that lacks first-class capabilities to defeat weapons of mass destruction and other threats might become a zero-war military, because future presidents may shy away from committing such forces to battle."[64]

Budget-Based Planning. Proponents of budget-based planning have contributed heavily to development of an anti-strategy by using faulty assumptions and wrongly applied analytical tools to keep defense spending within the limits of the politically defined glass ceiling. Moreover, the anti-strategy allowed to develop in the United States during the 1990s offers decision-makers no sense of the military risks facing the nation. Using the defense budget to define military strategy, or a means-ends process, avoided any consideration of risk. By definition the means-ends process—the reversal of an objectives-driven or ends-means coordination defense planning process—eliminates any strategy-force mismatch. Military risk in the anti-strategy is messy and unsightly. Hence, risk is pushed out of sight and out of mind, giving a false sense of security while the essence of military strength—trained personnel armed with the right weapons—is slowly whittled away.

A wide range of activities in the Executive Branch has led to the creation of an anti-strategy—a pressure cooker for defense spending that erects a glass ceiling every year that presents an image of the Administration striving heartily to achieve the needed military capabilities. Yet, no attempt has been made to design a military force structure sufficient to satisfy the national military strategy envisioned in the Bottom-Up or Quadrennial Defense Reviews—to do so would reveal military risks so severe that the glass ceiling on defense spending would be shattered.

The uniformed military has been placed in a very difficult position during the first six years of the Clinton Administration. Military officers instinctively seek to serve the President, the commander-in-chief, in defense of the nation. This submission to civil authorities is a crucial cornerstone of the American democracy, a strength so fundamental that countries around the world strive to emulate our success. At the same time, the uniformed military have a responsibility to Congress to explain defense programs and the associated military risks facing the country so that the people's senators and representatives can make informed judgments in providing for the

---

[64] Zalmay Khalilzad and David Ochmanek, "An Affordable Two-War Strategy," *Wall Street Journal* (March 13, 1997), p. A14.

---

nation's defense. Yet, the anti-strategy of the 1990s forbids strategy- or objectives-based planning that may call for different military forces and priorities in defense spending than those dictated by the Administration-imposed glass ceiling. Acceptance of the glass ceiling takes on the aura of rule of law for many in uniform—feeling themselves obliged to support the commander-in-chief, America's military works diligently to make the budget-based planning system work. The trouble is that Congress is often left out in the cold without an appreciation of the military risks facing the country. And those "risk assessments" that are made available by the Pentagon are the understated risks driven by budget-based planning and associated with the make-believe world of the anti-strategy.

This can sometimes lead to very bad and counterproductive decisions. The Air Force, for instance, in effect abandoned long-range airpower during the Quadrennial Defense Review at the very time when the need for global reach precision bombing emerged as a vital defense requirement to counter weapons of mass destruction and deny adversaries any realistic chance of locking out U.S. access to regional facilities. Short-range tactical fighters were protected in the Pentagon plan despite the obvious problems of operating from in-theater bases contaminated by biological and chemical attacks. An honest look at long-range precision strike aircraft was conducted by analysts from the Joint Staff, Office of the Secretary of Defense, and Institute for Defense Analyses in support of the Quadrennial Defense Review— the results showed that long-range precision strike was more cost-effective than any other force element. Nonetheless, the study's conclusions were deemed "politically incorrect" since they would lead to force structure choices that would be contrary to the views expressed by President Bill Clinton and Defense Secretary William S. Cohen. Trashed in the dark of night, the study results never saw the light of day. The anti-strategy had won one of its greatest victories by keeping the truth from members of Congress and the public—the fact that long-range air operations "could support U.S. national security at lower budget levels."[65]

France in the 1930s. This is not the first time that a great power has failed to recognize the changing face of war and adopted erroneous assumptions to preserve preferred strategies and military forces. French government officials and military leaders alike fell under the spell of a pervasive peace malaise in the 1930s after they had poured huge sums from the

---

[65] Scowcroft and others, *Final Report of the Independent Bomber Force Review Commission*, pp. 19-22.

national treasury into building an array of concrete bunkers, tank traps, pill boxes, and other military fortifications along its exposed border with Germany.

In the final analysis, the French unwittingly had developed their own version of an "anti-strategy" during the 1930s. It was an *anti*-strategy since it inhibited policy changes that would have defined a realistic set of military objectives around which to create a balanced offensive and defensive strategy. At the same time, the anti-strategy filtered the rapidly growing military threat looming next door in Germany and gave a "feel good" false sense of security to the French people. And the French military got so caught up in the bureaucratic method, inter-service rivalry, and just-on-the-horizon technologies that its procurement decisions were often shortsighted and sometimes counterproductive. The General Staff was bogged down in bureaucratic method and petty bickering; due to the financial strain of the Maginot Line, the Army was equipped with a great deal of 1918 vintage armament; pork barrel politics generated procurement delays and uneconomical production of tanks and other equipment; power political lobbies pushed new technologies over existing competitive aircraft thereby delaying production; intense inter-service rivalry based on the means of locomotion precluded doctrinal and procurement coordination between the Army and its air arm; and increased defense spending without a realistic strategic doctrine resulted in the squandering of resources on inappropriate armaments and military construction. When the Germans attacked, a French Army ready to fight World War One style infantry and artillery battles took to the field. While the French tanks were as good as, and sometimes better than, those of the Germans, they had few mobile anti-tank guns and land mines and their antiquated command procedures were tailored to slower moving infantry. When the assault came, French attempts to counterattack against German mechanized forces often were hours and sometimes even days late.

As Hitler's panzer forces exploited the speed, coordination, and firepower enjoyed by mechanized warfare supported from the air, the French found themselves outgunned, outnumbered, and out-thought. When the Germans broke out of the Ardennes Forest, the French Army could not respond in mass. With maneuver units deployed in Flanders, reserves already committed, and the Maginot Line "left like a stranded battleship," France's fate was sealed. Forty-three days after the German attack began in May 1940, the country of Napoleon lay prostrate. Occupied and without arms, France had been failed by its government, its army, and its people. Part of the reason for this debacle was tactical and can be explained in terms of what the French commanders did wrong and what the German generals did right. But the source of failure lies mostly with the self-imposed intellectual chains that restrained the French military from adopting a strategy geared to the realities of threat that mushroomed before them.

The bankruptcy of a generation of French military thought and preparations was expressed aptly by General Maurice Gamelin, the commander-in-chief, in response to a question by Winston Churchill. As the Germans rolled across northern France toward the English Channel, Churchill asked Gamelin when he was going to counterattack the enemy flank. "'Inferiority of numbers, inferiority of equipment, inferiority of method,'" General Gamelin replied, "and then a hopeless shrug of the shoulders."[66]

Is the United States on the verge of a bankruptcy of military thought by developing an unworkable strategy and a force structure inappropriate to meet the most dangerous and increasingly likely threats? A U.S. Senate majority report by the Committee on Government Affairs in January 1998 provides the answer: "The Clinton Administration's nonproliferation efforts have been inadequate.... The Clinton Administration has not been willing to take the tough actions necessary to back up rhetoric in executive orders and other statements. *By speaking loudly but carrying a small stick, the Clinton Administration risks its nonproliferation credibility and America's security.*"[67] [emphasis added]

"A Zero War Military"?[68]

Zalmay Khalilzad and David Ochmanek offered Americans a warning that following the present defense planning course, where a gap exists between strategy and forces, could lead us to a condition of being unable to satisfy our security commitments or our military tasks. "Indeed, a force of any size that lacks first-class capabilities to defeat weapons of mass destruction and other threats might become a zero-war military, because future presidents may shy away from committing such forces."[69]

Is the United States creeping slowly toward "a zero war military?" Does the current approach by the Clinton Administration sufficiently reduce the military risks confronting the nation?

---

[66] Alastair Horne, *To Lose a Battle* (Boston: Little, Brown, 1969), p. 394.

[67] *U.S., Senate, Proliferation Primer*, pp. 69, 1.

[68] Khalilzad and Ochmanek, "An Affordable Two-War Strategy," p. A14.

[69] *Ibid.*

Table 11.2
Are Military Risks Being Reduced?

Selected Military Risks	Clinton Administration Response
Time:	
— Strategic Warning and Time to Deploy	— Assumes 14 Days; Enemy Will Not Attack Until U.S. Forces Deployed
— Actual Airpower Deployment Rates of 100-200 Aircraft in 14 Days	— Assumes 1,000 Aircraft Deployed in 14 Days
— Ambiguous Warning May Delay U.S. Response	— Assumes Strategic Warning and Timely U.S. Decisions and Response
Access:	
— Hindered Access to Regional Seaports and Airfields	— Assumes Operation Desert Shield/Storm Conditions
— Obstructed Access to Regional Ports and Airfields	— Assumes No Obstructions; New Effort on Mine Countermeasures
— Politically Driven Denial of and Constraints On Theater Access for Land-Based Fighters	— Assumes Denials and Constraints Can Be Worked Around With Cruise Missiles, Carrier-Based Air, Non-Stealth Bombers
— U.S. Unable to Respond to 1996 Crisis in Northern Iraq, and, if required, Central Asia	— Ignores "defeat" of U.S. Interests; Claims Victory for Cruise Missile Shots 200 Miles Away
Weapons of Mass Destruction:	
— Biological and Chemical Warfare Attacks Against Seaports and Airfields	— Threaten Nuclear Response, Rely on Theater Missile Defense, Passive Defense
— State-Sponsored Terrorism Against U.S. and Allied Forces	— Force Protection Initiative Will Protect Troops

There is much at stake when allowing military risks to go unanswered. If Americans allow severe risks to the dual weight-bearing assumptions of U.S. military strategy to go unaddressed, the ultimate manifestation of those risks could be catastrophic. In a best-case scenario during crisis and war, the United States might be able to redress the aggression but it would do so at a far greater cost in American blood and treasure. Alternatively, in a worst-case, where the adversary achieves his initial military objectives and presents the U.S. with a fait accompli, Washington could be deterred from intervening since the perceived blood cost could be too high. Over time, the United States would slowly slip into being a country with global interests but regional military capabilities. With the cost of protecting security going up and emboldened enemies accelerating threats, the number of U.S. global interests deemed vital or very important will shrink. This is a classic picture of a declining power.

Andrew Marshall, director of the Pentagon's Office of Net Assessment, warns that the early lead by the United States, while the world is midway through a military revolution, is no guarantee of remaining on top. "Countries that have very good positions can lose them very rapidly," Mr. Marshall explains. "The British are an example."[70]

---

[70] Ricks, "How Wars Are Fought Will Change Radically," p. A1.

The New Face of War

Global Reconnaissance-Strike Complex

INTRODUCTION: PART IV

Part IV, taking a full accounting of the risks facing the current U.S. conventional military strategy, recommends that the United States create a Global Reconnaissance-Strike Complex to enact an integrated conventional-WMD strategy and supporting force structure. The proposed shift in strategy is aimed at reducing the military risks resulting from WMD proliferation that were uncovered in Part III—risks so far neither fully recognized nor acted upon in a comprehensive way by the Clinton Administration. In order to mitigate these risks, the United States must decrease dependence on warning time and theater access by increasing its global responsiveness and decreasing its theater footprint.

Chapter 12, "Massing Firepower, Not Forces," shows how a global precision strike strategy and capabilities will mitigate the strategic risks necessary to met the new challenges posed by WMD-armed adversaries. Fundamentally, the new U.S. strategy must be based on an integrated conventional-WMD warfare paradigm rather than the current Cold War–derived conventional strategy. The current strategy would achieve victory similar to the Persian Gulf War by withstanding the enemy's initial blows and then building up U.S. forces over some months, followed by a massive counter-offensive to retake lost territory. The proposed conventional-WMD strategy, on the other hand, would defeat the enemy at the outset of the conflict lessening the need for a lengthy buildup of forces to support a counterattack.

This strategy is based on a recognition of the intensification of the threat to the U.S. power projection capabilities by the proliferation of weapons of mass destruction. If a WMD-armed enemy successfully denies the United States strategic warning and ready access to the theater, long-range precision strike forces launched from bases beyond the reach of enemy missiles would be the weapons of choice. Hence, a "halt and enable" operational concept is proposed. The global precision strike forces would focus on two military tasks simultaneously: halting the invading forces and drawing down the enemy's WMD capabilities and other military forces sufficiently to enable U.S. tactical fighters, ground forces, and carrier battle groups to gain entrance to the theater.

A system-of-systems architecture of military capabilities, ranging from intelligence and communications assets to distributed ground combat cells, demonstrates how a Global Reconnaissance-Strike Complex can be built from existing resources. Long-range precision strike forces, the core element giving operational life to the "halt and enable" concept, serve as the centerpiece capabilities of the Global Reconnaissance-Strike Complex.

Chapter 13, "Getting From Here To There," examines the force structure issues associated with the reshaped conventional-WMD military strategy. How many of which kinds of forces are required to satisfy the invasion-halting and force deployment-enabling objectives of the "halt and enable" concept? Four avenues of inquiry are prosecuted: (1) bridging the gap in current global attack capabilities; (2) replacing current long-range precision strike forces during the 2016 to 2030 period; (3) changing the key functional entities and organizations to enliven sustained support for the Global Reconnaissance-Strike Complex; and (4) trading off force structure associated with the outdated Cold War-derived conventional strategy to free the resources needed to upgrade long-range precision strike capabilities.

CHAPTER 12

Massing Firepower, Not Forces

A "splintering" between the current U.S. conventional strategy and the need to find measures to cope with WMD proliferation dictates a shift in direction. What should the United States do if it is confronted by regional scenarios where, in the absence of sufficient strategic warning, it does not have enough time to deploy military forces and enemy WMD attacks against seaports and airfields deny unfettered access to the region of conflict?

Despite the looming regional WMD threats, American military strategy remains centered on stopping the initial enemy assault with a minimum loss of territory, a ponderous buildup of forces over time, and a massive air-land counter-offensive. Thus, new military strategy is needed to deal with weapons of mass destruction. This blueprint should focus on overcoming the existing dependencies on time and easy access for effective deployment of U.S. military forces. The strategy also should recognize that the killing power of weapons of *mass* destruction is so very threatening to U.S. forces and the militaries and populations of friendly countries that they must be neutralized in the earliest hours and days of an attack. In order to minimize the loss of territory and human life, an American response to a WMD-armed adversary's aggression must be fast, hard-hitting, and capable of halting an armed assault far short of the attacker's objectives.

Thus, the United States should focus on developing an integrated conventional-WMD strategy and a force structure that will mitigate the significant military risks associated with the current strategy by shifting the locus from the buildup and counter-offensive phases of conflict to the surprise attack and defensive stages. The integrated strategy should do two things in mitigating the strategic risks facing the United States. First, it should deny the enemy opportunities for exploiting the American dependencies on warning time and theater access by increasing global responsiveness and reducing the U.S. military's theater footprint (see Figure 12.1).[1]

---

[1] A theater "footprint" in strategy jargon includes all American military personnel, equipment, logistics, prepositioned supplies, bases, and other supporting infrastructure and consumables.

Figure 12.1
Mitigating Strategic Risks

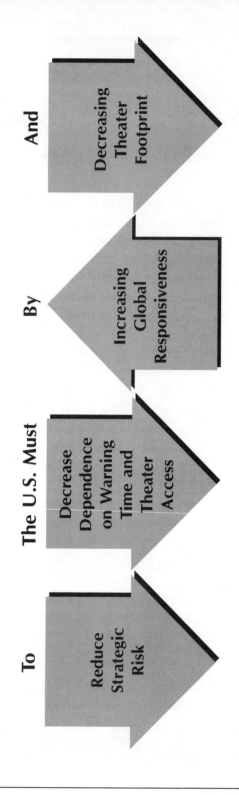

To
Reduce Strategic Risk

The U.S. Must
Decrease Dependence on Warning Time and Theater Access

By
Increasing Global Responsiveness

And
Decreasing Theater Footprint

Second, America's own asymmetric strategy should be created by radically increasing the military risks facing a WMD-armed adversary, including the denial of a quick victory. This proposed shift in strategy requires first and foremost a change in America's mental framework of how best to conduct successful military operations against WMD-armed adversaries.

Emerging technology is making possible the development of asymmetric operational strategies in which both the United States and its adversaries can use their strengths to exploit the other's weaknesses, and, as is the case in martial arts, turn the other's strengths against itself. Regional powers hostile to the United States, for instance, are pouring their limited resources into capabilities designed specifically to deny U.S. forces timely access to the theater. These actions promise to neutralize American strengths of moving massive contingents of air, land, and maritime forces across the oceans; sustaining tactical fighter operations from bases in the theater and aircraft carriers in close-in littoral waters; and dominating land warfare maneuver.

According to Chang Mengxiong, a former senior engineer of the Beijing Institute of System Engineering, the Chinese military could counter American conventional superiority by adopting methods that are "like a Chinese boxer with a knowledge of vital body points who can bring an opponent to his knees with a minimum of movement." The Chinese strategy for asymmetric warfare is focused on finding ways to leverage inexpensive but effective technology to defeat the more expensive and capable technology available to the United States. Captain Shen Zhongchang and his co-authors from the Chinese Navy Research Institute, for example, wrote an article about using highly accurate, land-based anti-ship missiles to defeat a large and powerful navy. The writers went on to discuss the benefits of attacking logistics bases and supply lines, with a particular focus on U.S. reinforcement and resupply operations during the Persian Gulf War.[2] China's keen interest in America's armed forces also is suggested by the fact that in the first half of 1998 the People's Liberation Army visited the U.S. Army Internet Web site more than any other user.[3]

To counter such deliberate attacks on its power projection strategy, the United States must also respond asymmetrically. That is, the U.S. must turn its unique—if heretofore under utilized—ability to strike from beyond the

---

[2] John Diamond, "Chinese Army Writings Reveal 'Very Unfriendly' Attitude Toward U.S.," *Miami Herald* (September 21, 1997).

[3] John McCaslin, "Inside the Beltway: Caught in the Web," *Washington Times* (July 1, 1998), p. A8.

region of conflict and, thus, the lethal radius of the enemy's anti-access weaponry. The combination of U.S. information and precision strike dominance—which together will provide the ability to locate and destroy virtually any military target on the earth's surface—can be used as a tool to deny the WMD-armed enemy his objectives. Long-range precision strike can do more. If the right kinds of forces are appropriately postured, the United States can turn the adversary's WMD against himself by striking his invading armored forces and interdicting his WMD *before* U.S. tactical fighters, troops, and ships are deployed to the theater in large numbers. Situational awareness provided by an array of sensors, rapid fusion through superior computing, and real-time communications can be linked directly to strike aircraft and unmanned platforms to the point that the United States can increase the tempo of warfare to confuse, disorient, and disorganize a regional adversary's forces in spite of their geographic advantage of proximity to the battle zone.

Mitigating strategic risks requires an assessment of the shift in military strategy and capabilities necessary to meet the new challenges posed by adversaries. Identifying the current forces most capable of providing the necessary military capabilities is an essential step. The graphic in Figure 12.2, for instance, depicts the comparative global responsiveness and theater footprint in terms of the number of personnel and arrival time of major force elements in the region of conflict. This power projection "aquarium" illustrates which force elements would be most useful for urgent counterforce[4] attacks against the enemy's assault forces, weapons of mass destruction, and other significant military forces—on-station maritime forces and long-range strike aircraft are available within hours; followed quickly by land-based tactical fighters, unless they are denied access to in-theater bases; and light ground combat units. Armored and mechanized divisions consume the most time to deploy.

Figure 12.3 illustrates the relative warfighting usefulness of major force types in a scenario where a lack of strategic warning enables the enemy's surprise attack and access denial operations prevent ready U.S. deployments to the theater and its littoral waters. Because of their dependence on in-theater bases, U.S. land-based tactical fighters and ground forces would be unable

---

[4] The term "urgent counterforce" is used to characterize U.S. anti-armor operations to halt an enemy's invading forces and counter-WMD, counter-conventional "anti-access" capabilities, offensive counter-air (airfield attack), and suppression of enemy air defenses to enable the deployment of U.S. tactical fighters, ground forces, and carrier battle groups to the region under attack.

Figure 12.2
Comparative Global Responsiveness and Theater Footprint

Figure 12.3

Warfighting Utility If Warning and Access Are Denied

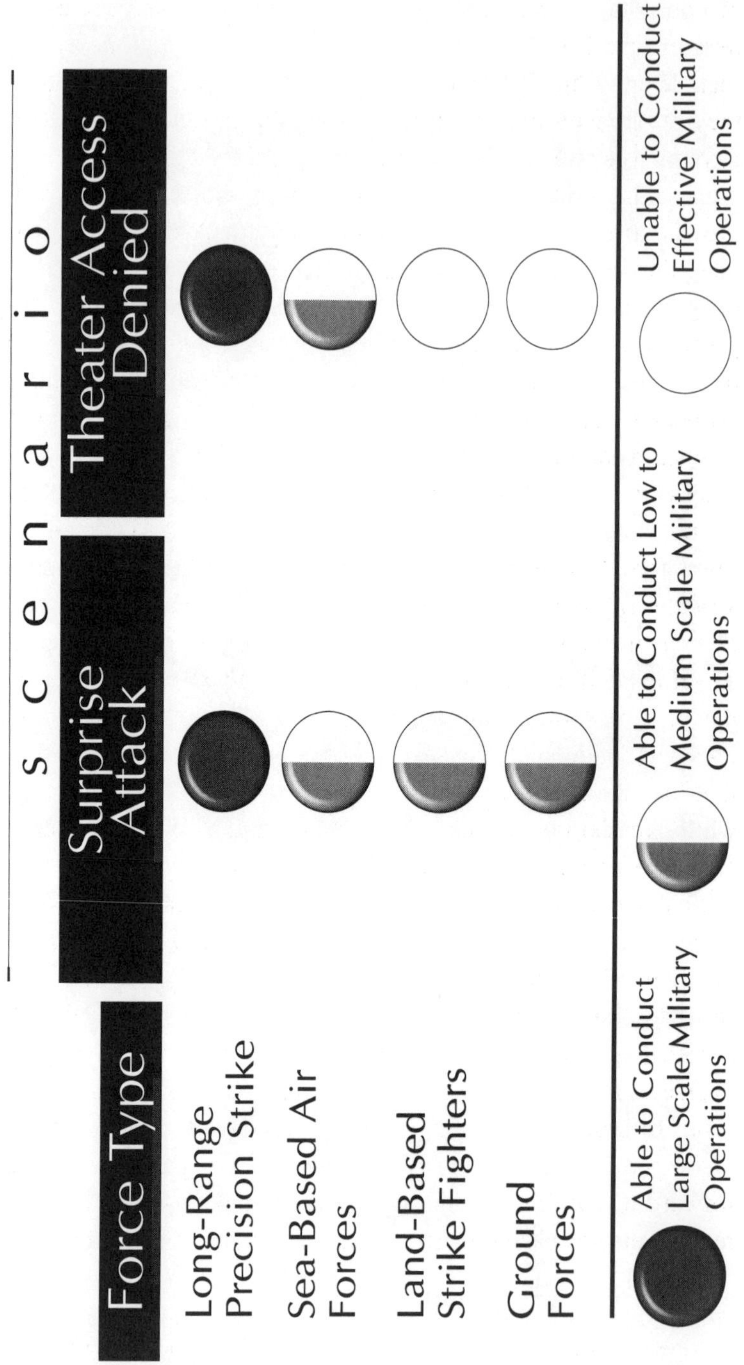

Force Type	Scenario	
	Surprise Attack	Theater Access Denied
Long-Range Precision Strike	● Able to Conduct Large Scale	● Able to Conduct Large Scale
Sea-Based Air Forces	◐	◐
Land-Based Strike Fighters	◐	○
Ground Forces	◐	○

● Able to Conduct Large Scale Military Operations

◐ Able to Conduct Low to Medium Scale Military Operations

○ Unable to Conduct Effective Military Operations

to conduct large-scale operations when they are denied access to essential reception facilities and bases. Under conditions of surprise attack, the usefulness of land-based air and land warfare forces would be limited because of their lengthy buildup times in the theater, especially ground forces. Unless they are already present in the region, aircraft carriers may require several days or weeks before they are present in the theater. Tomahawk land attack cruise missiles launched from submarines and surface ships, however, can provide a ready long-range precision strike capability aginst some fixed targets. Finally, when U.S. forces are denied strategic warning and face a surprise attack and anti-access operations are denying deployments, long-range precision strike platforms postured for global responsiveness in a matter of hours clearly become the weapon system of choice. "In the direct power projection role the Air Force forces can deter attack or inimical actions, provide a tailored response, or punch hard when required—over great distances—with quick response to decisions," General Russell E. Dougherty, former commander-in-chief of the Strategic Air Command, explains. "Air Force forces can provide a presence, or put ordnance on a target worldwide in a matter of hours, with or without reliance on any forward basing. Nothing else can match this reach, range and reaction time of mere hours."[5]

How well does the planned U.S. force for the coming decade satisfy the power projection capability needs for confronting WMD-armed adversaries? The National Defense Panel counselled in its December 1997 report that "we need greater mobility, precision, speed, stealth, and strike ranges while we sharply reduce our logistics footprint."[6] As illustrated in Figure 12.4, the currently planned U.S. force comes up short of the mark in four critical areas: (1) even with prepositioning equipment overseas and buying more airlift and sealift, the U.S. will still be unable to deploy sufficient numbers of ground, air, and maritime forces in time to be relevant to enemy surprise attacks (even when assuming access to the theater has not been denied); (2) thousands of friendly forces and civilian populations in the overseas theaters can be killed in the earliest hours of a surprise attack as a result of biological and chemical warfare attacks, and even nuclear strikes, while the U.S. is constrained from responding until its forces can move forward; (3) with a continuing emphasis on short-range tactical fighters that require theater basing or launch from carriers in the littoral, the U.S. must

---

[5] Russell R. Dougherty, General, U.S. Air Force (retired), "Projecting Power Without Bases," Statement Before the House Armed Services Committee (March 27, 1990). Photocopy.

[6] U.S., National Defense Panel, *Transforming Defense,* p. iii.

Figure 12.4

Reducing the U.S. Theater Footprint and Increasing Responsiveness

"We will need greater mobility, precision, speed, stealth, and strike ranges while we sharply reduce our logistics footprint"

National Defense Panel, 1997

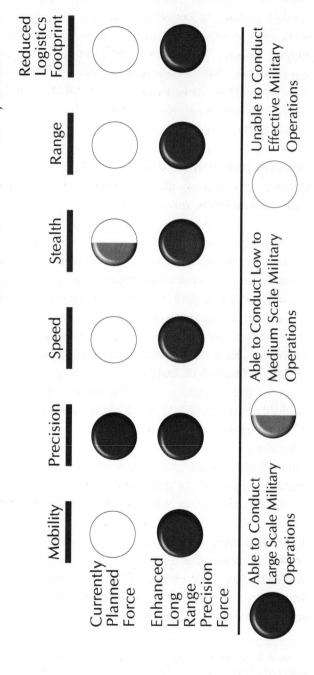

The New Face of War

first move forces into place, assuming access has not been denied, before undertaking combat operations; and (4) in spite of a lot of ink being spilled inside the Pentagon about reducing the logistics footprint, even a slimmed-down amount of supplies necessary to feed in-theater combat and combat support forces, arm them with aerial bombs and missiles and other munitions, and fuel their combat and support equipment would be enormous. An enhanced long-range precision strike force attacking from beyond the range of the adversary's delivery systems would satisfy all criteria for integrated conventional-WMD warfare.

Leveraging Long-Range Strike

General Ronald R. Fogleman, former Air Force chief-of-staff, drew the right lesson when he observed that:

> It was not until Desert Storm that we discovered conventional air operations could not only support a ground scheme of maneuver, but also directly achieve operational- and strategic-level objectives independent of ground forces, or even with ground forces in support.... The need for mass on the battlefield has changed, we don't need to occupy an enemy's country to defeat his strategy. We can reduce his combat capabilities, and in many instances defeat his armed forces from the air.[7]

Still, the United States is currently dependent on tactical fighters whose success hinges dependent on the use of foreign bases and waters. Even if the regional seaports, bases, and waters are open to American forces, the United States could be hard pressed to stop an armor-led invasion before the aggressor seized friendly territory, economic assets, and population.

Until recently, the accuracy and survivability limitations of long-range conventional bombers restricted their role as a theater strike asset. Today, with long-range, large payloads, and delivery of *precision weapons,* the bomber possesses many of the desired characteristics needed to answer the new challenges posed by WMD-armed adversaries attacking without warning. A series of graphics help to clarify the impact of technology in developing a long-range precision strike force.

---

[7] Ronald R. Fogleman, General, U.S. Air Force, Chief of Staff, "Aerospace Doctrine—More Than Just a Theory," presented at the Air Force Doctrine Seminar (Maxwell AFB, Ala.: unpublished, April 30, 1996). Photocopy.

Table 12.1 summarizes the challenges and desired force characteristics of modern long-range precision strike. Global responsiveness, independence from theater basing, and survivability of the attacking aircraft are prominent desired characteristics.

Figure 12.5 illustrates the extraordinary accuracy available to all long-range strike systems as a result of precision munitions. The illustration shows the results of an October 1996 live test of a B-2 strike against a simulated airfield. All bombs hit their targets in a single pass. Similar results can be achieved by B-52 and B-1 bombers armed with standoff missiles or when delivering bombs in an environment protected from enemy air defenses.

Figure 12.6 illustrates the phenomenal leap ahead in bombing accuracy available to global response precision strike systems. Using the Pentagon as a simulated target, a B-52 high altitude delivery of 500-pound bombs would achieve the bombing pattern shown on the left. Extrapolating the B-2's live test of GPS-aided bombs, all sixteen could hit inside the Pentagon's court yard from high altitude. This is an astounding leap in long-range precision strike capabilities that has emerged since the 1991 Gulf War. These capabilities provide the basis for conducting effective urgent counterforce strikes for long distance operations against the enemy's invading forces, WMD, and anti-access forces.

A military strategy designed to meet the new challenges of the twenty-first century must be successful independent of strategic warning, and it should be focused on *halting* an aggressor's assault while *enabling* the projection of U.S. forces threatened by enemy anti-access operations. Long-range precision strike would form the core capacity for designing rapid and effective U.S. asymmetric responses against the enemy's military forces, with a particular focus on WMD and conventional anti-access capabilities. The United States needs to leverage the diminished bomber force still available in 1998 for the urgent counterforce missions needed at the very outset of conflict in the coming decade.

Halt and Enable Operational Concept

The ability of the United States armed forces to halt an invasion quickly in the Persian Gulf or on the Korean peninsula is under severe stress. With seaports, airfields, and military bases held at risk by missiles, aircraft, and paramilitary super-terrorists armed with biological and chemical weapons, and perhaps a few nuclear weapons as well, the United States faces an uphill battle. The Persian Gulf War suggests some lessons for tomorrow's war.

Table 12.1
Modern Long-Range Precision Strike

Challenge	Desired Force Characteristic
Declining Defense Budgets	Cost-Effective Forces
Reduced Forward Presence	Global Responsiveness From U.S. Bases
Base Access Problems	Independence From Foreign/Theater Basing; Global Responsiveness
Proliferation of Weapons of Mass Destruction	Independence From Theater Basing; Minimal Personnel at Risk
Terrorism Against U.S. Forces Abroad Increasing	Independence From Theater Basing
Proliferation of Advanced Counter-Air and Sea Conventional Weapons	Stealth/Survivability; Long Range To Operate From Beyond Theater
U.S. Casualty Sensitivity Rising	Stealth/Survivability; Minimal Personnel at Risk
Surprise Attacks Likely	Global Responsiveness

Figure 12.5
B-2 Live Fire Test

Pre-Strike

Strike

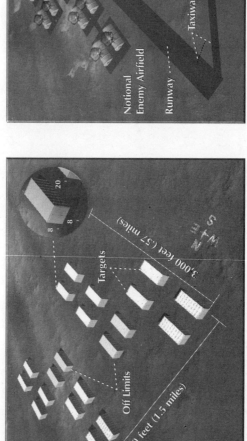

Target Array, Nellis AFB Range,
October 1996

Results With Potential Future
Application

The New Face of War

Figure 12.6
Long-Range Bomber Accuracy, Yesterday and Today

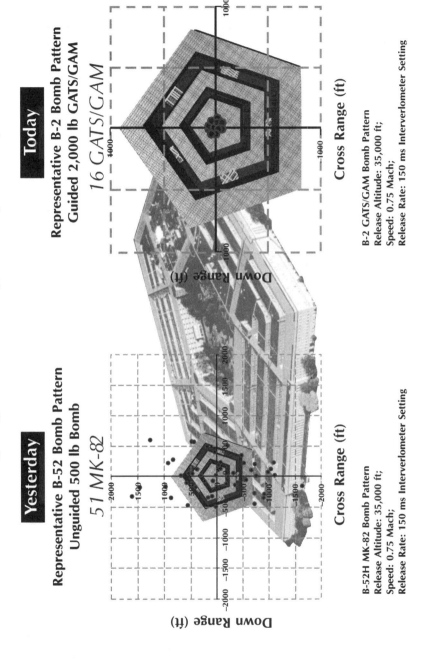

Today

Representative B-2 Bomb Pattern
Guided 2,000 lb GATS/GAM

16 GATS/GAM

Cross Range (ft)

Down Range (ft)

B-2 GATS/GAM Bomb Pattern
Release Altitude: 35,000 ft;
Speed: 0.75 Mach;
Release Rate: 150 ms Interverlometer Setting

Yesterday

Representative B-52 Bomb Pattern
Unguided 500 lb Bomb

51 MK-82

Cross Range (ft)

Down Range (ft)

B-52H MK-82 Bomb Pattern
Release Altitude: 35,000 ft;
Speed: 0.75 Mach;
Release Rate: 150 ms Interverlometer Setting

"Desert Storm, like all wars," says the Gulf War air commander General Charles A. Horner, "provides a valuable opportunity to learn how warfare may be changing. But it only provides the opportunity to learn.... Too often historians can show us examples of armed forces that did not learn or learned the wrong lessons."[8] In General Horner's view, "...it seems clear that we have squandered much of the valuable insight gained by Desert Storm."[9] Four lessons that Americans should have learned but failed to heed are directly relevant to future warfare:

- *"Surprise attack is inevitable and therefore must be hedged against."* Noting that Saddam Hussein had the opportunity to capture not only the majority of the world's oil supply but also the seaports and airfields necessary to deploy American forces, the Iraqi leader and others learned a valuable lesson: "Don't give the Americans six months." The friction of distance results in too few forces arriving too late to be relevant to the initial assault.

- *"Future adversaries will be armed with weapons of mass destruction... and the means to deliver them."* This means that the current U.S. strategy of deploying tactical fighters, ships, and troops into an overseas theater within range of WMD-armed missiles is no longer risk free.

- *"The revolutionary combination of stealth and precision must be exploited."* The F-117 stealth aircraft was equipped with precision weapons and its operations in Desert Storm "revolutionized warfare." The "multiplier effect" of stealth was calculated after the war for the Commission on Roles and Missions of the Armed Forces where it was found that each F-117 sortie in the critical first twenty-four hours of the war were "worth" sixteen nonstealth tactical fighter sorties.

- *"The need to minimize U.S. casualties effects planning, decision-making, and operational effectiveness."* The planning and execution of the air campaign emphasized tactics and systems that would minimize aircraft losses, although the effectiveness of the air attacks were limited to some extent by this approach. "We gave casualty avoidance priority over military effectiveness because it was the morally correct thing to do."[10]

---

[8] Charles A. Horner, General, U.S. Air Force (retired), "Lessons in Warfighting Operations From Desert Storm," *NATO's Sixteen Nations,* 1/97, p. 66.

[9] Charles A. Horner, General, U.S. Air Force (retired), "What We Should Have Learned in Desert Storm But Didn't." *Air Force Magazine* (December 1996), p. 52.

[10] *Ibid.,* pp. 52–55.

The New Face of War

Figure 12.7 illustrates an overarching strategy concept for the conduct of conventional-WMD warfare.[11] The Global Reconnaissance-Strike Complex should be incorporated into America's transoceanic power projection plans. The key operational component of this "Complex" of modern military weapons and technologies is a halt and enable concept—halt the enemy's invasion while enabling the deployment of U.S. forces to the region through a range of counter-military strikes against those capabilities most threatening to American expeditionary elements and which pose significant anti-access threats to arriving soldiers, planes, and ships.

Presented against the background of the actual deployment rates of key U.S. force elements following Iraq's August 1990 seizure of Kuwait, the graphic illustrates the need for operations in the critical first hours and days of an enemy assault to buy time for the buildup of "early" arriving American forces. This enabling function would continue throughout the hostilities to create a warfighting environment conducive to prosecution of U.S. combat operations. Since the Global Reconnaissance-Strike Complex would blunt the enemy's invading forces, including armored elements, there could be no need for a subsequent buildup of a huge American footprint similar to the Gulf War for the ground forces and logistics necessary to launch a counter-offensive. A sizable Army and Marine Corps presence in the theater may be needed as a protection force for key areas at risk, but their numbers would be no where close to those participating in the massive ground counter-offensive launched during Operation Desert Storm.

The enabling aspect of the new operational concept also includes strikes against enemy airfields (offensive counter-air mission) and against surface-to-air missiles, anti-aircraft guns, early warning and guidance radars, command and control centers, and other elements of the enemy's integrated air defense system (suppression of enemy air defenses or SEAD mission). Priority counterforce attention should be given to strikes against the enemy's WMD, advanced conventional weapons, and missiles that could provide the basis for asymmetric strikes or anti-access operations against U.S. deployments. Finally, this new strategy element is envisioned as a "joint operation" where the attacking platforms would be under the command and control of the theater combatant commander. To ensure that the requisite unity of command is preserved, this new strategy element, largely (but not solely) based on long-range strike aircraft launched from bases outside the theater

---

[11] Glenn C. Buchan, "The Use of Long-Range Bombers In a Changing World: A Classical Exercise of Systems Analysis" in *New Challenges for Defense Planning,* ed. by Paul K. Davis (Santa Monica, Calif.: RAND Corporation, 1994), pp. 411–12.

Figure 12.7
Global Reconnaissance-Strike Complex

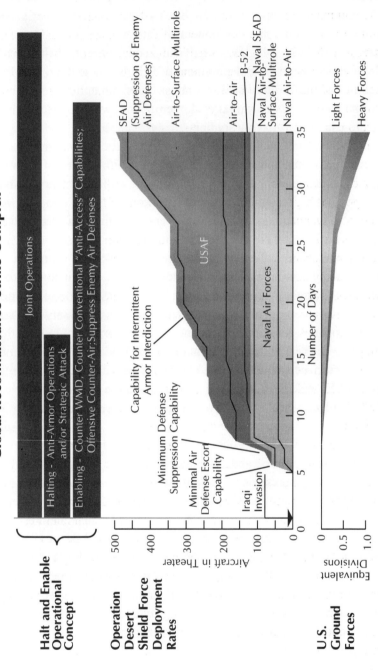

Source: As slightly modified from Glen C. Buchan, *The Use of Long-Range Bombers in a Changing World: A Classic Exercise of Systems Analysis in New Challenges for Defense Planning*; ed. by Paul K. Davis (Santa Monica, Calif.; RAND Corporation, 1994), p. 462.

The New Face of War

of conflict, must be integrated into the responsible commander's concept of operations.

The commanders-in-chief or "CINCs"—the combatant commanders responsible for the employment of American forces in support of U.S. military objectives—deal with new realities like the emergence of the WMD and missile threats through the development of concepts of operations. Whatever the specifics of the U.S. policy and strategy at the time, the CINCs will first look to the adversary's military capabilities and infrastructure. If the CINC is asked to use military force, his first steps will encompass actions against a set of high-threat (to the United States) targets and high-value (to the enemy) targets. The "high threat" to U.S. security interests are the enemy's military capabilities for invading and seizing the territory of its neighbors. The weapons of highest value to the enemy would include weapons of mass destruction, advanced conventional weapons, and ballistic and cruise missiles that can enable an enemy's air-ground conventional assault and enable anti-access operations to prevent the rapid arrival of U.S. forces.

Hence, a key aspect of a U.S. theater CINC's concept of operations is an analytic process based on the interaction at the strategic, operational, and tactical levels of warfare between operations (the shooters) and intelligence (the target locators and characterizers). A well-executed target-to-strategy planning approach will integrate intelligence considerations with factors important to effective strikes that will halt invading forces and counter the enemy's WMD and conventional anti-access forces.

Halt the Invasion. Stopping an invasion quickly is an essential military task in the CINC's concept of operations. To keep an invader from presenting the United States with a fait accompli, the enemy's seizure of territory and critical facilities must be blunted. Such action can also stiffen the backbone of the leadership of the countries under attack by the first-hand evidence of the U.S. willingness to fulfill its security commitments. The greater the advance made by the enemy the more sizable the U.S. military buildup necessary to restore lost territory and important economic assets seized by the enemy.[12]

Using a Global Reconnaissance-Strike Complex to implement an integrated conventional-WMD strategy is a far different operational element than contained in the current U.S. conventional strategy, which calls for stopping an enemy short of his objectives, stabilizing the battlefield, building up forces over time, and then launching a counter-offensive to "evict" the aggressor from the prizes of war seized in the initial assault. The United States has the

---

[12] Cohen, *Report of the Quadrennial Defense Review,* p. 13.

---

technological base to "defend" friends and allies by halting an invasion in its earliest hours. The rape, pillage, and mayhem following the Iraqi seizure of Kuwait can be prevented. Similarly, a North Korean gamble of invading the South can be answered quickly and with devastating results for Pyongyang. Three compelling reasons—moral, political, and military—underwrite a needed change in U.S. military strategy.

First, the current U.S. conventional strategy surrenders to the enemy the ability to win his military objectives early. This assumption of American powerlessness early in a conflict is based on outdated ideas of geography and the axiom that "the effect of force is in inverse proportion to the distance from its source."[13] Today, Americans have within their grasp the capacity to halt an enemy's aggression early in a conflict through long-range precision strikes. This capability is "defensive" rather than "evictive." If the United States has it within its capacity to assist in the defense of allies and deny the aggressor the anticipated fruit from assaulting neighboring countries, then Americans have a moral obligation to field those forces and minimize the extreme miseries of biological and chemical warfare and the numerous human casualties that could result.

Secondly, blunting the invasion can also stiffen the backbone of the leadership of the countries under attack by offering first-hand evidence of the U.S. willingness to remain steadfast in their defense. By reducing or even eliminating the prospective loss of territory resulting from an aggressors's assault, the political price that regional states might have to pay—allowing for American use of its seaports, airfields, and bases on its territory—will be less. The ready capability to blunt an invasion helps to deter adversaries and reassure friends. Halting the invasion contributes to U.S. access objectives.

Finally, the military imperative for stopping a WMD-armed enemy invasion looms in particular importance. WMD in the hands of an adversary enables anti-access operations to block U.S. deployment to the region. If Saddam Hussein would have waited a couple of years until he had a few nuclear weapons and more advanced dissemination capabilities for biological weapons, a very different outcome could have occurred. Not only would the U.S.-led buildup of Coalition forces have been retarded without the use of the Persian Gulf seaports at Al Jubayl and Ad Dammam, but the ultimate counteroffensive to evict the Iraqis from Kuwait could have been far more costly in

---

[13] Nicholas John Spykman, *America's Strategy in World Politics* (1942. Reprint: Archon Books, 1970), p. 165.

terms of American casualties. A similar plausible scenario could be posed for North Korea's potential uses of weapons of mass destruction.

Counter Weapons of Mass Destruction, Advanced Conventional Weapons, and Key Military Technologies. Another military task that needs to be reshaped and then built into the CINCs' concepts of operation is demilitarizing the enemy's weapons of mass destruction and other advanced weapons and support systems as quickly as possible. To limit dispersal of critical WMD assets and possible WMD retaliation, the initial counterforce strikes must be decisive. While many types of military forces may be required, land- and sea-based airpower will no doubt comprise the main strike force. American planners will want to destroy as many targets as they can as quickly as possible. This places a premium on surprise, lethality and payload. The 1997 Quadrennial Defense Review, for instance, called upon the armed forces to improve their capabilities to locate and destroy biological and chemical weapons "preferably before they can be used."[14] Counter-military operations are always a difficult task, one that can never be expected to reach 100 percent effectiveness. Nevertheless, after more than four decades of building targeting plans for nuclear warfare against the Soviet Union and Communist China, the United States has already developed many of the requisite targeting and campaign planning tools to conduct effective counter-WMD operations, especially when combined with the modern sensors, communications, and target acquisition systems available today. The initial task is to reduce the enemy's WMD and advanced conventional weapons sufficiently to relieve the stress on introducing U.S. tactical fighters, ground forces, and maritime elements to the theater. Countering the enemy's asymmetric anti-access capabilities through America's own asymmetric strikes is key to enabling the rapid deployment of U.S. expeditionary forces.

Peacetime intelligence collection and processing can greatly improve the identification of high-priority WMD targets and their location and acquisition for strike operations during the opening hours of a conflict. Intelligence about WMD targets offers clues about the enemy's intentions, provides vital input for attack planning, helps determine when and where to attack, facilitates precision strike operations, assists in minimizing collateral damage, and permits initiation of rapid counter-WMD operations. There is much WMD-armed adversaries can do to frustrate and complicate intelligence collection. Iraq learned from the Soviets how to deny locational cuing for their missile launchers. Some of the Iraqi practices included preparation of

---

[14] Cohen, *Report of the Quadrennial Defense Review,* p. 13.

---

ready-hide positions near launch points, rapid deployment, false targets, decoys, camouflage and deception practices, and good operations security, especially radio silence. In some cases, key documentation and machinery essential to Iraq's WMD program were moved out of buildings presumed to be on the Coalition's counter-military target list.

In order to neutralize such wartime measures, peacetime intelligence needs to analyze the entire lifetime of weapons of mass destruction and missiles to determine their location and vulnerabilities from the earliest stages of research and development through delivery or launch. Figure 12.8 provides an example of lifetime analysis of WMD and targeting opportunities. In peacetime, intelligence analysts should create data bases necessary for attack planning, including the location of WMD assets. During a crisis, targets can be reprioritized quickly as dictated by events.

The timelines associated with each target set define the counter-military problem for both the intelligence analysts and the operators. The timelines associated with the enemy's committed assets and their relocating to forward sites are one of the most stressful for U.S. attack operations planners. Enemy WMD and missile assets must emerge from concealment or forward storage depots prior to launch. This dwell time of the weapons at their launch sites could require only minutes to accomplish or, in some instances, hours.

Another important variable is distance of the target from the shoreline or political borders of its neighbors. The distance over land that must be covered to reach specific targets is very important in selecting the right strike platform for the mission.

In addition to the target timelines, an ability to relate the target sets to the distances from friendly assets greatly assists the battle managers in determining which of the available attack assets would be most effective against specific targets. When all of these factors—target sets, timelines, distances, and available attack assets—are combined, a potentially effective concept of operations begins to emerge.

System-of-Systems Architecture

The rationale for integrating a robust Global Reconnaissance-Strike Complex into the current military strategy is to mass firepower against the enemy's high-threat forces while minimizing the American in-theater footprint. When confronting a WMD-adversary, a CINC will be able to halt an enemy's invasion and reduce the number and effectiveness of his weapons of mass destruction, missiles, and advanced conventional weapons before large numbers of U.S. forces begin arriving in the theater under severe risk

Figure 12.8
Lifetime of WMD and Missile Systems

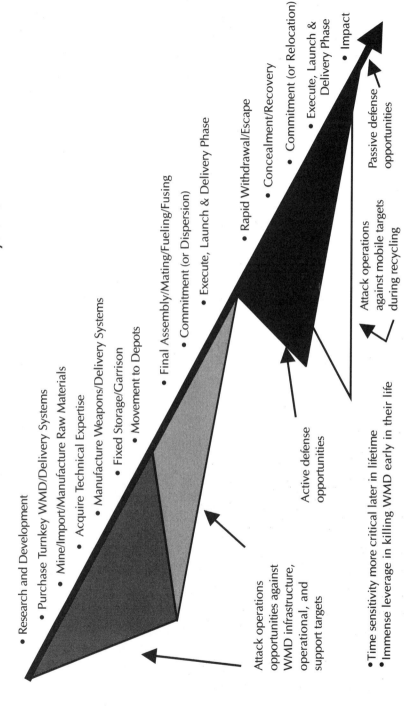

• Research and Development
• Purchase Turnkey WMD/Delivery Systems
• Mine/Import/Manufacture Raw Materials
• Acquire Technical Expertise
• Manufacture Weapons/Delivery Systems
• Fixed Storage/Garrison
• Movement to Depots
• Final Assembly/Mating/Fueling/Fusing
• Commitment (or Dispersion)
• Execute, Launch & Delivery Phase
• Rapid Withdrawal/Escape
• Concealment/Recovery
• Commitment (or Relocation)
• Execute, Launch & Delivery Phase
• Impact

Passive defense opportunities

Attack operations against mobile targets during recycling

Active defense opportunities

Attack operations opportunities against WMD infrastructure, operational, and support targets

• Time sensitivity more critical later in lifetime
• Immense leverage in killing WMD early in their life

conditions. To bridge the gap in the theater commander's military capabilities, the Global Reconnaissance-Strike Complex integrates a diverse set of eight main components: intelligence, surveillance, and reconnaissance (ISR); command, control, communications, computing, and intelligence (C4I); global precision strike platforms; precision strike weapons; theater enabling forces; carrier-based aircraft; distributed ground combat cells; and theater missile and air defenses. This is a system-of-systems architecture concept—the components make up a whole whose synergistic strengths are manifested in conducting "halt and enable" operations.

Intelligence, Surveillance, and Reconnaissance (ISR). The intelligence, surveillance, and reconnaissance assets providing a heightened battlefield awareness of the location of weapons, troops, and armored columns are important components of a combatant commander's concept of operations. The U.S. commander is also offered the ability to achieve dominant battlespace knowledge based on (1) an awareness of where things are, (2) an understanding of the relationships and related significance of the enemy's force elements, (3) how the units and weapons fit into the terrain and are constrained by it, (4) what the forces are trying to achieve, and (5) how the various military objectives relate to each other. The ability to quickly comprehend how the enemy's units and weapons relate to each other will provide the United States a tremendous leverage that can be exploited by precision munitions.[15] No other country is able to bring to the battlefield the integrated array of sensors positioned in space, air, ground, and at sea.[16] The United States will be able to select the highest payoff targets and develop an attack plan that goes after the enemy's strategy by turning his strengths against himself.[17]

---

[15] James Blaker, *Understanding the Revolution in Military Affairs: A Guide to America's 21st Century Defense*, ed. by Robert A. Manning (Washington, D.C.: Progressive Policy Institute, 1997), pp. 8–11.

[16] *Ibid.*, pp. 9–10.

[17] The objective is to *understand* what is occurring on the battlefield, not just *awareness*. Understanding confers *dominance* to U.S. planners whereas awareness, largely based on sensor-derived object locations with identification, gives battlefield advantage. Awareness answers "what," while understanding answers "why" (the enemy's intent). The key additive element is "knowledge," which is based on reasoning, context, experience, intuition, intangibles, and training. At its center, "understanding" is inferential and, when applied wisely, can illuminate though not fully dispel the fog of war. By concentrating on *understanding* rather than simple *awareness,* the United States will be able to build a more aggressive and creative approach and make information technology relevant to the warfighter's military tasks assigned through the development of the CINC's concept of operations. See U.S., Defense Science Board, *Tactics and Technology for 21st Century Military Superiority,* Vol. 1—Final Report, 1996 Summer Study Task Force (Washington, D.C.: Office of the Secretary of Defense, October 1996), pp. V-25/V-26.

The ability of the United States to collect and process data rapidly from a relatively large area (about 40,000 square miles) will permit the identification and location, with minimal processing delay, of virtually all friendly, neutral and opposing forces, military facilities, machinery, weapons, vehicles, and militarily significant units. Processing the data to provide an integrated fusion provides a battlespace picture in great detail. This dominant battlespace knowledge is an enormously important exploitable advantage—these "eyes and ears" enable the conduct of the anti-armor and counter-military operations. Over time, one should anticipate adversaries will adjust by taking actions to deny the United States such knowledge to the extent possible. Yet, even a grand "cat-and-mouse" game of a competition between "hiders" and "finders" promises to disrupt an adversary's invasion forces against neighbors and the flow of asymmetric attacks against U.S. deployments. As the adversary becomes better at "hiding," the U.S. can be expected to become better at "finding." The regional competition will favor the side that is most creative in understanding the other.[18]

The U.S. Air Force has already taken the initial steps to enhance battlefield awareness by developing the Information Superiority/Air Expeditionary Force (IS/AEF) concept. The "electronic triad," which it is often called, is built around the long-range sensors such as the Joint STARS—Joint Surveillance Target Attack Radar System (radar tracking of vehicle movement), AWACS—Airborne Warning and Control System (air superiority aircraft control), and Rivet Joint (electronic signals). While all three members of the ISR *troika* are important, the Joint STARS aircraft provides a key component of the ability to "see" the enemy's disposition over a wide area and to choose the time and place to attack them before they engage U.S. and friendly forces. The Joint STARS combines moving target indicators with synthetic aperture radar systems to produce images that allow U.S. strike platforms to single out individual vehicles. The radar can even distinguish between wheeled and tracked vehicles such as trucks and tanks. A key synergism of the sensor-to-shooter linkage is making it possible to interdict enemy armored columns before they engage allied forces.[19]

The IS/AEF is an important development in overcoming the WMD threat to America's power projection strategy. First, it is organized as expeditionary force, which makes it immediately available for worldwide deployment.

---

[18] U.S., National Defense University, *1997 Strategic Assessment* (Washington, D.C.: Government Printing Office, 1997), pp. 262–63.

[19] Loren Thompson, "Joint STARS Can Save Troops' Lives," *Air Force Times,* p. 46.

Second, it has a small footprint in or near the theater, which minimizes its exposure. And, third, the IS/AEF has both flexibility and versatility; it offers a readily adaptable resource for countering asymmetric threats. The three aircraft, for instance, offer shooters different battlefield pictures fused together into a single, multispectral picture of the battlespace. The fusion could be enriched easily by "plugging in" to U-2 reconnaissance aircraft, reconnaissance unmanned aerial vehicles (UAV), and space surveillance and communications systems. The Navy's E-2C Hawkeye air surveillance and P-3 Orion maritime surveillance could also tap in. Potential candidates to join the IS/AEF could include the Airborne Laser with its advanced surveillance and battle management systems; the Global Hawk and Dark Star high altitude, high endurance UAVs; and the highly advanced sensor systems of the F-22 tactical fighter. Unattended ground sensors used to monitor an enemy's underground weapons storage facilities and other installations also could become useful members.[20]

The high altitude (60,000-65,000 feet) Global Hawk will possess long endurance on-station times of more than twenty-four hours, be effective in all weather, encompass a 40,000 square nautical mile radar search footprint, and provide planners with spot radar resolution of one foot. The Dark Star will be a stealth technology UAV.[21]

New families of in-close sensors are being developed for detecting weapons of mass destruction and missiles. Even more advanced technologies available over the long term will allow detection of camouflaged targets. Advances in bringing data together from multiple sources and putting it into useable forms for military operations is making progress. The Navy, for instance, is creating new concepts for "net-centric" warfare schemes. This approach nets together electronically a suite of platforms and sensors with wide band communications links.[22] While fusion of the data makes progress, the military operator may draw great benefit from sensor data correlations.

---

[20] Robert Wall, "The Electronic Triad," *Air Force Magazine* (January 1998), pp. 54–58. See also U.S., National Defense University, *Strategic Assessment 1996,* pp. 186–87, and "The Future of Warfare," *Economist* (March 8, 1997), p. 21.

[21] John Entzminger, Deputy Director for Technology, Defense Airborne Reconnaissance Office, *The Past and Future of Airborne Reconnaissance* (Cambridge, Mass.: Center for International Studies, Massachusetts Institute of Technology, November 1997).

[22] Owen Cote and Harvey Sapolsky, *Antisubmarine Warfare After the Cold War* (Cambridge, Mass.: Center for International Studies, Massachusetts Institute of Technology, 1998), p. 18.

The New Face of War

Sensors based on satellites and UAVs can be used in mutually reinforcing ways. Satellites, for instance, can provide twenty-four-hour surveillance of a specific target. They can perform this function from a predictable location. The potential to have almost constant images from satellites of specific trouble spots in the world would give the United States a tremendous advantage.[23] UAVs, on the other hand, are mobile and can respond to rapidly changing events on the ground.

Some thought is being given to developing a "Modular Airborne Reconnaissance System" that would combine electro-optical, infrared, synthetic aperture radar, and signals intelligence. The candidate modules for such a system would include Global Hawk, Dark Star, and the manned U-2 reconnaissance aircraft.[24]

UAVs can also offer non-Western states a ready reconnaissance capability to very cheaply supplement the more sophisticated one-meter square satellite images available from commercial companies. While UAVs appear to offer an equalizing capacity in surveillance and reconnaissance capability to WMD-armed adversaries and other smaller countries, the integration of UAVs and ISR data is an enormously complex and challenging task.[25] While the U.S. and its allies can be expected to maintain their lead in these capabilities for some time in providing real-time targeting information, WMD-armed adversaries may soon achieve systems that are "good enough" to target U.S. forces deploying to the theater or present in littoral waters.

Another sensor platform of potentially great value is the Cobra Ball RC-135 aircraft that has been revamped to detect the launch of ballistic missiles and analyze their capabilities. Its advanced sensor suite can accurately locate a missile launch more than 260 miles away, mark the missile engine cutoff, and then quickly calculate its trajectory and impact point. Valuable information about its stability and accuracy can be gleaned from the reentry vehicle's speed of rotation, and any signals it receives from ground controllers can tell more about the missile's mission. These are valuable components of a theater ballistic missile defense system. Cobra Ball

---

[23] Walter Pincus, "Smaller Spy Satellites May Give U.S. Stealth Capability Over Trouble Spots," *Washington Post* (February 1, 1998), p. 9.

[24] David Mulholland, "Pentagon May Enhance UAV Role," *Defense News* (April 20–26, 1998), p. 38.

[25] International Institute for Strategic Studies, "The Future of Unmanned Aerial Vehicles," *Strategic Comments,* 3-10 (London, United Kingdom: December 1997).

---

is expected to provide a sound anti-Scud capability by using proven technology.[26]

Command, Control, Communications, Computing, and Intelligence (C4I). A second crucial element of the Global Reconnaissance-Strike Complex is the set of enhanced C4I communications and data links that are growing apace with dominant battlespace understanding and allowing the transmission of the information to where it is most needed, whether to the strike operations command posts or the top of the chain of command. The Global Command and Control System links the various military command centers of the United States and provides the warfighter with a fused picture of the battlespace. The commander can also talk to and coordinate a vast number of military assets at the same time.[27] Rapid fusion and dissemination of surveillance and targeting data can ensure greater battlefield awareness in the cockpit or other firing platform. Integrating Global Positioning System data into the overall C4I system gives strike platforms even greater visualization of the battlefield and lethal opportunities.

The C4I system element is important to targeting the right strike platforms at the right time. In the rapidly changing ground environment anticipated when WMD-adversaries take counter-actions against U.S. attacks, military commanders will need to be able to "read" the other side quickly and adapt rapidly to the newly emerging circumstances. This leads to the conclusion that the synergy between ISR and C4I is a special attribute that must be fully exploited.

Hence, the C4ISR system fuses both elements into one. These capabilities are based on more than a collection of hardware and software systems. Dominant battlespace understanding can only be achieved by integration of concepts, operational methods, people, training, and supporting systems and processes. C4ISR provides a usable picture of the battlespace to support targeting and strike operations as well as the bases for the commanders making informed and timely decisions. Integrating C4ISR into the CINC concept of operations is a key to enhancing U.S. urgent counterforce and counter-WMD capabilities and the basis for attacking the enemy's asymmetric strategy.[28]

---

[26] David A. Fulghum, "Cobra Ball Revamped For Battlefield Missions," *Aviation Week & Space Technology* (August 4, 1997), pp. 48–50.

[27] U.S., National Defense University, *Strategic Assessment 1996*, p. 187.

[28] William S. Cohen, Secretary of *Defense, Annual Report to the President and the Congress* (Washington, D.C.: Government Printing Office, 1997), pp. 229–30.

The Gulf War provided an unambiguous demonstration of the value of achieving information dominance in military operations. Satellite communications during the war were processed by 188 mobile ground stations, plus twelve commercial satellite terminals. Linkages to U.S. data bases and networks were complex—up to 700,000 telephone calls and 152,000 messages were handled every day. In order to conduct the forty-two-day air war, more than thirty million telephone calls were necessary. Citing these examples, Admiral David E. Jeremiah, former vice chairman of the Joint Chiefs of Staff, makes a strong case that communications technology has ushered in a new era. "Global dominance," Admiral Jeremiah argues, "will be achieved by those that most clearly understand the role of information and the power of knowledge that flows from it."[29]

The interface between man and machine is reaching revolutionary dimensions. With modern C4ISR today's military commander is increasingly able to simulate reality, identify and test alternatives, and inform his decision-making with precise costs, risks, and benefits of a range of different options. When confronting WMD-armed adversaries, the ability to create, disseminate, access, and use information to satisfy the commander's military objectives provides a decisive advantage. The revolution in information technologies is not about machines but how combatant commanders will conduct military operations. "It is time to come to grips with an intersection of technology and strategic thought," Admiral Jeremiah argues, "...in large measure...technology drives doctrine and tactics, and to a major degree drives strategy."[30]

Long-Range Precision Strike Platforms. With long-range strike capabilities from B-52, B-1, and B-2 bombers, and cruise missiles, the United States is able to launch attacks against the enemy's armored columns or WMD and other military forces from beyond the reach of enemy sensors and weapons. While the initial strikes can be launched from the United States, long-range strike aircraft would recover and then sustain operations from distant regional bases (e.g., Guam in the Pacific and Diego Garcia in the Indian Ocean). Overseas basing located near the enemy's key military capabilities but beyond the reach of his WMD-tipped missiles are necessary to increase sortie rates. The refueling, rearming, and turning of the long-range aircraft requires pre-designated bases where war reserve material can be

---

[29] As quoted in John G. Roos, "InfoTech InfoPower," *Armed Forces Journal International* (June 1994), p. 31.

[30] *Ibid.*

---

safely stored. It is not always possible to find the optimum base—geography sometimes works against the perfect or even second-best solutions.[31] The C4ISR and precision-munitions also are essential components in applying airpower's inherent characteristics of speed, range, flexibility, and versatility to attack enemy targets directly. With a zero delay in sensor-to-shooter information, manned aircraft can do their own spotting and attacking of targets not only in the close-in battle between land forces but deep into the enemy's rear areas.

With C4ISR providing a near-real-time global awareness, the U.S. is able to dominate the dimension of time by carefully selecting targets and integrating the campaign to strike the enemy throughout his territory. This asymmetric strategy invokes parallel warfare in which the enemy is attacked in depth and breadth with overwhelming force. The centers of gravity of the enemy's anti-access asymmetric strategy are the primary targets, including the critical points in his order of battle and infrastructure that underwrite his WMD threats to deny the U.S. access to regional seaports and airfields. The U.S. operations would be designed to give the enemy no time to adjust, adapt, or mount a counter-offensive.[32] Indeed, the air campaign would give the adversary nothing to attack. The objective is to strike all of the enemy's centers of gravity at once—in parallel—rather than serially where the adversary is given a chance to adapt to attacks against facilities low on the CINC's priority list. Three operational objectives can be expected to guide U.S. strike operations at the outset of a conflict: disrupt the enemy command and control, halt the invading forces, and ensure ready access to the region's ports and airfields.[33]

An entirely new concept of victory may be made possible by modern long-range strike capabilities. Is strategic success—halting an enemy invasion and enabling U.S. deployments by defeating a WMD-armed enemy's asymmetric strategy—possible through joint air operations alone? Is success

---

[31] The writer conducted a B-52 basing study for the Persian Gulf in 1980 and in Europe in 1984. The perfect basing scheme was elusive, compelling adoption of second-best forward bases. The B-2, however, needs much less parking area or special runways. Nevertheless, the prepositioning of fuel, weapons, aircraft support facilities, and base support are essential to timely deployment and sustained air operations.

[32] Richard Szafranski, Colonel, U.S. Air Force, "Parallel War and Hyperwar: Is Every Want a Weakness?," *Proceedings,* U.S. Naval Institute (April 1995).

[33] John T. Correll, "Deep Attack," *Air Force Magazine* (April 1996), p. 2 and "The Rediscovery of Strategic Airpower," *Air Force Magazine* (November 1996), pp. 24–31; and Glenn A. Kent, Lieutenant General, "The Relevance of High-Intensity Operations" (circa 1992). Photocopy.

possible by placing air operations at the centerpiece of strategy with other components providing essential combat support? Under what circumstances would such an air dominant strategy not be feasible when confronting a WMD-armed adversary?

Improving long-range strike force effectiveness by devising new tactics and operational concepts for the B-52 Stratofortress, B-1 Lancer, and B-2 Spirit are key aspects of the massing of firepower instead of forces. The B-1, for instance, has good self-defense capabilities derived from its supersonic speed and electronic warfare systems. Ninety-three Lancers are in service, forty of these can serve as conventionally armed intercontinental bombers. The aircraft will soon be capable of carrying a large payload of precision-guided bombs and missiles, including the Joint Standoff Weapon (JSOW), Joint Air-to-Surface Standoff Missile (JASSM), and the Joint Direct Attack Munition (JDAM).[34]

Long-range strike is a vital attribute when conducting operations against a WMD-armed adversary. The B-52, B-1, and B-2, for example, have unrefueled ranges of five to ten times greater than most tactical fighters and can respond to surprise aggression faster than any other force element. If the bombers are deployed forward in order to speed re-arming and refueling and thereby increase sortie rates, it greatly expands the number of potential basing options since airfields located in rearward areas can be used. Moreover, long-range also increases the number of countries that might agree to grant the U.S. access to their bases. Finally, the large payload of long-range bombers allows a small number of aircraft to assume a disproportionate share of the fighting. The B-2 Spirit stealth bomber carries sixteen precision delivery 2,000-pound bombs, for instance, while the stealth F-117 tactical fighter carries only two.[35] The B-52 and B-1 will require theater-based forces to enable their penetration to targets; they can also be used to launch cruise missiles and other standoff weapons.

Precision Strike Weapons. It is crucial to match the right weapons with the right delivery platform. The synergy of combining the long-range weapon-carriage of heavy bombers with the revolutionary precision accuracy of the new precision strike weapons provides the basis for developing a global response force. Precision-guided munitions (PGMs) are capable of

---

[34] Greg Caires, "Even Without Nukes, B-1s Can Still Deter—AF General Michael McMahan," *Defense Daily* (March 16, 1998).

[35] Scowcroft and others, *Final Report of the Independent Bomber Force Review Commission,* p. 8.

---

striking targets that can be located and characterized in sufficient detail anyplace in the world. Three main streams of technologies assures precision guidance: human-guided weapons, which include fiber-optic- and laser-guided bombs; signature-guided weapons, which use infrared radar reflection and acoustic homing; and location-directed, or those that know precisely where the target is and where the delivery bomb is located.[36] The reason for attacking with precision munitions is the efficiency obtained in strike operations. There are other important logistics benefits as well. According to the Defense Science Board, one ton of PGMs is equivalent to twelve to twenty tons of unguided munitions on a tonnage per target basis. With fewer misses, it stands to reason that fewer bombs and aircraft are needed to destroy the target. In addition, when taken in the totality of operations during the Gulf War, the use of PGMs saves as much as thirty-five to forty tons of fuel.[37]

Two kinds of weapons are of particular interest in the halt and enable operational concept. One set is the right weapons to halt the aggressor's armored invasion forces. The second set of munitions are those necessary to demilitarize an adversary's weapons of mass destruction, ballistic and cruise missiles, and conventional anti-access capabilities to levels that will *enable* the introduction of U.S. tactical fighters, ground forces, and carrier battle groups.

Since precision weapons make it possible to destroy virtually everything that can be targeted, it means American forces can strike air defense missile sites and radars, airfields, bridges, supply dumps, concentrations of parked vehicles, fixed command posts, and armored forces on the move. These targets will be vulnerable not just to large raids but small-scale ones as well. Precision weapons allow a significant increase in efficiency in the resources for such missions with fewer misses or bombs scattered across the landscape. In addition, there will be less collateral damage, which is always an important consideration and especially in situations with a high political context.

Three criteria help to assess the consequences of precision munitions: (1) the direct, first-order effects on the destruction of various classes of targets; (2) indirect effects such as delays and confusion; and (3) the direct

---

[36] U.S., National Defense University, *Strategic Assessment 1996,* p. 188.

[37] U.S., Defense Science Board, *Report of the Defense Science Board Task Force on Tactical Air Warfare* (Washington, D.C.: Office of the Secretary of Defense, November 1993), p. 17.

The New Face of War

and indirect effects after allowing for countermeasures and other adaptive responses by enemies, including virtual attrition resulting from inducing a diversion of enemy resources to active or passive defenses against these weapons.

The ability to make highly accurate attacks on locatable targets at any range has major implications for attacks against fixed facilities. These include WMD and WMD-related installations, including storage and garrison locations, command and control facilities, and other important targets. No less important is the target acquisition of wheeled and armored vehicles on the move by Joint STARS and other ISR sensors.

Especially if the enemy's routes of advance are known and monitored because they are restricted by terrain and a scarcity of roads, concentrations of vehicles will be subject to accurate fires delivered by precision strike platforms. The enemy will use counters, including attacks against surveillance sensors or control systems, active defenses and decoys, use of natural cover, and wider spacing of vehicles when on the move to reduce the chances of multiple kills by a single precision munition. Yet, the aggressor must be on the move to seize the territory of others, which means his forces will be more visible and sometimes in road march formation. This will enhance the defender's efforts to halt the enemy's invasion short of his objectives. It will lessen the chances of an adversary successfully presenting the United States with a fait accompli.[38]

Theater Enabling Aircraft. The stealth F-22 Raptor is a next generation air superiority fighter that will soon join the Air Force inventory. It is far more versatile than the F-15 aircraft it is replacing. The aircraft can cruise at supersonic speeds while using only slightly more fuel than consumed by a conventional tactical fighter to cruise at subsonic speeds. It has a low radar cross-section—on the order of an insect to a small bird—which allows it to penetrate an enemy's integrated air defense systems unnoticed; the aircraft's low drag gives it exceptional range and minimal refueling needs. Heat and other emissions from the aircraft are carefully managed. Using the latest computer technology, the F-22 has an integrated avionics suite that allows the pilot to manage information instead of operating multiple complicated sensors. With the on-board computers handling more of the sensor tasking, the pilot is freed to fly the airplane and fire the weapons.

---

[38] U.S., Commission on Integrated Long-Term Strategy, *The Future of Containment,* Report of the Offense-Defense Working Group (Washington, D.C.: Department of Defense, October 1988), pp. 54–70.

The sensors allow the F-22 to detect enemy aircraft at greater distances than conventional fighters; the F-22 also receives information from AWACS. The combination of supercruise, stealth, and integrated avionics makes the F-22 dominant over all other fighter aircraft in the world. It has been built to fight in a chemically contaminated environment. The F-22 also has an air-to-ground bombing capability, and it is highly deployable. A squadron of twenty-four aircraft equipped for thirty days of combat requires only eight C-141 air transports to carry the required support equipment and supplies.[39]

The multi-role F-22 is another centerpiece element of the Global Reconnaissance-Strike Complex. In halting the enemy, the F-22 provides essential leverage for long-range precision strike platforms arriving from bases outside the lethal radius of enemy WMD and other anti-access capabilities by (1) neutralizing the enemy air-to-air threat with highly aggressive air superiority concepts such as pin-down combat air patrols and strikes against enemy airfields and dispersal locations, (2) providing lethal suppression of enemy air defenses (SEAD) on the first day of the war and doing so autonomously, (3) enabling daytime B-2 direct attack operations (B-2 conducts autonomous missions at night with a limited standoff), (4) enabling B-52 and B-1 direct attack operations (day and night) as the air defense environment becomes less threatening, and (5) enabling the allocation of a maximum percentage of on-station aircraft carrier fighter-bombers to exercise strike operations by accepting both the air-to-air and lethal SEAD roles in support of naval air operations.

A second F-22 contribution to halting the enemy is through the protection of theater- and outside-the-theater based C4ISR systems. By neutralizing the enemy air-to-air and surface-to-air threats, the F-22 creates a buffer zone for airborne C4ISR systems, including Joint STARS, AWACS, Rivet Joint, and command and control platforms.

Finally, the F-22 can perform autonomous rapid-response interdiction and halt missions by filling in for bombers and aircraft carriers when not on station. Small and smart anti-armor munitions can be effectively exploited by the aircraft.

F-22 operations also involve the safe and timely deployment and employment of theater land, sea, and air reinforcements. Long-range precision

[39] Michael J. Costigan, Lieutenant Colonel, USAF, *The F-22: The Right Fighter for the Twenty-First Century?*, Air War College, Maxwell Paper No. 9 (Maxwell Air Force Base, Ala.: Air University, August 1997), pp. 1–13, and Loren B. Thompson, "F-22 Counters Emerging Missile Threat to U.S. Air Superiority," *ADTI Defense Issue Brief* (Arlington, Va.: Alexis de Tocqueville Institution, October 15, 1997).

strike and carrier-based aircraft need to be free of enemy attacks. Highly aggressive combat air patrol, offensive counter-air, and defensive counter-air missions will neutralize enemy WMD-armed aircraft. The F-22 must also ensure employment over enemy territory of the Airborne Laser. Similar functions are needed to provide freedom from the enemy's land-attack cruise missiles. The F-22's intra-theater speed, autonomous daytime strike capability, and integrated avionics allows the fusion and exploitation of multiple on- and off-board sensors.

In an urgent counterforce role, the F-22 offers a rapid response counter-WMD strike capability: direct, time-urgent precision attack of fixed facilities (e.g., WMD and missile research, production and storage facilities) and mobile and relocatable systems (e.g., missile transporter erector launchers and cruise missile launchers); and rapid response counter-conventional anti-access strike (e.g., shore- and patrol boat-based anti-ship cruise missiles).

The F-22 helps to mitigate the access problem of not being able to move large numbers of mostly strike fighters into the theater safely and quickly, including the substantial support necessary for sustained air operations. The U.S. can usually be assured of having a small number of fighters in a region such as those peacetime deployments in South Korea and Saudi Arabia. The F-22 allows the United States to leapfrog the access constraints for large numbers of fighters by importing its strike capability from outside the theater through enabling or leveraging the capabilities of otherwise limited theater strike assets such as non-stealth long-range bombers. The reason that the F-22 is the only fighter to perform this function is because it can handle, at once, the air superiority, lethal SEAD, and time-urgent, air-to-ground missions. Different specialized aircraft were once required for these functions—today they are all wrapped together in the F-22's twenty-first century capabilities.

The F-22 was developed to establish and maintain aggressive air superiority. By combining creative theater basing concepts such as shell games, small numbers of aircraft at multiple locations, and use of camouflage, concealment, and deception, it should be possible in most instances to maintain a small force of theater-based F-22s in the earliest days of a conflict. The point is that the aircraft is so capable in its air superiority role that only a few would be needed to enable long-range precision strike operations.

Carrier-Based Aircraft. Long-range precision strike aircraft and carrier-based fighter-bombers and Tomahawk cruise missiles used in tandem against a WMD-armed adversary could neutralize the enemy's anti-access operations against arriving U.S. forces. The cross-service synergies and complementarities could be essential in delivering the remote fires upon which expeditionary ground forces would be dependent. Air power debates of the past over the role of bombers versus carrier-based aircraft need to be precisely delivered into the trash can of "old think."

The United States faces adversaries with growing capabilities to attack the longstanding U.S. power projection strategy. To adapt appropriately and deliver America's own asymmetric blows to defeat the enemy's strategy, joint operations are essential. The operational synergies between long distance global response air forces and carrier-based tactical fighters and cruise missiles are important qualities of the emerging twenty-first century force posture. These aircraft can execute operations autonomously or in tandem. The operational synergies possible range across the conflict spectrum.

The value of cooperative bomber and carrier air operations could increase ordnance delivery rates early in a conflict while ground and air forces are deploying or are restricted from gaining access to regional bases by enemy access denial operations. Long-range B-52, B-1, and B-2 bombers could strike first, followed by surge air strikes from carriers for twenty-four to forty-eight hours. Once recycled, the bombers could strike the enemy again while carrier aircraft are repaired and turned for additional strikes. Widely dispersed Air Force F-22s operating in both air interceptor and suppression of enemy air defense roles could provide an extra dimension of air superiority in support of the attacking Navy and Marine Corps fighter-bombers. When armed and postured appropriately, the F-22 leverages both long-range precision strike and sea-based attack operations twenty-four hours a day.

Deploying long-range precision strike bombers and carrier-based aircraft together can strengthen the deterrent effect since aerial firepower is likely to be the determining element in land warfare. When striking enemy armored forces invading a neighbor, bombers and F/A-18s or other strike fighters can have a significant effect, especially if Joint STARS and Rivet Joint aircraft are available. Since these ISR assets are high-value targets to the enemy, combat air patrol by a mix of stealth F-22 and air superiority fighters from aircraft carriers also can be instrumental.

Similarly, surprise attacks against the enemy's WMD could be most useful in preventing the enemy from taking effective countermeasures. Long-range, stealthy, precision strike bombers could be most usefully employed before other forces deploy to theater, which would give the enemy strategic warning. If F-22s are over-taxed for limited periods, carrier-based aircraft could suppress enemy air defenses and conduct escort missions for non-stealthy B-52 and B-1 bombers.[40] Carrier-based aircraft can also support land-based surveillance and target acquisition aircraft (AWACS, Joint STARS, and Rivet Joint).[41]

The Global Reconnaissance-Strike Complex provides a joint strike mixing bowl that can be used to take advantage of cross-service synergies and complementarities. When retaliating against Baghdad's seizure of the Kurdish region around the city of Irbil in northern Iraq during September 1996, for instance, Air Force B-52s were escorted by Navy F-14 air superiority fighters to launch points for the bombers' conventional air-launched cruise missiles. Joint exercises also demonstrated the value of long-range bombers and naval air working together. In a 1993 exercise at the target range in Corsica, Navy F/A-18s first conducted SEAD missions. When B-1 bombers launched from bases in Kansas arrived on the scene, F-14s provided air cover for the B-1s penetrating to the target and delivery of their ordnance. A 1997 analysis shows that when two B-1 bombers join fifteen Navy strike fighters, the number of bombs dropped on the target set is increased by forty percent.[42]

Distributed Ground Combat Cells. Situations will arise in the future where air power alone may be unable to deal with potent military challenges. In these cases, compelling roles for U.S. ground forces in the theater may be beneficial, including (1) integrating with other Coalition forces, (2) filling in gaps and resolving ambiguities associated with remote sensors, (3) identifying noncombatants and fixing their locations to the extent possible, (4) securing points of debarkation for follow-on forces, (5) controlling territory for the time necessary to satisfy the CINC's concept of operations, (6) locating and neutralizing WMD, and (7) exploiting the gains achieved by long-range precision strike operations. To satisfy these roles, the rapid insertion of ground forces would be required. The new expeditionary force concept designed by the U.S. Defense Science Board in 1996 envisions light, agile, potent, and rapidly deployable ground forces. This is an

---

[40] Charles M. Perry, Laurence E. Rothenberg, and Jacquelyn K. Davis, *Airpower Synergies in the New Strategic Era: The Complementary Roles of Long-Range Bombers & Carrier-Based Aircraft* (McLean, Va.: Brassey's, 1997), pp. 49–82.

[41] Reuven Leopold, *Sea-Based Aviation and the Next U.S. Aircraft Carrier Design: The CVX* (Cambridge, Mass.: Center for International Studies, Massachusetts Institute of Technology, 1998), p. 11.

[42] Perry, Rothenberg, and Davis, *Airpower Synergies in the New Strategic Era,* p. 50.

---

enabling force in that it prepares the basis, together with long-range and carrier-based airpower, for the deployment of large numbers of U.S. tactical fighters and land warfare units. Key elements of this concept include a ground force that is distributed and disaggregated into ten- to twenty-man "combat cells." These "cells" would be empowered by battle dominant knowledge, supported by precision logistics, connected by robust communications, and dependent on remote fires from long-range precision strike aircraft that are effective against a variety of targets. By deploying the right suite of weapons, the enemy can be attacked when he presents the most lucrative targets and when they are most vulnerable.

The expeditionary force would contribute to halting the enemy's armored assaults, demilitarizing enemy WMD, and securing the in-theater ports of debarkation essential to deployment of U.S. forces. When necessary, the combat cells would coalesce into larger units. The concept is more about "massing fires, not forces" and extensive use of unmanned vehicles and robotics than traditional ground units and equipment. Low profile, responsive logistics provides the essential force sustaining consummables.

C4ISR capabilities that are focused on enabling land warfare can provide a comprehensive combat identification of the ground environment. This perspective can be created by fusing high resolution, multispectral, and geometrically diverse data from multiple sensors on a variety of platforms from satellites, aircraft, and unmanned aerial vehicles (UAV) to unattended ground sensors and micro air vehicles.

A robust information infrastructure is at the foundation of the expeditionary ground force concept. Multi-tiered communications networks of geosynchronous and low earth satellites, aircraft, and UAVs are essential. The personal information ensembles used by combat cell members will provide paging, conferencing, and imaging services. The wide band communication networks will enable the CINC to maintain centralized control and stay in the loop of the combat cell activities and, at the same time, give the on-the-scene freedom of action necessary to exploit enemy vulnerabilities. The command relationships that will permit the requisite freedom on the ground while giving the CINC enough information to direct long-range, precision strike air operations to halt invading forces and destroy WMD need to be examined in great detail to strike just the right balance.[43]

---

[43] U.S., Defense Science Board, *Tactics and Technology for 21st Century Military Superiority*, Vol. I—Final Report, 1996 Summer Study Task Force (Washington, D.C.: Office of the Secretary of Defense, October 1996).

The distributed ground combat cells are key components of the Global Reconnaissance-Strike Complex. Taking advantage of advances in C4ISR and precision weapons delivered from a long distance, the distributed combat cells can make significant contributions toward satisfying the halt and enable operational concept.

Theater Missile and Air Defenses. Theater missile defenses will be critical in future transoceanic deployments of American military power. With adversaries armed with WMD and the missiles to deliver them with sufficient accuracy at locations where U.S. and allied forces concentrate, effective missile defenses will be important capabilities for early force deployments into overseas theaters. Theater missile defenses will be needed to protect U.S. forces deployed to the crisis area; reassure coalition allies of the American capability and will to protect them against enemy missiles; enable U.S. reinforcements to pass through protected debarkation ports, airfields and staging areas; and assure timely air and sea transport to the crisis zone. Among the early arrivers in need of protection are aircraft carriers and other ships, IS/AEF expeditionary force and other ISR elements, F-22 air superiority fighters, and distributed ground combat cells.

In Northeast Asia, for example, a significant number of U.S. forces are at risk: about 35,000 U.S. military personnel and their families and 100 Air Force aircraft in South Korea; some 24,000 personnel are at risk in Japan along with seventy-eight Air Force aircraft and a Navy aircraft carrier battle group; and 29,000 troops and seventy Air Force aircraft are based in Okinawa. Sea-based upper tier and theater wide ballistic missile defenses promise to provide a significant reduction of those risks. Yet, threats from missile attacks cannot be eliminated. Significant questions remain open about the effectiveness of the U.S. missile defenses in terms of the number of enemy warheads that can penetrate the defenses and hit their designated targets.[44]

While the Defense Department has a multi-tiered array of missile defenses to protect troops overseas, much of it will not be fielded, at best, until sometime between 2005 and 2010. In the mid-1990s, according to a panel of military experts reporting in March 1998, the theater missile programs were plagued by a lack of aggressive management, too few tests, and unnecessarily tight schedules.[45]

---

[44] "Navy Theater Air Defense," Briefing at the National Defense University Foundation Breakfast Seminar (Washington, D.C.: Capitol Hill Club, May 2, 1996). Photocopy.

[45] Landay, "U.S. Missile Defense Drifting Off Target."

These difficulties mean that the theater missile defense component of the Complex may be a long time in coming. Meanwhile, this lack of robust theater missile defenses has opened a "window of opportunity" to countries wishing to exploit the time and access dependencies of the U.S. military strategy. With about $50 million, according to one Army study, a hostile non-Western country could equip itself with two fighter aircraft, four attack helicopters, ten utility helicopters, fifteen ballistic missiles with three launchers, 100 reconnaissance drones, and more than 100 off-of-the-shelf cruise missiles. Such capabilities make the U.S. armed forces, with a wealth of modern weapons, vulnerable to a "poor man's force." The Army report says that, "theater missiles, particularly when armed with a weapon of mass destruction, make it possible for a potential enemy to drive the cost of military action to a level where the United States may not be able to afford the political, diplomatic, and human price."[46]

There is no silver bullet solution to satisfying the theater defense mission. A range of tools with complementary capabilities are needed. As the menace of WMD-tipped ballistic and cruise missiles grows, active defenses should consist of space, air, ground, and sea-based systems, plus robust passive defense capabilities. The U.S. defensive posture must be based on achieving a very low leakage of enemy warheads through the theater protective shield. Yet, this level of protection is difficult to achieve and even harder to prove. This means that regional friends and allies of the United States may be reluctant to grant American forces access while the enemy is armed with WMD and the means to deliver them. Hence, even greater importance should be given to the urgent counterforce operations against an enemy's WMD, ballistic and cruise missiles, and strike aircraft.

A New Strategy Compass

The current U.S. conventional military strategy reeks of Cold War thinking and outdated concepts. A strong reluctance to reorient the nation's armed forces in new directions is evident throughout the Pentagon. The 1997 QDR validated the reluctance to change. Wishful thinking and the use of unrealistic planning assumptions has created a "Potemkin" strategy bound to collapse on its own faulty assumptions. Budget constraints reinforce the bunker mentality of hunkering down until the threatening fiscal barrage subsides.

---

[46] As quoted in Sandra I. Meadows, "Multi-Tiered Plan Aims at Thwarting Attacks on Battlefield, Continental U.S.," *National Defense* (May/June 1997), p.18.

Meanwhile, WMD proliferators are going about their business of unravelling the U.S. conventional strategy. In Washington, the military risks are ignored in the wonderland of a declared "strategic lull."

Redirecting U.S. strategy toward deterring and, if necessary, fighting and winning conventional-WMD conflicts will face some tough sledding in the face of those who simply want to stand pat. The burden of proof is placed on those who counsel change to meet the new threats and risks of WMD proliferation. Those seeking evidence for the strategy recommendations in this chapter need to look no further than Part II, which provides the details of global WMD proliferation, and Part III, which explains the profound implications of these deadly weapons on the current U.S. conventional strategy.

The Global Reconnaissance-Strike Complex is a simple mixing bowl concept that seeks to find the most feasible blend of offensive and defensive military forces to satisfy U.S. objectives. A combination of outstanding C4ISR capabilities, heavy bombers, precision strike weapons, carrier-based aircraft, distributed ground combat cells, and the stealth multi-role F-22 fighter enables long-range precision strike operations early in a conflict. The employment of strike platforms from bases beyond the lethal threat envelope of the enemy's WMD-tipped missile systems is necessitated by risks of no warning attacks and denial operations blocking U.S. entry to the region.

Secondly, the Global Reconnaissance-Strike Complex ensures an appropriate offense-defense balance tailored to the realities of the asymmetrical WMD threat to U.S. military strategy. During the Cold War, United States military doctrine and posture evolved to one that was wholly offensively oriented for nuclear contingencies and mostly defensively oriented for conventional conflicts. Offense and defense complement each other and are mutually reinforcing. Offensive capabilities can discourage aggression by denying quick victory while theater defenses can deny the full impact of enemy anti-access attacks designed to keep American military forces at bay for as long as possible. Balanced offense and defense capabilities should be developed as a central doctrinal and force structure concern in an integrated WMD-conventional strategy for the new era.[47]

---

[47] U.S., Commission on Integrated Long-Term Strategy, *The Furture of Containment,* p. 50, and Fred C. Ikle and Albert Wohlstetter, co-chairmen, *Discriminate Deterrence,* Report of the Commission on Integrated Long-Term Strategy (Washington, D.C.: Government Printing Office, June 1988), p. 65.

The current U.S. conventional strategy will not work against WMD-armed adversaries. An integrated conventional-WMD strategy, given life through a Global Reconnaissance-Strike Complex that assembles existing forces and those about to enter production, will work and mitigate the current military risks facing the United States. Force modernization and force structure adjustments are needed and can be realized by shifting defense resources from those forces arriving late in overseas theaters to those capable of early deployment to counter cross-border operations and neutralize the enemy's anti-access capabilities.

A less often stated moral imperative also drives the conclusion that the U.S. needs to strike the offending forces as early as possible from the initiation of hostilities: the sheer number of human casualties resulting from biological and chemical attacks, and perhaps even nuclear strikes, could number in the thousands, even tens of thousands. In the face of such threats, the United States cannot stand pat.

CHAPTER 13

Getting From Here To There

The United States needs to arm and organize itself differently from the Cold War and the transitional and somewhat confusing decade of the 1990s. New modernization guidelines are needed to shift military force structure toward an integrated conventional-WMD strategy for the early twenty-first century. Fundamentally, the United States needs to do two things. First, stop spending on military forces to support yesterday's conventional military strategy that offer marginal contributions to regional security in the new era. Secondly, start investing in the forces necessary to make the Global Reconnaissance-Strike Complex a practical centerpiece for revitalizing America's transoceanic power projection strategy. The halt and enable operational concept—stop the enemy's armored aggression and neutralize the adversary's WMD and advanced conventional military capabilities for denying U.S. forces access to overseas theaters—should provide the primary criteria for making modernization decisions and sizing military forces.

America's global strike capabilities are woefully inadequate for the tasks necessary to confront and defeat the strategic impact of WMD proliferation. Large gaps exist in the American capacity to project military forces across the oceans in a timely and effective way. With the current force structure, for example, the United States and its allies have no choice but to plan on losing the first battle. According to this "strategy," a subsequent buildup of U.S. ground, air, and maritime forces in the region eventually will provide the capacity to launch a counter-offensive, re-take lost territory, and restore the status quo ante. The United States needs to shift its thinking from accepting early defeat to winning the next first battle. Weapons of mass destruction and advanced conventional weapons in the hands of future adversaries could make the next first battle rapidly paced and very deadly—unless the United States adopts the right strategy and puts together the right force structure, it could also be the last battle. Modernization options needed to fight and win the next first battle are being left by the

---

wayside by the Pentagon because they conflict with the current strategy of accepting early defeat, building up forces, and launching a counter attack.

With a tip of the hat to the "contribution" of the heavy bombers to the current conventional strategy, for example, the Defense Department defines the "key" to success in halting armored invasions as being "land-based and carrier-based aircraft to interdict."[1] Yet, the presence of any significant WMD and advanced conventional weapons arsenal in an overseas theater would require the U.S. commanders to rethink their concepts of operation in terms of how they would deploy forces to the region and employ those air, ground, and maritime components most effectively. According to General Charles A. Horner, the air commander during the Persian Gulf War, "the proliferation of WMD and ballistic missiles means that our current strategy of pouring thousands of fighters and hundreds of thousands of troops into our enemy's back yard is no longer viable. The best hedge against the emerging threat is to shift as much of the power projection burden as we can—as fast as we can—to long-range systems able to fight effectively from beyond WMD range."[2] Or, as so bluntly put by Major General J. P. McConnell in the late 1950s over the prospect of fighter forces replacing long-range bombers for some missions: "Who owns the real estate that you plan to launch your force from? End of briefing!"[3]

One would think that the growing military risks resulting from attempts to employ short-range tactical fighters against armored forces spearheading an invasion by WMD-armed adversaries would prompt a shift in the operational approach and the forces employed. Nothing could be further from the truth. Congressman Duncan Hunter lamented in April 1998 that the United States planned on spending $350 billion through 2012 on tactical aircraft but "not a dime on procurement of long-range aircraft." General Larry Welch, former Air Force chief-of-staff, told the House Subcommittee on Military Procurement in April 1998 that "we could find nothing that we would call a long-term blueprint for the bomber force."[4] Indeed, the Defense Department's

---

[1] William J. Perry, Secretary of Defense, *Annual Report to the President and the Congress* (Washington, D.C.: Government Printing Office, 1996), p. 172.

[2] Horner, "What We Should Have Learned in Desert Storm But Didn't," pp. 53–54.

[3] General McConnell was chief of plans at the Strategic Air Command when he made these remarks. As quoted by Rudolph C. Koller, Jr., "Letters to the Editor," *Armed Forces Journal International* (October 1997), p. 4.

[4] U.S., House of Representatives, National Security Committee, Military Procurement Subcommittee, "Hearing on the Report of the Long-Range Airpower Review Panel" (April 1, 1998).

The New Face of War

preference for tactical fighters had trumped long-range bombers, sweeping them from all but a very modest modernization consideration.[5]

The difficulty is that, if surprise attack (a lack of strategic warning) and/ or enemy anti-access operations preclude a timely deployment of tactical fighters to the theater and its littoral waters, the U.S. military's default position is "no go" due to a lack of sufficient numbers of modern attack platforms. And if the U.S. continues its current approach of deemphasizing their capabilities in order to protect tactical fighter programs, long-range bombers would also be placed in a "no go" default position for want of imagination, doctrine, modern aircraft, and munitions. The United States has a glaring gap in its long-range precision strike capabilities, one resulting from inattention and an unwillingness to transform the nation's heavy bombers into the point of a spear for plausible regional scenarios against WMD-armed adversaries.

Quick response, urgent counterforce capabilities are necessary to satisfy an integrated conventional-WMD strategy. Only air power, and long-range precision strike in particular, can meet the required timelines for effective counter-military attack early in a conflict. There can be little doubt that the United States faces a significant global strike gap. Fundamentally, the options for restructuring the current force are limited to direct-attack, precision-equipped, non-stealthy bombers; cruise missile-equipped, non-stealthy bombers; and direct attack, precision-equipped, stealth bombers. How many long-range strike platforms are needed to satisfy the invasion-halting and force deployment-enabling objectives of the "halt and enable" operational concept? In order to create a viable Global Reconnaissance-Strike Complex, what would be the most effective phased transition to fielding the requisite forces? What military forces should be reduced to free the resources needed to field the urgent counterforce capabilities needed in the opening hours of a conflict?

These questions suggest four major lines of inquiry: (1) bridging the gap in long-range precision strike capabilities through upgrades to the seven components of the Global Reconnaissance-Strike Complex; (2) developing a long-range plan for a follow-on bomber (2016-2030); (3) defining the functional and organizational changes necessary to enact and facilitate the

---

[5] Upgrades of conventional bombers in 1998 were designed to keep them capable of employing the latest munitions and the ability to communicate with other forces. The B-52 and B-1 were being outfitted to deliver weapons in low-threat environments, including standoff munitions. See Cohen, *Annual Report to the President and the Congress* (1998), p. 38.

---

halt and enable operational concept; and (4) creating a framework for force structure tradeoffs to free resources for investment in the capabilities needed to revitalize America's capacity for timely projection of military power to troubled theaters overseas.[6]

Bridging the Global Strike Gap

The Global Reconnaissance-Strike Complex can be built in the near-term by jury-rigging current forces into long-range precision strike packages designed to halt armored invasion forces and neutralize enemy anti-access forces, enabling the timely deployment of U.S. troops and land- and carrier-based fighters to overseas theaters. To do better with existing forces, the strengths of high quality systems must leverage those with lesser qualities to produce greater contributions. The synergy and complementarity offered by the Global Reconnaissance-Strike Complex system-of-systems architecture will provide the needed capabilities. The subarchitectures for each element of the Complex provide useful decision-making frameworks for making force structure choices.

C4ISR. The U.S. armed forces are entering an information era where space-based systems are no longer considered as supporting functions for military operations but as critical intelligence and communication components of overall military capabilities. Space is rapidly becoming a vital national interest on a par with geographical areas of interest such as Northeast Asia or the Persian Gulf. As the U.S. becomes increasingly dependent on space over time, adversaries can be expected to exploit any vulnerabilities they discover. It is for this reason that the U.S. Space Command has developed a long-range plan for deploying a robust space warfighting system incrementally to protect military and civilian satellites in the opening decades of the twenty-first century.[7]

---

[6] A host of operationally based measures and investments will give the bombers greater capability in satisfying the "halt and enable" concept presented in the previous chapter: non-nuclear operational support for B-52, B-1, and B-2 bombers; all bombers capable of carrying the maximum practical number of the most effective munitions; capability to attack multiple high leverage targets per sortie by increasing the responsiveness of the mission planning system; assured C4ISR connectivity for battlefield awareness; better delivery accuracy for the B-1 and B-52 by improving the attack radar systems; and increase sortie rates through upgrading improved B-2 stealth maintenance and performance, mission planning, and additional support resources, especially at forward bases. See U.S., Panel to Review Long-Range Air Power, "Summary of the Principal Findings and Recommendations," March 1998 (Washington, D.C.: Hearings of the U.S. House National Security Committee, Military Procurement Subcommittee, April 1, 1998).

[7] Robert S. Dudney, "The New Space Plan," *Air Force Magazine* (July 1998), pp. 22–24.

The New Face of War

As a component of the Global Reconnaissance-Strike Complex, space forces provide the only means to attain wide area surveillance and reconnaissance to otherwise denied areas. The space-based C4ISR functions contribute to U.S. forces by maintaining global awareness of events as well as a means to command, control, and employ long-range precision strike forces and assess their effectiveness. Space forces make up the *reconnaissance* and *command and control* backbones of the Global Reconnaissance-Strike Complex—they provide the battlefield awareness essential for effective execution of the halt and enable operational concept.

Three space systems are particularly important to the Global Reconnaissance-Strike Complex: (1) the Space-Based Infrared System provides a single system-of-systems architecture of missile warning, missile defense, and intelligence applications—this multi-mission infrared detection system will provide timely information essential to effective long-range precision strike; (2) Military Satellite Communications provide medium data-rate communications to tactical forces worldwide—the Global Broadcast Service is a new element providing direct broadcast of digital multimedia information, including imagery and video from theater and theater interjection sites to users; and (3) the Global Positioning System provides navigation aids essential to current and planned precision guided munitions being acquired by the military services—the system will be used by all long-range precision strike elements.[8]

In the future it may also be possible—through a synergy of low earth orbits, geosynchronous orbits, and highly elliptical orbits similar to the Space-Based Infrared System—to position in space some functions now conducted on airborne platforms. The electronic triad of Joint STARS, AWACS, and Rivet Joint immediately come to mind as potential candidates. Migration of such systems from aircraft to space-based platforms would be of immediate significance to the Global Reconnaissance-Strike Complex and its long-range precision strike operations.

Long-Range Precision Strike. The 1998 President's Panel to Review Long-Range Air Power began a process to "recover" from the previous short-changing of long-range bombers in the CINCs' concepts of

---

[8] Cohen, *Annual Report to the President and the Congress* (1998), pp. 67–71; William Matthews, "Improved Space Assets Would Aid U.S. Forces In Persian Gulf Conflict," *Defense News* (February 23–March 1, 1998), p. 44; and Walter Pincus, "Pentagon Stresses Control of Space," *Washington Post* (March 15, 1998), p. A6.

---

operation, Joint Staff plans, and the Pentagon's modernization decisions.[9] In considering the role of long-range air power, General Welch, the panel chairman, and other members concluded:

- The Panel believes that long-range air power is an increasingly important element of U.S. military capability....
- The potential of the bomber force is multiplied by the addition of precision-guided munitions, both direct delivery and stand-off....
- The Panel believes that more attention is needed to exploit this expanded capability of the bomber force....
- In addition to their own attack capability, stealth aircraft can be employed to leverage the success of the rest of the bomber force and fighter fleets.[10]

The Panel's conclusions lead one to believe that a de facto decision already had been made in 1997 to abandon the bomber force and to rest the future of U.S. air power on short-range fighters. Indeed, one civilian "insider" working under contract to the Air Force during the Quadrennial Defense Review concluded that "in a nutshell, tactical air power...dominated the QDR."[11] One conclusion is unavoidable: unless the Long-Range Air Power Panel's recommendations, at minimum, are implemented, the U.S. long-range strike force faces near-term obsolescence and inevitable elimination from the American arsenal.

The Long-Range Air Power Panel's recommendations made it crystal clear that the bomber force should not be allowed to wither and die. "As these emerging long-range high payload attack systems are integrated into the force structure, there will be increasing demand for them," General

---

[9] The congressionally mandated Panel to Review Long-Range Air Power met to recommend how funds appropriated in 1997 for the B-2 might be best spent and to consider a the broader issues of long-range air power. Retired Air Force General Larry D. Welch served as chairman. Other members included Samuel D. Adcock, Senator James J. Exon, John S. Foster, Jr., Colonel Frederick L. Frostic, U.S. Air Force (retired), General Merrill A. McPeak, U.S. Air Force (retired), Walter E. Morrow, Jr., Donald B. Rice, and General Robert L. Rutherford, U.S. Air Force (retired). The panel's proceedings took place from late February through March 1998.

[10] U.S., Panel to Review Long-Range Air Power, "Summary of the Principal Findings and Recommendations."

[11] Paul Nagy, "One Insider's Look At the Quadrennial Defense Review," *MIT Security Studies Program Seminar,* rapporteur: Tim Wolters (Cambridge, Mass.: Massachusetts Institute of Technology, February 11, 1998).

The New Face of War

Welch expressed confidently, "the DoD [Department of Defense] needs a plan for maintaining the bomber force over the years through 2030."[12] The House National Security Committee agreed, stating in a May 1998 press release that "...the Committee directs the Secretary of the Air Force to report to Congress by March 1, 1999, on planned upgrades to the current bomber fleet, a funding profile for these upgrades, and a timeline for consideration of the acquisition of a follow-on bomber."[13]

The near-term U.S. bomber force consists of seventy-one B-52s, ninety-five B-1s, and twenty-one B-2s. Fifty-seven of the long-range bombers are used for training or assigned to an attrition reserve where they are kept in flyable condition and receive all upgrades. A total of 130 bombers—forty-four B-52s, seventy B-1s (twenty-two are nuclear capable), and sixteen B-2s—make up the primary mission aircraft available.

With B-2 production ending at just twenty-one aircraft, significant effort will be necessary to build precision strike capabilities into the two non-stealth bombers. Arming them with standoff weapons is one part of the answer; another response is providing them protection against enemy interceptors, surface-to-air missiles, and anti-aircraft artillery guns so that they can penetrate enemy-controlled airspace to the targets. These points suggest three conclusions.

First, the B-2 is best suited for halting the enemy's armored invasion since the delivery of an array of precision munitions requires direct attack where stealth is a premium in the face of mobile surface-to-air missiles (SAMs). Secondly, the B-52 and B-1 bombers are best suited for strikes against fixed WMD facilities and storage areas, which are more suitable for standoff attack. Hence, a rough division of labor is possible between the B-2 for "halt" missions and the B-52 and B-1 for "enabling" missions. Some amount of overlap is present in this general division of labor. The B-1, for example, could be used in anti-armor missions by delivery of munitions dispensers packed with submunitions that seek out and destroy armored vehicles. Some of the attacking B-2s could be assigned for suppression of enemy air defenses (radars and SAMs) to facilitate the counter-WMD and counter-military missions conducted by B-1 bombers. A third conclusion is a recognition that the F-22 will provide critical combat

---

[12] U.S., House of Representatives, National Security Committee, Military Procurement Subcommittee, "Hearing on the Report of the Long-Range Air Power Review Panel" (April 1, 1998).

[13] U.S., House of Representatives, National Security Committee, *Press Release* (May 6, 1998).

---

air patrol and suppression of enemy air defenses (SEAD) roles for B-52 and B-1 missions and B-2 daylight operations. How many B-52, B-1, and B-2 bombers and F-22 multi-role fighters are needed to create a Global Reconnaissance-Strike Complex that will be sufficiently robust to support the halt and enable operational concept in regions worldwide?

Halt the Invasion. Let us be clear about one thing: the B-2 is the most effective military option for substantially strengthening America's long-range precision strike force through 2030.[14] Since budget constraints preclude the production of a sufficient number of B-2s to protect the nation's interests, an aggressive and comprehensive long-range strike force enhancement program for B-52s and B-1s is required. The B-1 already has been shifted from nuclear to conventional missions. Avionics and weapon systems upgrades since 1993 have transformed the B-1 into a potent conventional bomber. As future modifications are made the B-1 will be capable of delivering a full family of precision and near-precision weapons.[15] B-2 upgrades also are necessary, and a replacement bomber must be developed and produced over the long-term.

The bomber force should be sized to execute the following missions from the United States initially and subsequently from regional bases such as Guam in the Pacific and Diego Garcia in the Indian Ocean: (1) *Halt* by minimizing damage and loss of territory by stopping an aggressor's invasion, and (2) *Enable* or facilitate the deployment and employment of U.S. theater-based forces by neutralizing enemy anti-access capabilities, including WMD and their delivery systems, air forces, anti-naval force capabilities on land and at sea, and air defenses. A great deal of analytical work has already been accomplished to identify the number of B-2s needed to satisfy these objectives. With some care, one can use these B-2 analytical results as a baseline for identifying the modernization needed by the current force of B-52s, B-1s, and B-2s.[16] Ideally, early success in the halt phase of the war could obviate the need for an eventual counter-offensive (and thus a massive theater buildup), although some lesser level of theater reinforcement

---

[14] The B-2 stealth bomber has two crew members, a payload in excess of 40,000 pounds, and an unrefueled range of 6,000 nautical miles (10,000 nautical miles with one refueling).

[15] John A. Tirpak, "B-1s for Theater War," *Air Force Magazine* (June 1998), pp. 27–28.

[16] The Middle East and Korea Peninsula provide two excellent notional scenarios for placing stress on the U.S. strategy and force structure to better understand the actions necessary to mitigate U.S. military risks. Plausible scenarios involving WMD proliferation are possible in other regions of the world as well.

The New Face of War

would be required. The strong preference for the B-2 in stopping armored invasions is based on its ability, as depicted in Figure 13.1, to spread numerous highly lethal submunitions from air-delivered dispensers in autonomous direct attacks at night. The B-1 could also deliver anti-armor munitions dispensers, although combat air patrol and SEAD support would have to be provided by the multi-role F-22 stealth fighter or carrier-based aircraft. The anti-armor force requirements are driven primarily by the sortie rate—largely the distance of external bases outside the range of the enemy's WMD-tipped missiles and strike aircraft—and coverage provided by precision weapons and their degree of tolerance for enemy countermeasures. Several analyses have answered the "how much is enough" question with regard to B-2s specialized in halting armored invasions:

- The RAND Corporation found that in order to render one division per day non-combat capable, sixty operational B-2s with the planned anti-armor weapons (Sensor-Fuzed Weapons) would be needed; this number could be halved to thirty aircraft by using advanced anti-armor weapons such as the Army-developed Brilliant Antiarmor Submunition (BAT).[17]
- BDM Federal examined the B-2s' armor halting capabilities in three Middle East scenarios: fourteen days' warning, surprise attack, and no warning combined with chemical strike against airfields. The planned force was found to be unable to stop an invasion in cases of surprise attack and no warning chemical attacks. In the absence of warning, for instance, forty B-2s would be needed to halt an Iraqi invasion of Saudi Arabia.[18]
- Welch and Associates postulated an objective of destroying 6,400 combat vehicles over thirty days to halt an armored invasion or about twenty sorties per day for five days. Seventy B-2s would be needed if they were based in the United States; forty aircraft were required when they had theater basing (Guam and Diego Garcia).[19]

Enable the Deployment of Theater-Access Dependent Forces. The B-52 and B-1 bombers will have a wide variety of conventional roles for

[17] Buchan, "The Use of Long-Range Bombers In a Changing World," pp. 432–34.

[18] BDM Federal, Inc., *Beyond the DoD Heavy Bomber Study* (McLean, Va.: 1996).

[19] Jasper Welch, "Bomber Forces for 'Cold Start' Conflicts," *Air Force Magazine* (December 1994).

Figure 13.1
Stop Armored Invasions

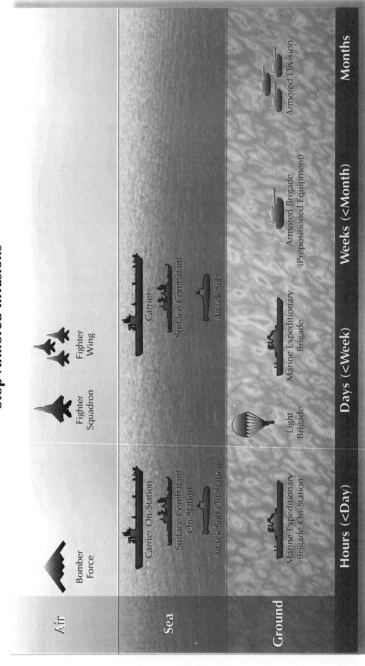

Source: Charles M. Perry, Robert L. Pfaltzgraf, and Joseph C. Conway, *Long-Range Bombers & the Role of Airpower in the New Century* (Washington, D.C.: Institute for Foreign Policy Analysis, 1995), p. 60.

The New Face of War

the first decade or so of the twenty-first century.[20] The B-52's conventional cruise missiles can be re-programmed right up to the moment of launch, which means newly emerging targets can be struck by re-directing the missiles while the aircraft are airborne. During the Gulf War, B-52s took off from Barksdale Air Force Base, Louisiana, to the Persian Gulf theater and launched conventional air launched cruise missiles before returning to Barksdale—a thirty-five-hour, non-stop combat mission. Thirty-five of the thirty-nine conventional cruise missiles were launched successfully for defense suppression purposes. They scored a seventy-six percent overall hit rate.[21] In September 1996, B-52s launched thirteen cruise missiles (another three failed prelaunch tests aboard the B-52s and were not launched). Of the thirteen that were fired, ten hit their targets.

The B-1 bomber has an integrated defense system with electronic jamming equipment, infrared countermeasures, radar location, and warning systems as well as a low radar cross section and the ability to penetrate enemy defenses at high speed. It can carry up to eighty-four 500-pound bombs and other munitions that require flying over the target to deliver them accurately. Plans are moving forward to equip the B-1 to carry twenty-four Joint Air-to-Surface Standoff Missiles and thirty wind-corrected munitions dispensers for anti-armor operations.[22]

The effectiveness of the B-52 and B-1 bombers, and cruise missiles, in locating and destroying weapons of mass destruction, countering conventional anti-access capabilities, and conducting offensive counter-air operations (airfield attack) is closely tied to the munitions delivered against the targets. The B-52 and B-1 will specialize in delivery of standoff weapons under the combat air patrol and SEAD protection of F-22 multi-role fighters. When they can be protected from enemy air defenses, the B-52 and B-1 also are capable of delivering a wide variety of direct attack weapons.

---

[20] The B-52 heavy bomber has an unrefueled combat radius in excess of 8,800 miles. The aircraft can carry up to twenty cruise missiles.

[21] *Putting Cruise Missiles in Perspective: A Comparison of Direct Delivered Ordnance and Cruise Missiles in Illustrative Combat Scenarios* (Arlington, Va.: SDS International, December 1996). Great credit goes to the aircrews who planned and flew the missions, and the vision and dedication to making the CALCM available offered by Major General John Borling, then the director of operations at the Strategic Air Command.

[22] Ronald R. Fogleman, General, USAF, U.S. Air Force Chief of Staff, "The Contribution of Long-Range Bombers to America's Deep Strike Capability," an address delivered to the Tocqueville Group in Washington, D.C. (September 13, 1996); Tirpak, "B-1s for Theater War," p. 31; and U.S. Air Force "Fact Sheets" on the B-52 and B-1 bombers.

Although best suited for urgent anti-armor missions, the B-2 also could conduct effective counter-WMD and counter-conventional anti-access missions. Several analysts estimated B-2 requirements to do the enabling function of attacks against WMD and other military capabilities:

- The Iris Corporation assessed the objective of striking 560 WMD aimpoints on one week and found that forty B-2s would be required when operating from the United States.[23]
- Welch and Associates found that a force of fifteen sorties per day would be needed to destroy the operational support for 500 enemy ballistic missiles in ten days. Fifty B-2s would be required if operating bases were located in the United States.[24]
- Burdeshaw Associates found that seventy U.S.-based B-2s would be needed to support the required nineteen sorties per day against Iranian WMD storage sites and missile garrison in five days.[25]
- Welch and Associates found that sixty to one hundred B-2s would be needed to support thirty sorties daily for ten days to neutralize twenty enemy airfields.[26]

Drawing from these analyses and adding a little "Kentucky windage," one can conclude that thirty B-2s armed with advanced anti-armor munitions would be needed to halt an invasion and another forty to fifty B-2s would be required to satisfy the counter-WMD and counter-military missions. It is unlikely the defense resources needed to expand the B-2 fleet will be made available. Yet, the requirement for a viable, modern long-range strike force will likely become increasingly urgent in the near-term. Thus, it will be of paramount importance to multiply to the greatest extent possible the capabilities of the bomber force, including B-52s, B-1s, and B-2s.

The United States can maximize the utility of the B-2 through technological upgrades and the development of innovative operational and organizational concepts. These capabilities will hedge against the B-52 and B-1 being unable to reach some targets deep into enemy territory or to neutralize

---

[23] Rebecca Grant, *Rethinking Defense* (Arlington, Va.: Air Force Association, 1997).

[24] Welch, "Bomber Forces for 'Cold Start' Conflicts."

[25] Burdeshaw Associates, Ltd., *Using Prompt Massive B-2 Firepower To Win Quickly, Decisively and With Few Casualties* (Bethesda, Md.: Burdeshaw Associates, 1994).

[26] Welch, "Bomber Forces for 'Cold Start' Conflicts."

The New Face of War

hardened and deeply buried targets (such as command centers) where their standoff weapons may be ineffective. Thus, a very aggressive enhancement program would be required for the B-2 to execute concurrent anti-armor and counter-WMD missions. Among the technological enhancements, particular attention should be given to producing more effective weapons, improving avionics to ensure a full battlefield awareness, maintaining low observability, and upgrading aircraft maintainability to increase its sortie rate. This course will require immediate research on and development of the next-generation global strike capabilities, with a goal of fielding a more cost-effective B-2 replacement by 2015. A lower cost, modified version of the B-2 (keeping the airframe and re-stuffing it with effective, less costly systems) needs to be built slowly from 1998 to 2015. In the meantime, a "virtual" expansion can be realized through upgrading the existing B-2 capabilities—especially a dramatic increase in sortie rates—and pressing the B-52 and B-1 into long-range precision strike operations.

The absence of a sufficient number of B-2s severely handicaps the development of a Global Reconnaissance-Strike Complex. Upgrading the B-52 and B-1 with standoff precision strike weapons is less than an optimal quick fix. Nonetheless, these three bombers could contribute to halting an invasion and conducting counterforce strike in parallel to enabling the deployment of short-range ground and air forces. The jury-rigged specialization arrangement of sixteen operational B-2s concentrating mostly on halting the invasion and B-52s and B-1s predominantly centered on interdiction against WMD and enemy anti-access capabilities provides a fundamental long-range precision strike force. This bomber triad is the minimum needed to underwrite a shift from the longstanding U.S. conventional military strategy to an integrated conventional-WMD strategy.

One extremely important way of expanding the capabilities of long-range bombers is to arm them with highly capable munitions. As RAND's Glenn C. Buchan says, "matching bombers and weapons is one of the most critical issues in structuring a bomber force for the new world."[27]

A Joint Family of Precision Weapons. As long as a target's location is known precisely and it is understood in detail, the United States has the technical capacity to destroy virtually any military-related facility in the world. Two kinds of weapons are of particular interest in developing a workable halt and enable operational concept—those needed to stop an aggressor's armored forces invading a neighbor's territory and those nec-

---

[27] Buchan, "Use of Long-Range Bombers in a Changing World," p. 423.

---

essary to demilitarize an adversary's weapons of mass destruction to the extent possible and destroy enemy anti-access capabilities to levels that will *enable* the introduction of U.S. tactical fighters, ground forces, and aircraft carriers and other ships. Air-launched missiles for standoff attack with high accuracy and lethality can underwrite many precision strikes deep into enemy territory with less risk to the U.S. aircraft. The greater the standoff range, however, the more costly will be the missile because of the complex accuracy improvements that would be required. This is an important consideration since conventional munitions effectiveness increases as weapon accuracy increases.[28]

Wind-Corrected Munitions Dispenser (WCMD). This is an Air Force system designed to get dispensers with submunitions close enough to their targets, including moving vehicles, so that terminal-guidance sensors will take over to produce a high probability of kill. Unguided munitions dispensers are unsuitable for high altitude delivery since the wind patterns can push them far off course and miss the target area. A tail kit installed on existing dispensers allows the WCMD to correct for wind drift. An inertial guidance kit, movable tail fins that pop out in flight, and a signal processor preserve high accuracy. The attacking aircraft does not have to overfly the target. When released at 40,000 feet, for instance, the WCMD steers to a target area nine miles away and about two or three miles cross-range. When released at 20,000 feet, the WCMD has a down-range distance of four to five miles and a cross-range of one to two miles. At 10,000 feet WCMD can guide the dispenser two to three miles down-range and about a mile cross-range. In addition to the CBU-97 Sensor Fuzed Weapon, the WCMD

---

[28] *Ibid.,* pp. 422–23. Long-range precision strike requirements can be effective with an array of specialized munitions designed specifically to neutralize or destroy specific classes of targets. The following four examples illustrate the growing non-nuclear lethality of American precision strike weapons: (1) *Advanced Unitary Penetrator*—This warhead is designed as a "bunker buster," which digs into the earth and explodes. The new penetrator weights 1,650 pounds and can dig twice as deep as its predecessor; (2) *Hard Target Strike Fuze*—This fuze is for use among weapons designed to destroy buried and hardened targets. The fuze is designed to sense voids, or air space, in chambers below the ground. The fuze counts rooms by sensing the voids as it passes through during penetration. The fuze is set to detonate at a particular floor or level underground; (3) *Joint Programmable Fuze*—This weapon's fuze has multiple settings on its delay before exploding (older fuzes have just one setting). The fuze can be programmed from the cockpit in some types of strike aircraft; and (4) *Proximity Sensor*—the DSU-33 sensor allows a bomb to detonate five to thirty-five feet above the ground, making it an ideal weapon for use against WMD-armed parked aircraft, vehicles, and other mobile equipment. The above-ground detonation allows the bomb fragments to be dispersed around the surrounding area rather than becoming buried in the ground. See Lisa Burgess, "Iraq Faces Much-Improved U.S. Air Strike Arsenal," *Defense News* (February 16–22, 1998), p. 14.

will be able to dispense the CBU-87 combined effects munitions (anti-matériel/anti-personnel) and CBU-89 Gator air-delivered mines.[29] The B-52, B-1, and B-2 can deliver the WCMD.

Sensor Fuzed Weapon (SFW). This wide area anti-armor cluster munition was specifically designed to attack moving vehicles. It dispenses smaller projectiles that fire *discriminately* at targets on the ground—under best-case conditions, a single SFW theoretically could disable about ten tanks in a single pass. Each SFW contains ten BLU-108 submunitions; each submunition contains four "Skeet" projectiles, an orientation and stabilization system, a radar altimeter, and a rocket motor. Each of these hockey-puck shaped projectiles forms and fires an explosively formed penetration warhead at a target using infrared sensors to locate a hot target such as tanks or armored vehicles. In sum, each tactical munitions dispenser contains 400 lethal projectiles. This weapon gives the Air Force an all-weather, twenty-four-hour, anti-armor capability. Each SFW released by the B-2 heavy bombers to halt an enemy invasion, for instance, could cover an area of about twenty football fields with forty of these top-attack projectiles. Since each B-2 would carry thirty-four Sensor Fuzed Weapons, 1,360 of the hockey-puck shaped lethal projectiles could be delivered against advancing enemy armor (the B-1 could deliver 1,200 projectiles). Eventually, all of the Sensor Fuzed Weapons will be equipped with the wind-corrected munitions dispenser tail kit assemblies. The potential load for this submunition is four in the F-16, twelve in the F-15E, ten for the A-10, sixteen for the B-52, thirty for the B-1, and thirty-four for the B-2 or eight more than the combined total of all three fighters and more than twice the carriage of the B-52.[30] If all sixteen B-2 bombers were fully loaded with SFW, the U.S. could strike the enemy armor with 21,760 lethal penetrators. This is an awesome anti-armor kill capacity.

Brilliant Antiarmor Submunition (BAT). This Army-developed submunition is a self-guided, anti-armor, top attack system that employs acoustic and infrared sensors. The BAT works autonomously to acquire, track, and home on to moving armored vehicles. Since BAT has a much larger

---

[29] *Combined-Effects Munitions*—The CBU-87 is a cluster dispenser weapon which includes both anti-matériel and anti-personnel bomblets. *Gator Mine*—This air-delivered mine includes capability against vehicles, light armor, and soft and relocatable targets. Tamar A. Mehuron, "USAF Almanac 1998," *Air Force Magazine* (May 1998), p. 159, and John Tirpak, "Brilliant Weapons," *Air Force Magazine* (February 1998), p. 51.

[30] Robert Wall, "The Devastating Impact of Sensor Fuzed Weapons," *Air Force Magazine* (March 1998), pp 28–32, and Mehuron, "USAF Almanac 1998," pp. 157–58.

"footprint," or area of coverage, than the Skeet submunition, it would improve the effectiveness of long-range bombers by a factor of two or three by reducing the number of aircraft needed to halt an armored invading force. The larger footprint makes BAT far less sensitive to enemy dispersal and vehicle interspersal than Skeet.[31] The BAT should be the anti-armor weapon of choice for bomber delivery.

Conventional Air Launched Cruise Missile (CALCM). This conventionally armed version of the nuclear air launched cruise missile (ALCM) is carried on B-52 bombers. The CALCM has a standoff range of about 750 miles, with a 2,000-pound warhead and a subsonic speed of 550 miles per hour. Each B-52 can carry twenty CALCMs. The conversion process from a nuclear to conventional role gives the CALCM an accuracy of less than forty feet of a precision aim point. Approximately 1,700 ALCMs were produced between 1976 and 1986. About 200 ALCMs have been converted to CALCMs and another 200 are available for conversion. Each missile is converted at a cost of about $150,000.[32]

Tomahawk Sea Launched Cruise Missile. Launched from submarines or surface ships, the 550 miles-per-hour Tomahawk has a cruise altitude of 50-100 feet and a range of about 1,000 miles. It delivers a 1,000-pound warhead or serves as a conventional submunition dispenser with incendiary, fragmentation, or armor piercing bomblets. Inertial and terrain contour matching guidance assures this $750,000 cruise missile precision accuracy.[33]

Joint Standoff Weapon (JSOW). This aerodynamically efficient, stealthy system is guided by an inertial navigation system and GPS. This glide weapon has a fifteen to forty nautical mile range, and it will probably comprise much of the early U.S. attack capability against enemy air defenses. It can disperse to attack fixed area and relocatable targets or dive onto the target with a 500-pound warhead. The JSOW can be launched by B-52, B-1, and B-2 bombers as well as by a number of fighter aircraft. The initial version will weigh about 1,000 pounds and have an accuracy of about

---

[31] Glenn C. Buchan and David R. Frelinger, *Providing an Effective Bomber Force for the Future,* RAND Congressional Testimony, prepared statement for the Senate Armed Services Committee (May 5, 1994), pp. 26–27.

[32] Bert H. Cooper, Jr., *Missiles for Standoff Attack: Air-to-Surface Munitions Programs* (Washington, D.C.: Congressional Research Service, Library of Congress, November 6, 1996), pp. 5–6; Tirpak, "Brilliant Weapons," pp. 49–50; and Mehuron, "USAF Almanac 1998," p. 155.

[33] U.S. Department of the Navy, "Tomahawk Cruise Missile," *Navy Fact File* (May 1998).

　　　　　　　　　　　　　　　　　　　　The New Face of War

thirty-five feet. The Navy envisions the JSOW delivering submunitions to attack fixed area targets, sensor-fuzed munitions to attack armored and mobile surface-to-air weapons, and a 500-pound single warhead with good accuracy against fixed targets. The Navy will buy some 17,800 JSOWs and the Air Force 6,000.[34] The JSOW gives the B-2 an autonomous direct attack capability at night by using the limited range stealth glide bombs in a SEAD role. By launching the stealth glide bomb against enemy air defenses to create protected penetration funnels for B-1s and other B-2s delivering anti-armor munitions, the JSOW adds an extra dimension to the Global Reconnaissance-Strike Complex.

Joint Air-to-Surface Standoff Missile (JASSM). This conventionally armed cruise missile is designed to attack heavily defended targets with high precision at ranges estimated to be about 180 miles with an accuracy of about eight feet. Launched from outside the enemy's area defenses, JASSM boasts automatic target recognition, autonomous guidance, precision accuracy, and a J-1000 warhead optimized for penetration and carrying a new high yield explosive. These characteristics give JASSM capabilities against heavily defended hard targets such as port facilities, hardened aircraft shelters, and underground command posts, as well as soft targets such as rail yards and roads. Production will begin in 2000 at a cost of about $400,000; the Air Force plans on buying 2,400 of these missiles and the Navy less than 1,000.[35] The JASSM can be carried by the B-52 and B-1 in conducting counter-WMD and other missions to neutralize an enemy's anti-access capabilities. The B-2 also can be armed with the JASSM.

Joint Direct Attack Munition (JDAM). The JDAM is equipped with a tail kit with an inertial guidance system and GPS guidance for general purpose and penetrator warheads, which will give it an accuracy of less than thirty-nine feet. The JDAM's accuracy is almost as good as the Laser Guided Bomb without requiring the delivery aircraft to overfly the target or wait for clear weather. This all-weather weapon solves the problem of weather-obscured targets that deny high precision from laser-guided weapons. The weapon will cost less than $10,000 each. The Air Force has ordered 62,000 and the Navy 25,000.[36] A 2,000-pound version will be delivered by B-52, B-1, and B-2 bombers (sixteen bombs) and the new F-22 stealth fighter will

---

[34] Cooper, *Missiles for Standoff Attack,* pp. 6–7, and Mehuron, "USAF Almanac 1998," p. 157.

[35] *Ibid.,* pp. 5–6, and Robert Holzer, "JASSM Winner Targets Extra Mission," *Defense News* (April 13–19, 1998), pp. 4, 26.

[36] Tirpak, "Brilliant Weapons," p. 53.

---

be able to deliver two of the 1,000-pound JDAMs. Small JDAMs in the 250-pound and 500-pound range could increase the lethality of the stealthy B-2 and the F-22, as well as the B-52 and B-1.

Figure 13.2 presents an overview of the value of selected precision weapons in satisfying the halt and enable operational concept.

F-22 Theater Enabling Fighter. The F-22 is revolutionary in providing the pilot superior battlefield awareness through use of a fully integrated avionics system. When combined with its stealth, supercruise, and first-look, first-shot, first-kill capabilities, the F-22 will be able to establish air superiority on the first day of conflict. The F-22 will play an essential role in protecting the "eyes and ears" provided by C4ISR systems in future scenarios as the enemy's capabilities to counter these U.S. systems increase. The aircraft also possesses an inherent multi-role capacity that will allow it to conduct comprehensive operations, including air-to-air, suppression of enemy air defenses, and offensive counter-air or airfield attack missions.

Simply put, a properly structured and postured F-22 force will establish and maintain an air dominance sufficient for a full scope of long-range precision strike operations. The F-22 counter-air and SEAD missions will create a protected environment for importing long distance bomber operations to the theater. In most theaters the U.S. has a small Air Force presence in peacetime. An emphasis on the F-22 mutli-role fighter in peacetime would ensure a ready capability to import long-range precision strike from the United States or from forward positions outside the reach of the enemy's WMD-armed missiles and aircraft. Hence, the F-22 could serve as an important enabling tool for long-range precision operations against enemy armored forces as well as WMD and anti-access capabilities.

Pointing out that "no U.S. soldier has been killed by hostile air power in over forty years," seven former Secretaries of Defense issued a statement in support of F-22 production in April 1998. "Even in a period of diminished threats, other nations will gradually overtake and surpass the fighting effectiveness of current U.S. fighters," the former Secretaries counselled. "Therefore, the stealth, agility, firepower and situational awareness embodied in the F-22 must be funded."[37]

In the final analysis, the F-22 is a key platform in leveraging long-range strike. It offers the opportunity to neutralize the enemy air-to-air threat

---

[37] Caspar Weinberger, Frank Carlucci, Donald Rumsfeld, Dick Cheney, Harold Brown, and James Schlesinger. "Seven Former Defense Secretaries Endorse Full Funding for F-22," press release (Arlington, Va.: Alexis de Tocqueville Institution, April 27, 1998).

Figure 13.2
Value of Selected Precision Weapons

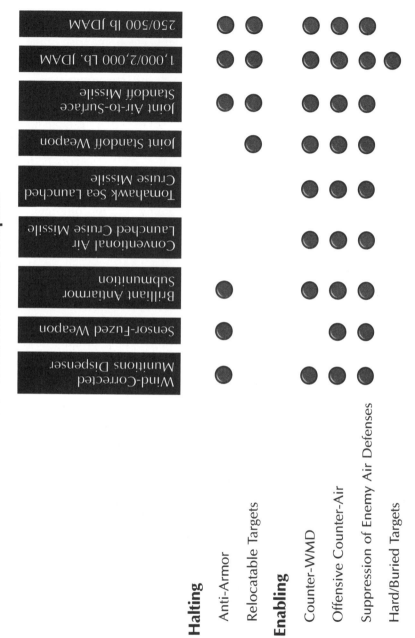

Halting

Anti-Armor

Relocatable Targets

Enabling

Counter-WMD

Offensive Counter-Air

Suppression of Enemy Air Defenses

Hard/Buried Targets

through an uncompromising air superiority concept afforded by a combination of stealth, supercruise, and integrated avionics. The F-22 can pin the adversary's air force down over his own territory, disallowing air cover for cross-border invasion forces. The F-22 creates a safe buffer for U.S. long-range precision strike forces and the airborne electronic triad of the AWACS, Joint STARS, and Rivet Joint. With an inherent capability for unescorted lethal SEAD, the F-22's combination of stealth, supercruise, and maneuverability will allow the aircraft to operate on air-to-ground strike missions in high threat environments as well as unescorted offensive counter-air missions (airfield attack).

Carrier-Based Aircraft. The operational flexibility, synergy, and complementarity between long-range precision strike assets and naval air needs to be fully exploited. Providing combat air patrol and suppression of enemy air defenses to supplement the F-22 enabling role for long-range precision strike is a particularly important mission. Over the long-term, however, offensive firepower in the fleet might be best concentrated in the delivery of cruise missiles. The closer aircraft carrier battle groups must press into littoral waters to enable strike aircraft to reach their targets, the greater the fraction of on board resources that must be applied to protect these vessels. This is a form of virtual attrition. It also increases the cost per sortie of weapons delivered from carrier battle groups against primary targets.[38]

The continuing proliferation of weapons of mass destruction and advanced conventional weapons and technologies can be expected to weaken the case for carrier-based strike operations over time. Until long-range precision strikes can reduce land-based anti-access capabilities—including ballistic and cruise missiles, patrol boats armed with anti-ship cruise missiles, and similar forces—the carrier battle groups may need to stay out of range. Submarines and mines also offer adversaries anti-access barriers that must be overcome to project American forces ashore. In the Global Reconnaissance-Strike Complex mixing bowl naval air helps to protect long-range precision strike operations and the B-52s, B-1s, and B-2s help enable naval air strikes by drawing down the enemy weapon systems denying the battle groups access to the theater.

Distributed Ground Combat Cells. This new expeditionary force concept focuses on the smallest fighting unit, the combat cell of ten to twenty soldiers or marines, to leverage remote fires such as long-range precision strike. These combat cells can ensure timely and effective precision strikes

---

[38] U.S., Commission on Integrated Long-Term Strategy, *Future of Containment*, p. 58.

The New Face of War

by fixing the location of enemy forces and reporting their posture when they are most vulnerable. These dispersed U.S. forces can also track and, when possible, tag enemy mobile targets with distinctive sensors to assist in targeting them by U.S. precision munitions. The combat cells, for instance, can call for urgent fires to engage fleeting targets such as missile transporter erector launchers. Battle damage assessment reports also can be sent by the combat cells.[39]

The on-the-scene ground combat cells help to ensure the effectiveness of long-range precision strike by fixing the location of targets as well as civilian populations to be protected. These "eyes and ears" on the ground can be very helpful supplements to the C4ISR complex by filling in details that will enrich the combatant commander's knowledge of the battlefield.

Theater Missile and Air Defenses. A critical combat mission is protection of U.S. forces, allies and friends, and other countries of vital interest to the United States from theater missile and air attack, including the minimization of the effects of damage caused by enemy attacks (passive defense). The problem with theater defense is the presence of a large number of uncertainties. The territory to be defended is not fixed. Threat scenarios vary widely, from terrorist attacks of a few missiles against urban centers to protracted military campaigns. The threats include long- and short-range ballistic missiles, low-flying cruise missiles, and modern strike aircraft armed with nuclear, biological, or chemical weapons, and advanced conventional weapons. The identity of allies where defenses may be needed are unknown ahead of time. Hence, one is unsure of the contributions to defense that they might make, the enemies that might be faced, and the capabilities of the missiles that might be in their arsenals. Given the unknowns involved and the potential uses of WMD, theater defense programs need to field the best possible capabilities quickly. These defense systems must be rapidly deployable. Protection of regional host countries may be a prerequisite to granting U.S. forces access to the country's seaports, airfields, and littoral waters.

Theater defenses are essential capabilities in the Global Reconnaissance-Strike Complex. While other elements of the Complex are centered on halting the enemy invasion and enabling the deployment of U.S. forces to the theater by neutralizing the enemy's anti-access capabilities, theater defense is centered on protection of the host government's capital and urban areas as well as seaports, airfields, and other facilities important

---

[39] U.S., Defense Science Board, *Tactics and Technology for 21st Century Military Superiority.*

for arriving American military forces. Since attack operations against the WMD-armed adversary's anti-access capabilities cannot be assumed to be 100 percent effective, theater ballistic missile and air defense (includes anti-cruise missile capabilities) systems are essential for the protection of the host government assets and arriving U.S. forces. The more effective these defenses, the less onerous will be the counter-WMD and counter-military operations designed to enable U.S. deployments. The "enabling" mission of long-range precision strike operations, therefore, is to draw down the enemy's anti-access capabilities to levels that can be handled confidently by theater defense systems. This is the epitome of the offense-defense synergy in modern warfare.

What Needs To Be Done. In order to bridge the global strike gap during the first decade or so of the twenty-first century, several upgrades to existing forces will be needed. Emphasis should be placed on low-cost, high-payoff modernization efforts—such as intensified development of precision munitions—that will produce the greatest synergies among long-range precision strike forces.

C4ISR. The battlefield awareness that can be achieved by a host of space-based, airborne, and unattended ground sensors will be challenged over time. To the extent possible, the U.S. should migrate its capabilities currently contained on airborne platforms to space, especially Joint STARS, AWACS, and Rivet Joint. Protection of C4ISR platforms against jamming and interdiction is essential.

Long-Range Precision Strike. B-2 bomber capabilities, following the guidance in the 1998 Long-Range Air Power Panel, need to be enhanced to strengthen both their near- and long-term warfare capacity. Enhancing the nation's current bomber fleet is the most cost-effective way of increasing their capacity for long-range strike. These enhancements should produce a "virtual increase" in the size of the fleet by increasing the bomber sortie rates and effectiveness per sortie. The Panel recommended improvements to enhance the B-2's maintainability, survivability, deployability, and connectivity.

- *Maintainability.* Decreasing the time needed for maintenance between sorties would increase sortie rates. The greatest benefits can be achieved by improving the maintainability of the aircraft's low-observable systems.
- *Survivability.* Observable maintainability and stealth performance will increase B-2 survivability and permit greater effectiveness per sortie even against improving air defenses.

The New Face of War

- *Deployability.* Enhancing the B-2's capability to deploy and operate from forward bases will reduce the flight time to target and return, thereby increasing the sortie rate. The shorter flight times will require less maintenance, further increasing sortie rates.
- *Connectivity.* Improving the connectivity of the B-2 will allow combatant commanders to get the most out of the aircraft. Updated target data, for example, could be sent to the aircraft en route to increase the lethality and effectiveness. Better connectivity would increase survivability as well since the aircrews would have a better situational awareness of potential threats. Decreasing mission planning times would increase sortie rates, and developing the most survivable aircraft routings would increase survivability.

In a letter to the Congress in March 1998, President Clinton certified that no additional B-2 bombers should be procured in 1998-99. Noting the recommendations of the Long-Range Air Power Panel, the President said that the "...recommendations for fully exploiting the potential of the current B-1, B-2, and B-52 bomber force, and for upgrading and sustaining the bomber force for the longer term...warrant careful review...."[40] Hence, modernization of the B-2 and procurement of standoff attack weapons for the B-1 and B-52 should receive priority attention.

A Joint Family of Precision Weapons. One of the keys to bridging the global strike gap is to match the highest quality munitions with the right long-range bomber. With precision-guided munitions—bombs, aerial dispensers with submunitions, and standoff weapons—the bomber force can readily adapt to new invasion-halting and WMD-destroying combat roles. Special attention should be given to four areas:

- *Enhanced Anti-Armor Submunitions.* In order to counter the enemy's countermeasures against aerial bombardment, such as dispersing armored vehicles over a wider area, U.S. anti-armor submunitions should be able to cover a greater amount of territory. The Army-developed Brilliant Antiarmor Submunition (BAT) should be adapted for aerial delivery while longer-term solutions to enemy countermeasures are pursued.
- *Cost-Effective Cruise Missiles.* Longer range, cost-effective cruise missiles could enhance B-52 and B-1 standoff attack capabilities,

---

[40] William J. Clinton, President, "Letter to the Congress of the United States" (Washington, D.C.: The White House, March 31, 1998).

especially during the early hours of an enemy's aggression. By being able to stand back and launch missiles, little or no F-22 support would be needed for some long-range precision strike missions. These two bombers also need to be outfitted with the capacity to deliver munitions dispensers and drop precision-guided bombs to augment the small B-2 force of sixteen aircraft. F-22 air-to-ground bombing would be needed in these second wave and later attacks after the enemy's air defenses have been torn down.

- *Precision Small Bombs.* All targets do not need to be hit with the 2,000- or 1,000-pound JDAMs. Smaller JDAM's on the order of 250- and 500-pound bombs can be very useful against fixed and relocatable targets, especially with GPS-aided accuracy. The B-52, B-1, and B-2 could carry many more of the smaller bombs per sortie and strike a larger number of enemy military capabilities.
- *F-22 Sized Specialized Weapons.* The F-22 possesses a highly advanced capacity to achieve a full battlefield awareness through its on-board sensors and connectivity to the C4ISR structure. This highly capable aircraft can already deliver two 1,000-pound JDAMs as well as its air superiority mission. By tailoring anti-radiation missiles and other special weapons for suppressing the enemy's air defenses, the F-22 could become a premier multi-role air defense fighter.

F-22 Theater Enabling Fighter. The Air Force needs to reconsider its entire tactical fighter modernization program in light of the Global Reconnaissance-Strike Complex and its halt and enable operational concept. A revitalized U.S. transoceanic power projection strategy hinges on the fielding of a dominant multi-role fighter that can do more for less, both in terms of dollars and theater presence. The F-22 is of such a higher quality than all other U.S. fighter forces that a smaller number of aircraft can replace the F-15, F-16, and F-117 inventory, as well as the prospective Joint Strike Fighter. This would not be a one-for-one replacement. A small number of F-22 multi-role fighters can allow the U.S. to accomplish its overall strategic objectives for much less—in both blood and treasure—than a much larger force of specialized aircraft. This leads to a recommendation to build between 500 and 1,000 F-22s and significantly cut the Joint Strike Fighter program.

The United States can field military forces in a high complexity mix due to technology. Budgetary remedies of the Cold War that emphasized high-low mixes, in terms of technological complexity and cost, do not necessarily fit the counter-WMD mission area. The proliferation of nuclear, biological, and chemical weapons, as well as advanced conventional weapons, and missiles has changed the threat calculus for regional conflict. Entirely new approaches are necessary to mitigate the risks imparted against the U.S. power projection strategy. Long-range, stealth, and precision weapons give the greatest value. The F-22 is a critical piece of the twenty-first century power projection puzzle. The United States cannot afford to make the same mistake with the F-22 that it made with the B-2 bomber.

Carrier-Based Aircraft. Ten aircraft carriers should be sustained as key components of the Global Reconnaissance-Strike Complex at least through 2015.

Distributed Ground Combat Cells. The distributed ground combat cells build on a host of new technologies to enable new concepts of operations and tactics. The subarchitecture for these small fighting units requires several enabling technologies: fires and lethality; battle management, command and control; information infrastructure; sensors and situation understanding; insertion, sustainment, and extraction; force survival; technologies to enhance exercises and training; and urban operations (including non-lethal weapons).[41]

The Defense Science Board task force examining combat cells concluded that it is a feasible concept but should be refined, tested and evolved into field capabilities over a twenty-year period. Extensive simulations, red teaming, and field experiments are needed to bring this capability into being. The possibility of leveraging long-range precision strike operations should be given priority attention in the testing and fielding of initial distributed ground combat cells. Initial units should be readied for deployment by 2005 or sooner, if possible. The real-time targeting information provided by the combat cells promises to make long-range precision strike operations more effective in quickly neutralizing enemy anti-access capabilities essential for the deployment of U.S. ground, air, and naval forces to the region.

Theater Missile and Air Defense. Intermediate-range missiles need to be destroyed in boost phase while the missile and its WMD-filled warhead is still over the enemy's territory. Higher altitude interceptors are needed for interdiction of enemy warheads in mid-course flight. Air defenses against cruise missiles and modern fighter bombers also are required.

---

[41] U.S., Defense Science Board, *Tactics and Technology for 21st Century Military Superiority*, pp. C-1/C-19.

Passive defenses need to be 100 percent. There can be no budgetary priority higher than protection of the individual soldier, airman, sailor, and marine.

Building a Follow-On Bomber

The Long-Range Air Power Panel recommended in its April 1998 report that the Defense Department should develop a plan to support and upgrade the existing bomber force. In addition, the Panel recommended the development of a blueprint for replacing the existing force over time. The approach envisaged would develop more advanced technologies that might lead to a next generation aircraft (a B-3) or a variant of the B-2—such as a B-2B—that incorporates upgrades to the current aircraft.[42] One estimate of the research and development cost for a new bomber runs as high as $40-$50 billion over fifteen to twenty years before the first aircraft could be delivered. If that amount was instead spent on the B-2, eighty to 100 B-2 bombers could be produced by 2010.

The U.S. needs to plan now for a bomber replacement for the 2016 to 2030 period. Despite the uncertainties looming over the long-term planning, the Air Force needs to decide quickly on which course to follow. Since the conduct of warfare will likely be transformed over the next twenty to thirty years as a result of the spread of the military technical revolution to non-Western countries, planners today need to have a vision of how future warfare might be waged. That is not an easy task.

Some in the defense community jumped the gun in their criticism of the Air Power Panel's recommendations for replacing the current bomber force. The editors of *Defense News,* for instance, missed the point by saying that the Air Force does not need a new bomber. "The United States can make do with its current long-range bombers," the editors opined. "The Air Force is extending the life of the B-52Hs through 2040.... Upgrades also continue on the B-1 bomber.... Further buttressing bombing the Air Forces's capability will be the multi-mission Joint Strike Fighter."[43] Who will volunteer to fly a ninety-year-old B-52 into conflict in 2040? Who owns the real estate from which the Joint Strike Fighter and other aircraft will launch from? Will there be sufficient time to deploy these aircraft and ready them to join the fight against the aggressor? Will they have to operate in an environment contaminated by chemical and biological agents as soon as they arrive?

---

[42] U.S., Panel to Review Long-Range Air Power, "Summary Report of the Principal Findings and Recommendations."

[43] "USAF Does Not Need B-3," *Defense News* [Editorial] (April 6-12, 1998), p. 18.

The New Face of War

Will host countries allow the fighters to use their airfields? Will the aggressor block the U.S. supply umbilical that runs though regional seaports, resulting in lesser munitions, fuel, and other combat support consummables? The editors got one thing right. The Air Force does not need a B-3. The next generation bomber should evolve through a series of upgrades to the B-2 to solve the problem of obsolescence that will improve its performance—a slow rate of production would add stealth bombers to the Global Reconnaissance-Strike Complex over time.

What Needs To Be Done. The country made a grave mistake in 1997 when it capped the number of B-2s at twenty-one. The "right thing to do" is to double or triple the B-2 buy over time. Unfortunately, this is extremely unlikely. Hence, we must turn to a host of second and third best measures to enhance the current fleet of bombers for the near-term and extend those capabilities into the long-range.

It may be possible to leverage the already expended research and development dollars for the B-2 in building a follow-on bomber. This would be especially useful since the nation's bomber industrial base largely has been eliminated. Using the same stealth airframe and low-observable technologies, the new aircraft could be "re-stuffed" with very capable system components, such as revolutionary avionics now in the F-22. This B-2B would cost less than the current version, which is optimized for penetrating advanced air defenses. The B-2B would satisfy the need for a bomber at least through 2030.

Adapting Planning Functions and Organizations

Global halting and enabling operations in the twenty-first century will rely on long-range aerial strike packages totally different from those experienced in the past. Adopting the Global Reconnaissance-Strike Complex as the centerpiece of U.S. military strategy means that it should serve as a guide to future concepts of operation, force development, and weapons procurement. "Are traditional organizational approaches adequate to meet the demands of the counterproliferation mission?," the late Major General Robert E. Linhard, the director of plans and policy at the U.S. Strategic Command, asked in July 1993. "Who should do the planning for direct military actions?," he asked. "When should planning be accomplished? Should options be preplanned?"[44] These questions are still open.

---

[44] Robert E. Linhard, Major General, USAF, "Counterproliferation Strategies: Countering Weapons of Mass Destruction" in *Counter-Proliferation: Deterring Emerging Nuclear Actors,* a Defense Nuclear Agency-Sponsored Strategic Options Assessments Conference Held at the U.S. Strategic Command (McLean, Va.: Strategic Planning International, Inc., July 7–8, 1993).

The basic problem is the continuing struggle inside the U.S. government between those organizations assigned geographical responsibilities and those given global functional tasks. The U.S. Strategic Command, sometimes inappropriately referred to as the successor to the Strategic Air Command (SAC), retains a potential role in planning conventional invasion-halting and counter-WMD enabling operations. Much of the planning needs to be done in advance to allow intelligence experts and aircrews time to sufficiently characterize the targets, locate key aimpoints, and assign them to the appropriate precision-delivery platforms and precision-guided munitions. The regional CINCs, however, are responsible for tasking forces to counter threats in their geographical area. Hence, a new organizational paradigm is needed to ensure planning coordination between the U.S. Strategic Command near Omaha, Nebraska, and the theater CINCs.[45]

Regional CINCs' Concepts of Operation. Forces, including people and equipment, carry out military or operational tasks as specified by a combatant commander in a concept of operations that ties together the weapons systems, support elements, and organizations necessary to satisfy an assigned mission. The CINC's concept of operations also can be seen as a road map for decisions on what needs to be done first and how best to do it when conflict begins or if directed to take military action in response to warning. In peacetime, the concept of operations is also a road map for employment planning, analysis, and force requirements validation. There are four steps to development of a CINC's concept of operations for dealing with WMD: (1) characterize the target, (2) task resources, (3) attack and kill (with minimum collateral damage), and (4) assess and report the results of the attack. The integration and harmonization of these elements is a function of the operations-intelligence interface.[46] This interface is as crucial given the WMD proliferation threat as the Cold War nuclear threat. The existence of WMD and the potential for anti-access operations directed at U.S. forces can have a substantial impact on the conduct of military operations. The CINC concepts of operation do not yet adequately address WMD

---

[45] The writer worked as a plans officer and special assistant to the commanders-in-chief of the Strategic Air Command and the U.S. European Command, experiencing first-hand the different planning approaches taken by global and regional CINCs.

[46] The operations-intelligence interface is the analytic process that (1) integrates intelligence considerations (target characteristics) with operational factors (operational tasks), (2) determines the degree or relevance the military tasks have to each target, and (3) compares relevant target characteristics with their operational attributes in order to provide an operations plan that supports the CINC concept of operations.

---

as a threat, in part because a fully developed operations-intelligence interface is lacking.

Characterize the Target. Characterizing the potential adversary's advanced weapons and WMD accurately is key to determining how best to deal with them. Especially important is the identification of the network of facilities and activities necessary to develop, acquire, sustain, and use WMD. This proliferation network can be used to cue intelligence, surveillance, and reconnaissance systems supporting preemptive or urgent counterforce attacks during wartime. In addition, peacetime target characterization offers clues about an adversary's intentions, helps reduce collateral damage, and allows rapid response to enemy actions.

Task Resources. The operations-intelligence interface is essential to bridging the peacetime function of target characterization with wartime attack and kill functions. Integration of all C4ISR support into the CINC's battle management system and making updated threat information available to decision-makers is an important interface role. The ISR systems play a key role in the tasking of resources to meet the specialized time constrained requirements inherent in many WMD targets.

Attack and Kill. This element of the operations-intelligence interface includes attack operations, theater active defense, and passive defense measures. WMD lethality, coupled with the speed of missile delivery systems, demands that the traditional means of selecting targets (that is, detect a target, make attack decisions, then attack) must be rejected in favor of a faster process of decide-detect-attack where the attack criteria are established ahead of time and an attack decision is preauthorized during peacetime. When wartime conditions evolve to the point that the attack criteria are fulfilled, the U.S. aircrews, missile launch crews, or special operations forces are directed to strike the offending forces quickly before they can be employed against friendly forces and populations. Reducing the time from detection to attack is crucial to WMD counterforce and active and passive defense operations.

Assess and Report. The last element in a CINC's concept of operations is the assessment and reporting process. Since future enemies can be expected to be armed with WMD and ballistic and cruise missiles to deliver them, it will be important to have accurate post-strike damage assessments. Good target characterization can help to define the criteria for making post-attack battle damage assessments.

Military action to locate and destroy WMD and their related facilities and activities requires special attention by the theater CINCs and at the national level. Military action against WMD requires substantially more planning and evaluation because of moral and political sensitivities surrounding such an attack, the potential consequences of unattended collateral damage (e.g., dispersal of hazardous materials from the target), and the potential lethality of WMD should we not take military action. Furthermore, there is often a limited window of opportunity for action—and an action delayed may be an option lost.

Counter-WMD Single Integrated Operations Plan (Counter-WMD SIOP). The Department of Defense holds a unique responsibility for developing plans and options involving direct military action. The armed forces could be asked to satisfy a range of tasks associated with weapons of mass destruction: (1) punish illegal proliferation and eliminate acquired capabilities, (2) preemptively destroy an adversary's most threatening forces, (3) deter the use of WMD that cannot be destroyed, (4) conduct urgent counterforce operations should deterrence fail, and (5) defend against WMD launched against U.S. forces and the militaries and populations of friends and allies in the overseas regions.[47]

A workable division of labor for nuclear planning was developed during the Cold War. The Joint Strategic Target Planning Staff (JSTPS), co-located at the Strategic Air Command headquarters, developed nuclear war plans against the Soviet Union and its Warsaw Pact allies and Communist China to satisfy many of the same tasks as those enumerated above, importantly including deterrence as the ultimate guarantor of peace. The theater nuclear CINCs, on the other hand, developed war plans for their geographic area of responsibility and coordinated them with the JSTPS to eliminate any overlap in the respective attack plans.

An analogous planning process could develop war plans against WMD-armed adversaries. The creation of a Counter-WMD SIOP would assure theater commanders of prompt, direct military actions against the enemy's WMD and WMD-related facilities by long-range precision strike forces from outside the region of conflict. The system-of-systems architecture underwriting the Global Reconnaissance-Strike Complex would allow more effective urgent counterforce operations without significant additional investments in invasion-halting and counter-WMD capabilities.

Two main target categories would be included in the Counter-WMD SIOP. The first target set would include infrastructure installations ranging from WMD research and development facilities to manufacturing and

---

[47] Linhard, "Counterproliferation Strategies: Countering Weapons of Mass Destruction."

assembly, as well as critical scientific-engineering and military manpower and forward storage sites. Committed assets, the second target category, are those WMD delivery platforms and munitions in transit to the battlefield for use against U.S. and other friendly forces and populations. Target characterization and selection of aimpoints in these two broad categories should be accomplished to the extent possible during peacetime.

Targeting WMD is a scientific-engineering task to achieve an understanding of the target's technological integration and to identify critical nodes for precision strike. On the basis of this scientific-engineering target analysis, the combatant commander could overlay the enemy's air defense architecture and assess the pros and cons of different ordnance choices. One of the most critical choices occurs when matching aircraft and munitions, especially when long-range precision strike can offer so much to a CINC's campaign plan in the earliest hours and days of a conflict. Data bases on WMD and advanced conventional weapons are essential to identifying the enemy's vulnerabilities from research and development through deployment to the field and launch. Attack plans can be created, awaiting essential updating during a crisis or conflict as the peacetime unknowns are transformed into known facts. As a crisis unfolds, key targets may be reprioritized as dictated by events and with special attention given to compressed timelines.

This dual track planning system offers an opportunity to develop and refine tactics, assign precision strike systems against specific targets, train forces and rehearse strike operations at unit level, and for sensitive high priority targets—including those that may threaten the dispersal of hazardous materials from the target onto civilian populations—the peacetime planning offers an opportunity to certify the aircrews or cruise missile teams to strike specific targets to minimize the chances of unwanted collateral damage.

Another reason for creating a dual track system is to involve the nation's political leaders in the strike planning for the highly critical and most sensitive WMD targets. The Counter-WMD SIOP would provide a means to inform the civilian leadership on the military strike options developed and to elicit feedback for final refinement and validation of the technical approach taken. These plans will encourage the military and civilian leadership to explore possible contingencies together and develop understandings that will avoid surprises should a crisis emerge or execution of counter-WMD strike plans is needed.

Today's regional WMD threat should be taken as seriously as the Soviet nuclear threat was taken during the Cold War. In order to elevate WMD to the level they deserve in the Defense Department, a national-level planning function should develop a Counter-WMD SIOP with separate annexes for each of the proliferating countries. The primary strike forces assigned should include the B-52, B-1, and B-2, air- and sea-launched cruise missiles, and available aircraft carriers. While the rigor and completeness of SIOP preparation to strike high-priority (most threatening to U.S. forces) targets would be planned jointly with the geographical CINC, sufficient flexibility also would be built into the planning process for theater forces to attack WMD and other military targets throughout the region of conflict.

The integration of the Counter-WMD SIOP and the theater CINCs' concepts of operation must be accomplished in peacetime and, when possible, the respective national-level and theater forces should conduct exercises to smooth their operational coordination. Distributed interactive simulation techniques should be used to train planners and command center personnel in coordinating attacks against the enemy's WMD and WMD-related facilities.

A Reconstituted and Restructured Strategic Air Command. On June 1, 1992, in haste, confusion, and in the midst of a national euphoria over the end of the Cold War, America disbanded the Strategic Air Command (SAC), sending the nation's bomber force into a status of being neither fish nor fowl. As clearly put by the 1997 Independent Bomber Force Review Commission, the Air Force merger of SAC and the Tactical Air Command in 1992 "was in reality much more akin to a hostile takeover." Dominated by tactical fighter generals, the Air Force subsequently denied funds for a new bomber program, reversed its support for the B-2, silenced internal advocacy for bombers, and eliminated "bomber-oriented officers." The Air Combat Command, as explained by the Gulf War air commander, General Charles Horner, ensured that the bomber-oriented officers were "funneled out of the Air Force."[48]

SAC's death knell left the nation without a bomber command for the first time since World War Two. Those responsible for the untimely death of SAC had their own personal agendas for eliminating the command. Leaving long-range bombers to die on the vine for want of a long-term modernization plan is a direct result of disbanding the nation's bomber command, SAC. The nation was ill-served.

---

[48] Scowcroft and others, *Final Report of the Independent Bomber Force Review Commission,* pp. 13–14, and Charles A. Horner, General, U.S. Air Force (retired), "Unmatched Survivability: The B-2 and Defense Entwined," *Washington Times* (June 13, 1995).

The New Face of War

With the end of the Cold War, SAC needed to be reorganized to place a far greater emphasis on conducting conventional operations. It was a big mistake to clean the slate so quickly. SAC was an icon of deterrence during the Cold War—it should be exercising that reputation today in new ways to dissuade today's proliferators and to convince them to keep their WMD holstered. SAC needs to be reconstituted into a twenty-first century organization that works closely with the geographical CINCs to ensure attack missions of the long-range precision strike forces are fully integrated into the regional concepts of operation. In addition, the restructured SAC would provide a single voice inside the Air Force to articulate the requirement for global precision strike.

In determining the future course of a Global Reconnaissance-Strike Complex, it may be helpful to quote the original mission statement of the Strategic Air Command as enunciated by General Carl Spaatz, the Commanding General of the Army Air Force, on March 12, 1946:

> The Strategic Air Command will be prepared to conduct long range offensive operations in any part of the world either independently or in cooperation with land and naval forces...to provide combat units capable of intense and sustained combat operations employing the latest and most advanced weapons.

It would be difficult to improve on these words as a mission statement for America's post–Cold War strategy needs. The United States needs a bomber command to deal effectively with the military threats looming ahead.

What Needs To Be Done. In order to organize the planning and operating functions for support of an integrated conventional-WMD strategy, the U.S. government needs to do five things:

- CINC war plans for counter-WMD operations should be integrated fully with the national-level Counter-WMD Single Integrated Operations Plan.
- A Counter-WMD SIOP should developed along the lines of the nuclear SIOP. Separate annexes or plans should be built for each WMD proliferator and transnational terrorist organization. The operations-intelligence interface, which is key to this process, should include representatives of the theater CINCs. National guidance should be developed to direct the Counter-WMD SIOP against specific target sets and others to be developed by the theater CINCs.

These two plans should be integrated for operational strikes against a WMD-adversary's entire military structure. To ensure bureaucratic wrangling does not sidetrack this initiative, the orders should be given by the President.

- The Joint Strategic Target Planning Staff (JSTPS) should be reestablished and co-located with a reconstituted Strategic Air Command. The JSTPS should build the Counter-WMD SIOP using (1) Navy aircraft carriers and cruise missiles from surface ships and submarines, and (2) Air Force long-range bombers and conventional air-launched cruise missiles. Other forces should be made available to the theater CINCs for execution of their concepts of operation.

- The Strategic Air Command should be reestablished as an Air Force operating command and a global long-range precision strike combat command during wartime. The U.S. Strategic Command should be disestablished. The new SAC should be a dual-role command to include execution of the nuclear SIOP and the Counter-WMD SIOP. SAC planning cells should be located with the regional CINC's staffs. The command should build a long-term bomber modernization plan. Other functions would include working inside the Air Force to field the precision-guided weapons and develop procedures for F-22 support of long-range precision strike operations, taking advantage of bomber and naval air complementarities, and wartime procedures for interface with distributed ground combat cells that may be in the field.

Freeing the Resources for Force Tradeoffs

The United States needs to change the way it fights wars, especially wars involving enemies armed with weapons of mass destruction and the means and will to deliver them. An entirely new concept of victory is needed. If the U.S. changes its warfighting strategy, it will need to procure the weapons necessary to execute the new strategy. This requires a political will to stop buying those forces we do not need and start buying those relevant to the new integrated conventional-WMD strategy where emphasis is placed on the early hours and days of the conflict.

The Global Reconnaissance-Strike Complex is supported by a system-of-systems architecture where long-range precision strike represents the core capabilities of a new strategy that masses firepower, not forces. *The New Face of War* asks Americans to dare to think that air power—long-range precision strike aircraft, carrier-based tactical air, theater enabling tactical air, and air- and sea-launched cruise missiles—can halt an armored invasion and at the same time attack the enemy's WMD and other systems posing anti-access threats to deploying U.S. forces.

Time is a scarcity when dealing with weapons of mass destruction. The "aquarium" graphic in Figure 13.3 offers a perspective on affordability and the weapons systems the United States should be buying and those of lesser significance in the new strategy. The forces available in a matter of hours are those maritime forces that may be on station or nearby and global strike aircraft. Tactical fighter wings and light brigades can be available within days to weeks; one armored brigade can be available in weeks or less than a month. Deployment of armored divisions, including support forces, would take months. In terms of cost, one finds that the manpower- and capital stock-intensive armored divisions are most expensive along with carrier battle groups that are not on station when a crisis breaks out. While tactical fighter wings in the aquarium appear to be cost-effective, they are dependent on theater operating bases and seaports and airfields for resupply. The existing military force structure reflects the traditional conventional strategy of giving ground to the initial attack, stabilizing the battlefield, building up forces, and launching a ground counter-offensive. Hence, theater-base dependent and late arriving forces are the ones that should be reduced to free the resources needed to create a robust long-range precision strike force. This means that U.S. force structure emphasis should be shifted from (1) ground forces to air power, (2) short-range air power to long-range precision strike, and (3) airborne to space-based C4ISR.

What Needs To Be Done. By continuing to invest in forces that do not account for the lack of strategic warning that allows insufficient time to deploy to overseas theaters and the anti-access opportunities that WMD and advanced conventional weapons offer regional adversaries, the United States exposes the Achilles heel of its strategy. Encouraged by such actions, adversaries are offered incentives to pursue asymmetric strategies vis-à-vis the U.S. transoceanic power projection strategy. The reality of potential regional warfare reflects a distinct shift (1) from close combat to long-range precision strike, and (2) from emphasis on a lengthy overseas build-up of forces and a land warfare-dominant counter-offensive to early precision strike attacks to halt the enemy's armored forces and to interdict his anti-access forces to enable the deployment of U.S. forces to the theater of conflict.

Five specific changes in defense spending should be taken to stop procurement programs for the military forces supporting the currently mori-

Figure 13.3
Perspectives on Relative Affordability

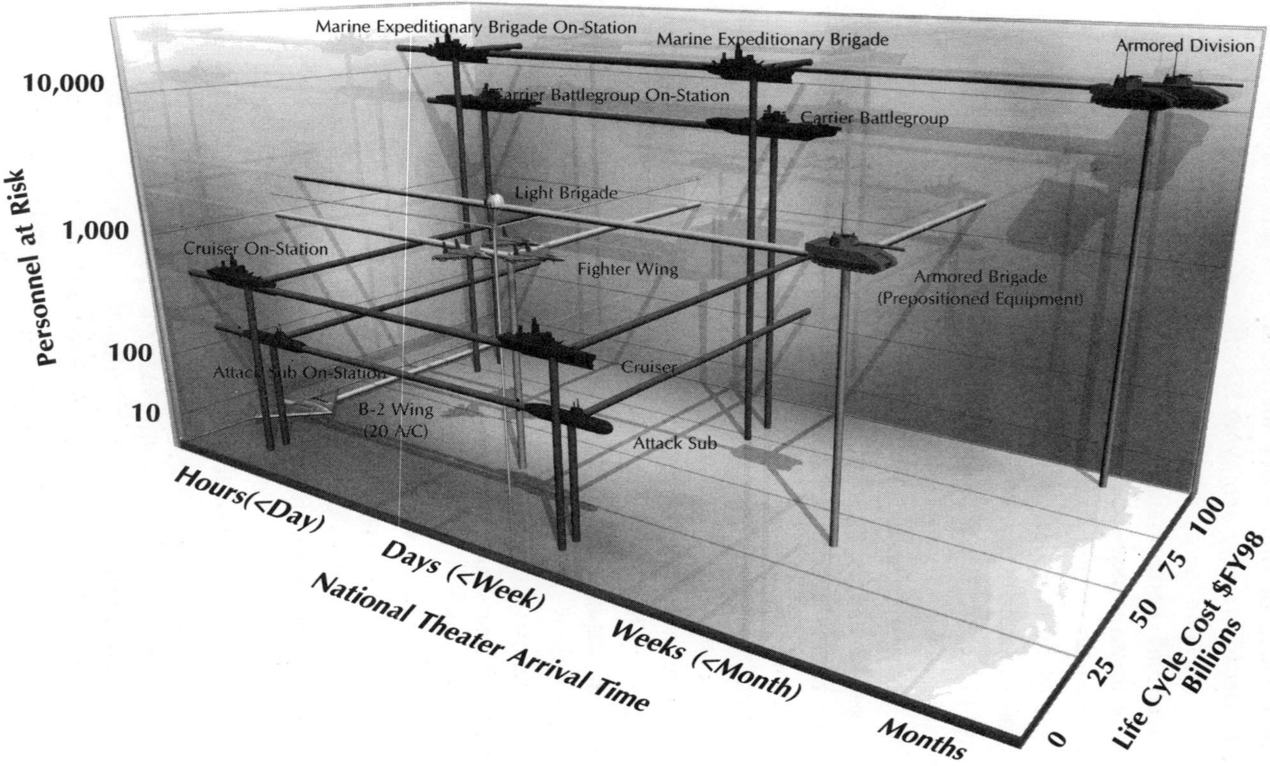

The New Face of War

bund, Cold War–derived conventional strategy. The resources freed should be applied to the creation of a Global Reconnaissance-Strike Complex with "first responder" long-range precision strike forces as the tip of the spear in a modernized conventional-WMD strategy:

- Cut at least two heavy armored and mechanized Army divisions.
- Reduce Air Force tactical fighter procurement by cutting the number of Joint Strike Fighters planned (protect and expand F-22 buys).
- Streamline the Pentagon staff by slashing numerous senior positions in the Office of the Secretary of Defense (OSD); the Secretary should place greater reliance on the uniformed Joint Staff.
- Reduce, consolidate, and reengineer the multitude of defense agencies that consume defense dollars.
- Close military bases with due consideration given to easing the impact of the prospective closures on the surrounding American communities.

The resources freed by these cuts should be reinvested in long-range precision strike forces—upgrading and expanding the heavy bomber force; developing precision munitions to give the bombers far greater anti-armor and counter-military effectiveness; producing F-22s for multi-role missions and weapons to match its operations; and moving C4ISR from airborne platforms to space. The Air Force should consider reshaping its tactical fighter force structure by reducing Joint Strike Fighter buys and moving toward far greater numbers of F-22s than now planned.

The willingness to make the suggested cuts rests on accurate perceptions of the military risks facing the United States and U.S. military capabilities. In order to create a more realistic planning environment in the Pentagon, two steps are vital.

- Abandon the budget-based planning currently used in the Pentagon in favor of an objectives-based planning approach that accounts for the military risks facing the nation—report these military risks accurately to the Congress.
- Adopt realistic strategy and force structure planning assumptions to serve as a tool for obtaining more accurate analyses—report the planning assumptions used to the Congress.

Reducing Military Risks

The Pentagon's 1997 Quadrennial Defense Review signs up to an outdated conventional warfare concept that is "designed to get the maximum number of young men and women within range of enemy fire as quickly as possible."[49] This strategy postulates that the U.S. and its allies will lose the early battles but, after giving ground, they will eventually hold against the enemy's initial assault and then build-up forces and launch a manpower-intensive land maneuver-dominated counter-offensive to restore lost territory.

> The security environment between now [1997] and 2015 will...likely be marked by the absence of a 'global peer competitor'.... Furthermore, it is likely that no regional power or coalition will amass sufficient conventional military strength in the next 10 to 15 years to defeat our armed forces, *once the full military potential of the United States is mobilized and deployed to the region of conflict.*[50] [emphasis added]

The main strategic challenge when confronting WMD-armed adversaries is bringing the "full military potential of the United States" to bear in time to be relevant to forces inimical to U.S. interests. It is no wonder the Secretary of Defense has been left hat in hand trying to close bases and find other ways to pay for this strategic albatross. Missing from the Defense Department's planning is a realistic assessment of the military risks facing the United States.[51] Also absent is a practical strategy and force structure to reduce those risks.

In its December 1997 report to Congress, the National Defense Panel presented the most comprehensive military risk assessment conducted since the Bush Administration. Despite the ominous warnings indicated by

---

[49] An unidentified retired Air Force general as quoted by Philip Gold, "What the Air Force Can Do For You," *Washington Times* (July 6, 1998), p. A17.

[50] Cohen, *Report of the Quadrennial Defense Review,* pp. 4–5.

[51] An eighteen-member team of eleven colonels, three civilian government strategists, and four government contractors conducted a force transformation exercise in April 1997 with a particular focus on technology and major changes needed in the military. They concluded that the U.S. should cancel its two-war strategy and cut three Navy aircraft carrier battle groups, three Army divisions, one Marine Corps expeditionary force, and six Air Force fighter wings. The savings would be used to buy twenty more B-2 bombers, 200 uninhabited air combat vehicles (an armed strike platform), five arsenal ships, and national and theater missile defenses, as well as other advanced weapons systems. See Jeff Erlich, "Officers Propose Counter to QDR," *Defense News* (May 19–25, 1997), pp. 4, 27.

these risks, no perceptible change has been detected in the nation's military strategy and forces. Here are a few samples of the risks that will face Americans during the first decade of the twenty-first century:

- **Politics:** "For political (domestic or regional) reasons, allies might be coerced not to grant the United States access to their sovereign territory." (pg. 12)
- **Geography:** "Geographical realities are putting greater demands on power projection capabilities. For example, as oil and gas fields in Central Asia gain in strategic value, we may need to project power greater distances, farther from littorals or established bases." (pg. 13)
- **Growing Anti-Access Threat:** "Hostile forces might threaten punitive strikes (perhaps using weapons of mass destruction) against nations considering an alliance with the United States." (pg. 12)
  - "Even if we retain the necessary bases and port infrastructure to support forward deployed forces, they will be vulnerable to strikes that could reduce or neutralize their utility." (pg. 13)
  - "...constraints on forward...basing and advanced technologies threaten to impede our access to key regions." (pg. 13)
  - Enemies could employ "weapons of mass destruction and ballistic and cruise missiles to neutralize forward ports, bases, and prepositioned assets and to inflict heavy casualties on us and our allies." (pg. 11)
- **Force Procurement:** "Current force structures and information architectures extrapolated to the future may not suffice to meet successfully the conditions of future battles." (pg. iii)
  - "The procurement budgets of the services are focused primarily on current systems and do not adequately support the central thrust of their visions. In light of these factors, the Panel questions the procurement plans for Army equipment, Navy ships, and tactical aircraft of all three services." (pg. iii)
- **Transoceanic Power Projection:** "In short, we must radically alter the way in which we project power...there is a high premium on forces that can deploy rapidly, seize the initiative, and achieve our objective with minimal risk of heavy casualties." (pg. 33)
  - "We must be able to project military power much more rapidly into areas where we may not have stationed forces." (pg. 33)
- **Long-Range Precision Strike Forces:** "Air forces would place greater emphasis on operating at extended ranges, relying heavily on

long-range aircraft and extended-range unmanned systems, employing advanced precision and brilliant munitions and based outside the theater of operations."[52] (pg. 34)

Despite an excellent framework for assessing the risks and designing measures to mitigate them, the NDP analysis was flawed by two glaring problems. First, the Panel bought into the Clinton Administration's view that the United States is in a "strategic lull" and that significant risks are unlikely to appear before 2015. Second, the NDP did not, except in the most general of terms, offer force structure choices to reduce the military risks defined in its final report. Rather, it offered a somewhat vague "transformation strategy" that would apply billions of dollars each year to advanced technologies to create a military force structure relevant to the threats prognosticated for 2015 and beyond.

The graphic presented in Figure 13.4 compares the threats and risks postulated by the Department of Defense and the National Defense Panel based on the absence of a "peer competitor" until at least 2015. A third risk assessment is drawn from the proliferation data and analysis present in Parts II and III of this writing. A combination of the ongoing proliferation of WMD and advanced conventional weapons and technologies, the shadow of Gulf War Syndrome lingering over future military operations, and the potential use of terrorism as a weapon of war lead to the conclusion that the United States will face severe threats to its current strategy at least a decade earlier than prognosticated by the Defense Department and the National Defense Panel. Thus, the idea that the United States is in the midst of a "strategic lull" is foolhardy, especially when WMD and advanced conventional weapons proliferation are intensifying threats to the U.S. strategy. The nuclear tests by India and Pakistan in 1998 expose the inherent weaknesses of the argument that the United States has until about 2015 to straighten out its post-Cold War strategy and force structure.

The threats and risks to U.S. regional security interests exist now, and they are accelerating. Current WMD programs in several countries will gain fruition around 2005. It is for this reason that the Global Reconnaissance-Strike Complex capability line in Figure 13.4 ramps upward sharply from 2005 to 2015 and at a lesser rate of growth until 2030. By way of comparison, the QDR capability line represents a simple linear extension of

---

[52] U.S., National Defense Panel, *Transforming Defense* (page numbers indicated in text).

The New Face of War

Figure 13.4
Long-Range Strike Force Enhancements

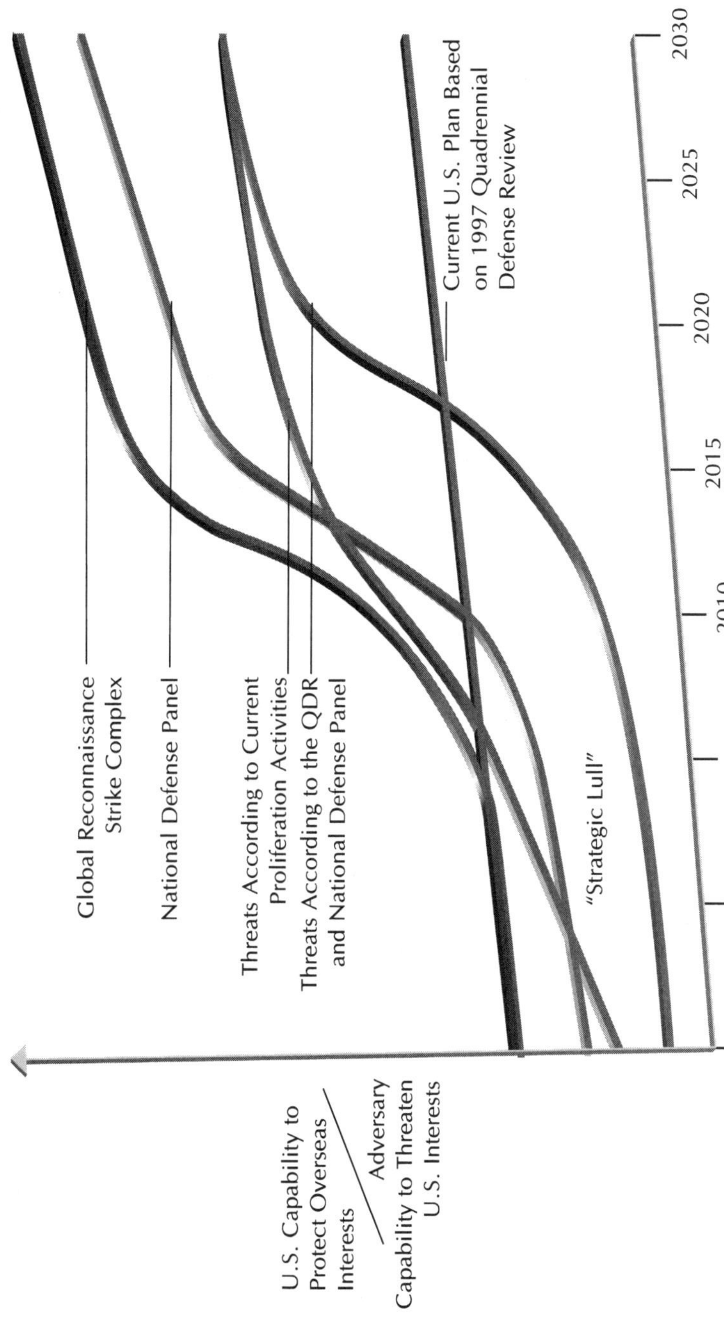

Global Reconnaissance
Strike Complex

National Defense Panel

Threats According to Current
Proliferation Activities

Threats According to the QDR
and National Defense Panel

Current U.S. Plan Based
on 1997 Quadrennial
Defense Review

"Strategic Lull"

U.S. Capability to
Protect Overseas
Interests

Adversary
Capability to Threaten
U.S. Interests

1995   2000   2005   2010   2015   2020   2025   2030

the 1997 Pentagon analysis, and the NDP "transformation strategy" line lags behind the Global Reconnaissance-Strike Complex by about five years.

By creating the Global Reconnaissance-Strike Complex in the near-term, the United States will be in far better position to mitigate the military risks associated with WMD proliferation and the spread of advanced conventional weapons and technology. In future warfare, long-range precision strike operations will be highly compressed temporally and centered on quickly striking the enemy's centers of gravity, including those that might allow the use of nuclear, biological, and chemical weapons against U.S. forces and regional friends and allies. The Global Reconnaissance-Strike Complex will make possible strategic attacks that will revitalize U.S. transoceanic power projection operations similar to the manner in which naval gunfire prepares the way and supports amphibious operations.

The bomber force has untapped potential in numbers of supported aircraft, payloads of the best munitions, target acquisition and delivery accuracy (B-1 and B-52), sortie rates, and survivable access to targets. In order to generate the sortie rates needed for the bomber force to provide the needed weight of effort for the halt and enable concept, forward basing and extensive support at overseas bases is required. To mold the bomber force into the cutting edge of the Global Reconnaissance-Strike Complex, the aircraft require increased operational attention, investment upgrades, and precision and specialized munitions with increased standoff, accuracy, and lethality against both "halt" and "enable" targets, including hardened and deep underground facilities.[53]

The Global Reconnaissance-Strike Complex breaks with modern classical warfare by advocating new conceptual approaches and enhanced long-range operational capabilities that will be relevant to theater warfare in the early twenty-first century. Americans have an opportunity to shape the future by freeing themselves from the shackles of yesterday's military strategy by daring to embrace a new operational concept that could save thousands of lives. Long-range precision strike offers an opportunity to turn the strengths of WMD-armed adversaries against themselves.

---

[53] U.S., Panel to Review Long-Range Air Power, "Summary of the Principal Findings and Recommendations."

PART V

The Eleventh Plague

INTRODUCTION: PART V

Tenth Plague: the Death of the First-Born

At midnight the Lord slew every first-born in the land of Egypt, from the first-born of the Pharaoh on the throne to the first-born of the prisoner in the dungeon, as well as all the first-born animals. Pharaoh arose in the night, he and all his servants and all the Egyptians; and there was loud wailing throughout Egypt, for there was not a house without its dead.

— The Book of Exodus

Like deadly clouds from the heavens, biological, radiological, and chemical toxins will be rained upon America's uniformed men and women in the next war and in the ones thereafter. Unlike the Lord's Tenth Plague wracked upon the Egyptians, the man-made poisons of the Eleventh Plague will be non-discriminatory, killing every man, woman, child, and animal in their path. Unless we find effective ways to protect America's military on foreign shores, we can be assured of a loud wailing throughout the United States as we mourn the fallen.

CHAPTER 14

Conclusion
Immunizing U.S. Strategy Against Weapons of Mass Destruction

Weapons of mass destruction have transformed both the tempo and character of regional warfare. As a result, transoceanic power projection in the twenty-first century must be conducted in a totally different way than in the past. For American forces to be successful, they must be relatively unaffected by a lack of strategic warning and by enemy anti-access operations in overseas theaters. To meet the exigencies of time and access in future crises and conflicts, the U.S. should shift its strategy toward a Global Reconnaissance-Strike Complex in which a long-range precision strike force is capable of sustaining operations from beyond the theater of conflict. High U.S. casualties must be avoided.

Military risks will increase as a result of an intensified competition between U.S. power projection and the capacity of regional adversaries to deny the United States access through threats and uses of a growing array of modern weapons. Despite the clear and present danger of the expanding WMD and advanced conventional weapons arsenals in East Asia, South Asia, and the Middle East, the potential operational degradation of U.S. military forces has been largely understated by the Pentagon. Biological and chemical weapons threaten the current U.S. power projection strategy through their potential for attacks against large ground formations, tactical air forces positioned at fixed bases and aboard aircraft carriers, and regional seaports and airfields. While some progress has been made in resolving these problems, significant gaps in our knowledge about WMD warfare produce a reluctance to shift the nation's military strategy in new directions.

Nevertheless, enough is already known about this new form of warfare to begin devising innovative approaches to regional security. The denial of the weight-bearing pillars of the current U.S. power projection strategy—time and access—is shifting the center of theater warfare from close combat to long-range precision strike operations.[1] These long distance strikes must be properly synchronized with ground and naval operations to obtain a fundamental unity of effort and combined arms synergy. A Global Reconnaissance-Strike Complex[2] would serve as the correct mixing bowl to create just the right blend of forces needed to respond to crises and conflict worldwide. Standoff warfare is the right vaccine needed to immunize U.S. strategy against weapons of mass destruction.

Technology finally has caught up with past visions of what air power, especially long-range bomber operations, can contribute to modern warfare. When organized and armed with precision munitions for long-range strike, even the geriatric B-52, along with its more youthful B-1 and B-2 partners, can contribute significantly to America's early power projection operations. Halting the enemy's invasion and demilitarizing his WMD to levels that can be handled by U.S. active and passive defenses are prerequisites for the introduction of large numbers of tactical fighters, land warfare units, and naval forces to the region. The nearly 100,000 U.S. Gulf War veterans falling ill after the conflict, plus thousands more from other Coalition members, should sound a loud klaxon of alarm about the dangers of inserting American forces into biologically and chemically contaminated environments. In some cases, aerial victory early in a conflict may obviate the need for follow-on deployments to the theater. Depending on the number and disposition of the enemy's WMD, protracted U.S. operations against weapons of mass destruction and other anti-access military forces may be necessary. Yet, with proper peacetime intelligence analysis and characterization of the WMD target base, long-range precision strike operations will offer significant opportunities for success. Since the attacking aircraft would be launching from bases outside the lethal range of the enemy's WMD, firing standoff weapons, or relying on stealth or limited theater support for penetration of enemy defenses, the interdiction operations would be largely unimpeded. In those instances where the bombers could be placed at risk, stealth F-22 fighters and other defensive systems could ensure their protection.

With the advent of precision weapons, the need for mass of friendly forces on the ground has lessened dramatically. A Global Reconnaissance-Strike Complex tailored specifically to defeat the enemy's WMD-based

---

[1] Michael G. Vickers, *Warfare in 2020: A Primer* (Washington, D.C.: Center for Strategic and Budgetary Assessments, 1996), pp. 3–5.

[2] A system-of-systems architecture consisting of C4ISR, long-range precision strike aircraft, precision strike weapons, theater enabling aircraft, carrier-based aircraft, distributed ground combat cells, and theater missile and air defenses. *See* Chapter 12.

anti-access asymmetric strategy can operate effectively from outside the theater. The time dimension can be dominated through the careful selection of targets. Locating and destroying WMD throughout the breadth and depth of the enemy's territory will significantly overwhelm the capacity to deny the U.S. access for its tactical fighters, ground forces, and maritime forces. Such a dominance in the air will enable the deployment of all of America's military forces.[3]

The Global Reconnaissance-Strike Complex also hedges against ambiguous warning and surprise. Under the current strategy adversaries are rewarded for denying the United States strategic warning. "As I look at the world today," CIA director George Tenet observed in November 1997, "it is clear to me that the potential for dangerous surprise is as great as ever."[4] This condition requires improved responses to ambiguous signals, especially when confronting WMD-adversaries. The enemy's military readying moves may be deliberately deceptive or shrouded in the noise of shifting forces to deal with internal or regional troubles. These ambiguities cannot only delay the American response, but regional allies and friends may hesitate or be unwilling to grant the U.S. access to their military facilities. This places pressure on the intelligence and warning system and even greater stress on the ability to decide quickly on appropriate and effective responses to ambiguous signals.[5] Long-range precision strike elements can move forward during a crisis when the warning signals are most ambiguous. Forward bases located outside the reach of the adversary's WMD-tipped missiles place U.S. forces in position to respond quickly, if needed. Their ability to rapidly deploy should also reassure friends and allies in the region.

A properly structured and postured Global Reconnaissance-Strike Complex would also encourage a new strategic approach. During the Cold War, four phases of warfare evolved over time: (1) surprise attack—avoid quick defeat and deny the enemy an opportunity to present the United States with a fait accompli; (2) strategic defense—stabilize the battlefield and minimize territorial loss by halting the enemy's advance; (3) buildup—amass large numbers of forces and logistics; and (4) counter-offensive—retake lost ground

---

[3] Fogleman, "Aerospace Doctrine—More Than Just a Theory."

[4] George Tenet, "Does America Need the CIA?," remarks at the Gerald Ford Library Conference in Ann Arbor, Michigan (November 19, 1997) in *Periscope* (newsletter of the Association of Former Intelligence Officers), Vol. 22, No. 2 (1998).

[5] Albert and Roberta Wohlstetter, *Responding to Ambiguous Signals of Soviet Imminent or Future Power Projection,* Vol. I (Marina del Rey, Calif.: Pan Heuristics, Inc., 1982), pp. 1–8.

through coordinated air-land operations and re-establish the status quo ante. This Cold War conflict model was used successfully in the Gulf War, and it is still the Defense Department's basis for the major force planning scenarios in which the fourth phase, the counter-offensive, is ascribed the greatest importance.

According to this manpower-intensive paradigm, close combat is mandatory to inflict a decisive defeat on the enemy; only the ground operation would produce a lasting effect and provide for post-war stability. Since the land counter-offensive is the key to victory in this warfare style, ground forces, especially armored and mechanized divisions, need to be deployed to the theater as rapidly as possible.[6]

This is precisely the wrong warfare model for dealing with a WMD-armed adversary. The most critical phases of warfare in the new era include coping with the surprise attack by halting the enemy's invasion with minimum loss of territory and stabilizing the battlefield. The United States should be focusing its strategy in the post–Cold War era on the earliest hours and days of a conflict—when tremendous losses can be experienced in terms of territory, lives, and resources, especially at the hands of WMD-armed adversaries. Even with a subsequent buildup to amass and provide the means for counterattack, numerous friendly casualties could be inflicted early in the conflict. The greater the initial losses, the greater the subsequent buildup required and the more arduous the counter-offensive to retake lost ground.[7]

The right military strategy for operations against WMD-armed adversaries is to contain an aggressor's land assault with long-range precision strikes. Halting the invasion from the air is the only way to contain an invasion quickly and keep large numbers of U.S. forces out of reach of the enemy's WMD. The B-52, B-1, and B-2 bombers, armed with precision munitions, and fully leveraged by the inherently multi-role F-22—the collective centerpieces of the Global Reconnaissance-Strike Complex—provide the essential capability. Recognizing that the opening phases of a war are far more important than a delayed land warfare counter-offensive—after months of building up combat and support elements—should lead to a shift of resources from ground forces to air forces and from short-range tactical fighters to long-range precision strike. Of the Army's ten active divisions,

---

[6] Rebecca Grant, *Airpower and the Total Force: The Gift of Time* (Arlington, Va.: IRIS Independent Research, 1997), pp. 16–17.

[7] Philip Gold, "A New Paradigm in Warfare," *Washington Times* (August 19, 1997), p. A15.

The New Face of War

for example, six are heavy armored and mechanized units. They consume a disproportionate share of the Army's budget. While some level of heavy maneuver forces will be needed on many battlefields for the foreseeable future, their potential delayed arrival time in many plausible fast-breaking scenarios make them questionable assets in the current U.S. conventional strategy. Continued heavy emphasis on them represents an unacceptably high opportunity cost.

The Army has set unrealistic and unattainable deployment goals for armored and mechanized divisions in major regional conflicts. Assuming *unlimited* sealift and airlift capacity, the Army would send three and one-third divisions of 70,000 combat and 190,000 support forces to a theater anywhere in the world in thirty days. A five and one-third division combat force—80,000 combat troops and their equipment (up to 6,000,000 square feet)—would be assembled in-theater within seventy-five days. Early arriving forces would include one light division and one mechanized brigade to any region in fifteen days. Not only is existing and planned lift capacity insufficient to support such a deployment, but the reserve components upon which the Army depends may be unable to deploy in time to satisfy planning for the first of two major theater wars.

Equipment stored overseas is not invulnerable to attack, especially when the enemy is armed with biological and chemical weapons and strike platforms within range of the storage sites. If everything goes right, the Army could meet its deployment schedule for combat forces but not for support forces in the first of the two-war planning scenario. Even for a single conflict, assuming deployment in a benign environment, it would take ninety to 100 days to deploy 260,000 combat and support troops and their equipment to Korea or the Middle East. For a second conflict, beginning forty-five days from the start of the first war, more than six months could be needed to deploy the planned-for combat and support forces.[8] The next war, quite simply, will be decided long before then.

The Army deployment schedule is a clear reflection of Cold War thinking and shows a reluctance to adapt strategy and forces to meet new threats. The armed forces need to be restructured with modern equipment to meet the most serious challenges they are likely to face. For the foreseeable future the most significant military threats will occur early in a conflict. The initial stages of conflict are the most dangerous since time is a scarcity and

---

[8] U.S., Congress, Congressional Budget Office, *Structuring the Active and Reserve Army for the 21st Century* (Washington, D.C.: Government Printing Office, December 1997), pp. 15–19.

---

enemy access denial operations via the threat and use of WMD can disrupt and block U.S. deployments to the theater. Priority attention should be given to the resources needed for the critical opening hours and days of a conflict by paring down the Army's armored and mechanized divisions. Cuts in the number of divisions and their support would free up resources for application to halting the enemy's invasion early in the conflict and destroying weapons of mass destruction. "The brunt of short-term restructuring should occur in the Army's armored and mechanized divisions," David Ochmanek, a former senior defense analyst in the Office of the Secretary of Defense, observes. "The alternatives—cutting budgets and forces across the board, settling for a scaled-back strategy, or continuing to starve modernization—are surely riskier."[9]

The United States plays right into the hands of the WMD proliferators by retaining a conventional warfare strategy that depends on a large contingent of land forces for execution of a counter-offensive after some weeks and months of buildup, and by assuming a benign environment to assure force deployment overseas as planned. Beginning with rather crude and intermittent anti-access barriers in the near-term, one should anticipate that the rogue regimes and other countries hostile toward the United States will, over time, build increasingly effective obstructions to America's overseas deployments.[10] Even the most marginally successful anti-access effort would send the Army's deployment schedule off track, inflicting severe consequences in terms of significant losses of territory, high civilian and military casualties, and seizure of valuable resources that can be used to strengthen the aggressor.

The Air Force faces a similar disparity between planned tactical fighter deployments and actual performance when the chips were down in 1990 and 1994. While about 700 tactical fighters are to be deployed in fourteen days of strategic warning—at least as in the baseline case used in the 1995 *Heavy Bomber Force Study*—only about 150 fighters were deployed to the Persian Gulf during the first two weeks in response to Saddam Hussein's seizure of Kuwait in August 1990 and again in the Iraqi crisis of 1994.[11] In

---

[9] David Ochmanek, "Time to Restructure U.S. Defense Forces," *Issues in Science and Technology* (Winter 1995–96), p. 41.

[10] Andrew F. Krepinevich, Jr., "The Future of Tactical Aviation," testimony before the AirLand Subcommittee, Senate Armed Services Committee (Washington, D.C.: Center for Strategic and Budgetary Assessments, March 5, 1997). Photocopy.

[11] Guthe, *A Precisely Guided Analytic Bomb,* p. 21, and Buchan, "Use of Long-Range Bombers in a Changing World," pp. 411–12.

both cases, the United States was granted access to bases in the region. On the other hand, the absence of base access denied the United States an opportunity to challenge Iraq's seizure of the northern Kurdish region in 1996. The 1997-98 U.N. inspections crisis in Iraq again confronted the Air Force with limited access to regional airfields, making the entire operation dependent on two potentially vulnerable aircraft carriers.

Unless they are nearby when a conflict breaks out, aircraft carriers could take days and even weeks to arrive. Barring anti-access obstructions or missile threats to carriers located in littoral waters, naval air strikes could be executed relatively soon. If sustained bombing operations and firepower are needed, aircraft carriers, however, would not be the weapon system of choice. Even for maintaining a prolonged presence in overseas theaters, naval forces end up grinding down equipment and morale while accelerating costs. Keeping a sizable force in the Persian Gulf to convince Saddam Hussein to cooperate with U.N. weapons inspectors, for instance, will cost the United States $1.3 billion in 1998. Increasing morale problems and costs convinced some in the Pentagon to urge a paring of the deployed forces to one aircraft carrier instead of two. "It will be difficult to deter Saddam Hussein on the cheap," John Hillen of the Council on Foreign Relations observes. "You have to be excessively creative to not wear out our forces by keeping them in the Persian Gulf, but at the same time to keep enough there to deter Saddam."[12]

A de facto global reconnaissance-strike complex was created in June 1998 when the American force presence in the Persian Gulf was cut in half. The force reductions included one aircraft carrier, thirty-six tactical fighters, six F-117 stealth fighters, six B-52 and two B-1 bombers, and aerial tankers and other support aircraft. One carrier battle group remained in the Gulf with an increased ability to launch cruise missiles. Defense Secretary William S. Cohen stressed that "the bomber force can go back in very quickly. We will have far more prepositioned equipment. We will have a rapid-deployable force ready to go and be there within 48 hours should it become necessary."[13]

A "virtual presence" of ready, quick responding long-range precision strike systems armed with precision-guided munitions could keep the pressure on Saddam Hussein at a far less cost and with a lesser strain on

---

[12] As quoted by Rowan Scarborough, "Pentagon Asks Gulf Cuts for Morale, Cost," *Washington Times* (May 7, 1998), p. A6.

[13] Charles Aldinger, "Cohen Warns Saddam About New Provocation," *Washington Times* (May 26, 1998), p. A13; and Dana Priest, "U.S. Cuts Forces in Persian Gulf," *Washington Post* (May 27, 1998), pp. A1, A2.

U.S. military personnel. The formation of a Global Reconnaissance-Strike Complex would allow the prepositioning of some aircraft at forward bases beyond the range of enemy missiles as well as the subsequent deployment of second wave forces ready to launch from the United States. Such a tiered force deployment would relieve the pressure on naval assets and allow the U.S. Navy far more flexibility in maintaining a presence in the Persian Gulf.

A robust long-range precision strike force—the point of the Global Reconnaissance-Strike Complex spear—would mitigate the problems associated with early deployment schedules for the Army's heavy divisions and hundreds of Air Force, Navy, and Marine Corps tactical fighters positioned on land and at sea. Within hours and armed with the precision munitions and other support, long-range strike aircraft can blunt invading forces and enable U.S. military deployments through attacks on the aggressor's arsenal of WMD and other military forces. Thousands of armored vehicles and WMD targets could be destroyed or damaged, severely weakening the enemy's military capabilities, while U.S. readying activities for heavy divisions and tactical fighters are underway. As Army armored and mechanized forces, Air Force tactical fighters, and Navy carrier battle groups move toward the theater of conflict, the long-range precision strike bombers and cruise missiles will enable the force projection and continue to take the fight directly to the WMD-armed enemy.

The United States has within its technological and fiscal grasp to create a robust Global Reconnaissance-Strike Complex from existing forces and those entering production. These early invasion-halting and regional deployment-enabling forces can be upgraded over time by carefully exploiting the joint warfighting synergies inherent in integrated C4ISR and air, ground, and maritime operations.

Americans should have learned from the events leading to and during the Gulf War that the face of warfare changed dramatically with the proliferation of nuclear, biological, and chemical weapons. For instance, Saddam Hussein bombed the Kurdish village of Halabjah in northern Iraq on March 16, 1988. Five thousand of the 85,000 civilian inhabitants died immediately from the massive use of chemical weapons, including mustard gas and nerve agents. By 1998, 40,000 people remained in the bombed out buildings of Halabjah when Dr. Christine Gosden, a British genetics expert, documented the effects of the chemical attacks a decade after they occurred:

The New Face of War

- Terrible skin scarring from mustard gas, which often progresses to cancer;
- People's eyes were affected with corneal scarring, impaired vision or blindness;
- Breathing in the vapors caused severe respiratory damage;
- Breast, skin, and childhood cancers occurred at three times the rate of a neighboring city that was not gassed;
- Stillbirths, infant deaths, cerebral palsy, Down's syndrome, and other mental disabilities occur with greater frequency than in cities that were not gassed;
- Children have a far greater rate of being born with cleft palates, harelips, major heart defects, and other malformations;
- Neurological and psychiatric consequences are severe, including neuromuscular damage leaving persons unable to control their limbs, suffering from severe depression, and suicide is common; and
- The chemicals, especially mustard gas, caused occurrences of genetic mutations leaving it open to question whether anyone of reproductive age will have an abnormal child.

In short, the people of Halabjah still suffer from the "eleventh plague" of chemical attacks that hit them a decade ago. *"In innocent men, women and children, these chemical weapons have planted genetic time bombs,"* Dr. Gosden explains. *"Their effects go on and on, ruining lives long after the shells have gone off and destroying future generations."*[14]

If America has within its grasp the capability to strike a WMD-armed adversary decisively from beyond the WMD delivery range, why should the core military strategy still entail sending thousands of Americans into a proliferator's backyard where they might come under biological and chemical warfare attacks? Why not create a Global Reconnaissance-Strike Complex to revitalize America's transoceanic power projection strategy?

---

[14] Dr. Christine Gosden, "'We've Got to Try to Do Something,'" *USA Weekend* (May 15–17, 1998), pp. 14, 16.

SELECTED BIBLIOGRAPHY

The writings listed have been used in making this book. By no means is this selected bibliography a complete record of all the documents and electronic sources consulted by the writer. These references are representative of the range of sources consulted in thinking through the implications of the global proliferation of weapons of mass destruction and advanced conventional weapons and technologies. Learning about and assessing the impact of these new weapons on the U.S. transoceanic power projection strategy are prerequisites for comprehending the significance of the military risks facing the United States and what Americans should be doing to mitigate them.

"A Future Look At 'Weapons of Mass Disruption.'" *Defense Week* (November 24, 1997).

Albright, David and Hibbs, Mark. "Iraq and the Bomb: Were They Even Close?" *Bulletin of the Atomic Scientists* (March 1991).

Albright, David. "A Proliferation Primer." *Bulletin of Atomic Scientists* (June 1993).

Albright, David; Berkhout, Frans; and Walker, William. "Fact Sheet: Plutonium and Highly Enriched Uranium 1996: World Inventories, Capabilities and Policies" (March 13, 1997). Photocopy.

————. *Plutonium and Highly Enriched Uranium 1996: World Inventories, Capabilities and Policies* (Stockholm International Peace Institute and Oxford University Press, 1997). Photocopy.

Aldinger, Charles. "Cohen Warns Saddam About New Provocation." *Washington Times* (May 26, 1998).

Alger, John I. *Definitions and Doctrine of the Military Art: Past and Present.* U.S. Military Academy History Series. Edited by Thomas E. Griess. Wayne, N.J.: Avery Publishing Group, 1985.

Allison, Graham. "Testimony to the Senate Committee on Government Affairs, Permanent Subcommittee on Investigations." Cambridge, Mass.: Harvard University, March 13, 1996. Photocopy.

American Defense Preparedness Association and National Security Industrial Association. *Proceedings: "NBC 2000—New Challenges/New Capabilities*. Worldwide Chemical Conference XV and NBC Symposium. Fort McClellan, Ala.: June 24–27, 1997.

"Americans Unmoved By Washington's Big Stories." *Pew Research Center* (April 11, 1997).

Anderson, John Ward and Khan, Kamran. "Pakistan Again Explodes Bomb." *Washington Post* (May 31, 1998).

———. "Pakistan Sets Off Nuclear Blasts." *Washington Post* (May 29, 1998).

"Anthrax: Iraq's Doomsday Option?" *Washington Times* (November 9, 1997).

"Anti-HIV Mix Found in Gulf Veterans." *Washington Times* (August 1, 1997).

Asghar, Raja. "Pakistan Seeks U.N. Help Over Indian Missile Threat." *Washington Times* (June 14, 1997).

Aspin, Les, Representative. Chairman, House Armed Services Committee. "An Approach to Sizing American Conventional Forces For the Post-Soviet Era—Four Illustrative Options." Washington, D.C: February 25, 1992. Photocopy.

Aspin, Les, Secretary of Defense. *Report of the Bottom-Up Review.* Washington, D.C.: Department of Defense, October 1993. Photocopy.

———. *Force Structure Excerpts—Bottom-Up Review.* News Release No. 403-93. Washington, D.C.: Office of the Secretary of Defense (Public Affairs), September 1, 1993.

———. Remarks Before the Committee on International Security and Arms Control, National Academy of Sciences. Washington, D.C.: December 7, 1993. Photocopy.

Assessment of the Impact of Chemical and Biological Weapons on Joint Operations in 2010 (The CB 2010 Study): A Summary Report. McLean, Va.: Booz, Allen & Hamilton, October 1997.

Atkinson, Rick. *Crusade: The Untold Story of the Persian Gulf War.* Boston: Houghton Mifflin, 1993.

Bailey, Kathleen C. *The UN Inspections in Iraq: Lessons for On-Site Verification.* Boulder: Westview Press, 1995.

Barry, John. "Unearthing the Truth." *Newsweek* (March 2, 1998).

Baruah, Amit. "Pakistan Tests 1,500 km Range Missile." *The Hindu* (India) (February 11, 1998).

BDM Federal, Inc. *Beyond the DoD Heavy Bomber Study.* McLean, Va.: 1996.

Bennett, Bruce. "Implications of Proliferation of New Weapons on Regional Security." 11th Conference on Korea-U.S. Security Studies on "The Search for Peace and Security in Northeast Asia Toward the 21st Century" (Seoul, Korea: October 24–25, 1996). Santa Monica, Calif.: RAND Corporation.

Blair, David. "How to Defeat the United States: The Operational Effects of the Proliferation of Weapons of Precise Destruction." *Fighting Proliferation: New Concerns for the Nineties.* Edited by Henry Sokolski. Washington, D.C.: Government Printing Office (Air University Press), September 1996.

Blaker, James. *Understanding the Revolution in Military Affairs: A Guide to America's 21st Century Defense.* Edited by Robert A. Manning. Washington, D.C.: Progressive Policy Institute, January 1997.

Blanche, Ed. "Reports Show Gaps in U.S. Security." *Jane's Intelligence Review and Jane's Sentinel Pointer* (October 1997).

Blank, Stephen. "Russia's Clearance Sale." *Jane's Intelligence Review* (November 1997).

―――. "China Acquires Arms Technology." *Jane's Intelligence Review and Jane's Sentinel Pointer* (November 1997).

Blazer, Ernest. "Inside the Ring: Unready Signs." *Washington Times* (October 2, 1997).

―――. "Inside the Ring." *Washington Times* (November 6, 1997).

Bluth, Christoph. "Russia's Nuclear Forces: A Clear and Present Danger." *Jane's Intelligence Review* (December 1997).

"Both India and Pakistan Reject U.N. Call to Sign Nuclear Treaty." *Armed Forces Presswire* (June 7, 1998).

Bowen, Wyn and Shepard, Stanley. "Living Under the Red Missile Threat." *Jane's International Defence Review* (December 1996).

Bowie, Christopher J. and others. *The New Calculus*. MR-149-AF. Santa Monica, Calif.: RAND Corporation, 1993.

Broad, William J. and Miller, Judith. "Iraq's Deadliest Arms: Puzzles Breed Fears." *New York Times* (February 26, 1998).

Brodie, Bernard and Brodie, Fawn M. *From Crossbow to H-Bomb*. Bloomington: Indiana University Press, 1973.

Brody, Richard. "The 1973 War—Summary." *Responding to Ambiguous Warning Signals of Soviet Imminent or Future Power Projection*. Vol. II—Case Studies. Marina del Rey, Calif.: Pan Heuristics, Inc., May 1982.

Brown, David. "Independent Panel Recommended To Oversee Probe of Gulf War Illness." *Washington Post* (November 9, 1997).

Bruce, James and Starr, Barbara. "US Exploits Images of Military Rebirth... As Iraq Rejects UN Resolution on Oil Sales." *Jane's Defence Weekly* (May 6, 1995).

Buchan, Glenn C. and Frelinger, David R. *Providing an Effective Bomber Force for the Future*. RAND Congressional Testimony. Prepared Statement for the Senate Armed Services Committee. Santa Monica, Calif.: RAND Corporation, May 5, 1994.

Buchan, Glenn C. "The Use of Long-Range Bombers In a Changing World: A Classical Exercise of Systems Analysis." *New Challenges for Defense Planning*. Edited by Paul K. Davis. Santa Monica, Calif.: RAND Corporation, 1994.

Buell, Thomas B. and others. *The Second World War: Europe and the Mediterranean*. U.S. Military Academy History Series. Edited by Thomas E. Griess. Wayne, N.J.: Avery Publishing Group, 1984.

Bukharin, Oleg. "Problems of Nuclear Terrorism." *The Monitor*. 3-2. Center for International Trade and Security at the University of Georgia (Spring 1997).

Burdeshaw Associates, Ltd. *Using Prompt Massive B-2 Firepower To Win Quickly, Decisively and With Few Casualties.* Bethesda, Md.: Burdeshaw Associates, 1994.

Burgess, Lisa. "Iraq Faces Much-Improved U.S. Airstrike Arsenal." *Defense News* (February 16–22, 1998).

Bushinsky, Jay. "UN Inspections Won't Harm Saddam's Bio-Warfare Ability." *Jerusalem Post* (December 7, 1997).

Caires, Greg. "Even Without Nukes, B-1s Can Still Deter—AF General Michael McMahan." *Defense Daily* (March 16, 1998).

Carr, Caleb. "Terrorism As Warfare: The Lessons of Military History." *World Policy Journal.* 13-4. Winter 1996/97.

Chace, James. "The Pentagon's Superpower Fantasy?" *New York Times* (March 16, 1992).

Chandler, Robert W. *Tomorrow's War, Today's Decisions: Iraqi Weapons of Mass Destruction and the Implications of WMD-Armed Adversaries for Future U.S. Military Strategy.* McLean, Va.: AMCODA Press, 1996.

Charnetski, Joanne and Rauf, Tariq. "Let Canada Cremate Nuclear Swords." *Defense News* (October 3–9, 1994).

"Chemical Risk to Gulf Troops Was Forecast." *USA Today* (August 14, 1997).

Cheney, Richard, Secretary of Defense. Transmittal Letter to Senator Sam Nunn for a Report Outlining the Defense Department's *Plan for Deployment of Theater and National Ballistic Missile Defenses.* Washington, D.C.: July 2, 1992. Photocopy.

"China Acquires Arms Technology." *Jane's Intelligence Review and Jane's Sentinel Pointer* (November 1997).

"CIA Reports China Built Missile Plant in Pakistan." *Reuters* (June 24, 1997).

"CIA 'Very Concerned' By Russian Nuclear Safeguards." *Russia Today* (December 4, 1997).

Clinton, William J., President. "Letter to the Congress of the United States." Washington, D.C.: The White House, March 31, 1998.

Cochran, Thomas B. "Nuclear Weapons and Fissile Material Security in Russia." Testimony Before the Committee on Foreign Affairs, Subcommittee on International Security, International Organizations and Human Rights. National Resource Defense Council, Inc., June 27, 1994. Photocopy.

Cohen, Eliot. "Calling Mr. X." *New Republic* (January 19, 1998).

Cohen, William S., Secretary of Defense. *Annual Report to the President and the Congress.* Washington, D.C.: Government Printing Office, 1998.

———. *Annual Report to the President and the Congress.* Washington, D.C.: Government Printing Office, 1997.

———. *Report of the Quadrennial Defense Review.* Washington, D.C.: Department of Defense, May 1997.

Collins, John M.; Davis, Zachary S; and Bowman, Steven R. *Nuclear, Biological, and Chemical Weapons Proliferation: Potential Military Countermeasures.* Washington, D.C.: Congressional Research Service, Library of Congress, June 28, 1994.

"Congressional News." *Air Force Magazine* (June 1997).

Conrad, Scott W. *Moving the Force: Desert Storm and Beyond.* McNair Paper 32. Institute for National Strategic Studies. National Defense University. Washington, D.C.: Government Printing Office, December 1994.

Cooper, Bert H., Jr. *Missiles for Standoff Attack: Air-to-Surface Munitions Programs.* Washington, D.C.: Congressional Research Service, Library of Congress, November 6, 1996.

Cooper, Kenneth J. "India Conducts 2nd Round of Nuclear Tests." *Washington Post* (May 14, 1998).

———. "Leader Says India Has A 'Credible' Deterrent." *Washington Post* (June 17, 1998).

———. "Premier Says India Capable of 'Big Bomb.'" *Washington Post* (May 16, 1998).

Cooper, Pat and Holzer, Robert. "Shalikashvili: Plan for Terror." *Defense News* (August 12–18, 1996).

Cordesman, Anthony H. *Weapons of Mass Destruction in Iraq: A Summary of Biological, Chemical, Nuclear* and *Delivery Efforts and Capabilities*. Washington, D.C.: Center for Strategic and International Studies, November 12, 1996.

Correll, John T. "Backing Up On Strategy." *Air Force Magazine* (June 1996).

―――. "Deep Attack." *Air Force Magazine* (April 1996).

―――. "Fallout From Khobar Towers." *Air Force Magazine* (September 1997).

―――. "The Rediscovery of Strategic Airpower." *Air Force Magazine* (November 1996).

Costigan, Michael J., Lieutenant Colonel, U.S. Air Force. *The F-22: The Right Fighter for the Twenty-First Century?* Air War College, Maxwell Paper No. 9. Maxwell Air Force Base, Ala.: Air University, August 1997.

Cote, Owen and Sapolsky, Harvey. *Antisubmarine Warfare After the Cold War*. Cambridge, Mass.: Center for International Studies, Massachusetts Institute of Technology, 1998.

Courter, Jim and Thompson, Loren. *Deep-Attack Weapons Mix Study: Bias May Produce Flawed B-2 Analysis*. Arlington, VA.: Alexis de Toqueville Institution, 1996.

Croddy, Eric. "Putting the Lid Back On the Chemical Box." *Jane's Intelligence Review* (January 1998).

Crossette, Barbara and others. "U.S. Says Iraq Aided Production of Chemical Weapons in Sudan." *New York Times* (August 25, 1998).

Crossette, Barbara. "Experts Doubt Iraq's Claims On A-Bomb." *New York Times* (August 30, 1995).

Daigneault, Joseph J.; Welander, Robert; and White, Pete. *USPACOM Study Program: Chemical Warfare Analysis*. Prepared for the Director, Defense Nuclear Agency. Alexandria,Va.: Defense Technical Information Center, March 25, 1988. Redacted copy.

Darilek, Richard E. "What Drives North Korea's Nuclear Program." *Adjusting to Change: Understanding Proliferation Risks.* A Defense Nuclear Agency-Sponsored Strategic Options Assessments Conference. McLean, Va.: Strategic Planning International, Inc., 1994.

Davis, Zachary S. "Weapons of Mass Destruction: New Terrorist Threat?" *The Monitor.* 3-2. Center for International Trade and Security at the University of Georgia (Spring 1997).

"Defense & Diplomacy—Gulf War Logs." *Washington Post* (December 14, 1996).

Deutch, John M., Deputy Secretary of Defense. *Report on Nonproliferation and Counterproliferation Activities and Programs.* Washington, D.C.: Department of Defense, May 1994.

Diamond, John. "Chinese Army Writings Reveal 'Very Unfriendly' Attitude Toward U.S." *Miami Herald* (September 21, 1997).

———. "U.S. Housing to Be Safer At Saudi Desert Air Base." *Washington Times* (December 30, 1997).

"DIA: N. Korea Threat Declining As Economic Collapse Nears." *Defense Week* (January 12, 1998).

Dougherty, Russell E., General, U.S. Air Force (retired). "Projecting Power Without Bases." Statement Before the House Armed Services Committee, March 27, 1990. Photocopy.

Dudney, Robert S. "The New Space Plan." *Air Force Magazine* (July 1998).

Dunn, L. and others. *Global Proliferation: Dynamics, Acquisition Strategies, and Responses.* Vol. IV——Biological Weapons Proliferation. Newington, Va.: Center for Verification Research, December 1992.

———. *Global Proliferation: Dynamics, Acquisition Strategies, and Responses.* Vol. V—Missile Proliferation. Newington, Va.: Center for Verification Research, December 1992.

Ebert, Barbara. "Iraq: Its Nuclear Past As a Way of Assessing Its Nuclear Future." Vienna, Va.: Science Applications International Corporation, April 1994. Photocopy.

Eddington, Patrick G. *Gassed in the Gulf: The Inside Story of the Pentagon-CIA Cover-Up of the Gulf War Syndrome.* Washington, D.C.: Insignia Publishing Company, 1997.

Eisenstadt, Michael. *Like a Phoenix From the Ashes? The Future of Iraqi Military Power*. Policy Paper No. 36. Washington, D.C.: Washington Institute for Near East Policy, 1993.

———. *"The Sword of the Arabs:" Iraq's Strategic Weapons*. Policy Paper No. 21. Washington, D.C.: Washington Institute for Near East Policy, 1990.

Eisenstein, Maurice. *Early Entry Forces: An Annotated Briefing on the Question of New and Nonconventional Threats*. Santa Monica, Calif.: RAND Corporation, undated.

Ellsworth, Robert; Goodpaster, Andrew; and Hauser, Rita, co-chairs. *America's National Interests*. A Report from the Commission on America's National Interests. Cambridge, Mass.: Harvard University Center for Science and International Affairs, 1996.

Entzminger, John. Deputy Director for Technology, Defense Airborne Reconnaissance Office. *The Past and Future of Airborne Reconnaissance*. Cambridge, Mass.: Center for International Studies, Massachusetts Institute of Technology, November 1997.

Erlich, Jeff. "Ballistic Threats Trigger Interest in Missile Defense." *Defense News* (April 22–28, 1996).

———. "Diplomats Work to Fill 'Empty' Wassenaar Arrangement." *Defense News* (June 9–15, 1997).

———. "New U.S. Nuclear Policy Maintains Ambiguity." *Defense News* (January 5–11, 1998).

———. "Officers Propose Counter to QDR." *Defense News* (May 19–25, 1997).

———. "Storm Brews As Congress Awaits QDR." *Defense News* (May 12–18, 1997).

———. "U.S. Officials To Study Cruise Missile Threat." *Defense News* (June 16–22, 1997).

Faleh, Waiel. "Iraqis Remain in Kurd City Despite Order." *Washington Times* (September 2, 1996).

———. "Saddam Attacks Kurds in Safe Haven." *Washington Times* (September 1, 1996).

Finnegan, Philip and Holzer, Robert. "Politics Foul Strike Plans Against Iraq." *Defense News* (February 23–March 1, 1998).

Finnegan, Philip. "Limited U.S. Action May Boost Iraqi Biological Threats." *Defense News* (September 23–29, 1996).

———. "Saddam's Bio-Chem Arsenal Could Snarl U.S. Gulf Plans." *Defense News* (September 30–October 6, 1996).

———. "U.N. Woes May Allow Bio-Chem Revival in Iraq." *Defense News* (November 18–24, 1996).

Fisher, Richard D. and Dori, John T. *The Strategic Implications of China's Nuclear Aid to Pakistan.* Executive Memorandum No. 532. Washington, D.C.: Heritage Foundation, June 16, 1998.

Fogleman, Ronald R., General, U.S. Air Force Chief of Staff. "Aerospace Doctrine—More Than Just a Theory." Presented at the Air Force Doctrine Seminar. Maxwell AFB, Ala.: April 30, 1996. Photocopy.

———. "The Contribution of Long-Range Bombers to America's Deep Strike Capability." An address delivered to the Tocqueville Group. Washington, D.C.: September 13, 1996. Photocopy.

Ford, James L. "Nuclear Smuggling: How Serious a Threat?" *Strategic Forum.* No. 59. Washington, D.C.: National Defense University, January 1996.

Ford, Peter. "Russia Races U.S. in Military Sales." *Washington Times* (September 1, 1997).

Foss, Christopher. "Latest Brazilian Rocket Revealed." *Jane's Defence Weekly* (May 14, 1997).

Fox, Eugene and Orman, Stanley. "Cruise Missile Threat Grows." *Defense News* (September 30-October 6, 1996).

Fulghum, David A. "Cobra Ball Revamped For Battlefield Missions." *Aviation Week & Space Technology* (August 4, 1997).

"GAO Ties Gulf War Illness to Nerve Gas." *Washington Times* (June 15, 1997).

George, Alan. "Saddam Stockpiled 'Cancer Time Bombs.'" *Washington Times* (October 17, 1996).

Gerth, Jeff and Broder, John M. "The White House Dismissed Warning on China Satellite Deal." *New York Times* (June 1, 1998).

Gerth, Jeff and Miller, Judith. "Funds for Terrorists Traced To Persian Gulf Businessmen." *New York Times* (August 14, 1996).

Gerth, Jeff. "China Buying U.S. Computers, Raising Fears of Enhanced Nuclear Weapons." *New York Times* (June 19, 1997).

Gertz, Bill. "Arms Agency Finds Beijing Broke Pledge." *Washington Times* (August 16, 1997).

———. "China Assists Iran, Libya on Missiles." *Washington Times* (June 16, 1998).

———. "China Joins Forces With Iran on Short-Range Missile." *Washington Times* (June 17, 1997).

———. "China Sold Iran Missile Technology." *Washington Times* (November 21, 1996).

———. "Export Controls Need Checking, Expert Says." *Washington Times* (June 18, 1997).

———. "Horror Weapons." *Air Force Magazine* (January 1996).

———. "Missile-Related Technology Sold to Beijing By Belarus." *Washington Times* (June 12, 1997).

———. "New Chinese Missiles Target All of East Asia." *Washington Times* (July 10, 1997).

———. "N. Korea Fires New Cruise Missile." *Washington Times* (June 30, 1997).

———. "N. Korea Targets U.S. GIs." *Washington Times* (October 22, 1997).

———. "Russia, China Aid Iran's Missile Program." *Washington Times* (September 10, 1997).

———. "Russia Disregards Pledge to Curb Iran Missile Output." *Washington Times* (May 22, 1997).

———. "Russian Missile Assurance Challenged." *Washington Times* (June 6, 1997).

———. "Russian Renegades Pose Nuke Danger." *Washington Times* (October 22, 1996).

————. "Russian Smuggling Ring Arms Kurd Rebels in Turkey." *Washington Times* (June 23, 1997).

————. "Russia Sells China High-Tech Artillery." *Washington Times* (July 3, 1997).

————. "Russia Sells Missiles to Iran." *Washington Times* (April 16, 1997).

————. "'Suitcase' Weapons Exist, Built for 'Terrorist Purposes.'" *Washington Times* (October 3, 1997).

————. "Supercomputer Diversion Prompts Criminal Probe, Senate Panel Told." *Washington Times* (June 12, 1997).

————. "Technology Transfers Detailed for Senate." *Washington Times* (May 22, 1998).

————. "Terrorism and the Force." *Air Force Magazine* (February 1997).

————. "U.S. Protests Kazakh's Plans to Sell Iran Advanced Missiles." *Washington Times* (June 4, 1997).

Gold, Philip. "A New Paradigm in Warfare." *Washington Times* (August 19, 1997).

————. "What the Air Force Can Do For You." *Washington Times* (July 6, 1998).

Goodpaster, Andrew J., General, U.S. Army (retired). "New Patterns of Peace and Security: Implications for the U.S. Military." *Bulletin.* 8-11. Washington, D.C.: Atlantic Council of the United States, December 3, 1997.

Gordon, Michael and Trainor, Bernard E., General. *The Generals' War: The Inside Story of the Conflict in the Gulf.* Boston: Little, Brown, 1995.

Gormley, Dennis M. Remarks at the "Conference on Nuclear Non-Proliferation: Enhancing the Tools of the Trade." Carnegie Endowment for International Peace. Washington, D.C.: June 10, 1997.

Gormley, Dennis M. and McMahon, K. Scott. "Proliferation of Land-Attack Cruise Missiles: Prospects and Policy Implications." *Fighting Proliferation: New Concerns for the Nineties.* Edited by Henry Sokolski. Washington, D.C.: Government Printing Office, September 1996.

Gosden, Christine, Dr. Remarks on *60 Minutes*. CBS Television (February 28, 1998).

———. "We've Got to Try to Do Something." *USA Weekend* (May 15–17, 1998).

Goshko, John M. "U.N. Teams Find No Sign of Iraqi Nuclear Arms." *Washington Post* (April 14, 1998).

———. "Iraqi Nerve Gas Tests Confirmed." *Washington Post* (June 25, 1998).

Gosoroski, David M. "Sentry Duty in Saudi." *Veterans of Foreign Wars* (September 1996).

Graham, Bradley. "Pentagon's Plan for Future Draws Heavily From Cold War Past." *Washington Post* (May 11, 1997).

———. "U.S. Forces Better Equipped for Chemical, Biological Warfare." *Washington Post* (February 8, 1998).

Graham, Thomas. "Conventional Response." *Defense News* (February 23–March 1, 1998).

Grant, Rebecca. *Airpower and the Total Force: The Gift of Time.* Arlington, Va.: IRIS Independent Research, 1997

———. *Rethinking Defense.* Arlington, Va.: Air Force Association, 1997.

Grimmett, Richard F. *Conventional Arms Transfers to Developing Nations, 1987–1994.* Washington, D.C.: Congressional Research Service, Library of Congress, August 4, 1995.

"Gulf War Provides Ample Information for Chinese Military Thinkers." *Inside Missile Defense* (March 12, 1997).

Gunaratna, Rohan. "Illicit Weapons Trade in South Asia." *Janes Intelligence Review and Jane's Sentinel Pointer* (October 1997).

Guthe, Kurt. *A Precisely Guided Analytic Bomb: The Defense Department's Heavy Bomber Force Study.* Fairfax, Va.: National Institute for Public Policy, September 1996.

Hanchette, John and Brewer, Norm. "U.N., Intelligence Reports Show Iraq Could Have Spread Deadly Aflatoxin." *Gannett News Service* (December 7, 1996).

Hanley, Charles J. "Iran's Nuclear Effort Behind Schedule." *Washington Times* (May 5, 1997).

————. "General Warns On Iran Nukes." *Washington Times* (June 27, 1997).

Hargrove, Thomas and Stempel, Guido H., III. "Poll Says Americans Suspect Worst of Their Government." *Washington Times* (July 5, 1997).

Harman, Jane and Kyl, Jon. "Make Russia Face Reality." *Defense News* (October 20–26, 1997).

Harrison, Selig S. "India's Muscle Flexing Is Over: Let the Bargaining Begin." *Washington Post* (May 17, 1998).

Harvey, Don. "Intelligence Notebook: Terrorism." *Periscope*. Newsletter of the Association of Former Intelligence Officers (July 1996).

Hashim, Ahmed. "New Sino-Russian Partnership." *Jane's Intelligence Review and Jane's Sentinel Pointer* (September 1997).

"Health Aspects of Chemical and Biological Weapons." Geneva: World Health Organization, 1970. As quoted in L. Dunn and others. *Global Proliferation: Dynamics, Acquisition Strategies, and Responses.* Volume IV: Biological Weapons Proliferation. Newington, Va.: Center for Verification Research, December 1992.

Heivilin, Donna. *Gulf War Illnesses: Reexamination of Research Emphasis and Improved Monitoring of Clinical Progress Needed.* Testimony Before the Senate Committee on Veterans Affairs. GAO/ T-NSIAD-97-191. Washington, D.C.: General Accounting Office, June 25, 1997.

Hitchens, Theresa. "U.S. Must Spell Out Bio War Response." *Defense News* (September 11–17, 1995).

Hoffman, David. "Russia Expanding Role in Iranian Power Plant." *Washington Post* (February 22, 1998).

————. "Russia's Missile Gyroscopes Were Sold to Iraq." *Washington Post* (September 12, 1997).

————. "Yeltsin Approves Doctrine of Nuclear First Use If Attacked." *Washington Post* (May 10, 1997).

Holzer, Robert. "Antiterror Plans May Endanger U.S. Forces." *Defense News* (September 2–8, 1996).

——. "Dangerous Waters: Submarines, New Mines Imperil Ill-Prepared U.S. Navy Fleet." *Defense News* (May 4–10, 1998).

——. "JASSM Winner Targets Extra Mission." *Defense News* (April 13–19, 1998).

Horne, Alastair. *To Lose a Battle.* Boston: Little, Brown, 1969.

Horner, Charles, A., General, U.S. Air Force (retired). "Lessons in Warfighting Operations From Desert Storm." *NATO's Sixteen Nations*, 1/97.

——. "Unmatched Survivability: The B-2 and Defense Entwined." *Washington Times* (June 13, 1995).

——. "What We Should Have Learned in Desert Storm But Didn't." *Air Force Magazine* (December 1996).

Hough, Harold. "Could Israel's Nuclear Assets Survive a First Strike?" *Jane's Intelligence Review* (September 1997).

——. "Iran Targets the Arabian Peninsula." *Jane's Intelligence Review* (October 1996).

Hull, Andrew and Markov, David. "A Changing Market in the Arms Bazaar." *Jane's Intelligence Review* (March 1997).

——. "Trends in the Arms Market—Part One." *Jane's Intelligence Review* (April 1997).

——. "Trends in the Arms Market—Part Two." *Jane's Intelligence Review* (May 1997).

Hunter, Tom. "Russia's Mafiyas: The New Revolution." *Jane's Intelligence Review* (June 1997).

Huntington, Samuel P. *Clash of Civilizations and the Remaking of World Order.* New York: Simon & Schuster, 1996.

"Hyperbolic Missile." *Aviation Week & Space Technology* (July 7, 1997).

Ibrahim, Youssef M. "Saudi Exile Warns More Attacks Planned." *New York Times* (July 11, 1996).

Ikle, Fred C. and Wohlstetter, Albert, co-chairmen. *Discriminate Deterrence.* Report of the Commission on Integrated Long-Term Strategy. Washington, D.C.: Government Printing Office, January 1988.

Infield, Glen B. *Disaster At Bari.* New York: Macmillan, 1971.

International Atomic Energy Agency. "Fact Sheet" (January 1994).

———. *IAEA Inspections and Iraq's Nuclear Capabilities.* Vienna, Austria: April 1992.

International Institute for Strategic Studies. "The Future of Unmanned Aerial Vehicles." *Strategic Comments.* 3-10. London, United Kingdom: December 1997.

"Interview: Rolf Ekeus." *Dallas Morning News* (December 21, 1997).

"Iran's Weapons Development, Limping Poor Economy Saps Alleged Nuclear Program." *MSNBC* (December 10, 1997).

"Iraq-Backed Kurds Celebrate Triumph." *Washington Times* (September 11, 1996).

"Iraq Finally Admits Building Biological Weapon Arsenal." *Jane's Defence Weekly* (July 15, 1995).

"Iraq Likely Has Hidden Missiles, Inspector Says." *Washington Times* (December 19, 1996).

Isby, David C. "The Residual Iraqi 'Scud' Force." *Jane's Intelligence Review* (March 1995).

Israel, David. Assistant for Theater Missile Defense. "An SDIO In TMD Counterforce." Washington, D.C.: Strategic Defense Initiative Organization, June 1992. Photocopy.

"Israel Warns Syria on New Nerve Gas." *Washington Times* (April 30, 1997).

Jehl, Douglas. "Faction of Kurds Supported By Iraq Takes Rival's City." *New York Times* (September 10, 1996).

———. "U.S. Military in Saudi Arabia Digs Into the Sand." *New York Times* (November 9, 1996).

Kan, Shirley A. "China's Compliance With Nonproliferation Commitments." A paper delivered at the Nonproliferation Policy Forum. Washington, D.C.: January 21, 1998.

———. *Chinese Proliferation of Weapons of Mass Destruction: Background and Analysis.* Washington, D.C.: Congressional Research Service, Library of Congress, September 13, 1996. Photocopy.

Karniol, Robert. "China Supplied Iran With Decontamination Agent." *Jane's Defence Weekly* (April 30, 1997).

Katzman, Kenneth. *Persian Gulf Armed Forces*. No. 95-390 F. Washington, D.C.: Congressional Research Service, Library of Congress, March 13, 1995.

Katzman, Kenneth and Shinn, Rinn-Sup. *North Korea: Military Relations With the Middle East*. Washington, D.C.: Congressional Research Service, Library of Congress, September 27, 1994.

Kay, David A. "Denial and Deception Practices of WMD Proliferators: Iraq and Beyond." *Weapons Proliferation in the 1990s*. Edited by Brad Roberts. Cambridge, Mass.: MIT Press, 1995.

Kay, David; Lehman, Ronald F.; and Woolsey, R. James. "First the Treaty, Then the Hard Work." *Washington Post* (April 13, 1997).

Keller, William W. "The Political Economy of Conventional Arms Proliferation." *Current History* (April 1997).

Kelley, Jack. "Warning Plentiful in Saudi Bombing." *USA Today* (August 26, 1996).

Kent, Glenn A., Lieutenant General, U.S. Air Force (retired). "The Relevance of High-Intensity Operations." Circa 1992. Photocopy.

Khalilzad, Zalmay and Ochmanek, David. "An Affordable Two-War Strategy." *Wall Street Journal* (March 13, 1997).

————. "Rethinking US Defence Planning." *Survival*. 39-1 (Spring 1997).

Kim Sang-Beom. "For the Record." *East Asian Review* (Winter 1997).

Kincade, William. *Nuclear Proliferation: Diminishing Threat?* INSS Occasional Paper 6. U.S. Air Force Academy, Colo.: Institute for National Security Studies, December 1995.

Kissinger, Henry. "India and Pakistan: After the Explosions." *Washington Post* (June 9, 1998).

Kitfield, James. "Counterproliferation." *Air Force Magazine* (October 1995).

Koller, Rudolph C., Jr. "Letters to the Editor." *Armed Forces Journal International* (October 1997).

Krepinevich, Andrew F., Jr. *Testimony Before the AirLand Subcommittee, Senate Armed Services Committee of the Future of Tactical Aviation*. Washington, D.C.: Center for Strategic and Budgetary Assessments, March 5, 1997.

———. "The Future of Tactical Aviation." Testimony Before the AirLand Subcommittee, Senate Armed Services Committee. Washington, D.C.: Center for Strategic and Budgetary Assessments, March 5, 1997. Photocopy.

Landay, Jonathan S. "Iran May Pose First Test of Chemical-Arms Ban." *Christian Science Monitor* (April 28, 1997).

———. "U.S. Defense Drifting Off Target." *Christian Science Monitor* (March 26, 1998).

"Lebed Again Says Russia Has Lost Some of Its Nuclear Weapons." *Reuters Information Service* (September 19, 1997).

Lebed, Alexander, General, Russian Army (retired). Remarks on *60 Minutes*, CBS Television (September 7, 1997).

Lennox, Duncan. "Iran's Ballistic Missile Projects: Uncovering the Evidence." *Jane's Intelligence Review* (June 1998).

Leopold, Reuven. *Sea-Based Aviation and the Next U.S. Aircraft Carrier Design: The CVX.* Cambridge, Mass.: Center for International Studies, Massachusetts Institute of Technology, 1998.

Linhard, Robert E., Major General, U.S. Air Force. "Counterproliferation Strategies: Countering Weapons of Mass Destruction." *Counter-Proliferation: Deterring Emerging Nuclear Actors.* A Defense Nuclear Agency-Sponsored Strategic Options Assessments Conference. McLean, Va.: Strategic Planning International, Inc., July 7–8, 1993.

Loh, John M., General, U.S. Air Force. "Bomber Requirements." Presentation to the Subcommittee on Nuclear Deterrence, Arms Control and Defense Intelligence, Senate Armed Services Committee. May 5, 1994. Photocopy.

Lozlow, Chris. "The Bombing of Khobar Towers: Who Did It, and Who Funded It." *Jane's Intelligence Review* (December 1997).

Lugar, Richard, Senator. Remarks on *ABC News* (Television) (October 2, 1997).

Luttwak, Edward N. "A Post-Heroic Military Policy." *Foreign Affairs.* 75-4 (July/August 1996).

Mandel, Robert. "Chemical Warfare: Act of Intimidation or Desperation?" *Armed Forces & Society.* 19-2 (Winter 1993).

Marshall, Toni. "India Announces Nuclear Tests: Move Could Spark Response By Its Bitter Rival, Pakistan." *Washington Times* (May 12, 1998).

Matthews, William. "Improved Space Assets Would Aid U.S. Forces In Persian Gulf Conflict." *Defense News* (February 23–March 1, 1998).

Maze, Rick. "Pentagon Ups Number of Troops Exposed to Toxic Weapons in Persian Gulf." *Army Times* (July 21, 1997).

McCaslin, John. "Inside the Beltway." *Washington Times* (July 1, 1998).

Meadows, Sandra I. "Logistics Load Makes Land Force Too Slow for 21st Century Warfare." *National Defense* (September 1997).

———. "Multi-Tiered Plan Aims at Thwarting Attacks on Battlefield, Continental U.S." *National Defense* (May/June 1997).

———. "U.S. Forces Prepare for Future Chemical, Biological Blitzkrieg." *National Defense* (September 1997).

Mehuron, Tamar A. "USAF Almanac 1998." *Air Force Magazine* (May 1998).

Meselson, Matthew. "How Serious Is the Biological Weapons Threat?" *Defense & Arms Control Studies Seminar.* Cambridge, Mass.: Center for International Studies, Massachusetts Institute of Technology, November 29, 1995.

Meyers, Steven Lee. "U.S. Calls Alert As Iraqis Strike a Kurd Enclave." *New York Times* (September 1, 1996).

———. "Pentagon Sees A New Threat By Iraq Forces." *New York Times* (August 31, 1996).

Millot, Marc Dean; Mollander, Roger; and Wilson, Peter A. *"The Day After..." Study: Nuclear Proliferation in the Post–Cold War World.* Vol. I—Summary Report. Santa Monica, Calif.: RAND Corporation, 1993.

Mintz, John and Smith, R. Jeffrey. "Military Underestimated Terrorists, Perry Says." *Washington Post* (July 10, 1996).

Mintz, John. "Sale of Aircraft and Machinery Shows Perils of Exporting Technology." *Washington Post* (June 7, 1998).

Mitchell, Alison. "U.S. Prepares Further Action Against Iraq As Clinton Vows He Will Extract 'a Price.'" *New York Times* (September 4, 1996).

Moodie, Michael. "Beyond Proliferation: The Challenge of Technology Diffusion." *Washington Quarterly* (Spring 1995).

Mulholland, David. "Pentagon May Enhance UAV Role." *Defense News* (April 20–26, 1998).

Murphy, James M., Major, U.S. Army. "...FROM THE SEA: Chemical and Biological Concerns." Newport, R.I.: Naval War College, June 17, 1994.

Nagler, Robert G. and others. *Ballistic Missile Proliferation: An Emerging Threat 1992*. Arlington, Va.: Systems Planning Corporation, October 1992.

Nagy, Paul. "One Insider's Look At the Quadrennial Defense Review." *MIT Security Studies Program Seminar*. Rapporteur: Tim Wolters. Cambridge, Mass.: Massachusetts Institute of Technology, February 11, 1998.

"National Security For Sale?" *Detroit News* [Editorial] (May 24, 1998).

"Navy Theater Air Defense." Briefing at the National Defense University Foundation Breakfast Seminar. Washington, D.C.: Capitol Hill Club, May 2, 1996. Photocopy.

Nelan, Bruce W. "How the Attack On Iraq Is Planned." *Time* (February 23, 1998).

———. "The Price of Fanaticism." *Time* (April 3, 1995).

Nerlich, Uwe. *Nuclear Non-State Actors: Lessons from the RAF-GDR Connection?* Ebenhausen, Germany: Stiftung Wissenschaft und Politk (SW), Forsdhungsinstitut fur Internationale Politik und Sicherheit, August 1993.

Novichkov, Nikolai. "Russia Details Illegal Deliveries to Armenia." *Jane's Defence Weekly* (April 16, 1997).

"Nuclear Taiwan." *CQ Washington Alert* (December 22, 1997).

"Nuclear Watchdog Unleashes New Powers to Stall Evaders." *Jane's Defence Weekly* (April 8, 1995).

Nunn, Sam. "Terrorism Meets Proliferation: A Post–Cold War Convergence of Threats." *The Monitor.* Center for International Trade and Security at the University of Georgia (Spring 1997).

Ochmanek, David and Sokolsky, Richard. "Employ Nuclear Deterrence." *Defense News* (January 12–18, 1998).

Ochmanek, David. "Time to Restructure U.S. Defense Forces." *Issues in Science and Technology* (Winter 1996–97).

Opall, Barbara. "DoD Lifts Code Limits in New Export Drive." *Defense News* (June 9–15, 1997).

———. "Israel Awaits NATO Summit Before Pressing Washington On Russia-Iran Missile Effort." *Defense News* (July 7–13, 1997).

Osullivan, Arieh. "Mordechai Favors 'Pre-emptive Strikes' Against Missiles." *Jerusalem Post* (October 28, 1997).

"Pakistan's New Danger Weapon Is 'Confirmed.'" *Jane's Defence Weekly* (December 3, 1997).

Payne, Keith B. *Deterrence in the Second Nuclear Age.* Lexington: University of Kentucky Press, 1996.

Perry, Charles M.; Pfaltzgraf, Robert L.; and Conway, Joseph C. *Long-Range Bombers & the Role of Airpower in the New Century.* Washington, D.C.: Institute for Foreign Policy Analysis, 1995.

Perry, Charles M.; Rothenberg, Laurence E.; and Davis, Jacquelyn K. *Airpower Synergies in the New Strategic Era: The Complementary Roles of Long-Range Bombers & Carrier-Based Aircraft.* McLean, Va.: Brassey's, 1997.

Perry, William J., Secretary of Defense. *Annual Report to the President and the Congress.* Washington, D.C.: Government Printing Office, 1996.

———. Preface. U.S. Department of Defense. *Proliferation: Threat and Response.* Washington, D.C.: Government Printing Office, April 1996.

———. "Preventive Defense." *Washington Times* (November 10, 1996).

———. Remarks on Weapons of Mass Destruction at the Georgetown University. Washington, D.C.: Department of Defense, April 18, 1996.

————. "Report to the President on the Protection of U.S. Forces Deployed Abroad." *Defense Issues*. 11-80. Washington, D.C.: Office of the Assistant Secretary of Defense for Public Affairs, September 16, 1996.

"Persian Gulf Vets Still Searching for Answers." *Checkpoint*. A publication of the Veterans of Foreign Wars (January/February 1997).

Peters, F. Whitten, Acting Secretary of the Air Force, and Ryan, Michael E., General, Chief of Staff of the Air Force. Testimony Before the Senate Armed Services Committee, February 12, 1998. Photocopy.

Peters, John E. "Technology and Advances in Foreign Military Capabilities." *Fletcher Forum in World Affairs* (Winter/Spring 1995).

Pillsbury, Michael. As quoted in "Gulf War Provided Ample Information for Chinese Military Thinkers." *Inside Missile Defense* (March 12, 1997).

Pincus, Walter. "Pentagon Stresses Control of Space." *Washington Post* (March 15, 1998).

————. "Smaller Spy Satellites May Give U.S. Stealth Capability Over Trouble Spots." *Washington Post* (February 1, 1998).

————. "Pentagon, CIA Differ on Missile Threat." *Washington Post* (June 7, 1998).

Pine, Art. "U.S. Hints It Would Bomb Libyan Weapons Facility." *Los Angeles Times* (April 11, 1996).

Plato. *Republic*. Book II.

Plaxe, Jack. "Libya's Role in International Terrorism." *Counterterrorism & Security Report*. 4-4. Winter 1996.

Poneman, Daniel. Special Assistant to the President. Letter to Robert Gallucci, Department of State, and Ashton Carter, Department of Defense. Subject: "Agreed Definitions." Washington, D.C.: National Security Council, February 18, 1994.

Powell, Colin L., General, U.S. Army. Chairman, Joint Chiefs of Staff. "The Base Force—A Total Force." A Briefing for Presentation to the Senate Appropriations Sub-Committee on Defense, 1991. Photocopy.

Priest, Dana. "Gas Exposure in Gulf War Revised." *Washington Post* (July 24, 1997).

————. "Poison Gas Exposure Estimate Is Growing." *Washington Post* (October 2, 1996).

————. "U.S. Cuts Forces in Persian Gulf." *Washington Post* (May 27, 1998).

Purver, Ron. *Chemical and Biological Terrorism: The Threat According to Open Literature.* Ottawa: Canadian Security Intelligence Service, June 1995.

————. *Report on Conference, "Preventing Super-Terrorism: Threats and Responses," at Tel Aviv University and the Center for Technological Education, Holon, Israel, 11–13 March 1997.* Ottawa: Canadian Security Intelligence Service, 1997.

Putting Cruise Missiles in Perspective: A Comparison of Direct Delivered Ordnance and Cruise Missiles in Illustrative Combat Scenarios. Arlington, Va.: SDS International, December 1996.

Raghunanshi, Vivek. "India Denies Deployment of Prithvi Near Pakistan." *Defense News* (June 16–23, 1997).

Ramachandran, Hari. "India Criticizes Big Five on China." *Washington Times* (June 6, 1998).

Ranger, Robin and Wiencek, David. *The Devil's Brew II: Weapons of Mass Destruction and International Security.* Lancaster, United Kingdom: Centre for Defence and International Security Studies, Lancaster University, 1997.

Ranger, Robin. Editor. *The Devil's Brews I: Chemical and Biological Weapons and Their Delivery Systems.* Bailrigg Memorandum 16. Lancaster, United Kingdom: Centre for Defence and International Security Studies, Lancaster University, 1996.

Rathmell, Andrew, Dr. "Chemical Weapons in the Middle East: Lessons From Iraq." *Jane's Intelligence Review* (December 1995).

Rattray, Gregory J. *Explaining Weapons Proliferation: Going Beyond the Security Dilemma.* INSS Occasional Paper No. 1. U.S. Air Force Academy, Colo.: Institute for National Security Studies, July 1994.

Richter, Paul. "U.S. Germ War Defenses Porous, Officials Warn Pentagon." *Los Angeles Times* (December 28, 1997).

Ricks, Thomas E. "How Wars Are Fought Will Change Radically, Pentagon Planner Says." *Wall Street Journal* (July 5, 1994).

Riley, Joyce. R.N., B.S.N. Letter to "Dear Gulf War Veteran and/or Supporter." Sugarland, Tex.: American Gulf War Veterans Association,1996.

———. "Reasons for the Cover-Up of 'Gulf War Syndrome.'" *Gulf War Syndrome*. Information packet. Sugarland, Tex.: American Gulf War Veterans Association, 1996.

Roberts, Guy B. *Five Minutes Past Midnight: The Clear and Present Danger of Nuclear Weapons Grade Fissile Materials*. INSS Occasional Paper 8. U.S. Air Force Academy, Colo.: Institute for National Security Studies, February 1996.

Rodriguez, Paul M. "Pentagon Denies Use of Compounds." *Washington Times* (August 15, 1997).

Roos, John G. "InfoTech InfoPower." *Armed Forces Journal International* (June 1994).

Rosenthal, A. M. "The Chosen Weapon." *New York Times* (October 17, 1997).

Russia. Foreign Intelligence Service Report. *A New Challenge After the Gulf War*. U.S. Foreign Broadcast Information Service. *Proliferation Issues*. JPRS-TND-93-007. March 5, 1993.

"Russia's Defence Minister Denies Nuclear Bombs Are Missing." *Reuters* (September 5, 1997).

"Saddam Hopes BW Confession Is Enough To Convince USA." *Jane's Defence Weekly* (September 2, 1995).

Sam Nunn Policy Forum. *Terrorism, Weapons of Mass Destruction, and U.S. Security*. Athens, Ga.: University of Georgia, April 28, 1997.

Sandrock, John H. *Arms Control and Nonproliferation: South Asia*. McLean, Va.: Science Applications International Corporation, November 19, 1993.

———. "South Asian Proliferation Drivers." *Adjusting to Change: Understanding Proliferation Risks*. A Defense Nuclear Agency-Sponsored Strategic Options Assessments Conference. McLean, Va.: Strategic Planning International, Inc., 1994.

Scarborough, Rowan. "China Helps Iran Develop Chemical Arms." *Washington Times* (April 11, 1997).

———. "Iraq 'Show' Riles Joint Chiefs." *Washington Times* (February 4,1998).

———. "Pentagon Asks Gulf Cuts for Morale, Cost." *Washington Times* (May 7, 1998).

Schlesinger, James. "Statement Before the National Security Committee, House of Representatives." February 12, 1997. Photocopy.

Schmitt, Eric. "Clinton, Claiming Success, Asserts Most Iraqi Troops Have Left Kurds' Enclave." *New York Times* (September 5, 1996).

Scowcroft, Brent and others. *Final Report of the Independent Bomber Force Review Commission.* Presented to The Honorable Duncan Hunter, Chairman, Military Procurement Subcommittee of the Committee on National Security, House of Representatives. Washington, D.C.: July 23, 1997.

"Security Council Informed of Missile Test Last Fall." *Washington Post* (February 14, 1998).

Shaud, John. "The Other Side of Khobar Towers." *Washington Times* (August 26, 1997).

Shenon, Philip. "Ex-C.I.A. Analysts Assert Cover-Up." *New York Times* (October 30, 1996).

———. "Half of Gulf-Illness Panel Now Calls Gas a Possible Factor." *New York Times* (August 19, 1997).

———. "Legacy of Illness for Unit That Blew Up Bunkers." *New York Times* (August 11, 1996).

———. "Many Veterans of the Gulf War Detail Illnesses From Chemicals." *New York Times* (September 20, 1996).

———. "Report Shows U.S. Was Told in 1991 of Chemical Arms." *New York Times* (August 28, 1996).

———. "Study Links Chemicals to Sick Veterans." *New York Times* (June 15, 1997).

———. "U.S. Jets Pounded Iraqi Arms Depot Storing Nerve Gas." *New York Times* (October 3, 1996).

———. "U.S. Widens Search For Gulf Veterans Near Depot Blast." *New York Times* (October 23, 1996).

Sheppard, Ben. "Too Close for Comfort: Ballistic Ambitions in South Asia." *Jane's Intelligence Review* (January 1998).

Sherman, Jason. "Iranian Impact." *Armed Forces Journal International* (January 1998).

Shuey, Robert. *Ballistic and Cruise Missile Forces of Foreign Countries.* Washington, D.C.: Congressional Research Service, Library of Congress, updated October 25, 1996.

Shy, John. "First Battles in Retrospect." *America's First Battles: 1776–1965.* Edited by Charles E. Heller and William A. Stofft. Lawrence, Kan.: University of Kansas Press, 1986.

Sieff, Martin and Kaplan, Refet. "Experts: U.S. Should've Seen Attack Coming." *Washington Times* (September 3, 1996).

Sieff, Martin. "Albright Oks Saddam's Ouster." *Washington Times* (March 27, 1997).

Siegel, Adam B. *Basing and Other Constraints on Land-Based Aviation Contributions to U.S. Contingency Operations.* Alexandria, Va.: Center for Naval Analyses, 1995.

"Sloppily and Unreliable." *Washington Post* [Editorial] (April 11, 1997).

Smith, R. Jeffrey and Frankel, Glenn. "Saddam's Nuclear-Weapons Dream: A Lingering Nightmare." *Washington Post* (October 13, 1991).

Smith, R. Jeffrey and Hoffman, David. "No Support Found for Report of Lost Russian Suitcase-Sized Nuclear Weapons." *Washington Post* (September 5, 1997).

Smith, R. Jeffrey. "Clinton Changes Nuclear Strategy." *Washington Post* (December 7, 1997).

———. "Iraq Had Program For Germ Warfare." *Washington Post* (July 6, 1995).

———. "Iraq's Drive for a Biological Arsenal." *Washington Post* (November 21, 1997).

———. "Iraq's Nuclear Prowess Underestimated by U.S." *Washington Post* (October 13, 1991).

———. "2 Panels Reject Iraqi Claim on Arms." *Washington Post* (February 20, 1998).

Spranza, Francis. "The Will of Allah?" *Aviation Security International.* (1997).

Spykman, Nicholas John. *America's Strategy in World Politics.* 1942. Reprint: Archon Books, 1970.

Starr, Barbara. "Egypt and Syria Are BW Capable, Says Agency." *Jane's Defence Weekly* (August 21, 1996).

———. "Interview." *Jane's Defence Weekly* (August 14, 1996).

———. "Iran Has Vast Stockpiles of CW Agents, Says CIA." *Jane's Defence Weekly* (August 14, 1996).

Stogel, Stewart. "Iraq Fired Scuds At Israeli Reactor." *Washington Times* (January 1, 1998).

Strobel, Warren P. "U.S. Launches Second Attack on Iraq." *Washington Times* (September 4, 1996).

"Sudan Seeking Chemical Weapons." *Arabic News* (October 25, 1997).

Sullivan, Kevin. "N. Korea Admits Selling Missiles." *Washington Post* (June 17, 1998).

Sundarji, Krishnaswami, General, Army of India (retired). Remarks at the U.S. *International Conference on Controlling Arms.* Richmond, Va.: Defense Nuclear Agency, June 7–10, 1993.

———. "Strategic Stability in the Early 2000s: An Indian View of a South Asian Model." *NATO Advanced Research Workshop: Strategic Stability in the Post–Cold War World and the Future of Nuclear Disarmament.* Edited by Melvin L. Best, Jr., John Hughes-Wilson, and Andrei A. Piontkowsky. Brussels, Belgium: NATO Scientific and Environmental Affairs Division, April 6–10, 1995.

Sun Tzu. *The Art of War.* Translated by Samuel B. Griffith. New York: Oxford University Press, 1977.

Swamy, M. R. Narayan. "India Lashes West for 'Hypocrisy' of Anti-Nuclear Stance." *Washington Times* (May 21, 1998).

"Syria to Make Chemical Bomblets for 'Scud Cs.'" *Jane's Defence Weekly* (September 3, 1997).

Szafranski, Richard, Colonel, U.S. Air Force. "Parallel War and Hyperwar: Is Every Want a Weakness?" *Proceedings*. U.S. Naval Institute (August 1995).

"Team Was Close to Uncovering Iraqi Nerve Gas, Report Says." *USA Today* (November 3, 1997).

"Tehran Deal To Help With Libyan Missile." *The Times* (London) (November 21, 1997).

"Tehran Warns Israel Against Attack On Its Ballistic Missiles." *Arabic News* (October 30, 1997).

Teischer, Howard. "The Naive Hope That Allowed Hussein to Weigh Mass Murder." *Los Angeles Times* (September 10, 1995).

Tenet, George. "Does America Need the CIA?" Remarks at the Gerald Ford Library Conference in Ann Arbor, Michigan (November 19, 1997). *Periscope*. Newsletter of the Association of Former Intelligence Officers (April 1998).

"The Big, Mean War Machine." *U.S. News & World Report* (February 28, 1994).

"The Future of Warfare." *Economist* (March 8, 1997).

The Global Positioning System: Civil and Military Uses. MIT Security Studies Conference Series. Cambridge, Mass.: Massachusetts Institute of Technology, Security Studies Program, 1997.

"The Pentagon's Quadrennial Riddle." *Washington Times* [Editorial] (June 2, 1997).

The Plutonium Trade: A Troubling New Era of Proliferation. Greenpeace International, March 1, 1993.

"The Threat of Chemical/Biological Terrorism." *Commentary*. No. 60. Ottawa, Canada: Canadian Security Intelligence Service, August 1995.

Thompson, Loren. "Airborne Laser Makes Sense for Missile Defense." *Defense Week* (February 17, 1998).

———. "F-22 Counters Emerging Missile Threat to U.S. Air Superiority." *ADTI Defense Issue Brief*. Arlington, Va.: Alexis de Tocqueville Institution, October 15, 1997.

———. "Joint STARS Can Save Troops' Lives." *Air Force Times* (January 12,1998).

Timmerman, Kenneth R. "A Nuclear Iraq—Again." *Wall Street Journal* (November 12, 1993).

———. "Missile Threat From Iran." *Reader's Digest* (January 1998).

Tirpak, John A. "B-1s for Theater War." *Air Force Magazine* (June 1998).

———. "Brilliant Weapons." *Air Force Magazine* (February 1998).

———. "The NDP and the Transformation Strategy." *Air Force Magazine* (March 1998).

"Transportable Station Receives Satellite Imagery." *Jane's International Defense Review* (February 1997).

Truesdell, Amy. "Cruise Missiles: The Discriminating Weapons of Choice?" *Jane's Intelligence Review* (February 2, 1997).

Tucker, Jonathan B. "Chemical/Biological Terrorism: Coping with a New Threat." *Politics and the Life Sciences* (September 1996).

———. "The Biological Weapons Threat." *Current History* (April 1997).

Tuite, James J., III. "Persian Gulf Syndrome and the Delayed Toxic Effects of Chemical Agent Exposure." March 1995. Photocopy.

Turbiville, Graham H., Jr. *Weapons Proliferation and Organized Crime: The Russian Military and Security Force Dimension.* INSS Occasional Paper 10. U.S. Air Force Academy, Colo.: Institute for National Security Studies, June 1996.

"20,800 Gulf Vets Exposed To Nerve Agents." *Veterans of Foreign Wars* (December 1996).

United Nations, Security Council. *Consolidated Report On the First Two IAEA Inspections Under Security Council Resolution 687 (1991) of Iraqi Nuclear Capabilities.* U.N. Doc. S/22788 (July 15, 1991).

———. *First Report on the Sixth IAEA On-Site Inspection in Iraq Under Security Council Resolution 687 (1991).* U.N. Doc. S/23122 (October 8, 1991).

————. *Fourth Report of the Executive Chairman of the Special Commission Established By the Secretary-General Pursuant to Paragraph 9 (b) (i) of Security Council Resolution 687 (1991), On the Activities of the Special Commission.* U.N. Doc. S/24984 (December 17, 1992).

————. *Ninth Report of the Executive Chairman of the Special Commission Established By the Secretary-General Pursuant to Paragraph 9 (b) (i) of Security Council Resolution 687 (1991), On the Activities of the Special Commission.* U.N. Doc. S/1995/494 (June 20, 1995).

————. *Report by the Executive Chairman of the Special Commission Established by the Secretary-General Pursuant to Paragraph 9 (b) (i) Security Council Resolution 687 (1991).* U.N. Doc. S/23165 (October 25, 1991).

————. *Report of the Executive Chairman of the Special Commission Established By the Secretary-General Pursuant to Paragraph 9 (b) (i) of Security Council Resolution 687 (1991).* U.N. Doc. S/23268 (December 4, 1991).

————. *Report of the Secretary-General On the Activities of the Special Commission Established By the Secretary-General Pursuant to Paragraph 9 (b) (i) of Resolution 687 (1991).* U.N. Doc. S/1996/258 (April 11, 1996).

————. *Report of the Secretary-General On the Activities of the Special Commission Established By the Secretary-General Pursuant to Paragraph 9 (b) (i) of Resolution 687 (1991).* U.N. Doc. S/1997/301 (April 11, 1997).

————. *Report of the Secretary-General on the Status of the Implementation of the Special Commissions Plan for the Ongoing Monitoring and Verification of Iraq's Compliance with Relevant Parts of Section C of Security Council Resolution 687 (1991).* U.N. Doc. S/1995/864 (October 11, 1995).

————. *Report of the Secretary-General on the Status of the Implementation of the Special Commission's Plan for the Ongoing Monitoring and Verification of Iraq's Compliance With Relevant Parts of Section C of Security Council Resolution 687 (1991).* U.N. Doc. S/1995/284 (April 10, 1995).

————. *Report of the Seventh IAEA On-Site Inspection in Iraq Under Security Council Resolution 687 (1991).* U.N. Doc. S/23215 (May 22, 1992).

————. *Report of the Status of Compliance By Iraq With the Obligation Placed Upon It Under Section C of Security Council Resolution 687 (1991) and Resolutions 707 (1991) and 715 (1991).* U.N. Doc. S/23993 (May 22, 1992).

————. *Report on the Twelfth IAEA On-Site Inspection in Iraq Under Security Council Resolution 687 (1991)* (May 26–June 4, 1992). U.N. Doc. S/24223 (July 2, 1992).

————. *Report to the Secretary-General On Activities of the Special Commission Established By the Secretary-General Pursuant to Paragraph 9 (b) (i) of Resolution 687 (1991).* U.N. Doc. S/1996/848 (October 11, 1996).

————. *Seventh Report of the Executive Chairman of the Special Commission Established By the Secretary-General Pursuant to Paragraph 9 (b) (i) of Security Council Resolution 687 (1991), On the Activities of the Special Commission.* U.N. Doc. S/1994/750 (June 24, 1994).

————. Special Commission on Iraq. Information Paper (October 16, 1995). Photocopy.

————. Special Commission on Iraq. "Major Sites Associated with Iraq's Past WMD Programs." New York: UNSCOM, October 3, 1995. Photocopy.

————. Special Commission on Iraq. *Report of the Secretary-General,* U.N. Doc. S/1996/258 (April 11, 1996).

————. *Tenth Report of the Executive Chairman of the Special Commission Established By the Secretary-General Pursuant to Paragraph 9 (b) (i) of Security Council Resolution 687 (1991), and Paragraph 3 of Resolution 699 (1991) On the Activities of the Special Commission.* U.N. Doc. S/1995/1038 (December 17, 1995).

————. *Third Report By the Executive Chairman of the Special Commission Established By the Secretary-General Pursuant to Paragraph 9 (b) (i) of Security Council Resolution 687 (1991).* U.N. Doc. S/24108 (June 16, 1992).

"U.N. Official: Iraq Worked On Radiological Arms." *Washington Post* (November 8, 1995).

"USAF Does Not Need B-3." *Defense News* [Editorial] (April 6–12, 1998).

U.S. Arms Control and Disarmament Agency. "Chemical Weapon Convention: A Balance Between Obligations and the Needs of States Parties." *Occasional Paper*. Washington, D.C.: January 5, 1993.

———. *World Military Expenditures and Arms Transfers 1995*. Washington, D.C.: Government Printing Office, 1996.

U.S. Central Intelligence Agency. "The Acquisition of Technology Relating to Weapons of Mass Destruction and Advanced Conventional Weapons." Reprinted in *Inside Missile Defense* (July 16, 1997).

U.S. Commission on Integrated Long-Term Strategy. *The Future of Containment*. Report of the Offense-Defense Working Group. Washington, D.C.: Department of Defense, October 1988.

U.S. Commission on Roles and Missions of the Armed Forces. *Directions of Defense*. Washington, D.C.: Government Printing Office, May 24, 1995.

———. *Future Bomber Force*. Arlington, Va.: Aerospace Education Foundation, May 1995.

U.S. Congress. Congressional Budget Office. *Moving U.S. Forces: Options for Strategic Mobility*. Washington, D.C.: Government Printing Office, February 1997.

———. Congressional Budget Office. *Structuring the Active and Reserve Army for the 21st Century*. Washington, D.C.: Government Printing Office, December 1997.

———. House of Representatives. National Security Committee. Military Procurement Subcommittee. "Hearing on the Report of the Long-Range Airpower Review Panel." Washington, D.C.: April 1, 1998.

———. House of Representatives. National Security Committee. *Press Release*, May 6, 1998.

———. Office of Technology Assessment. *Technologies Underlying Weapons of Mass Destruction*. OTA-BP-ISC-115. Washington, D.C.: Government Printing Office, December 1993.

———. Senate. Committee on Governmental Affairs. *The Proliferation Primer.* A Majority Report of the Subcommittee on International Security, Proliferation, and Federal Services. Washington, D.C.: January 1998.

———. Senate. Committee on Banking, Housing, and Urban Affairs. *United States Dual-Use Exports to Iraq and Their Impact on the Health of the Persian Gulf War Veterans.* 103d Cong., 2d sess. Washington, D.C.: Government Printing Office, 1994.

———. Senate. Committee on Banking, Housing and Urban Affairs. *U.S. Chemical and Biological Warfare-Related Dual Use Exports to Iraq and Their Possible Impact on the Health Consequences of the Persian Gulf War.* 103d Cong., 2d sess. May 25, 1994.

U.S. Defense Science Board. *Investments for 21st Century Military Superiority.* Washington, D.C.: Office of the Secretary of Defense, November 1995.

———. *Tactics and Technology for 21st Century Military Superiority.* Vol. I—Final Report, 1996 Summer Study Task Force. Washington, D.C.: Office of the Secretary of Defense, October 1996.

———. *Report of the Defense Science Board Task Force on Tactical Air Warfare.* Washington, D.C.: Office of the Secretary of Defense, November 1993.

U.S. Department of Defense. Background Briefing on the Counterproliferation Initiative. Attributable to a "Senior Defense Official." Transcript ID No. 1020543. Washington, D.C.: Department of Defense, December 7, 1993.

———. *Compendium of the Defense Counterproliferation Initiative Conference.* Held at the Los Alamos National Laboratory, New Mexico. Washington, D.C.: Department of Defense, May 6–7, 1994.

———. *Compendium of the Second Annual Counterproliferation Conference.* Held at the National Defense University. Washington, D.C.: Department of Defense, October 26–27, 1995.

———. *Conduct of the Persian Gulf War.* Washington, D.C.: Government Printing Office, April 1992.

———. *Defense Almanac 1997.* Washington, D.C.: Government Printing Office, 1997.

————. *Proliferation: Threat and Response.* Washington, D.C.: Government Printing Office, April 1996.

————. *Proliferation: Threat and Response.* Washington, D.C.: Government Printing Office, November 1997.

————. *Report of Activities and Programs for Countering Proliferation and NBC Terrorism.* Washington, D.C.: Department of Defense, May 1997.

U.S. Department of Justice. Federal Bureau of Investigation. *Terrorism in the United States: 1995.* Washington, D.C.: Government Printing Office, 1997.

U.S. Department of State. *Patterns of Global Terrorism: 1996.* Washington, D.C.: April 1997.

U.S. Department of the Air Force. *Gulf War Air Power Survey: A Statistical Compendium and Chronology.* Vol. V. Washington, D.C.: Government Printing Office, 1993.

————. *Gulf War Air Power Survey: Operations and Effects and Effectiveness.* Vol. II, Part 1. Washington, D.C.: Government Printing Office, 1993.

————. *Gulf War Air Power Survey: Operations and Effects and Effectiveness.* Vol. II, Part 2. Washington, D.C.: Government Printing Office, 1993.

————. *Gulf War Air Power Survey: Planning and Command and Control.* Vol. I, Part 1. Washington, D.C.: Government Printing Office, 1993.

————. *Gulf War Air Power Survey: Summary Report.* Washington, D.C.: Government Printing Office, 1993.

U.S. Department of the Army. *Handbook: Medical Management of Biological Casualties.* Second edition. Fort Detrick, Md.: Medical Research Institute of Infectious Diseases, 1996.

————. *Medical Management of Chemical Casualties.* Second edition. Aberdeen Proving Ground, Md.: Medical Research Institute of Chemical Defense, 1995.

————. Vice Chief of Staff. "Chemical Functional Area Assessment." Washington, D.C.: The Pentagon, May 23, 1997. Photocopy.

U.S. Department of the Navy. "Tomahawk Cruise Missile," *Navy Fact File* (May 1998).

U.S. Foreign Broadcast Information Service. *Proliferations Issues—Russian Federation: Foreign Intelligence Service Report—A New Challenge After the Cold War: Proliferation of Weapons of Mass Destruction.* JPRS-TND-93-007. March 5, 1993.

U.S. General Accounting Office. *Arms Control: U.S. and International Efforts to Ban Biological Weapons.* GAO/NSIAD-93-113. Washington, D.C.: General Accounting Office, 1992.

————. *Bottom-Up Review: Analysis of DOD War Game to Test Key Assumptions.* GAO/NSIAD-96-170. Washington, D.C.: General Accounting Office, 1996.

————. *Combatting Terrorism: Status of DOD Efforts to Protect Its Forces Overseas.* GAO/NSIAD-97-207. Washington, D.C.: General Accounting Office, July 1997.

————. *Export Controls: Change in Export Licensing Jurisdiction for Two Sensitive Dual-Use Items.* GAO/NSIAD-97-24. Washington, D.C.: General Accounting Office, January 1997.

————. *Export Controls: Sale of Telecommunications Equipment to China.* GAO/NSIAD-97-5. Washington, D.C.: General Accounting Office, November 1996.

————. *Export Controls: Sensitive Machine Tool Exports to China.* GAO/ NSIAD-97-4. Washington, D.C.: General Accounting Office, November 1996.

————. *Gulf War Illnesses' Improved Monitoring of Clinical Progress and Reexamination of Research Emphases Are Needed.* GAO/ NSIAD-97-163. Washington, D.C.: General Accounting Office, June 1997.

————. *Gulf War Illnesses: Public and Private Efforts Relating to Exposures of U.S. Personnel to Chemical Attacks.* Washington, D.C.: General Accounting Office, October 1997.

————. *Military Exports: Offset Demands Continue to Grow.* Washington, D.C.: General Accounting Office, 1996.

————. *Nuclear Nonproliferation: Status of U.S. Efforts to Improve Nuclear Material Controls in Newly Independent States.* GAO/NSIAD/RCED-96-89. Washington, D.C.: General Accounting Office, March 1996.

U.S. Joint Chiefs of Staff. *Joint Doctrine for Nuclear, Biological, and Chemical (NBC) Defense.* Joint Pub. 3-11. Washington, D.C.: Joint Staff, April 15, 1994.

————. *National Military Strategy of the United States of America 1997.* Washington, D.C.: Government Printing Office, 1997.

U.S. National Defense Panel. *Transforming Defense: National Security in the 21st Century.* Arlington, Va.: December 1997.

U.S. National Defense University. Center for Counterproliferation Research. *The Impact of the Proliferation of Nuclear, Biological, and Chemical (NBC) Weapons on U.S. Army Doctrine, Operating Principles, and Capabilities.* Third Workshop: "Unit Operations." Washington, D.C.: March 16, 1995.

————. *1997 Strategic Assessment.* Washington, D.C.: Government Printing Office, 1997.

————. *Strategic Assessment 1996.* Washington, D.C.: Government Printing Office, 1996.

U.S. Panel to Review Long-Range Air Power. "Summary of the Principal Findings and Recommendations" (March 1998). Washington, D.C.: Hearings of the U.S. House National Security Committee, Military Procurement Subcommittee, April 1, 1998.

U.S. *Presidential Advisory Committee on Gulf War Veterans' Illnesses: Final Report.* Washington, D.C.: Government Printing Office, December 1996).

————. *Presidential Advisory Committee on Gulf War Veterans' Illnesses: Special Report.* Washington, D.C.: Government Printing Office, October 1997.

"U.S. Raises Estimate of Troops Near Iraqi Chemical Arms." *Washington Post* (June 27, 1997).

"U.S., Russia Still At Odds Over Iran." *Reuters* (January 16, 1998).

"U.S. Tells Gulf Veterans of Exposure During War." *Washington Times* (July 25, 1997).

U.S. White House. "U.S. Policy on Counterterrorism." Presidential Decision Directive 39 (partially declassified and released on January 1, 1997). Washington, D.C.: June 21, 1995.

van Creveld, Martin. *Nuclear Proliferation and the Future of Conflict.* New York: Free Press, 1993.

Venter, Al J. "Biological Warfare Atrocities Revealed." *Jane's Intelligence Review and Jane's Sentinel Pointer* (March 1998).

———. "Experts Differ On Iraq's A-bomb Threat." *Jane's Intelligence Review and Jane's Sentinel Pointer* (June 1998).

———. "Iran Still Exporting Terrorism to Spread Its Islamic Vision." *Jane's Intelligence Review* (November 1997).

———. "How Saddam Almost Built His Bomb." *Jane's Intelligence Review* (December 1997).

———. "Sverdlovsk Outbreak: A Portent of Disaster." *Jane's Intelligence Review*, 10-5 (May 1998).

Vickers, Michael. "QDR Fails to Boldly Confront Future." *Defense News* (June 16–22, 1997).

———. *Warfare in 2020: A Primer.* Washington, D.C.: Center for Strategic and Budgetary Assessments, October 1996.

Wall, Robert. "The Devastating Impact of Sensor Fuzed Weapons." *Air Force Magazine* (March 1998).

———. "The Electronic Triad." *Air Force Magazine* (January 1998).

Warden, John A., III. *The Air Campaign: Planning for Combat.* Washington, D.C.: National Defense University Press, 1988.

"War Games to Include Cruise Missile Threats." *Aviation Week & Space Technology* (July 14, 1997).

Washburn, Jennifer. "Unethical Arms Sales." *Washington Times* (May 14, 1997).

Weaver, Greg and Glaes, J. David. *Inviting Disaster: How Weapons of Mass Destruction Undermine U.S. Strategy for Projecting Military Power.* McLean, Va.: AMCODA Press, 1997.

Webster, William H. and others. *Russian Organized Crime.* Washington, D.C.: Center for Strategic and International Studies, 1997.

Weinberger, Caspar; Carlucci, Frank; Rumsfeld, Donald; Cheney, Dick; Perry, William; Brown, Harold; and Schlesinger, James. "Seven Former Defense Secretaries Endorse Full Funding for F-22." Press release. Arlington, Va.: Alexis de Tocqueville Institution, April 27, 1998.

Weiner, Tim. "Iraq Pulling Out, But Leaving Spies Behind, U.S. Says." *New York Times* (September 6, 1996).

―――. "US Spy Halted Taiwan N-bomb." *New York Times* (December 22, 1997).

Welch, Jasper. "Bomber Forces for 'Cold Start' Conflicts." *Air Force Magazine* (December 1994).

Weldon, Curt, Representative. Remarks on *60 Minutes*. CBS Television (September 7, 1997).

―――. "Word For Word." *Defense News* (August 5–11, 1996).

White, Deedee. *Characterization and Historical Review of Chemical/ Biological Weapons: Mid-Term Review*. San Diego, Calif.: Science Applications International Corporation, 1992.

Wickersham, Frank G., III. "Technology Fault Lines." McLean, Va.: Strategic Planning International, Inc., November 9, 1994.

Wiencek, David G. *Dangerous Arsenals: Missile Threats In and From Asia*. Bailrigg Memorandum 22. Lancaster, United Kingdom: Centre for Defence and International Studies, Lancaster University.

Wilkening, Dean and Watman, Kenneth. *Nuclear Deterrence In a Regional Context*. Santa Monica, Calif.: RAND Corporation, 1995.

Woellert, Lorraine. "After Atomic Tests, Economic Fallout?" *Washington Times* (May 13, 1998).

Wohlstetter, Albert and Roberta. *Responding to Ambiguous Signals of Soviet Imminent or Future Power Projection*. Vol. I. Marina del Rey, Calif.: Pan Heuristics, Inc., 1982.

Woolsey, R. James. Remarks at the National Defense University Foundation and American Defense Preparedness Association Breakfast Seminar. Washington, D.C.: Capitol Hill Club, April 24, 1997.

Yengst, W. C. and others. *Dispersal of Hazardous Gases*. McLean, Va.: Science Applications International Corporation, September 1994.

Zelikow, Philip. "Offensive Military Options." *New Nuclear Nations: Consequences for U.S. Policy*. Edited by Robert D. Blackwill and Albert Carnesale. New York: Council on Foreign Relations, 1993.

Zimmerman, Peter D. "Proliferation: Bronze Medal Technology Is Enough." *Orbis* (Winter 1994).

INDEX

toxicity, 65–66
bubonic plague, 57, 63, 66, 68, 79
    plague-infected fleas, 58
camel pox, 72, 74
cholera, 57, 66, 192
clostridium perfringens, 70–71, 73
Deer Fly Fever (Tularemia), 64
dysentery, 57
dysentery cholera, 58
epidemic haemorrhagia fever, 57
fungus aspergillus, 73
gas gangrene, 57
glanders, 189
hemorrhagic conjunctivitis, 72, 74
influenza, 57
mad cow disease, 79
measles, 79
mycotoxins, 70
pneumonia, 79
Q-fever, 63, 68, 189
rabbit fever (Tularemia), 64
ricin, 66, 70, 72, 188–90
rotavirus, 72, 74
smallpox, 57–58, 65
thyroid, 58
tricothecene mycotoxins, 73–74
tularemia, 57, 63–66
typhoidal tularmia, 66
Venezuelan Equine Encephalitis, 63, 65
viral hemorrhagic fever, 63
Biological weapons, 57–79
aerial bombs, 75
artillery shells, 74
attacks on U.S. forces, 11–12
eight basic steps, 66
missile warheads, 69, 72–73, 75,
    137, 149
    bomblets, 63
    cluster munitions, 69, 120
proliferation of, 5–7, 16, 60 fig. 3.1,
    66–70
remotely piloted vehicles, 74, 140
rockets, 74
sprayers, 69, 74, 212, 215
terrorists, 9, 185, 188–90
Biological Weapons Convention, 57, 61
Biosafety, Levels 3 and 4, 69
Biotechnology industry, 59, 68
Black market, arms sales, 103–04, 189, 255
Iraq, 208–19
growing world market, 109–10
suppliers and buyers: China, Iran,
    North Korea, 117
Blair, David, 9, 259

Blanck, Ronald, 154, 166
Blix, Hans, 46
"Blowback," 151–76
definition, 151n
from Coalition bombing, 83, 164–66
Bolivia,
grey and black arms market, 110
Bombers, long-range (B-52, B-1, B-2),
    240, 357
cruise missile carrier (B-52), 242–43
enable naval air strikes, 370
follow-on bomber,
    B-3, 376–77
    B-2B, 376–77
halt armored invasions, 358–59
killing of B-2 (1997), 294, 298–99
long-range strike, 339, 357, 382,
    392, 400
modernization, 376
precision strike capabilities, 17, 320,
    322 fig, 12.5, 323 fig. 12.6,
    365–68, 398
precision strike requirements, 361–63
President's Long-Range Airpower
    Panel, 372–73, 376–77
power projection, 240–45, 339,
    344–45, 359, 361, 403
Bosnia, 110, 186
Bihac (town), 145
Bottom-Up Review, 269–70, 301
as criteria for Heavy Bomber Force
    Study, 298
enhanced passive defenses, 285
underfunded, 293
Botulinum toxin. See also biological warfare
    agents.
Aum Shinrikyo (Japan), 191
ease of production, 189
filled in bombs and missile warheads,
    73, 75–76, 211
Iraqi production, 70–72, 211
Japanese production, World War II, 57
Persian Gulf War threat, 213–14
toxicity, 65–66
Brazil, 120, 218
long-range artillery rocket, 115
missile technology transfer, 143
Brilliant Antiarmor Submunition (BAT), 359,
    365–66, 373
Britain, 52, 66, 304, 404
anthrax experiments, 64
arms sales, 104, 109, 137
British Library, 191
discover Iraqi chemical mines, 162

Nuclear Non-Proliferation Treaty,
28, 279
nuclear weapons, 26
protection against cyanide in World
War I, 82
U.N. inspection crisis (1997-98),
238, 243
U.N. panel on Iraqi VX production, 101
V-1 and V-2 missile attacks in World
War II, 135
Broad, William, 75
Bubonic plague, 57, 63, 66, 68, 79. *See also*
biological warfare agents.
plague-infected fleas, 58
Buchan, Glenn, 298, 363
Budget-based planning, 14, 301–02
Quadrennial Defense Review (1997),
270–71
shift to objectives-based planning, 387
shrouds military risks, 198, 300
Bulgaria, 66, 83
grey and black arms market, 110
Burdeshaw Associates, 362
Bush Administration, 173, 213, 388
Bush, George, 216, 277
Butler, Richard, 100
"Buzz Bombs," 135

Cable News Network (CNN), 174, 227, 245
Cambodia (Kampuchea), 73
Camel pox, 72, 74. *See also* biological
warfare agents.
Canada,
Canadian Security Intelligence Service,
192n
export of portable satellite ground
station, 115
Capitol Hill, 269, 272
Carl Vinson, 240
CBS, 192
Center for Policy Research, 194
Central Asia, 389
Central Intelligence Agency,
chemical blowback from Coalition
bombing, 164
chemical exposure model, Khamisiyah
(Iraq), 157
defector (Taiwan), 33
Director of Central Intelligence, 39, 126
Gulf War Syndrome, 152, 171, 173
intelligence estimate, Iraq (1989-90), 53
missile estimate, North Korea, 124
Chad, 82
Challenger, main battle tank, Britain, 108

Chang, Hsien-yi, 33
Chang, Mengxiong, 313
Chechnya, 52, 186
Chemex process, 47
Chemical terrorism, 9, 188, 190–92
Chemical warfare agents, 12, 86–91, 149
chlorine gas, 82, 91, 97
chloropicrin, 82
cyanide, 82, 85, 90–92, 188
GB/GF mixture (Iraq), 99, 155–56
GF, nerve agent, 87–88, 155, 215
lewisite, 82, 90, 92, 161
mustard gas, 85–86, 96
Bari Harbor (Italy), World War II,
245–46, 247 fig. 10.9
detection of, Persian Gulf War,
161, 165, 169
ease of production, 92, 94–95
effects of mustard vapor, 89
table 4.4
historical uses, (1915-91), 82–83
Iran, 85
Iran-Iraq War (1980-88), 214
Iraq, 96–97, 99, 100 table 4.6
Iraq's use against Kurdish civilians,
(1988), 215, 403–05
Libya, 83
probable uses in Persian Gulf War,
157, 174
terrorism, 188
toxicity, 90
phosgene, 82, 85, 87, 91
phosphorus trichloride, 97
pulmonary agents, 91
sarin (GB), nerve agent, 66, 87, 167
Aum Shinrikyo, 52, 191-92
detection of, Persian Gulf War, 165
exposure of U.S. forces,
Khamisiyah (1991), 155–57
Iraq, 96, 99, 100 table 4.6, 215
Syria, 83
terrorism, 188
soman (GD), nerve agent, 87, 95, 215
tabun (GA), nerve agent, 87
Aum Shinrikyo, 191
ease of production, 91–95
Iraq, 96–97
use in Iran-Iraq War
(1980-88), 214
use in Soviet-Afghan War
(1979-88), 82
VX, nerve agent, 66, 87, 255
Iraq, 79, 96–97, 99, 215

thinking, 7, 348–49, 401
U.S. planning factors, 7, 387
Command, Control, Communications,
Computers, Intelligence, Surveillance, and
Reconnaissance (C4ISR), 332–38, 342,
346–47, 354–55, 368, 371–72,
379, 385
Commission on Roles and Missions of the
Armed Forces, 324
Comprehensive Test Ban Treaty, 26, 28
Congress, U.S., 270, 283, 297, 301–02, 387.
See also House of Representatives
and Senate.
Independent Bomber Force Review
Commission, report, 265
killing the B-2 bomber (1997), 299
National Defense Panel, report, 388
non/counterproliferation, report, 292–93
Contaminated environments, 21, 81, 151, 176
biologically and chemically, 11–12, 249,
255, 285–88, 292, 342, 398
Conventional Air Launched Cruise Missile
(CALCM), 243, 361, 366, 382
Coordinating Committee for Multilateral
Export Controls (COCOM), 103, 106
Corsica, 345
Council on Foreign Relations, 403
Counterproliferation, 277, 280, 287
definition, 268n
Initiative, 268, 293–95
Counter-stealth radars, 108
Counter-terrorism policy, U.S., 181–82
Counter-Weapons of Mass Destruction Single
Integrated Operational Plan, 380–84
Courter, Jim, 299
Croatia, 118
Crime syndicates,
cooperation: American, Russian,
Sicilian, Columbian, 37
Cruise missiles, 39, 135–40
definition, 119n
Global Positioning System,
guidance, 122
proliferation of, 9, 21, 107, 122–23,
139 fig. 6.5, 226
U.S., 17, 343,
Conventional air-launched, 243,
361, 366, 382
Tomahawk sea-launched, 83, 111,
317, 382
Cryptological equipment, 108
Cuba, 142
Cullinan, Dennis, 166

Cyanide, 82, 85, 90–92, 188. *See also*
chemical warfare agents.
Czechoslovakia, former, 169
anti-chemical defense unit, 164
detection of mustard gas, Persian Gulf
War, 169
detection of sarin, Persian Gulf War,
154, 165
fissile material, smuggling
intercepts, 36
Czech Republic, 36
ministry of defense, 154
sale of counter-stealth radar, 108

Dassault, 109
Decontamination, chemical and biological
agents, 64, 251, 285–87, 296
Deep Attack Weapons Mix Study
(DAWMS), 299
Deer Fly Fever (Tularemia), 64. *See also*
biological warfare agents.
Defense conversion, 103
Defense Intelligence Agency, 43, 210, 213
Defense News, 376
Defense Science Board, 286, 340, 345, 375
Deoxyribonucleic acid (DNA), 215
Department of Commerce, 113–14
Department of Defense,
airpower deployment rates,
assumptions, 230 fig. 10.1
airpower deployment rates, assumptions versus reality, 237 fig. 10.5
analytical assumptions, 17, 231, 235,
236 fig, 10.4, 238, 240
antiterrorism, 182, 184
chemical-biological defense
spending, 286
cruise missile defenses, 140
detailed guidance on Heavy Bomber
Force Study, 298
developing military plans, 380–382
follow-on bomber force plan, 357
Gulf War Syndrome, 151–76
Inspector General, Defense Criminal
Investigation Service, 176
over reliance on short-range
aircraft, 352
restructure armed forces, 269–73, 400
seven former Secretaries of Defense
endorse F-22 procurement, 368
upgrades to current bomber force, 376
Department of Energy, 53
Department of State, 53–54
Deterrence, 293

The New Face of War